"JAMES HERRIOT HAS DONE IT AGAIN!

Here is 'the warm and joyful sequel to *All Creatures Great and Small*,' as the publishers truthfully say . . . Human beings just naturally respond to a writer as lovable, wholesome, eloquent, humorous and well stocked with anecdotes as James Herriot . . . His readers will not be surprised to hear that he is just as delightful in multidimensional life as he is on the flat printed page. That is superlative praise . . . Blow the bugles again, for here is more of the best!"
—*Chicago Tribune Book World*

"A WARM, RICH BOOK ILLUMINATED BY AN ABIDING LOVE FOR HUMANITY."
—*Omaha World-Herald*

"A very warm, very engaging read, and as Herriot tells anecdote after anecdote the reader falls totally under his spell, wishing only that he could read faster to get to the good things he knows —and he's right—that lie ahead . . . A thoroughly charming book."
—*Associated Press*

Bantam Books by James Herriot
Ask your bookseller for the books you have missed

ALL CREATURES GREAT AND SMALL
ALL THINGS BRIGHT AND BEAUTIFUL
ALL THINGS WISE AND WONDERFUL
JAMES HERRIOT'S YORKSHIRE
THE LORD GOD MADE THEM ALL

All Things Bright and Beautiful

JAMES HERRIOT

BANTAM BOOKS
NEW YORK · TORONTO · LONDON · SYDNEY · AUCKLAND

ALL THINGS BRIGHT AND BEAUTIFUL
*A Bantam Book / published by arrangement with
St. Martin's Press, Inc.*

PRINTING HISTORY

St. Martin's edition published August 1974

*A Fall 1974 selection of the Book-Of-The-Month, Reader's
Digest, Newsweek Condensed Books and The Catholic Digest
book clubs.*

An excerpt appeared in Reader's Digest, December 1974

Serialized in the New York Post, March 1975

*Bantam edition / September 1975
39 printings through April 1990*

ISBN 0-553-24851-0

*Bantam Books are published by Bantam Books, a division of Bantam
Doubleday Dell Publishing Group, Inc. Its trademark, consisting of the
words "Bantam Books" and the portrayal of a rooster, is Registered in U.S.
Patent and Trademark Office and in other countries. Marca Registrada.
Bantam Books, 666 Fifth Avenue, New York, New York 10103.*

With love
to
MY WIFE

and to

MY MOTHER
In dear old Glasgow town

All things bright and beautiful,
   All creatures great and small,
All things wise and wonderful,
   The Lord God made them all.
Cecil Frances Alexander 1818-1895

1

As I crawled into bed and put my arm around Helen it occurred to me, not for the first time, that there are few pleasures in this world to compare with snuggling up to a nice woman when you are half frozen.

There weren't any electric blankets in the thirties. Which was a pity because nobody needed the things more than country vets. It is surprising how deeply bone-marrow cold a man can get when he is dragged from his bed in the small hours and made to strip off in farm buildings when his metabolism is at a low ebb. Often the worst part was coming back to bed; I often lay exhausted for over an hour, longing for sleep but kept awake until my icy limbs and feet had thawed out.

But since my marriage such things were but a dark memory. Helen stirred in her sleep—she had got used to her husband leaving her in the night and returning like a blast from the North Pole—and instinctively moved nearer to me. With a sigh of thankfulness I felt the blissful warmth envelop me and almost immediately the events of the last two hours began to recede into unreality.

It had started with the aggressive shrilling of the bedside phone at one a.m. And it was Sunday morning, a not unusual time for some farmers after a late Saturday night to have a look round their stock and decide to send for the vet.

This time it was Harold Ingledew. And it struck me right away that he would have just about had time to get back to his farm after his ten pints at the Four

Horse Shoes where they weren't too fussy about closing time.

And there was a significant slurr in the thin croak of his voice.

"I 'ave a ewe amiss. Will you come?"

"Is she very bad?" In my semi-conscious state I always clung to the faint hope that one night somebody would say it would wait till morning. It had never happened yet and it didn't happen now: Mr. Ingledew was not to be denied.

"Aye, she's in a bad way. She'll have to have summat done for 'er soon."

Not a minute to lose, I thought bitterly. But she had probably been in a bad way all the evening when Harold was out carousing.

Still, there were compensations. A sick sheep didn't present any great threat. It was worst when you had to get out of bed facing the prospect of a spell of sheer hard labour in your enfeebled state. But in this case I was confident that I would be able to adopt my half-awake technique; which meant simply that I would be able to go out there and deal with the emergency and return between the sheets while still enjoying many of the benefits of sleep.

There was so much night work in country practice that I had been compelled to perfect this system as, I suspect, had many of my fellow practitioners. I had done some sterling work while in a somnambulistic limbo.

So, eyes closed, I tiptoed across the carpet and pulled on my working clothes. I effortlessly accomplished the journey down the long flights of stairs but when I opened the side door the system began to crumble, because even in the shelter of the high-walled garden the wind struck at me with savage force. It was difficult to stay asleep. In the yard as I backed out of the garage the high branches of the elms groaned in the darkness as they bent before the blast.

Driving from the town I managed to slip back into my trance and my mind played lazily with the phenomenon of Harold Ingledew. This drinking of his was so out of character. He was a tiny mouse of a man about seventy years old and when he came into the surgery on an occasional market day it was difficult to extract more than a few muttered words from him. Dressed in his best suit, his scrawny neck protruding from a shirt collar several sizes too big for him, he was the very picture of a meek and solid citizen; the watery blue eyes and fleshless cheeks added to the effect and only the brilliant red colouration of the tip of his nose gave any hint of other possibilities.

His fellow smallholders in Therby village were all steady characters and did not indulge beyond a social glass of beer now and then, and his next door neighbour had been somewhat bitter when he spoke to me a few weeks ago.

"He's nowt but a bloody nuisance is awd Harold."

"How do you mean?"

"Well, every Saturday night and every market night he's up roarin' and singin' till four o'clock in the mornin'."

"Harold Ingledew? Surely not! He's such a quiet little chap."

"Aye, he is for the rest of t'week."

"But I can't imagine him singing!"

"You should live next door to 'im, Mr. Herriot. He makes a 'ell of a racket. There's no sleep for anybody till he settles down."

Since then I had heard from another source that this was perfectly true and that Mrs. Ingledew tolerated it because her husband was entirely submissive at all other times.

The road to Therby had a few sharp little switchbacks before it dipped to the village and looking down I could see the long row of silent houses curving away to the base of the fell which by day hung in peaceful green majesty over the huddle of roofs but now bulked black and menacing under the moon.

As I stepped from the car and hurried round to the back of the house the wind caught at me again, jerking me to wakefulness as though somebody had thrown a bucket of water over me. But for a moment I forgot the cold in the feeling of shock as the noise struck me. Singing . . . loud raucous singing echoing around the old stones of the yard.

It was coming from the lighted kitchen window.

"JUST A SONG AT TWILIGHT, WHEN THE LIGHTS ARE LOW!"

I looked inside and saw little Harold sitting with his stockinged feet extended towards the dying embers of the fire while one hand clutched a bottle of brown ale.

"AND THE FLICKERING SHADOWS SOFTLY COME AND GO!" He was really letting it rip, head back, mouth wide.

I thumped on the kitchen door.

"THOUGH THE HEART BE WEARY, SAD THE DAY AND LONG!" replied Harold's reedy tenor and I banged impatiently at the woodwork again.

The noise ceased and I waited an unbelievably long time till I heard the key turning and the bolt rattling back. The little man pushed his nose out and gave me a questioning look.

"I've come to see your sheep," I said.

"Oh aye." He nodded curtly with none of his usual diffidence. "Ah'll put me boots on." He banged the door in my face and I heard the bolt shooting home.

Taken aback as I was I realised that he wasn't being deliberately rude. Bolting the door was proof that he was doing everything mechanically. But for all that he had left me standing in an uncharitable spot. Vets will tell you that there are corners in farm yards which are colder than any hill top and I was in one now. Just beyond the kitchen door was a stone archway leading to the open fields and through this black opening there whistled a Siberian draught which cut effortlessly through my clothes.

I had begun to hop from one foot to the other when the singing started again.

"THERE'S AN OLD MILL BY THE STREAM, NELLIE DEAN!"

Horrified, I rushed back to the window. Harold was

back in his chair, pulling on a vast boot and taking his time about it. As he bellowed he poked owlishly at the lace holes and occasionally refreshed himself from the bottle of brown ale.

I tapped on the window. "Please hurry, Mr. Ingledew."

"WHERE WE USED TO SIT AND DREAM, NELLIE DEAN!" bawled Harold in response.

My teeth had begun to chatter before he got both boots on but at last he reappeared in the doorway.

"Come on then," I gasped. "Where is this ewe? Have you got her in one of these boxes?"

The old man raised his eyebrows. "Oh, she's not 'ere."

"Not here?"

"Nay, she's up at t'top buildings."

"Right back up the road, you mean?"

"Aye, ah stopped off on t'way home and had a look at 'er."

I stamped and rubbed my hands. "Well, we'll have to drive back up. But there's no water, is there? You'd better bring a bucket of warm water, some soap and a towel."

"Very good." He nodded solemnly and before I knew what was happening the door was slammed shut and bolted and I was alone again in the darkness. I trotted immediately to the window and was not surprised to see Harold seated comfortably again. He leaned forward and lifted the kettle from the hearth and for a dreadful moment I thought he was going to start heating the water on the ashes of the fire. But with a gush of relief I saw him take hold of a ladle and reach into the primitive boiler in the old black grate.

"AND THE WATERS AS THEY FLOW SEEM TO MURMUR SWEET AND LOW!" he warbled, happy at his work, as he unhurriedly filled a bucket.

I think he had forgotten I was there when he finally came out because he looked at me blankly as he sang.

"YOU'RE MY HEART'S DESIRE, I LOVE YOU,

NELLIE DEAN!" he informed me at the top of his voice.

"All right, all right," I grunted. "Let's go." I hurried him into the car and we set off on the way I had come.

Harold held the bucket at an angle on his lap, and as we went over the switchbacks the water slopped gently on to my knee. The atmosphere in the car soon became so highly charged with beer fumes that I began to feel lightheaded.

"In 'ere!" the old man barked suddenly as a gate appeared in the headlights. I pulled on to the grass verge and stood on one leg for a few moments till I had shaken a surplus pint or two of water from my trousers. We went through the gate and I began to hurry towards the dark bulk of the hillside barn, but I noticed that Harold wasn't following me. He was walking aimlessly around the field.

"What are you doing, Mr. Ingledew?"

"Lookin' for t'ewe."

"You mean she's outside?" I repressed an impulse to scream.

"Aye, she lambed this afternoon and ah thowt she'd be right enough out 'ere." He produced a torch, a typical farmer's torch—tiny and with a moribund battery—and projected a fitful beam into the darkness. It made not the slightest difference.

As I stumbled across the field a sense of hopelessness assailed me. Above, the ragged clouds scurried across the face of the moon but down here I could see nothing. And it was so cold. The recent frosts had turned the ground to iron and the crisp grass cowered under the piercing wind. I had just decided that there was no way of finding an animal in this black wasteland when Harold piped up.

"She's over 'ere."

And sure enough when I groped my way towards the sound of his voice he was standing by an unhappy looking ewe. I don't know what instinct had brought him to her but there she was. And she was obviously in trouble; her head hung down miserably and when I put my hand on her fleece she took only a few faltering steps instead of galloping off as a healthy sheep would. Beside her, a tiny lamb huddled close to her flank.

I lifted her tail and took her temperature. It was normal. There were no signs of the usual post-lambing ailments; no staggering to indicate a deficiency, no discharge or accelerated respirations. But there was something very far wrong.

I looked again at the lamb. He was an unusually early arrival in this high country and it seemed unfair to bring the little creature into the inhospitable world of a Yorkshire March. And he was so small . . . yes . . . yes . . . it was beginning to filter through to me. He was too damn small for a single lamb.

"Bring me that bucket, Mr. Ingledew!" I cried. I could hardly wait to see if I was right. But as I balanced the receptacle on the grass the full horror of the situation smote me. I was going to have to strip off.

They don't give vets medals for bravery but as I pulled off my overcoat and jacket and stood shivering in my shirt sleeves on that black hillside I felt I deserved one.

"Hold her head," I gasped and soaped my arm quickly. By the light of the torch I felt my way into the vagina and I didn't have to go very far before I found what I expected; a woolly little skull. It was bent downwards with the nose under the pelvis and the legs were back.

"There's another lamb in here," I said. "It's laid wrong or it would have been born with its mate this afternoon."

Even as I spoke my fingers had righted the presentation and I drew the little creature gently out and deposited him on the grass. I hadn't expected him to be alive after his delayed entry but as he made contact with the cold ground his limbs gave a convulsive twitch and almost immediately I felt his ribs heaving under my hand.

For a moment I forgot the knife-like wind in the

thrill which I always found in new life, the thrill that
was always fresh, always warm. The ewe, too,
seemed stimulated because in the darkness I felt her
nose pushing interestedly at the new arrival.

But my pleasant ruminations were cut short by a
scuffling from behind me and some muffled words.

"Bugger it!" mumbled Harold.

"What's the matter?"

"Ah've kicked bucket ower."

"Oh no! Is the water all gone?"

"Aye, nowt left."

Well this was great. My arm was smeared with
mucus after being inside the ewe. I couldn't possibly
put my jacket on without a wash.

Harold's voice issued again from the darkness.
"There's some watter ower at building."

"Oh good. We've got to get this ewe and lambs
over there anyway." I threw my clothes over my
shoulder, tucked a lamb under each arm and began
to blunder over the tussocks of grass to where I
thought the barn lay. The ewe, clearly feeling better without her uncomfortable burden, trotted behind
me.

It was Harold again who had to give me directions.

"Ower 'ere!" he shouted.

When I reached the barn I cowered thankfully
behind the massive stones. It was no night for a stroll
in shirt sleeves. Shaking uncontrollably I peered at the
old man. I could just see his form in the last faint radiance of the torch and I wasn't quite sure what he
was doing. He had lifted a stone from the pasture
and was bashing something with it; then I realised
he was bending over the water trough, breaking the
ice.

When he had finished he plunged the bucket into
the trough and handed it to me.

"There's your watter," he said triumphantly.

I thought I had reached the ultimate in frigidity but
when I plunged my hands into the black liquid with
its floating icebergs I changed my mind. The torch
had finally expired and I lost the soap very quickly.

When I found I was trying to work up a lather with one of the pieces of ice I gave it up and dried my arms.

Somewhere nearby I could hear Harold humming under his breath, as comfortable as if he was by his own fireside. The vast amount of alcohol surging through his blood stream must have made him impervious to the cold.

We pushed the ewe and lambs into the barn which was piled high with hay and before leaving I struck a match and looked down at the little sheep and her new family settled comfortably among the fragrant clover. They would be safe and warm in there till morning.

My journey back to the village was less hazardous because the bucket on Harold's knee was empty. I dropped him outside his house then I had to drive to the bottom of the village to turn; and as I came past the house again the sound forced its way into the car.

"IF YOU WERE THE ONLY GIRL IN THE WORLD AND I WERE THE ONLY BOY!"

I stopped, wound the window down and listened in wonder. It was incredible how the noise reverberated around the quiet street and if it went on till four o'clock in the morning as the neighbours said, then they had my sympathy.

"NOTHING ELSE WOULD MATTER IN THE WORLD TODAY!"

It struck me suddenly that I could soon get tired of Harold's singing. His volume was impressive but for all that he would never be in great demand at Covent Garden; he constantly wavered off key and there was a grating quality in his top notes which set my teeth on edge.

"WE WOULD GO ON LOVING IN THE SAME OLD WAY!"

Hurriedly I wound the window up and drove off. As the heaterless car picked its way between the endless flitting pattern of walls I crouched in frozen immobility behind the wheel. I had now reached the state of total numbness and I can't remember much about my return to the yard at Skeldale House, nor my automatic actions of putting away the car, swinging shut the creaking doors of what had once been the old coach house, and trailing slowly down the long garden.

But a realisation of my blessings began to return when I slid into bed and Helen, instead of shrinking away from me as it would have been natural to do, deliberately draped her feet and legs over the human ice block that was her husband. The bliss was unbelievable. It was worth getting out just to come back to this.

I glanced at the luminous dial of the alarm clock. It was three o'clock and as the warmth flowed over me and I drifted away, my mind went back to the ewe and lambs, snug in their scented barn. They would be asleep now, I would soon be asleep, everybody would be asleep.

Except, that is, Harold Ingledew's neighbours. They still had an hour to go.

2

I had only to sit up in bed to look right across Darrowby to the hills beyond.

I got up and walked to the window. It was going to be a fine morning and the early sun glanced over the weathered reds and greys of the jumbled roofs, some of them sagging under their burden of ancient tiles, and brightened the tufts of green where trees pushed upwards from the gardens among the bristle of chimney pots. And behind everything the calm bulk of the fells.

It was my good fortune that this was the first thing I saw every morning; after Helen, of course, which was better still.

Following our unorthodox tuberculin testing honeymoon we had set up our first home on the top of Skeldale House. Siegfried, my boss up to my wedding and now my partner, had offered us free use of these empty rooms on the third storey and we had gratefully accepted; and though it was a makeshift arrangement there was an airy charm, an exhilaration in our high perch that many would have envied.

It was makeshift because everything at that time had a temporary complexion and we had no idea how long we would be there. Siegfried and I had both volunteered for the R.A.F. and were on deferred service but that is all I am going to say about the war. This book is not about such things which in any case were so very far from Darrowby; it is the story of the months I had with Helen between our marriage and my call-up and is about the ordinary things which have always made up our lives; my work, the animals, the Dales.

This front room was our bed-sitter and though it was not luxuriously furnished it did have an excellent bed, a carpet, a handsome side table which had belonged to Helen's mother and two armchairs. It had an ancient wardrobe, too, but the lock didn't work and the only way we kept the door closed was by jamming one of my socks in it. The toe always dangled outside but it never seemed of any importance.

I went out and across a few feet of landing to our kitchen-dining room at the back. This apartment was definitely spartan. I clumped over bare boards to a bench we had rigged against the wall by the window. This held a gas ring and our crockery and cutlery. I seized a tall jug and began my long descent to the main kitchen downstairs because one minor snag was that there was no water at the top of the house. Down two flights to the three rooms on the first storey then down two more and a final gallop along the passage to the big stone-flagged kitchen at the end.

I filled the jug and returned to our eyrie two steps at a time. I wouldn't like to do this now whenever I needed water but at that time I didn't find it the least inconvenience.

Helen soon had the kettle boiling and we drank our first cup of tea by the window looking down on the long garden. From up here we had an aerial view of the unkempt lawns, the fruit trees, the wisteria climbing the weathered brick towards our window, and the high walls with their old stone copings stretching away to the cobbled yard under the elms. Every day I went up and down that path to the garage in the yard but it looked so different from above.

"Wait a minute, Helen," I said. "Let me sit on that chair."

She had laid the breakfast on the bench where we ate and this was where the difficulty arose. Because it was a tall bench and our recently acquired high stool fitted it but our chair didn't.

"No, I'm all right, Jim, really I am." She smiled at

me reassuringly from her absurd position, almost at eye level with her plate.

"You can't be all right," I retorted. "Your chin's nearly in among your corn flakes. Please let me sit there."

She patted the seat of the stool. "Come on, stop arguing. Sit down and have your breakfast."

This, I felt, just wouldn't do. I tried a different tack.

"Helen!" I said severely. "Get off that chair!"

"No!" she replied without looking at me, her lips pushed forward in a characteristic pout which I always found enchanting but which also meant she wasn't kidding.

I was at a loss. I toyed with the idea of pulling her off the chair, but she was a big girl. We had had a previous physical try-out when a minor disagreement had escalated into a wrestling match and though I thoroughly enjoyed the contest and actually won in the end I had been surprised by her sheer strength. At this time in the morning I didn't feel up to it. I sat on the stool.

After breakfast Helen began to boil water for the washing-up, the next stage in our routine. Meanwhile I went downstairs, collected my gear, including suture material for a foal which had cut its leg and went out the side door into the garden. Just about opposite the rockery I turned and looked up at our window. It was open at the bottom and an arm emerged holding a dishcloth. I waved and the dishcloth waved back furiously. It was the start to every day.

And, driving from the yard, it seemed a good start. In fact everything was good. The raucous cawing of the rooks in the elms above as I closed the double doors, the clean fragrance of the air which greeted me every morning, and the challenge and interest of my job.

The injured foal was at Robert Corner's farm and I hadn't been there long before I spotted Jock, his sheep dog. And I began to watch the dog because behind a vet's daily chore of treating his patients there is always the fascinating kaleidoscope of animal personality and Jock was an interesting case.

A lot of farm dogs are partial to a little light relief from their work. They like to play and one of their favourite games is chasing cars off the premises. Often I drove off with a hairy form galloping alongside and the dog would usually give a final defiant bark after a few hundred yards to speed me on my way. But Jock was different.

He was really dedicated. Car chasing to him was a deadly serious art which he practised daily without a trace of levity. Corner's farm was at the end of a long track, twisting for nearly a mile between its stone walls down through the gently sloping fields to the road below and Jock didn't consider he had done his job properly until he had escorted his chosen vehicle right to the very foot. So his hobby was an exacting one.

I watched him now as I finished stitching the foal's leg and began to tie on a bandage. He was slinking about the buildings, a skinny little creature who without his mass of black and white hair would have been an almost invisible mite, and he was playing out a transparent charade of pretending he was taking no notice of me—wasn't the least bit interested in my presence, in fact. But his furtive glances in the direction of the stable, his repeated criss-crossing of my line of vision gave him away. He was waiting for his big moment.

When I was putting on my shoes and throwing my wellingtons into the boot I saw him again. Or rather part of him; just a long nose and one eye protruding from beneath a broken door. It wasn't till I had started the engine and begun to move off that he finally declared himself, stealing out from his hiding place, body low, tail trailing, eyes fixed intently on the car's front wheels, and as I gathered speed and headed down the track he broke into an effortless lope.

I had been through this before and was always afraid he might run in front of me so I put my foot down and began to hurtle downhill. This was where Jock came into his own. I often wondered how he'd fare against a racing greyhound because by golly he could run. That sparse frame housed a perfect physical machine and the slender limbs reached and flew again and again, devouring the stony ground beneath, keeping up with the speeding car with joyful ease.

There was a sharp bend about half way down and here Jock invariably sailed over the wall and streaked across the turf, a little dark blur against the green, and having craftily cut off the corner he reappeared like a missile zooming over the grey stones lower down. This put him into a nice position for the run to the road and when he finally saw me on to the tarmac my last view of him was of a happy, panting face looking after me. Clearly he considered it was a job well done and he would wander contentedly back up to the farm to await the next session, perhaps with the postman or the baker's van.

And there was another side to Jock. He was an outstanding performer at the sheepdog trials and Mr. Corner had won many trophies with him. In fact the farmer could have sold the little animal for a lot of money but couldn't be persuaded to part with him. Instead he purchased a bitch, a scrawny little female counterpart of Jock and a trial winner in her own right. With this combination Mr. Corner thought he could breed some world-beating types for sale. On my visits to the farm the bitch joined in the car-chasing but it seemed as though she was doing it more or less to humour her new mate and she always gave up at the first bend leaving Jock in command. You could see her heart wasn't in it.

When the pups arrived, seven fluffy black balls tumbling about the yard and getting under everybody's feet, Jock watched indulgently as they tried to follow him in his pursuit of my vehicle and you could almost see him laughing as they fell over their feet and were left trailing far behind.

It happened that I didn't have to go there for about ten months but I saw Robert Corner in the market occasionally and he told me he was training the pups and they were shaping well. Not that they needed much training; it was in their blood and he said they had tried to round up the cattle and sheep nearly as soon as they could walk. When I finally saw them they were like seven Jocks—meagre, darting little creatures flitting noiselessly about the buildings—and it didn't take me long to find out that they had learned more than sheep herding from their father. There was something very evocative about the way they began to prowl around in the background as I prepared to get into my car, peeping furtively from behind straw bales, slinking with elaborate nonchalance into favourable positions for a quick getaway. And as I settled in my seat I could sense they were all crouched in readiness for the off.

I revved my engine, let in the clutch with a bump and shot across the yard and in a second the immediate vicinity erupted in a mass of hairy forms. I roared on to the track and put my foot down and on either side of me the little animals pelted along shoulder to shoulder, their faces all wearing the intent fanatical expression I knew so well. When Jock cleared the wall the seven pups went with him and when they reappeared and entered the home straight I noticed something different. On past occasions Jock had always had one eye on the car—this was what he considered his opponent; but now on that last quarter mile as he hurtled along at the head of a shaggy phalanx he was glancing at the pups on either side as though they were the main opposition.

And there was no doubt he was in trouble. Superbly fit though he was, these stringy bundles of bone and sinew which he had fathered had all his speed plus the newly minted energy of youth and it was taking every shred of his power to keep up with them. Indeed there was one terrible moment when he stumbled and was engulfed by the bounding creatures around him; it seemed that all was lost but there was a core of steel in Jock. Eyes popping, nostrils dilated, he fought his way through the pack until by the time we reached the road he was once more in the lead.

But it had taken its toll. I slowed down before driving away and looked down at the little animal standing with lolling tongue and heaving flanks on the grass verge. It must have been like this with all the other vehicles and it wasn't a merry game any more. I suppose it sounds silly to say you could read a dog's thoughts but everything in his posture betrayed the mounting apprehension that his days of supremacy were numbered. Just round the corner lay the unthinkable ignominy of being left trailing in the rear of that litter of young upstarts and as I drew away Jock looked after me and his expression was eloquent.

"How long can I keep this up?"

I felt for the little dog and on my next visit to the farm about two months later I wasn't looking forward to witnessing the final degradation which I felt was inevitable. But when I drove into the yard I found the place strangely unpopulated.

Robert Corner was forking hay into the cow's racks in the byre. He turned as I came in.

"Where are all your dogs?" I asked.

He put down his fork. "All gone. By gaw, there's a market for good workin' sheep dogs. I've done right well out of t'job."

"But you've still got Jock?"

"Oh aye, ah couldn't part with t'awd lad. He's over there."

And so he was, creeping around as of old, pretending he wasn't watching me. And when the happy time finally arrived and I drove away it was like it used to be with the lean little animal haring along by the side of the car, but relaxed, enjoying the game, winging effortlessly over the wall and beating the car down to the tarmac with no trouble at all.

I think I was as relieved as he was that he was left alone with his supremacy unchallenged; that he was still top dog.

3

This was my third spring in the Dales but it was like the two before—and all the springs after. The kind of spring, that is, that a country vet knows; the din of the lambing pens, the bass rumble of the ewes and the high, insistent bawling of the lambs. This, for me, has always heralded the end of winter and the beginning of something new. This and the piercing Yorkshire wind and the hard, bright sunshine flooding the bare hillsides.

At the top of the grassy slope the pens, built of straw bales, formed a long row of square cubicles each holding a ewe with her lambs and I could see Rob Benson coming round the far end carrying two feeding buckets. Rob was hard at it; at this time of the year he didn't go to bed for about six weeks; he would maybe take off his boots and doze by the kitchen fire at night but he was his own shepherd and never very far from the scene of action.

"Ah've got a couple of cases for you today, Jim." His face, cracked and purpled by the weather, broke into a grin. "It's not really you ah need, it's that little lady's hand of yours and right sharpish, too."

He led the way to a bigger enclosure, holding several sheep. There was a scurry as we went in but he caught expertly at the fleece of a darting ewe. "This is the first one. You can see we haven't a deal o' time."

I lifted the woolly tail and gasped. The lamb's head was protruding from the vagina, the lips of the vulva clamped tightly behind the ears, and it had swollen enormously to more than twice its size. The

18

eyes were mere puffed slits in the great oedematous
ball and the tongue, blue and engorged, lolled from
the mouth.

"Well I've seen a few big heads, Rob, but I think
this takes the prize."

"Aye, the little beggar came with his legs back. Just
beat me to it. Ah was only away for an hour but he
was up like a football. By hell it doesn't take long. I
know he wants his legs bringin' round but what can I
do with bloody great mitts like mine." He held out his
huge hands, rough and swollen with the years of
work.

While he spoke I was stripping off my jacket and
as I rolled my shirt sleeves high the wind struck like a
knife at my shrinking flesh. I soaped my fingers
quickly and began to feel for a space round the
lamb's neck. For a moment the little eyes opened
and regarded me disconsolately.

"He's alive, anyway," I said. "But he must feel terrible and he can't do a thing about it."

Easing my way round, I found a space down by
the throat where I thought I might get through. This
was where my "lady's hand" came in useful and I
blessed it every spring; I could work inside the ewes
with the minimum of discomfort to them and this
was all-important because sheep, despite their out-
door hardiness, just won't stand rough treatment.

With the utmost care I inched my way along the
curly wool of the neck to the shoulder. Another push
forward and I was able to hook a finger round the
leg and draw it forward until I could feel the flexure
of the knee; a little more twiddling and I had hold
of the tiny cloven foot and drew it gently out into the
light of day.

Well that was half the job done. I got up from the
sack where I was kneeling and went over to the bucket of warm water; I'd use my left hand for the other
leg and began to soap it thoroughly while one of the
ewes, marshalling her lambs around her, glared at me
indignantly and gave a warning stamp of her foot.

Turning, I kneeled again and began the same procedure and as I once more groped forward a tiny lamb dodged under my arm and began to suck at my patient's udder. He was clearly enjoying it, too, if the little tail, twirling inches from my face, meant anything.

"Where did this bloke come from?" I asked, still feeling round.

The farmer smiled. "Oh that's Herbert. Poor little youth's mother won't have 'im at any price. Took a spite at him at birth though she thinks world of her other lamb."

"Do you feed him, then?"

"Nay, I was going to put him with the pet lambs but I saw he was fendin' for himself. He pops from one ewe to t'other and gets a quick drink whenever he gets chance. I've never seen owt like it."

"Only a week old and an independent spirit, eh?"

"That's about the size of it, Jim. I notice 'is belly's full every mornin' so I reckon his ma must let him have a do during the night. She can't see him in the dark—it must be the look of him she can't stand."

I watched the little creature for a moment. To me he seemed as full of knock-kneed charm as any of the others. Sheep were funny things.

I soon had the other leg out and once that obstruction was removed the lamb followed easily. He was a grotesque sight lying on the strawed grass, his enormous head dwarfing his body, but his ribs were heaving reassuringly and I knew the head would shrink back to normal as quickly as it had expanded. I had another search round inside the ewe but the uterus was empty.

"There's no more, Rob," I said.

The farmer grunted. "Aye, I thowt so, just a big single 'un. They're the ones that cause the trouble."

Drying my arms, I watched Herbert. He had left my patient when she moved round to lick her lamb and he was moving speculatively among the other ewes. Some of them warned him off with a shake of the head but eventually he managed to sneak up on a big, wide-bodied sheep and pushed his head underneath her. Immediately she swung round and with a fierce upward butt of her hard skull she sent the little animal flying high in the air in a whirl of flailing legs. He landed with a thud on his back and as I hurried towards him he leaped to his feet and trotted away.

"Awd bitch!" shouted the farmer and as I turned to him in some concern he shrugged. "I know, poor little sod, it's rough, but I've got a feelin' he wants it this way rather than being in the pen with the pet lambs. Look at 'im now."

Herbert, quite unabashed, was approaching another ewe and as she bent over her feeding trough he nipped underneath her and his tail went into action again. There was no doubt about it—that lamb had guts.

"Rob," I said as he caught my second patient. "Why do you call him Herbert?"

"Well that's my youngest lad's name and that lamb's just like 'im the way he puts his head down and gets stuck in, fearless like."

I put my hand into the second ewe. Here was a glorious mix up of three lambs; little heads, legs, a tail, all fighting their way towards the outside world and effectively stopping each other from moving an inch.

"She's been hanging about all morning and painin'," Rob said. "I knew summat was wrong."

Moving a hand carefully around the uterus I began the fascinating business of sorting out the tangle which is just about my favourite job in practice. I had to bring a head and two legs up together in order to deliver a lamb; but they had to belong to the same lamb or I was in trouble. It was a matter of tracing each leg back to see if it was hind or fore, to find if it joined the shoulder or disappeared into the depths.

After a few minutes I had a lamb assembled inside with his proper appendages but as I drew the legs into view the neck telescoped and the head slipped back; there was barely room for it to come through the pelvic bones along with the shoulders and I had to coax it through with a finger in the eye socket.

This was groaningly painful as the bones squeezed my hand but only for a few seconds because the ewe gave a final strain and the little nose was visible. After that it was easy and I had him on the grass within seconds. The little creature gave a convulsive shake of his head and the farmer wiped him down quickly with straw before pushing him to his mother's head.

The ewe bent over him and began to lick his face and neck with little quick darts of her tongue; and she gave the deep chuckle of satisfaction that you hear from a sheep only at this time. The chuckling continued as I produced another pair of lambs from inside her, one of them hind end first, and, towelling my arms again, I watched her nosing round her triplets delightedly.

Soon they began to answer her with wavering, high-pitched cries and as I drew my coat thankfully over my cold-reddened arms, lamb number one began to struggle to his knees; he couldn't quite make it to his feet and kept toppling on to his face but he knew where he was going, all right: he was headed for that udder with a singleness of purpose which would soon be satisfied.

Despite the wind cutting over the straw bales into my face I found myself grinning down at the scene; this was always the best part, the wonder that was always fresh, the miracle you couldn't explain.

I heard from Rob Benson again a few days later. It was a Sunday afternoon and his voice was strained, almost panic stricken.

"Jim, I've had a dog in among me in-lamb ewes. There was some folk up here with a car about dinner time and my neighbour said they had an Alsatian and it was chasing the sheep all over the field. There's a hell of a mess—I tell you I'm frightened to look."

"I'm on my way." I dropped the receiver and hurried out to the car. I had a sinking dread of what would be waiting for me; the helpless animals lying with their throats torn, the terrifying lacerations of limbs and abdomen. I had seen it all before. The ones which didn't have to be slaughtered would need stitching and on the way I made a mental check of the stock of suture silk in the boot.

The in-lamb ewes were in a field by the roadside and my heart gave a quick thump as I looked over the wall; arms resting on the rough loose stones I gazed with sick dismay across the pasture. This was worse than I had feared. The long slope of turf was dotted with prostrate sheep—there must have been about fifty of them, motionless woolly mounds scattered at intervals on the green.

Rob was standing just inside the gate. He hardly looked at me. Just gestured with his head.

"Tell me what you think. I daren't go in there."

I left him and began to walk among the stricken creatures, rolling them over, lifting their legs, parting the fleece of their necks to examine them. Some were completely unconscious, others comatose; none of them could stand up. But as I worked my way up the field I felt a growing bewilderment. Finally I called back to the farmer.

"Rob, come over here. There's something very strange."

"Look," I said as the farmer approached hesitantly. "There's not a drop of blood nor a wound anywhere and yet all the sheep are flat out. I can't understand it."

Rob bent over and gently raised a lolling head. "Aye, you're right. What the hell's done it, then?"

At that moment I couldn't answer him, but a little bell was tinkling far away in the back of my mind. There was something familiar about that ewe the farmer had just handled. She was one of the few able to support herself on her chest and she was lying there, blank-eyed, oblivious of everything; but . . . that drunken nodding of the head, that watery nasal discharge . . . I had seen it before. I knelt down and as I put my face close to hers I heard a faint bubbling —almost a rattling—in her breathing. I knew then.

"It's calcium deficiency," I cried and began to gallop down the slope towards the car.

Rob trotted alongside me. "But what the 'ell? They get that after lambin', don't they?"

"Yes, usually," I puffed. "But sudden exertion and stress can bring it on."

"Well ah never knew that," panted Rob. "How does it happen?"

I saved my breath. I wasn't going to start an exposition on the effects of sudden derangement of the parathyroid. I was more concerned with wondering if I had enough calcium in the boot for fifty ewes. It was reassuring to see the long row of round tin caps peeping from their cardboard box; I must have filled up recently.

I injected the first ewe in the vein just to check my diagnosis—calcium works as quickly as that in sheep —and felt a quiet elation as the unconscious animal began to blink and tremble, then tried to struggle on to its chest.

"We'll inject the others under the skin," I said. "It'll save time."

I began to work my way up the field. Rob pulled forward the fore leg of each sheep so that I could insert the needle under the convenient patch of un-woolled skin just behind the elbow; and by the time I was half way up the slope the ones at the bottom were walking about and getting their heads into the food troughs and hay racks.

It was one of the most satisfying experiences of my working life. Not clever, but a magical transfiguration; from despair to hope, from death to life within minutes.

I was throwing the empty bottles into the boot when Rob spoke. He was looking wonderingly up at the last of the ewes getting to its feet at the far end of the field.

"Well Jim, I'll tell you. I've never seen owt like that afore. But there's one thing bothers me." He turned to me and his weathered features screwed up in puzzlement. "Ah can understand how gettin' chased by a dog could affect some of them ewes, but why should the whole bloody lot go down?"

"Rob," I said. "I don't know."

And, thirty years later, I still wonder. I still don't know why the whole bloody lot went down.

I thought Rob had enough to worry about at the time, so I didn't point out to him that other complications could be expected after the Alsatian episode. I wasn't surprised when I had a call to the Benson farm within days.

I met him again on the hillside with the same wind whipping over the straw bale pens. The lambs had been arriving in a torrent and the noise was louder than ever. He led me to my patient.

"There's one with a bellyful of dead lambs, I reckon," he said, pointing to a ewe with her head drooping, ribs heaving. She stood quite motionless and made no attempt to move away when I went up to her; this one was really sick and as the stink of decomposition came up to me I knew the farmer's diagnosis was right.

"Well I suppose it had to happen to one at least after that chasing round," I said. "Let's see what we can do, anyway."

This kind of lambing is without charm but it has to be done to save the ewe. The lambs were putrid and distended with gas and I used a sharp scalpel to skin the legs to the shoulders so that I could remove them and deliver the little bodies with the least discomfort to the mother. When I had finished, the ewe's head was almost touching the ground, she was panting rapidly and grating her teeth. I had nothing to offer her—no wriggling new creature for her to lick and revive her interest in life. What she needed was an injection of penicillin, but this was 1939 and the antibiotics were still a little way round the corner.

"Well I wouldn't give much for her," Rob grunted. "Is there owt more you can do?"

"Oh, I'll put some pessaries in her and give her an injection, but what she needs most is a lamb to look after. You know as well as I do that ewes in this condition usually give up if they've nothing to occupy them. You haven't a spare lamb to put on her, have you?"

"Not right now, I haven't. And it's now she needs it. Tomorrow'll be too late."

Just at that moment a familiar figure wandered into view. It was Herbert, the unwanted lamb, easily recognisable as he prowled from sheep to sheep in search of nourishment.

"Hey, do you think she'd take that little chap?" I asked the farmer.

He looked doubtful. "Well I don't know—he's a bit old. Nearly a fortnight and they like 'em newly born."

"But it's worth a try isn't it? Why not try the old trick on her?"

Rob grinned. "O.K., we'll do that. There's nowt to lose. Anyway the little youth isn't much bigger than a new-born 'un. He hasn't grown as fast as his mates." He took out his penknife and quickly skinned one of the dead lambs, then he tied the skin over Herbert's back and round his jutting ribs.

"Poor little bugger, there's nowt on 'im," he muttered. "If this doesn't work he's going in with the pet lambs."

When he had finished he set Herbert on the grass and the lamb, resolute little character that he was, bored straight in under the sick ewe and began to suck. It seemed he wasn't having much success because he gave the udder a few peremptory thumps with his hard little head; then his tail began to wiggle.

"She's lettin' him have a drop, any road," Rob laughed.

Herbert was a type you couldn't ignore and the big sheep, sick as she was, just had to turn her head for a look at him. She sniffed along the tied-on skin in a non-committal way then after a few seconds she gave a few quick licks and the merest beginning of the familiar deep chuckle.

I began to gather up my gear. "I hope he makes it," I said. "Those two need each other." As I left the pen Herbert, in his new jacket, was still working away.

For the next week I hardly seemed to have my coat on. The flood of sheep work was at its peak and I spent hours of every day with my arms in and out of buckets of hot water in all corners of the district —in the pens, in dark nooks in farm buildings or very often in the open fields, because the farmers of those days didn't find anything disturbing in the sight of a vet kneeling in his shirt sleeves for an hour in the rain.

I had one more visit to Rob Benson's place. To a ewe with a prolapsed uterus after lambing—a job whose chief delight was comparing it with the sweat of replacing a uterus in a cow.

It was so beautifully easy. Rob rolled the animal on to her side then held her more or less upside down by tying a length of rope to her hind legs and passing it round his neck. In that position she couldn't strain and I disinfected the organ and pushed it back with the minimum of effort, gently inserting an arm at the finish to work it properly into place.

Afterwards the ewe trotted away unperturbed with her family to join the rapidly growing flock whose din was all around us.

"Look!" Rob cried. "There's that awd ewe with Herbert. Over there on t'right—in the middle of that bunch." They all looked the same to me but to Rob, like all shepherds, they were as different as people and he picked out these two effortlessly.

They were near the top of the field and as I wanted to have a close look at them we manoevered them into a corner. The ewe, fiercely possessive, stamped her foot at us as we approached, and Herbert, who had discarded his woolly jacket, held close to the flank of his new mother. He was, I noticed, faintly obese in appearance.

"You couldn't call him a runt now, Rob," I said.

The farmer laughed. "Nay, t'awd lass has a bag like a cow and Herbert's gettin' the lot. By gaw, he's in clover is that little youth and I reckon he saved the ewe's life—she'd have pegged out all right, but she never looked back once he came along."

I looked away, over the noisy pens, over the hundreds of sheep moving across the fields. I turned to the farmer. "I'm afraid you've seen a lot of me lately, Rob. I hope this is the last visit."

"Aye well it could be. We're getting well through now . . . but it's a hell of a time, lambin', isn't it?"

"It is that. Well I must be off—I'll leave you to it." I turned and made my way down the hillside, my arms raw and chafing in my sleeves, my cheeks whipped by the eternal wind gusting over the grass. At the gate I stopped and gazed back at the wide landscape, ribbed and streaked by the last of the winter's snow, and at the dark grey banks of cloud riding across on the wind followed by lakes of brightest blue; and in seconds the fields and walls and woods burst into vivid life and I had to close my eyes against the sun's glare. As I stood there the distant uproar came faintly down to me, the tumultuous harmony from deepest bass to highest treble; demanding, anxious, angry, loving.

The sound of the sheep, the sound of spring.

4

As the faint rumbling growl rolled up from the rib cage into the ear pieces of my stethoscope the realisation burst upon me with uncomfortable clarity that this was probably the biggest dog I had ever seen. In my limited past experience some Irish Wolfhounds had undoubtedly been taller and a certain number of Bull Mastiffs had possibly been broader, but for sheer gross poundage this one had it. His name was Clancy.

It was a good name for an Irishman's dog and Joe Mulligan was very Irish despite his many years in Yorkshire. Joe had brought him in to the afternoon surgery and as the huge hairy form ambled along, almost filling the passage, I was reminded of the times I had seen him out in the fields around Darrowby enduring the frisking attentions of smaller animals with massive benignity. He looked like a nice friendly dog.

But now there was this ominous sound echoing round the great thorax like a distant drum roll in a subterranean cavern, and as the chest piece of the stethoscope bumped along the ribs the sound swelled in volume and the lips fluttered over the enormous teeth as though a gentle breeze had stirred them. It was then that I became aware not only that Clancy was very big indeed but that my position, kneeling on the floor with my right ear a few inches from his mouth, was infinitely vulnerable.

I got to my feet and as I dropped the stethoscope into my pocket the dog gave me a cold look—a sideways glance without moving his head; and there was a chilling menace in his very immobility. I didn't mind my patients snapping at me but this one, I felt sure, wouldn't snap. If he started something it would be on a spectacular scale.

I stepped back a pace. "Now what did you say his symptoms were Mr. Mulligan?"

"Phwaat's that?" Joe cupped his ear with his hand. I took a deep breath. "What's the trouble with him?" I shouted.

The old man looked at me with total incomprehension from beneath the straightly adjusted cloth cap. He fingered the muffler knotted immediately over his larynx and the pipe which grew from the dead centre of his mouth puffed blue wisps of puzzlement.

Then, remembering something of Clancy's past history, I moved close to Mr. Mulligan and bawled with all my power into his face. "Is he vomiting?"

The response was immediate. Joe smiled in great relief and removed his pipe. "Oh aye, he's womitin' sorr. He's womitin' bad." Clearly he was on familiar ground.

Over the years Clancy's treatment had all been at long range. Siegfried had told me on the first day I had arrived in Darrowby two years ago that there was nothing wrong with the dog which he had described as a cross between an Airedale and a donkey, but his penchant for eating every bit of rubbish in his path had the inevitable result. A large bottle of bismuth, mag carb mixture had been dispensed at regular intervals. He had also told me that Clancy, when bored, used occasionally to throw Joe to the ground and worry him like a rat just for a bit of light relief. But his master still adored him.

Prickings of conscience told me I should carry out a full examination. Take his temperature, for instance. All I had to do was to grab hold of that tail, lift it and push a thermometer into his rectum. The dog turned his head and met my eye with a blank stare; again I heard the low booming drum roll and the upper lip lifted a fraction to show a quick gleam of white.

"Yes, yes, right, Mr. Mulligan," I said briskly. "I'll get you a bottle of the usual."

In the dispensary, under the rows of bottles with their Latin names and glass stoppers I shook up the mixture in a ten ounce bottle, corked it, stuck on a label and wrote the directions. Joe seemed well satisfied as he pocketed the familiar white medicine but as he turned to go my conscience smote me again. The dog did look perfectly fit but maybe he ought to be seen again.

"Bring him back again on Thursday afternoon at two o'clock," I yelled into the old man's ear. "And please come on time if you can. You were a bit late today."

I watched Mr. Mulligan going down the street, preceded by his pipe from which regular puffs rose upwards as though from a departing railway engine. Behind him ambled Clancy, a picture of massive calm. With his all-over covering of tight brown curls he did indeed look like a gigantic Airedale.

Thursday afternoon, I ruminated. That was my half day and at two o'clock I'd probably be watching the afternoon cinema show in Brawton.

The following Friday morning Siegfried was sitting behind his desk, working out the morning rounds. He scribbled a list of visits on a pad, tore out the sheet and handed it to me.

"Here you are, James, I think that'll just about keep you out of mischief till lunch time." Then something in the previous day's entries caught his eye and he turned to his younger brother who was at his morning task of stoking the fire.

"Tristan, I see Joe Mulligan was in yesterday afternoon with his dog and you saw it. What did you make of it?"

Tristan put down his bucket. "Oh, I gave him some of the bismuth mixture."

"Yes, but what did your examination of the patient disclose?"

"Well now, let's see." Tristan rubbed his chin. "He looked pretty lively, really."

"Is that all?"

"Yes . . . yes . . . I think so."

Siegfried turned back to me. "And how about you, James? You saw the dog the day before. What were your findings?"

"Well it was a bit difficult," I said. "That dog's as big as an elephant and there's something creepy about him. He seemed to me to be just waiting his chance and there was only old Joe to hold him. I'm afraid I wasn't able to make a close examination but I must say I thought the same as Tristan—he did look pretty lively."

Siegfried put down his pen wearily. On the previous night, fate had dealt him one of the shattering blows which it occasionally reserves for vets—a call at each end of his sleeping time. He had been dragged from his bed at 1 a.m. and again at 6 a.m. and the fires of his personality were temporarily damped.

He passed a hand across his eyes. "Well God help us. You, James, a veterinary surgeon of two years experience and you, Tristan, a final year student can't come up with anything better between you than the phrase 'pretty lively'. It's a bloody poor thing! Hardly a worthy description of clinical findings is it? When an animal comes in here I expect you to record pulse, temperature and respiratory rate. To auscultate the chest and thoroughly palpate the abdomen. To open his mouth and examine teeth, gums and pharynx. To check the condition of the skin. To catheterise him and examine the urine if necessary."

"Right," I said.

"O.K.," said Tristan.

My partner rose from his seat. "Have you fixed another appointment?"

"I have, yes." Tristan drew his packet of Woodbines from his pocket. "For Monday. And since Mr. Mulligan's always late for the surgery I said we'd visit the dog at his home in the evening."

"I see." Siegfried made a note on the pad, then he looked up suddenly. "That's when you and James are going to the young farmers' meeting, isn't it?"

The young man drew on his cigarette. "That's right. Good for the practice for us to mix with the young clients."

"Very well," Siegfried said as he walked to the door. "I'll see the dog myself."

On the following Tuesday I was fairly confident that Siegfried would have something to say about Mulligan's dog, if only to point out the benefits of a thorough clinical examination. But he was silent on the subject.

It happened that I came upon old Joe in the market place sauntering over the cobbles with Clancy inevitably trotting at his heels.

I went up to him and shouted in his ear. "How's your dog?"

Mr. Mulligan removed his pipe and smiled with slow benevolence. "Oh foine, sorr, foine. Still womitin' a bit, but not bad."

"Mr. Farnon fixed him up, then?"

"Aye, gave him some more of the white medicine. It's wonderful stuff, sorr, wonderful stuff."

"Good, good," I said. "He didn't find anything else when he examined him?"

Joe took another suck at his pipe. "No he didn't now, he didn't. He's a clever man, Mr. Farnon—I've niver seen a man work as fast, no I haven't."

"What do you mean?"

"Well now he saw all he wanted in tree seconds, so he did."

I was mystified. "Three seconds?"

"Yes," said Mr. Mulligan firmly. "Not a moment more."

"Amazing. What happened?"

Joe tapped out his pipe on his heel and without haste took out a knife and began to carve a refill from an evil looking coil of black twist. "Well now I'll tell ye. Mr. Farnon is a man who moves awful sudden, and that night he banged on our front door and jumped into the room." (I knew those cottages. There was no hall or lobby—you walked straight from the street into the living room.) "And as he came in he was pullin' his thermometer out of its case. Well now Clancy was lyin' by the fire and he rose up in a flash and he gave a bit of a wuff, so he did."

"A bit of a wuff, eh?" I could imagine the hairy monster leaping up and baying into Siegfried's face. I could see the gaping jaws, the gleaming teeth.

"Aye, just a bit of a wuff. Well, Mr. Farnon just put the thermometer straight back in its case turned round and went out the door."

"Didn't he say anything?" I asked.

"No, divil a word. Just turned about like a soldier and marched out the door, so he did."

It sounded authentic. Siegfried was a man of instant decision. I put my hand out to pat Clancy but something in his eyes made me change my mind.

"Well, I'm glad he's better," I shouted.

The old man ignited his pipe with an ancient brass lighter, puffed a cloud of choking blue smoke into my face and tapped a little metal lid on to the bowl. "Aye, Mr. Farnon sent round a big bottle of the white stuff and it's done 'im good. Mind yous," he gave a beatific smile, "Clancy's allus been one for the womitin', so he has."

Nothing more was said about the big dog for over a week, but Siegfried's professional conscience must have been niggling at him because he came into the dispensary one afternoon when Tristan and I were busy at the tasks which have passed into history— making up fever drinks, stomach powders, boric acid pessaries. He was elaborately casual.

"Oh by the way, I dropped a note to Joe Mulligan. I'm not entirely convinced that we have adequately explored the causes of his dog's symptoms. This womiting . . . er, vomiting is almost certainly due to depraved appetite but I just want to make sure. So I have asked him to bring him round tomorrow afternoon between two and two thirty when we'll all be here."

No cries of joy greeted his statement, so he continued. "I suppose you could say that this dog is to some degree a difficult animal and I think we should plan accordingly." He turned to me. "James, when he arrives you get hold of his back end, will you?"

"Right," I replied without enthusiasm.

He faced his brother. "And you, Tristan, can deal with the head. O.K.?"

"Fine, fine," Tristan muttered, his face expressionless.

His brother continued. "I suggest you get a good grip with your arms round his neck and I'll be ready to give him a shot of sedative."

"Splendid, splendid," said Tristan.

"Ah well, that's capital." My partner rubbed his hands together. "Once I get the dope into him the rest will be easy. I do like to satisfy my mind about these things."

It was a typical Dales practice at Darrowby; mainly large animal and we didn't have packed waiting rooms at surgery times. But on the following afternoon we had nobody in at all, and it added to the tension of waiting. The three of us mooched about the office, making aimless conversation, glancing with studied carelessness into the front street, whistling little tunes to ourselves. By two twenty-five we had all fallen silent. Over the next five minutes we consulted our watches about every thirty seconds, then at exactly two thirty Siegfried spoke up.

"This is no damn good. I told Joe he had to be here before half past but he's taken not a bit of notice. He's always late and there doesn't seem to be any way to get him here on time." He took a last look out of the window at the empty street. "Right we're not waiting any longer. You and I, James, have got that colt to cut and you, Tristan, have to see that beast of Wilson's. So let's be off."

Up till then, Laurel and Hardy were the only people I had ever seen getting jammed together in doorways but there was a moment when the three of us gave a passable imitation of the famous comics as we all fought our way into the passage at the same time. Within seconds we were in the street and Tristan was roaring off in a cloud of exhaust smoke. My colleague and I proceeded almost as rapidly in the opposite direction.

At the end of Trengate we turned into the market place and I looked around in vain for signs of Mr. Mulligan. It wasn't until we had reached the outskirts of the town that we saw him. He had just left his house and was pacing along under a moving pall of blue smoke with Clancy as always bringing up the rear.

"There he is!" Siegfried exclaimed. "Would you believe it? At the rate he's going he'll get to the surgery around three o'clock. Well we won't be there and it's his own fault." He looked at the great curly-coated animal tripping along, a picture of health and energy. "Well, I suppose we'd have been wasting our time examining that dog in any case. There's nothing really wrong with him."

For a moment he paused, lost in thought, then he turned to me.

"He does look pretty lively, doesn't he?"

5

"Them masticks," said Mr. Pickersgill judicially, "is a proper bugger."

I nodded my head in agreement that his mastitis problem was indeed giving cause for concern; and reflected at the same time that while most farmers would have been content with the local word "felon" it was typical that Mr. Pickersgill should make a determined if somewhat inaccurate attempt at the scientific term.

He didn't usually go too far off the mark—most of his efforts were near misses or bore obvious evidence of their derivation—but I could never really fathom where he got the masticks. I did know that once he fastened on to an expression it never changed; mastitis had always been "them masticks" with him and it always would be. And I knew, too, that nothing would ever stop him doggedly trying to be right. This, because Mr. Pickersgill had what he considered to be a scholastic background. He was a man of about sixty and when in his teens he had attended a two week course of instruction for agricultural workers at Leeds University. This brief glimpse of the academic life had left an indelible impression on his mind, and it was as if the intimation of something deep and true behind the facts of his everyday work had kindled a flame in him which had illumined his subsequent life.

No capped and gowned don ever looked back to his years among the spires of Oxford with more nostalgia than did Mr. Pickersgill to his fortnight at Leeds and his conversation was usually laced with references to a godlike Professor Malleson who had apparently been in charge of the course.

"Ah don't know what to make of it," he continued. "In ma college days I was allus told that you got a big swollen bag and dirty milk with them masticks but this must be another kind. Just little bits of flakes in the milk off and on—neither nowt nor something, but I'm right fed up with it, I'll tell you."

I took a sip from the cup of tea which Mrs. Pickersgill had placed in front of me on the kitchen table. "Yes, it's very worrying the way it keeps going on and on. I'm sure there's a definite factor behind it all —I wish I could put my finger on it."

But in fact I had a good idea what was behind it. I had happened in at the little byre late one afternoon when Mr. Pickersgill and his daughter Olive were milking their ten cows. I had watched the two at work as they crouched under the row of roan and red backs and one thing was immediately obvious; while Olive drew the milk by almost imperceptible movements of her fingers and with a motionless wrist, her father hauled away at the teats as though he was trying to ring in the new year.

This insight coupled with the fact that it was always the cows Mr. Pickersgill milked that gave trouble was enough to convince me that the chronic mastitis was of traumatic origin.

But how to tell the farmer that he wasn't doing his job right and that the only solution was to learn a more gentle technique or let Olive take over all the milking?

It wouldn't be easy because Mr. Pickersgill was an impressive man. I don't suppose he had a spare penny in the world but even as he sat there in the kitchen in his tattered, collarless flannel shirt and braces he looked, as always, like an industrial tycoon. You could imagine that massive head with its fleshy cheeks, noble brow and serene eyes looking out from the financial pages of the Times. Put him in a bowler and striped trousers and you'd have the perfect chairman of the board.

I was very chary of affronting such natural dignity and anyway, Mr. Pickersgill was fundamentally a fine stocksman. His few cows, like all the animals of that fast-dying breed of small farmer, were fat and sleek and clean. You had to look after your beasts when they were your only source of income and somehow Mr. Pickersgill had brought up a family by milk production eked out by selling a few pigs and the eggs from his wife's fifty hens.

I could never quite work out how they did it but they lived, and they lived graciously. All the family but Olive had married and left home but there was still a rich decorum and harmony in that house. The present scene was typical. The farmer expounding gravely, Mrs. Pickersgill bustling about in the background, listening to him with quiet pride. Olive, too, was happy. Though in her late thirties, she had no fears of spinsterhood because she had been assiduously courted for fifteen years by Charlie Hudson from the Darrowby fish shop and though Charlie was not a tempestuous suitor there was nothing flighty about him and he was confidently expected to pop the question over the next ten years or so.

Mr. Pickersgill offered me another buttered scone and when I declined he cleared his throat a few times as though trying to find words. "Mr. Herriot," he said at last, "I don't like to tell nobody his job, but we've tried all your remedies for them masticks and we've still got trouble. Now when I studied under Professor Malleson I noted down a lot of good cures and I'd like to try this 'un. Have a look at it."

He put his hand in his hip pocket and produced a yellowed slip of paper almost falling apart at the folds. "It's an udder salve. Maybe if we gave the bags a good rub with it it'd do t'trick."

I read the prescription in the fine copperplate writing. Camphor, eucalyptus, zinc oxide—a long list of the old familiar names. I couldn't help feeling a kind of affection for them but it was tempered by a growing disillusion. I was about to say that I didn't think rubbing anything on the udder would make the slightest difference when the farmer groaned loudly.

The action of reaching into his hip pocket had brought on a twinge of his lumbago and he sat very upright, grimacing with pain.

"This bloody old back of mine! By gaw, it does give me some stick, and doctor can't do nowt about it. I've had enough pills to make me rattle but ah get no relief."

I'm not brilliant but I do get the odd blinding flash and I had one now.

"Mr. Pickersgill," I said solemnly, "You've suffered from that lumbago ever since I've known you and I've just thought of something. I believe I know how to cure it."

The farmer's eyes widened and he stared at me with a childlike trust in which there was no trace of scepticism. This could be expected, because just as people place more reliance on the words of knacker men and meal travellers than their vets' when their animals are concerned it was natural that they would believe the vet rather than their doctor with their own ailments.

"You know how to put me right?" he said faintly.

"I think so, and it has nothing to do with medicine. You'll have to stop milking."

"Stop milking! What the 'ell. . . ?"

"Of course. Don't you see, it's sitting crouched on that little stool night and morning every day of the week that's doing it. You're a big chap and you've got to bend to get down there—I'm sure it's bad for you."

Mr. Pickersgill gazed into space as though he had seen a vision. "You really think . . ."

"Yes, I do. You ought to give it a try, anyway. Olive can do the milking. She's always saying she ought to do it all."

"That's right, Dad," Olive chimed in. "I like milking, you know I do, and it's time you gave it up— you've done it ever since you were a lad."

"Dang it, young man, I believe you're right! I'll

pack it in, now—I've made my decision!" Mr. Pickersgill threw up his fine head, looked imperiously
around him and crashed his fist on the table as though
he had just concluded a merger between two oil com-
panies.

I stood up. "Fine, fine. I'll take this prescription
with me and make up the udder salve. It'll be ready
for you tonight and I should start using it immediately."

It was about a month later that I saw Mr. Pickersgill. He was on a bicycle, pedalling majestically
across the market place and he dismounted when he
saw me.

"Now then, Mr. Herriot," he said, puffing slightly.
"I'm glad I've met you. I've been meaning to come
and tell you that we don't have no flakes in the milk
now. Ever since we started with t'salve they began
to disappear and milk's as clear as it can be now."

"Oh, great. And how's your lumbago?"

"Well I'll tell you, you've really capped it and I'm
grateful. Ah've never milked since that day and I
hardly get a twinge now." He paused and smiled
indulgently. "You gave me some good advice for me
back, but we had to go back to awd Professor Malleson to cure them masticks, didn't we?"

My next encounter with Mr. Pickersgill was on the
telephone.

"I'm speaking from the cossack," he said in a subdued shout.

"From the what?"

"The cossack, the telephone cossack in t'village."

"Yes indeed," I said, "And what can I do for you?"

"I want you to come out as soon as possible, to
treat a calf for semolina."

"I beg your pardon?"

"I 'ave a calf with semolina."

"Semolina?"

"Aye, that's right. A feller was on about it on t'wireless the other morning."

"Oh! Ah yes, I see." I too had heard a bit of the

farming talk on Salmonella infection in calves. "What makes you think you've got this trouble?"

"Well it's just like that feller said. Me calf's bleeding from the rectum."

"From the. . . ? Yes, yes, of course. Well I'd better have a look at him—I won't be long."

The calf was pretty ill when I saw him and he did have rectal bleeding, but it wasn't like Salmonella.

"There's no diarrhoea, you see, Mr. Pickersgill," I said. "In fact, he seems to be constipated. This is almost pure blood coming away from him. And he hasn't got a very high temperature."

The farmer seemed a little disappointed. "Dang, I thowt it was just same as that feller was talking about. He said you could send samples off to the labrador."

"Eh? To the what?"

"The investigation labrador—you know."

"Oh yes, quite, but I don't think the lab would be of any help in this case."

"Aye well, what's wrong with him, then? Is something the matter with his rectrum?"

"No, no," I said. "But there seems to be some obstruction high up his bowel which is causing this haemorrhage." I looked at the little animal standing motionless with his back up. He was totally preoccupied with some internal discomfort and now and then he strained and grunted softly.

And of course I should have known straight away —it was so obvious. But I suppose we all have blind spells when we can't see what is pushed in front of our eyes, and for a few days I played around with that calf in a haze of ignorance, giving it this and that medicine which I'd rather not talk about.

But I was lucky. He recovered in spite of my treatment. It wasn't until Mr. Pickersgill showed me the little roll of necrotic tissue which the calf had passed that the thing dawned on me.

I turned, shame-faced, to the farmer. "This is a bit of dead bowel all telescoped together—an intussusception. It's usually a fatal condition but fortunately in this case the obstruction has sloughed away and your calf should be all right now."

"What was it you called it?"

"An intussusception."

Mr. Pickersgill's lips moved tentatively and for a moment I thought he was going to have a shot at it. But he apparently decided against it. "Oh," he said. "That's what it was, was it?"

"Yes, and it's difficult to say just what caused it."

The farmer sniffed. "I'll bet I know what was behind it. I always said this one 'ud be a weakly calf. When he was born he bled a lot from his biblical cord."

Mr. Pickersgill hadn't finished with me yet. It was only a week later that I heard him on the phone again.

"Get out here, quick. There's one of me pigs going bezique."

"Bezique?" With an effort I put away from me a mental picture of two porkers facing each other over a green baize table. "I'm afraid I don't quite . . ."

"Aye, ah gave him a dose of worm medicine and he started jumpin' about and rollin' on his back. I tell you he's going proper bezique."

"Ah! Yes, yes I see, right. I'll be with you in a few minutes."

The pig had quieted down a bit when I arrived but was still in considerable pain, getting up, lying down, trotting in spurts round the pen. I gave him half a grain of morphine hydrochloride as a sedative and within a few minutes he began to relax and finally curled up in the straw.

"Looks as though he's going to be all right," I said. "But what's this worm medicine you gave him?"

Mr. Pickersgill produced the bottle sheepishly.

"Bloke was coming round sellin' them. Said it would shift any worms you cared to name."

"It nearly shifted your pig, didn't it?" I sniffed at the mixture. "And no wonder. It smells almost like pure turpentine."

"Turpentine! Well by gaw is that all it is? And bloke said it was summat new. Charged me an absorbent price for it too."

I gave him back the bottle. "Well never mind, I don't think there's any harm done, but I think the dustbin's the best place for that."

As I was getting into my car I looked up at the farmer. "You must be about sick of the sight of me. First the mastitis, then the calf and now your pig. You've had a bad run."

Mr. Pickersgill squared his shoulders and gazed at me with massive composure. Again I was conscious of the sheer presence of the man.

"Young feller," he said. "That don't bother me. When there's stock there's trouble and ah know from experience that trouble allus comes in cyclones."

6

I knew I shouldn't do it, but the old Drovers' Road beckoned to me irresistibly. I ought to be hurrying back to the surgery after my morning call but the broad green path wound beguilingly over the moor top between its crumbling walls and almost before I knew, I was out of the car and treading the wiry grass.

The wall skirted the hill's edge and as I looked across and away to where Darrowby huddled far below between its folding green fells the wind thundered in my ears; but when I squatted in the shelter of the grey stones the wind was only a whisper and the spring sunshine hot on my face. The best kind of sunshine—not heavy or cloying but clear and bright and clean as you find it down behind a wall in Yorkshire with the wind singing over the top.

I slid lower till I was stretched on the turf, gazing with half closed eyes into the bright sky, luxuriating in the sensation of being detached from the world and its problems.

This form of self-indulgence had become part of my life and still is; a reluctance to come down from the high country; a penchant for stepping out of the stream of life and loitering on the brink for a few minutes as an uninvolved spectator.

And it was easy to escape, lying up here quite alone with no sound but the wind sighing and gusting over the empty miles and, far up in the wide blue, the endless brave trilling of the larks.

Not that there was anything unpleasant about going back down the hill to Darrowby even before I was married. I had worked there for two years before Helen arrived, and Skeldale House had become home and the two bright minds in it my friends. It didn't bother me that both the brothers were cleverer than I was. Siegfried—unpredictable, explosive, generous; I had been lucky to have him as a partner. As a city bred youth trying to tell expert stock farmers how to treat their animals I had needed all his skill and guidance behind me. And Tristan; a rum lad as they said, but very sound. His humour and zest for life had lightened my days.

And all the time I was adding practical experience to my theory. The mass of facts I had learned at college were all coming to life, and there was the growing realisation, deep and warm, that this was for me. There was nothing else I'd rather do.

It must have been fifteen minutes later when I finally rose, stretched pleasurably, took a last deep gulp of the crisp air and pottered slowly back to the car for the six mile journey back down the hill to Darrowby.

When I drew up by the railings with Siegfried's brass plate hanging lopsidedly atop mine by the fine Georgian doorway I looked up at the tall old house with the ivy swarming untidily over the weathered brick. The white paint on windows and doors was flaking and that ivy needed trimming but the whole place had style, a serene unchangeable grace.

But I had other things on my mind at the moment. I went inside, stepping quietly over the coloured tiles which covered the floor of the long passage till I reached the long offshoot at the back of the house. And I felt as I always did the subdued excitement as I breathed the smell of our trade which always hung there; ether, carbolic and pulv aromat. The latter was the spicy powder which we mixed with the cattle medicines to make them more palatable and it had a distinctive bouquet which even now can take me back thirty years with a single sniff.

And today the thrill was stronger than usual because my visit was of a surreptitious nature. I almost tiptoed along the last stretch of passage, dodged quickly round the corner and into the dispensary. Gingerly I opened the cupboard door at one end and pulled out a little drawer. I was pretty sure Siegfried had a spare hoof knife hidden away within and I had to suppress a cackle of triumph when I saw it lying there; almost brand new with a nicely turned gleaming blade and a polished wooden handle.

My hand was outstretched to remove it when a cry of anger exploded in my right ear.

"Caught in the act! Bloody red-handed, by God!" Siegfried, who had apparently shot up through the floorboards, was breathing fire into my face.

The shock was so tremendous that the instrument dropped from my trembling fingers and I cowered back against a row of bottles of formalin bloat mixture.

"Oh hello, Siegfried," I said with a ghastly attempt at nonchalance. "Just on my way to that horse of Thompson's. You know—the one with the pus in the foot. I seem to have mislaid my knife so I thought I'd borrow this one."

"Thought you'd nick it, you mean! My spare hoof knife! By heaven, is nothing sacred, James?"

I smiled sheepishly. "Oh you're wrong. I'd have given it back to you straight away."

"A likely story!" Siegfried said with a bitter smile. "I'd never have seen it again and you know damn well I wouldn't. Anyway, where's your own knife? You've left it on some farm, haven't you?"

"Well as a matter of fact I laid it down at Willie Denholm's place after I'd finished trimming his cow's overgrown foot and I must have forgotten to pick it up." I gave a light laugh.

"But God help us, James, you're always forgetting to pick things up. And you're always making up the deficiency by purloining my equipment." He stuck his chin out. "Have you any idea how much all this is costing me?"

"Oh but I'm sure Mr. Denholm will drop the knife in at the surgery the first time he's in town."

Siegfried nodded gravely. "He may, I'll admit that, he may. But on the other hand he might think it is the ideal tool for cutting up his plug tobacco. Remember when you left your calving overall at old Fred Dobson's place? The next time I saw it was six months later and Fred was wearing it. He said it was the best thing he'd ever found for stooking corn in wet weather."

"Yes, I remember. I'm really sorry about it all." I fell silent, breathing in the pungency of the pulv aromat. Somebody had let a bagful burst on the floor and the smell was stronger than ever.

My partner kept his fiery gaze fixed on me for a few moments more then he shrugged his shoulders. "Ah well, there's none of us perfect, James. And I'm sorry I shouted at you. But you know I'm deeply attached to that knife and this business of leaving things around is getting under my skin." He took down a Winchester of his favourite colic draught and polished it with his handkerchief before replacing it carefully on its shelf. "I tell you what, let's go and sit down for a few minutes and talk about this problem."

We went back along the passage and as I followed him into the big sitting room Tristan got up from his favourite chair and yawned deeply. His face looked as boyish and innocent as ever but the lines of exhaustion round his eyes and mouth told an eloquent story. Last night he had travelled with the darts team from the Lord Nelson and had taken part in a gruelling match against the Dog and Gun at Drayton. The contest had been followed by a pie and peas supper and the consumption of something like twelve pints of bitter a man. Tristan had crawled into bed at 3 a.m. and was clearly in a delicate condition.

"Ah, Tristan," Siegfried said. "I'm glad you're here because what I have to say concerns you just as much as James. It's about leaving instruments on farms and you're as guilty as he is." (It must be remembered that before the Veterinary Surgeons' act of 1948 it was quite legal for students to treat cases and they regularly did so. Tristan in fact had done much sterling work when called on and was very popular with the farmers.)

"Now I mean this very seriously," my partner said, leaning his elbow on the mantelpiece and looking from one of us to the other. "You two are bringing me to the brink of ruin by losing expensive equipment. Some of it is returned but a lot of it is never seen again. What's the use of sending you to visits when you come back without your artery forceps or scissors or something else? The profit's gone, you see?"

We nodded silently.

"After all, there's nothing difficult about bringing your instruments away, is there? You may wonder why I never leave anything behind—well I can tell you it's just a matter of concentration. When I lay a thing down I always impress on my mind that I've got to lift it up again. That's all there is to it."

The lecture over, he became very brisk. "Right, let's get on. There's nothing much doing, James, so I'd like you to come with me to Kendall's of Brookside. He's got a few jobs including a cow with a tumour to remove. I don't know the details but we may have to cast her. You can go on to Thompson's later." He turned to his brother. "And you'd better come too, Tristan. I don't know if we'll need you but an extra man might come in handy."

We made quite a procession as we trooped into the farm yard and Mr. Kendall met us with his customary ebullience.

"Hello, 'ello, we've got plenty of man power today, I see. We'll be able to tackle owt with this regiment."

Mr. Kendall had the reputation in the district of being a "bit clever" and the phrase has a different meaning in Yorkshire from elsewhere. It meant he was something of a know-all; and the fact that he considered himself a wag and legpuller of the first degree didn't endear him to his fellow farmers either.

I always felt he was a good-hearted man, but his conviction that he knew everything and had seen it all before made him a difficult man to impress.

"Well what d'you want to see first, Mr. Farnon?" he asked. He was a thick-set little man with a round, smooth-skinned face and mischievous eyes.

"I believe you have a cow with a bad eye," Siegfried said. "Better begin with that."

"Right squire," the farmer cried, then he put his hand in his pocket. "But before we start, here's something for you." He pulled forth a stethoscope. "You left it last time you were 'ere."

There was a silence, then Siegfried grunted a word of thanks and grabbed it hastily from his hand.

Mr. Kendall continued. "And the time afore that you left your bloodless castrators. We did a swop over, didn't we? I gave you back the nippers and you left me the earphones." He burst into a peal of laughter.

"Yes, yes, quite," Siegfried snapped, glancing uneasily round at us, "but we must be getting on. Where is. . . ?"

"You know lads," chuckled the farmer, turning to us. "Ah don't think I've ever known 'im come here without leaving summat."

"Really?" said Tristan interestedly.

"Aye, if I'd wanted to keep 'em all I'd have had a drawerful by now."

"Is that so?" I said.

"Aye it is, young man. And it's the same with all me neighbours. One feller said to me t'other day, 'He's a kind man is Mr. Farnon—never calls without leavin' a souvenir.'" He threw back his head and laughed again.

We were enjoying the conversation but my partner was stalking up the byre. "Where's this damn cow, Mr. Kendall? We haven't got all day."

The patient wasn't hard to find; a nice light roan cow which looked round at us carefully, one eye almost closed. From between the lashes a trickle of tears made a dark stain down the hair of the face, and there was an eloquent story of pain in the cautious movements of the quivering lids.

"There's something in there," murmured Siegfried.

"Aye, ah know!" Mr. Kendall always knew. "She's got a flippin' great lump of chaff stuck on her eyeball but I can't get to it. Look here." He grabbed the cow's nose with one hand and tried to prise the eyelids apart with the fingers of the other, but the third eyelid came across and the whole orbit rolled effortlessly out of sight leaving only a blank expanse of white sclera.

"There!" he cried. "Nowt to see. You can't make her keep her eye still."

"I can, though." Siegfried turned to his brother. "Tristan, get the chloroform muzzle from the car. Look sharp!"

The young man was back in seconds and Siegfried quickly drew the canvas bag over the cow's face and buckled it behind the ears. From a bottle of spirit he produced a small pair of forceps of an unusual type with tiny jaws operated by a spring. He poised them just over the closed eye.

"James," he said, "Give her about an ounce."

I dribbled the chloroform on to the sponge in the front of the muzzle. Nothing happened for a few moments while the animal took a few breaths then her eyes opened wide in surprise as the strange numbing vapour rolled into her lungs.

The whole area of the affected eye was displayed, with a broad golden piece of chaff splayed out across the dark cornea. I only had a glimpse of it before Siegfried's little forceps had seized it and whisked it away.

"Squeeze in some of that ointment, Tristan," said my partner. "And get the muzzle off, James, before she starts to rock."

With the bag away from her face and the tormenting little object gone from her eye the cow looked around her, vastly relieved. The whole thing had taken only a minute or two and was as slick a little exhibition as you'd wish to see, but Mr. Kendall didn't seem to think a great deal of it.

"Aye right," he grunted. "Let's get on with t'next job."

As we went down the byre I looked out and saw a horse being led across the yard. Siegfried pointed to it.

"Is that the gelding I operated on for fistulous withers?" he asked.

"That's the one." The farmer's voice was airy.

We went out and Siegfried ran his hand over the horse's shoulders. The broad fibrous scar over the withers was all that was left of the discharging, stinking sinus of a few weeks back. Healing was perfect. These cases were desperately difficult to treat and I remembered my partner cutting and chiselling at the mass of necrotic tissue, curetting deeply till only healthy flesh and bone remained. His efforts had been rewarded; it was a brilliant success.

Siegfried gave the gelding a final pat on the neck. "That's done rather well."

Mr. Kendall shrugged and turned back towards the byre. "Aye, not so bad, I suppose." But he really wasn't impressed.

The cow with the tumour was standing just inside the door. The growth was in the perineal region, a smooth round object like an apple projecting from the animal's rear end, clearly visible an inch to the right of the tail.

Mr. Kendall was in full cry again. "Now we'll see what you're made of. How are you chaps going to get that thing off, eh? It's a big 'un—you'll need a carving knife or a hack saw for t'job. And are you goin' to put her to sleep or tie her up or what?" He grinned and his bright little eyes darted at each of us in turn.

Siegfried reached out and grasped the tumour, feeling round the base with his fingers. "Hmm . . . yes . . . hmm . . . bring me some soap and water and a towel, will you please?"

"I have it just outside t'door." The farmer scuttled into the yard and back again with the bucket.

"Thank you very much," Siegfried said. He washed his hands and gave them a leisurely towelling. "Now I believe you have another case to see. A scouring calf, wasn't it?"

The farmer's eyes widened. "Yes, I 'ave. But how about getting this big lump off the cow first?"

Siegfried folded the towel and hung it over the half door. "Oh, I've removed the tumour," he said quietly.

"What's that?" Mr. Kendall stared at the cow's backside. We all stared at it. And there was no doubt about it—the growth was gone. And there was another funny thing—there wasn't even a scar or mark remaining. I was standing quite close to the animal and I could see exactly to a fraction of an inch where that big ugly projection had been; and there was nothing, not a drop of blood, nothing.

"Aye," Mr. Kendall said irresolutely. "You've er . . . you've removed . . . you've removed it, aye, that's right." The smile had vanished from his face and his entire personality seemed suddenly deflated. Being a man who knew everything and was surprised by nothing he was unable to say, "When the devil did you do it? And how? And what on earth have you done with it?" He had to maintain face at all costs, but he was rattled. He darted little glances around the byre, along the channel. The cow was standing in a clean-swept stall with no straw and there was nothing lying on the floor there or anywhere. Casually, as though by accident, he pushed a milking stool to one side with his foot—still nothing.

"Well now, perhaps we can see the calf." Siegfried began to move away.

Mr. Kendall nodded. "Yes . . . yes . . . the calf. He's in t'corner there. I'll just lift bucket first."

It was a blatant excuse. He went over to the bucket and as he passed behind the cow he whipped out his spectacles, jammed them on his nose and directed a piercing glare at the cow's bottom. He only took an instant because he didn't want to show undue concern, but when he turned back towards us his face registered utter despair and he put his spectacles away with a weary gesture of defeat.

As he approached I turned and brushed against my partner.

"Where the hell is it?" I hissed.

"Up my sleeve," murmured Siegfried without moving his lips or changing expression.

"What. . . ?" I began, but Siegfried was climbing over a gate into the makeshift pen where the calf was cornered.

He was in an expansive mood as he examined the little creature and injected it. He kept up a steady flow of light conversation and Mr. Kendall, showing great character, managed to get his smile back on and answer back. But his preoccupied manner, the tortured eyes and the repeated incredulous glances back along the byre floor in the direction of the cow betrayed the fact that he was under immense strain.

Siegfried didn't hurry over the calf and when he had finished he lingered a while in the yard, chatting about the weather, the way the grass was springing, the price of fat bullocks.

Mr. Kendall hung on grimly but by the time Siegfried finally waved farewell the farmer's eyes were popping and his face was an anguished mask. He bolted back into the byre and as the car backed round I could see him bent double with his glasses on again, peering into the corners.

"Poor fellow," I said. "He's still looking for that thing. And for God's sake where is it, anyway?"

"I told you, didn't I?" Siegfried removed one arm from the wheel and shook it. A round fleshy ball rolled down into his hand.

I stared at it in amazement. "But . . . I never saw you take it off . . . what happened?"

"I'll tell you." My partner smiled indulgently. "I was fingering it over to see how deeply it was attached when I felt it begin to move. The back of it was merely encapsulated by the skin and when I gave another squeeze it just popped out and shot up my sleeve. And after it had gone the lips of the skin sprang back together again so that you couldn't see where it had been. Extraordinary thing."

Tristan reached over from the back seat. "Give it to me," he said. "I'll take it back to college with me and get it sectioned. We'll find out what kind of tumour it is."

His brother smiled. "Yes, I expect they'll give it some fancy name, but I'll always remember it as the only thing that shook Mr. Kendall."

"That was an interesting session in there," I said. "And I must say I admired the way you dealt with that eye, Siegfried. Very smooth indeed."

"You're very kind, James," my partner murmured. "That was just one of my little tricks—and of course the forceps helped a lot."

I nodded. "Yes, wonderful little things. I've never seen anything like them. Where did you get them?"

"Picked them up on an instrument stall at the last Veterinary Congress. They cost me a packet but they've been worth it. Here, let me show them to you." He put his hand in his breast pocket, then his side pockets, and as he continued to rummage all over his person a look of sick dismay spread slowly across his face.

Finally he abandoned the search, cleared his throat and fixed his eyes on the road ahead.

"I'll er . . . I'll show you them some other time, James," he said huskily.

I didn't say anything but I knew and Siegfried knew and Tristan knew.

He'd left them on the farm.

7

One of the nicest things about my married life was that my new wife got on so well with the Farnon brothers. And this was fitting because both of them had done their utmost to further my suit, Siegfried by means of some well-timed kicks in the pants, Tristan by more subtle motivation. The young man had been reassuring when I consulted him in the dispensary about my wooing that early summer morning.

"Well, it's a good sign." Tristan reluctantly expelled a lungful of Woodbine smoke and looked at me with wide, encouraging eyes.

"You think so?" I said doubtfully.

Tristan nodded. "Sure of it. Helen just rang you up, did she?"

"Yes, out of the blue. I haven't seen her since I took her to the pictures that night and it's been hectic ever since with the lambing—and suddenly there she was asking me to tea on Sunday."

"I like the sound of it," Tristan said. "But of course you don't want to get the idea you're home and dry or anything like that. You know there are others in the field?"

"Hell, yes, I suppose I'm one of a crowd."

"Not exactly, but Helen Alderson is really something. Not just a looker but . . . mm-mm, very nice. There's a touch of class about that girl."

"Oh I know, I know. There's bound to be a mob of blokes after her. Like young Richard Edmundson—I hear he's very well placed."

"That's right," Tristan said. "Old friends of the family, big farmers, rolling in brass. I understand old

56

man Alderson fancies Richard strongly as a son-in-law."

I dug my hands into my pockets. "Can't blame him. A ragged arsed young vet isn't much competition."

"Well, don't be gloomy, old lad, you've made a bit of progress, haven't you?"

"In a way," I said with a wry smile. "I've taken her out twice—to a dinner dance which wasn't on and to a cinema showing the wrong film. A dead loss the first time and not much better the second. I just don't seem to have any luck there—something goes wrong every time. Maybe this invitation is just a polite gesture—returning hospitality or something like that."

"Nonsense!" Tristan laughed and patted me on the shoulder. "This is the beginning of better things. You'll see—nothing will go wrong this time."

And on Sunday afternoon as I got out of the car to open the gate to Heston Grange it did seem as if all was right with the world. The rough track snaked down from the gate through the fields to Helen's home slumbering in the sunshine by the curving river, and the grey-stoned old building was like a restful haven against the stark backcloth of the fells beyond.

I leaned on the gate for a moment, breathing in the sweet air. There had been a change during the last week; the harsh winds had dropped, everything had softened and greened and the warming land gave off its scents. On the lower slopes of the fell, in the shade of the pine woods, a pale mist of bluebells drifted among the dead bronze of the bracken and their fragrance came up to me on the breeze.

I drove down the track among the cows relishing the tender young grass after their long winter in the byres and as I knocked on the farmhouse door I felt a surge of optimism and well-being. Helen's younger sister answered and it wasn't until I walked into the big flagged kitchen that I experienced a qualm. Maybe it was because it was so like that first disastrous time I had called for Helen; Mr. Alderson was there by the fireside, deep in the Farmer and Stockbreeder as before, while above his head the cows in the vast oil painting still paddled in the lake of startling blue under the shattered peaks. On the whitewashed wall the clock still tick-tocked inexorably.

Helen's father looked up over his spectacles just as he had done before. "Good afternoon, young man, come and sit down." And as I dropped into the chair opposite to him he looked at me uncertainly for a few seconds. "It's a better day," he murmured, then his eyes were drawn back irresistibly to the pages on his knee. As he bent his head and started to read again I gained the strong impression that he hadn't the slightest idea who I was.

It came back to me forcibly that there was a big difference in coming to a farm as a vet and visiting socially. I was often in farm kitchens on my rounds, washing my hands in the sink after kicking my boots off in the porch, chatting effortlessly to the farmer's wife about the sick beast. But here I was in my good suit sitting stiffly across from a silent little man whose daughter I had come to court. It wasn't the same at all.

I was relieved when Helen came in carrying a cake which she placed on the big table. This wasn't easy as the table was already loaded; ham and egg pies rubbing shoulders with snowy scones, a pickled tongue cheek by jowl with a bowl of mixed salad, luscious looking custard tarts jockeying for position with sausage rolls, tomato sandwiches, fairy cakes. In a clearing near the centre a vast trifle reared its cream-topped head. It was a real Yorkshire tea.

Helen came over to me. "Hello, Jim, it's nice to see you—you're quite a stranger." She smiled her slow, friendly smile.

"Hello, Helen. Yes, you know what lambing time's like. I hope things will ease up a bit now."

"Well I hope so too. Hard work's all right up to a point but you need a break some time. Anyway, come and have some tea. Are you hungry?"

"I am now," I said, gazing at the packed foodstuffs. Helen laughed. "Well come on, sit in. Dad, leave your precious Farmer and Stockbreeder and come over here. We were going to sit you in the dining room, Jim, but Dad won't have his tea anywhere but in here, so that's all about it."

I took my place along with Helen, young Tommy and Mary her brother and sister, and Auntie Lucy, Mr. Alderson's widowed sister who had recently come to live with the family. Mr. Alderson groaned his way over the flags, collapsed onto a high-backed wooden chair and began to saw phlegmatically at the tongue.

As I accepted my laden plate I can't say I felt entirely at ease. In the course of my work I had eaten many meals in the homes of the hospitable Dalesmen and I had discovered that light chatter was not welcomed at table. The accepted thing, particularly among the more old-fashioned types, was to put the food away in silence and get back on the job, but maybe this was different. Sunday tea might be a more social occasion; I looked round the table, waiting for somebody to lead the way.

Helen spoke up. "Jim's had a busy time among the sheep since we saw him last."

"Oh yes?" Auntie Lucy put her head on one side and smiled. She was a little bird-like woman, very like her brother and the way she looked at me made me feel she was on my side.

The young people regarded me fixedly with twitching mouths. The only other time I had met them they had found me an object of some amusement and things didn't seem to have changed. Mr. Alderson sprinkled some salt on a radish, conveyed it to his mouth and crunched it impassively.

"Did you have much twin lamb disease this time, Jim?" Helen asked, trying again.

"Quite a bit," I replied brightly. "Haven't had much luck with treatment, though. I tried dosing the ewes with glucose this year and I think it did a bit of good."

Mr. Alderson swallowed the last of his radish. "I think nowt to glucose," he grunted. "I've had a go with it and I think nowt to it."

"Really?" I said. "Well now that's interesting. Yes . . . yes . . . quite."

I buried myself in my salad for a spell before offering a further contribution.

"There's been a lot of sudden deaths in the lambs," I said. "Seems to be more Pulpy Kidney about."

"Fancy that," said Auntie Lucy, smiling encouragingly.

"Yes," I went on, getting into my stride. "It's a good job we've got a vaccine against it now."

"Wonderful things, those vaccines," Helen chipped in. "You'll soon be able to prevent a lot of the sheep diseases that way." The conversation was warming up.

Mr. Alderson finished his tongue and pushed his plate away. "I think nowt to the vaccines. And those sudden deaths you're on about—they're caused by wool ball on t'stomach. Nowt to do wi' the kidneys."

"Ah yes, wool ball eh? I see, wool ball." I subsided and decided to concentrate on the food.

And it was worth concentrating on. As I worked my way through I was aware of a growing sense of wonder that Helen had probably baked the entire spread. It was when my teeth were sinking into a poem of a curd tart that I really began to appreciate the miracle that somebody of Helen's radiant attractiveness should be capable of this.

I looked across at her. She was a big girl, nothing like her little wisp of a father. She must have taken after her mother. Mrs. Alderson had been dead for many years and I wondered if she had had that same wide, generous mouth that smiled so easily, those same warm blue eyes under the soft mass of black-brown hair.

A spluttering from Tommy and Mary showed that they had been appreciatively observing me gawping at their sister.

"That's enough, you two," Auntie Lucy reproved.

"Anyway you can go now, we're going to clear the table."

Helen and she began to move the dishes to the scullery beyond the door while Mr. Alderson and I returned to our chairs by the fireside.

The little man ushered me to mine with a vague wave of the hand. "Here . . . take a seat, er . . . young man."

A clattering issued from the kitchen as the washing-up began. We were alone.

Mr. Alderson's hand strayed automatically towards his Farmer and Stockbreeders but he withdrew it after a single hunted glance in my direction and began to drum his fingers on the arm of the chair, whistling softly under his breath.

I groped desperately for an opening gambit but came up with nothing. The ticking of the clock boomed out into the silence. I was beginning to break out into a sweat when the little man cleared his throat.

"Pigs were a good trade on Monday," he vouch-safed.

"They were, eh? Well, that's fine—jolly good."

Mr. Alderson nodded, fixed his gaze somewhere above my left shoulder and started drumming his fingers again. Once more the heavy silence blanketed us and the clock continued to hammer out its message.

After several years Mr. Alderson stirred in his seat and gave a little cough. I looked at him eagerly.

"Store cattle were down, though," he said.

"Ah, too bad, what a pity," I babbled. "But that's how it goes, I suppose, eh?"

Helen's father shrugged and we settled down again. This time I knew it was hopeless. My mind was a void and my companion had the defeated look of a man who has shot his conversational bolt. I lay back and studied the hams and sides of bacon hanging from their hooks in the ceiling, then I worked my way along the row of plates on the big oak dresser to a gaudy calendar from a cattle cake firm which dangled from a nail on the wall. I took a chance then and stole a glance at Mr. Alderson out of the corner of my eye and my toes curled as I saw he had chosen that precise moment to have a sideways peep at me. We both looked away hurriedly.

By shifting round in my seat and craning my neck I was able to get a view of the other side of the kitchen where there was an old-fashioned roll top desk surmounted by a wartime picture of Mr. Alderson looking very stern in the uniform of the Yorkshire Yeomanry, and I was proceeding along the wall from there when Helen opened the door and came quickly into the room.

"Dad," she said, a little breathlessly. "Stan's here. He says one of the cows is down with staggers."

Her father jumped up in obvious relief. I think he was delighted he had a sick cow and I, too, felt like a released prisoner as I hurried out with him.

Stan, one of the cowmen, was waiting in the yard.

"She's at t'top of t'field, boss," he said. "I just spotted 'er when I went to get them in for milkin'."

Mr. Alderson looked at me questioningly and I nodded at him as I opened the car door.

"I've got the stuff with me," I said. "We'd better drive straight up."

The three of us piled in and I set course to where I could see the stretched-out form of a cow near the wall in the top corner. My bottles and instruments rattled and clattered as we bumped over the rig and furrow.

This was something every vet gets used to in early summer; the urgent call to milk cows which have collapsed suddenly a week or two after being turned out to grass. The farmers called it grass staggers and as its scientific name of hypomagesaemia implied it was associated with lowered magnesium level in the blood. An alarming and highly fatal condition but fortunately curable by injection of magnesium in most cases.

Despite the seriousness of the occasion I couldn't

repress a twinge of satisfaction. It had got me out of the house and it gave me a chance to prove myself by doing something useful. Helen's father and I hadn't established anything like a rapport as yet, but maybe when I gave his unconscious cow my magic injection and it leaped to its feet and walked away he might look at me in a different light. And it often happened that way; some of the cures were really dramatic.

"She's still alive, any road," Stan said as we roared over the grass. "I saw her legs move then."

He was right, but as I pulled up and jumped from the car I felt a tingle of apprehension. Those legs were moving too much.

This was the kind that often died; the convulsive type. The animal, prone on her side, was pedalling frantically at the air with all four feet, her head stretched backwards, eyes staring, foam bubbling from her mouth. As I hurriedly unscrewed the cap from the bottle of magnesium lactate she stopped and went into a long, shuddering spasm, legs stiffly extended, eyes screwed tightly shut; then she relaxed and lay inert for a frightening few seconds before recommencing the wild thrashing with her legs.

My mouth had gone dry. This was a bad one. The strain on the heart during these spasms was enormous and each one could be her last.

I crouched by her side, my needle poised over the milk vein. My usual practice was to inject straight into the blood stream to achieve the quickest possible effect, but in this case I hesitated. Any interference with the heart's action could kill this cow; best to play safe—I reached over and pushed the needle under the skin of the neck.

As the fluid ran in, bulging the subcutaneous tissues and starting a widening swelling under the roan-coloured hide, the cow went into another spasm. For an agonising few seconds she lay there, the quivering limbs reaching desperately out at nothing, the eyes disappearing deep down under tight-twisted lids. Helplessly I watched her, my heart thudding, and this time as she came out of the rigor and started to

move again it wasn't with the purposeful peddling of
before; it was an aimless laboured pawing and as
even this grew weaker her eyes slowly opened and
gazed outwards with a vacant stare.

I bent and touched the cornea with my finger,
there was no response.

The farmer and cowman looked at me in silence as
the animal gave a final jerk then lay still.

"I'm afraid she's dead, Mr. Alderson," I said.

The farmer nodded and his eyes moved slowly
over the still form, over the graceful limbs, the fine
dark roan flanks, the big, turgid udder that would
give no more milk.

"I'm sorry," I said. "I'm afraid her heart must have
given out before the magnesium had a chance to
work."

"It's a bloody shame," grunted Stan. "She was a
right good cow, that 'un."

Mr. Alderson turned quietly back to the car. "Aye
well, these things happen," he muttered.

We drove down the field to the house.

Inside, the work was over and the family was collected in the parlour. I sat with them for a while but
my overriding emotion was an urgent desire to be
elsewhere. Helen's father had been silent before but
now he sat hunched miserably in an armchair taking
no part in the conversation. I wondered whether he
thought I had actually killed his cow. It certainly
hadn't looked very good, the vet walking up to the
sick animal, the quick injection and hey presto, dead.
No, I had been blameless but it hadn't looked good.

On an impulse I jumped to my feet.

"Thank you very much for the lovely tea," I said,
"but I really must be off. I'm on duty this evening."

Helen came with me to the door. "Well it's been
nice seeing you again, Jim." She paused and looked
at me doubtfully. "I wish you'd stop worrying about
that cow. It's a pity but you couldn't help it. There
was nothing you could do."

"Thanks, Helen, I know. But it's a nasty smack for
your father isn't it?"

She shrugged and smiled her kind smile. Helen was always kind.

Driving back through the pastures up to the farm gate I could see the motionless body of my patient with her companions sniffing around her curiously in the gentle evening sunshine. Any time now the knacker man would be along to winch the carcase on to his wagon. It was the grim epilogue to every vet's failure.

I closed the gate behind me and looked back at Heston Grange. I had thought everything would be all right this time but it hadn't worked out that way.

The jinx was still on.

8

"Monday morning disease" they used to call it. The almost unbelievably gross thickening of the hind limb in cart horses which had stood in the stable over the weekend. It seemed that the sudden suspension of their normal work and exercise produced the massive lymphangitis and swelling which gave many a farmer a nasty jolt right at the beginning of the week.

But it was Wednesday evening now and Mr. Crump's big Shire gelding was greatly improved.

"That leg's less than half the size it was," I said, running my hand over the inside of the hock, feeling the remains of the oedema pitting under my fingers. "I can see you've put in some hard work here."

"Aye, ah did as you said." Mr. Crump's reply was typically laconic, but I knew he must have spent hours fomenting and massaging the limb and forcibly exercising the horse as I had told him when I gave the arecoline injection on Monday.

I began to fill the syringe for a repeat injection. "He's having no corn, is he?"

"Nay, nowt but bran."

"That's fine. I think he'll be back to normal in a day or two if you keep up the treatment."

The farmer grunted and no sign of approval showed in the big, purple-red face with its perpetually surprised expression. But I knew he was pleased all right; he was fond of the horse and had been unable to hide his concern at the animal's pain and distress on my first visit.

I went into the house to wash my hands and Mr.

66

Crump led the way into the kitchen, his big frame lumbering clumsily ahead of me. He proffered soap and towel in his slow-moving way and stood back in silence as I leaned over the long shallow sink of brown earthenware.

As I dried my hands he cleared his throat and spoke hesitantly. "Would you like a drink of ma wine?"

Before I could answer, Mrs. Crump came bustling through from an inner room. She was pulling on her hat and behind her her teen-age son and daughter followed, dressed ready to go out.

"Oh Albert, stop it!" she snapped, looking up at her husband. "Mr. Herriot doesn't want your wine. I wish you wouldn't pester people so with it!"

The boy grinned. "Dad and his wine, he's always looking for a victim." His sister joined in the general laughter and I had an uncomfortable feeling that Mr. Crump was the odd man out in his own home.

"We're going down t'village institute to see a school play, Mr. Herriot," the wife said briskly. "We're late now so we must be off." She hurried away with her children, leaving the big man looking after her sheepishly.

There was a silence while I finished drying my hands, then I turned to the farmer. "Well, how about that drink, Mr. Crump?"

He hesitated for a moment and the surprised look deepened. "Would you . . . you'd really like to try some?"

"I'd love to. I haven't had my evening meal yet—I could just do with an aperitif."

"Right, I'll be back in a minute." He disappeared into the large pantry at the end of the kitchen and came back with a bottle of amber liquid and glasses.

"This is ma rhubarb," he said, tipping out two good measures.

I took a sip and then a good swallow, and gasped as the liquid blazed a fiery trail down to my stomach.

"It's strong stuff," I said a little breathlessly, "but the taste is very pleasant. Very pleasant indeed."

Mr. Crump watched approvingly as I took another drink. "Aye, it's just right. Nearly two years old."

I drained the glass and this time the wine didn't burn so much on its way down but seemed to wash around the walls of my empty stomach and send glowing tendrils creeping along my limbs.

"Delicious," I said. "Absolutely delicious."

The farmer expanded visibly. He refilled the glasses and watched with rapt attention as I drank. When we had finished the second glass he jumped to his feet.

"Now for a change I want you to try summat different." He almost trotted to the pantry and produced another bottle, this time of colourless fluid. "Elderflower," he said, panting slightly.

When I tasted it I was amazed at the delicate flavour, the bubbles sparkling and dancing on my tongue.

"Gosh, this is terrific! It's just like champagne. You know, you really have a gift—I never thought home made wines could taste like this."

Mr. Crump stared at me for a moment then one corner of his mouth began to twitch and incredibly a shy smile spread slowly over his face. "You're about fust I've heard say that. You'd think I was trying to poison folks when I offer them ma wine—they always shy off but they can sup plenty of beer and whisky."

"Well they don't know what they're missing, Mr. Crump." I watched while the farmer replenished my glass. "I wouldn't have believed you could make stuff as good as this at home." I sipped appreciatively at the elderflower. It still tasted like champagne.

I hadn't got more than half way down the glass before Mr. Crump was clattering and clinking inside the pantry again. He emerged with a bottle with contents of a deep blood red. "Try that," he gasped.

I was beginning to feel like a professional taster and rolled the first mouthful around my mouth with eyes half closed. "Mm, mm, yes. Just like an excellent port, but there's something else here—a fruitiness in the background—something familiar about it—it's . . . it's . . ."

"Blackberry!" shouted Mr. Crump triumphantly. "One of t'best I've done. Made it two back-ends since —it were a right good year for it."

Leaning back in the chair I took another drink of the rich, dark wine; it was round-flavoured, warming, and behind it there was always the elusive hint of the brambles. I could almost see the heavy-hanging clusters of berries glistening black and succulent in the autumn sunshine. The mellowness of the image matched my mood which was becoming more expansive by the minute and I looked round with leisurely appreciation at the rough comfort of the farmhouse kitchen; at the hams and sides of bacon hanging from their hooks in the ceiling, and at my host sitting across the table, watching me eagerly. He was, I noticed for the first time, still wearing his cap.

"You know," I said, holding the glass high and studying its ruby depths against the light, "I can't make up my mind which of your wines I like best. They're all excellent and yet so different."

Mr. Crump, too, had relaxed. He threw back his head and laughed delightedly before hurriedly refilling both of our tumblers. "But you haven't started yet. Ah've got dozens of bottles in there—all different. You must try a few more." He shambled again over to the pantry and this time when he reappeared he was weighed down by an armful of bottles of differing shapes and colours.

What a charming man he was, I thought. How wrong I had been in my previous assessment of him; it had been so easy to put him down as lumpish and unemotional but as I looked at him now his face was alight with friendship, hospitality, understanding. He had cast off his inhibitions and as he sat down surrounded by the latest batch he began to talk rapidly and fluently about wines and wine making.

Wide-eyed and impassioned he ranged at length over the niceties of fermentation and sedimentation, of flavour and bouquet. He dealt learnedly with the relative merits of Chambertin and Nuits St. George, Montrachet and Chablis. Enthusiasts are appealing but a fanatic is irresistible and I sat spellbound while Mr. Crump pushed endless samples of his craft in front of me, mixing and adjusting expertly.

"How did you find that 'un?"

"Very nice . . ."

"Bit sweet, maybe?"

"Well, perhaps . . ."

"Right, try some of this with it." The meticulous addition of a few drops of nameless liquid from the packed rows of bottles. "How's that?"

"Marvellous!"

"Now this 'un. Perhaps a bit sharpish, eh?"

"Possibly . . . yes . . ."

Again the tender trickling of a few mysterious droplets into my drink and again the anxious enquiry.

"Is that better?"

"Just right."

The big man drank with me, glass by glass. We tried parsnip and dandelion, cowslip and parsley, clover, gooseberry, beetroot and crab apple. Incredibly we had some stuff made from turnips which was so exquisite that I insisted on a refill.

Everything gradually slowed down as we sat there. Time slowed down till it was finally meaningless. Mr. Crump and I slowed down and our speech and actions became more and more deliberate. The farmer's visits to the pantry developed into laboured, unsteady affairs; sometimes he took a roundabout route to reach the door and on one occasion there was a tremendous crash from within and I feared he had fallen among his bottles. But I couldn't be bothered to get up to see and in due course he reappeared, apparently unharmed.

It was around nine o'clock that I heard the soft knocking on the outer door. I ignored it as I didn't want to interrupt Mr. Crump who was in the middle of a deep exposition.

"Thish," he was saying, leaning close to me and tapping a bulbous flagon with his forefinger. "Thish is, in my 'pinion, comp'rable to a fine Moselle. Made it lash year and would 'preciate it if you'd tell me what you think." He bent low over the glass, blinking, heavy-eyed as he poured.

"Now then, wha' d'you say? Ish it or ishn't it?"

I took a gulp and paused for a moment. It all tasted the same now and I had never drunk Moselle anyway, but I nodded and hiccuped solemnly in reply.

The farmer rested a friendly hand on my shoulder and was about to make a further speech when he, too, heard the knocking. He made his way across the floor with some difficulty and opened the door. A young lad was standing there and I heard a few muttered words.

"We 'ave a cow on calving and we 'phoned surgery and they said vitnery might still be here."

Mr. Crump turned to face me. "It's the Bamfords of Holly Bush. They wan' you to go there—jush a mile along t'road."

"Right," I heaved myself to my feet then gripped the table tightly as the familiar objects of the room began to whirl rapidly around me. When they came to rest Mr. Crump appeared to be standing at the head of a fairly steep slope. The kitchen floor had seemed perfectly level when I had come in but now it was all I could do to fight my way up the gradient.

When I reached the door Mr. Crump was staring owlishly into the darkness.

"'Sraining," he said. "'sraining like 'ell."

I peered out at the steady beat of the dark water on the cobbles of the yard, but my car was just a few yards away and I was about to set out when the farmer caught my arm.

"Jus' minute, can't go out like that." He held up a finger then went over and groped about in a drawer. At length he produced a tweed cap which he offered me with great dignity.

I never wore anything on my head whatever the

weather but I was deeply touched and wrung my
companion's hand in silence. It was understandable
that a man like Mr. Crump who wore his cap at all
times, indoors and out, would recoil in horror from
the idea of anybody venturing uncovered into the
rain.

The tweed cap which I now put on was the biggest
I had ever seen; a great round flat pancake of a thing
which even at that moment I felt would keep not
only my head but my shoulders and entire body dry
in the heaviest downpour.

I took my leave of Mr. Crump with reluctance and
as I settled in the seat of the car trying to remember
where first gear was situated I could see his bulky
form silhouetted against the light from the kitchen;
he was waving his hand with gentle benevolence and
it struck me as I at length drove away what a deep
and wonderful friendship had been forged that night.

Driving at walking pace along the dark narrow
road, my nose almost touching the windscreen, I was
conscious of some unusual sensations. My mouth and
lips felt abnormally sticky as though I had been
drinking liquid glue instead of wine, my breath
seemed to be whistling in my nostrils like a strong
wind blowing under a door, and I was having difficulty focusing my eyes. Fortunately I met only one
car and as it approached and flashed past in the
other direction I was muzzily surprised by the fact
that it had two complete sets of headlights which
kept merging into each other and drawing apart
again.

In the yard at Holly Bush I got out of the car,
nodded to the shadowy group of figures standing
there, fumbled my bottle of antiseptic and calving
ropes from the boot and marched determinedly into
the byre. One of the men held an oil lamp over a cow
lying on a deep bed of straw in one of the standings;
from the vulva a calf's foot protruded a few inches
and as the cow strained a little muzzle showed momentarily then disappeared as she relaxed.

Far away inside me a stone cold sober veterinary

surgeon murmured: "Only a leg back and a big roomy cow. Shouldn't be much trouble." I turned and looked at the Bamfords for the first time. I hadn't met them before but it was easy to classify them; simple, kindly, anxious-to-please people—two middle-aged men, probably brothers, and two young men who would be the sons of one or the other. They were all staring at me in the dim light, their eyes expectant, their mouths slightly open as though ready to smile or laugh if given half a chance.

I squared my shoulders, took a deep breath and said in a loud voice: "Would you please bring me a bucket of hot water, some soap and a towel." Or at least that's what I meant to say, because what actually issued from my lips was a torrent of something that sounded like Swahili. The Bamfords, poised, ready to spring into action to do my bidding, looked at me blankly. I cleared my throat, swallowed, took a few seconds' rest and tried again. The result was the same—another volley of gibberish echoing uselessly round the cow house.

Clearly I had a problem. It was essential to communicate in some way, particularly since these people didn't know me and were waiting for some action. I suppose I must have appeared a strange and enigmatic figure standing there, straight and solemn, surmounted and dominated by the vast cap. But through the mists a flash of insight showed me where I was going wrong. It was over-confidence. It wasn't a bit of good trying to speak loudly like that. I tried again in the faintest of whispers.

"Could I have a bucket of hot water, some soap and a towel, please." It came out beautifully though the oldest Mr. Bamford didn't quite get it first time. He came close, cupped an ear with his hand and watched my lips intently. Then he nodded eagerly in comprehension, held up a forefinger at me, tiptoed across the floor like a tight rope walker to one of the sons and whispered in his ear. The young man turned and crept out noiselessly, closing the door behind him with the utmost care; he was back in less

than a minute, padding over the cobbles daintily in
his heavy boots and placing the bucket gingerly in
front of me.

I managed to remove my jacket, tie and shirt quite
efficiently and they were taken from me in silence
and hung up on nails by the Bamfords who were
moving around as though in church. I thought I was
doing fine till I started to wash my arms. The soap
kept shooting from my arms, slithering into the dung
channel, disappearing into the dark corners of the
byre with the Bamfords in hot pursuit. It was worse
still when I tried to work up to the top of my arms.
The soap flew over my shoulders like a live thing, at
times cannoning off the walls, at others gliding down
my back. The farmers never knew where the next
shot was going and they took on the appearance of a
really sharp fielding side crouching around me with
arms outstretched waiting for a catch.

However I did finally work up a lather and was
ready to start, but the cow refused firmly to get to
her feet, so I had to stretch out behind her face down
on the unyielding cobbles. It wasn't till I had got
down there that I felt the great cap dropping over
my ears; I must have put it on again after removing
my shirt though it was difficult to see what purpose
it might serve.

Inserting a hand gently into the vagina I pushed
along the calf's neck, hoping to come upon a flexed
knee or even a foot, but I was disappointed; the leg
really was right back, stretching from the shoulder
away flat against the calf's side. Still, I would be all
right—it just meant a longer reach.

And there was one reassuring feature; the calf was
alive. As I lay, my face was almost touching the rear
end of the cow and I had a close up of the nose
which kept appearing every few seconds; it was
good to see the little nostrils twitching as they sought
the outside air. All I had to do was get that leg round.

But the snag was that as I reached forward the
cow kept straining, squeezing my arm cruelly against

her bony pelvis, making me groan and roll about in agony for a few seconds till the pressure went off. Quite often in these crises my cap fell on to the floor and each time gentle hands replaced it immediately on my head.

At last the foot was in my hand—there would be no need for ropes this time—and I began to pull it round. It took me longer than I thought and it seemed to me that the calf was beginning to lose patience with me because when its head was forced out by the cow's contractions we were eye to eye and I fancied the little creature was giving me a disgusted "For heaven's sake get on with it" look.

When the leg did come round it was with a rush and in an instant everything was laid as it should have been.

"Get hold of the feet," I whispered to the Bamfords and after a hushed consultation they took up their places. In no time at all a fine heifer calf was wriggling on the cobbles shaking its head and snorting the placental fluid from its nostrils.

In response to my softly hissed instructions the farmers rubbed the little creature down with straw wisps and pulled it round for its mother to lick.

It was a happy ending to the most peaceful calving I have ever attended. Never a voice raised, everybody moving around on tiptoe. I got dressed in a cathedral silence, went out to the car, breathed a final goodnight and left with the Bamfords waving mutely.

To say I had a hangover next morning would be failing even to hint at the utter disintegration of my bodily economy and personality. Only somebody who had consumed two or three quarts of assorted home made wines at a sitting could have an inkling of the quaking nausea, the raging inferno within, the jangling nerves, the black despairing outlook.

Tristan had seen me in the bathroom running the cold tap on my tongue and had intuitively administered a raw egg, aspirins and brandy which, as I came downstairs, lay in a cold, unmoving blob in my outraged stomach.

"What are you walking like that for, James?" asked Siegfried in what sounded like a bull's bellow as I came in on him at breakfast. "You look as though you'd pee'd yourself."

"Oh it's nothing much." It was no good telling him I was treading warily across the carpet because I was convinced that if I let my heels down too suddenly it would jar my eyeballs from their sockets. "I had a few glasses of Mr. Crump's wine last night and it seems to have upset me."

"A few glasses! You ought to be more careful—that stuff's dynamite. Could knock anybody over." He crashed his cup into its saucer then began to clatter about with knife and fork as if trying to give a one man rendering of the Anvil Chorus. "I hope you weren't any the worse to go to Bamford's."

I listlessly crumbled some dry toast on my plate. "Well I did the job all right, but I'd had a bit too much—no use denying it."

Siegfried was in one of his encouraging moods. "By God, James, those Bamfords are very strict methodists. They're grand chaps but absolutely dead nuts against drink—if they thought you were under the influence of alcohol they'd never have you on the place again." He ruthlessly bisected an egg yolk. "I hope they didn't notice anything. Do you think they knew?"

"Oh maybe not. No, I shouldn't think so." I closed my eyes and shivered as Siegfried pushed a forkful of sausage and fried bread into his mouth and began to chew briskly. My mind went back to the gentle hands replacing the monstrous cap on my head and I groaned inwardly.

Those Bamfords knew all right. Oh yes, they knew.

9

The silver haired old gentleman with the pleasant face didn't look the type to be easily upset but his eyes glared at me angrily and his lips quivered with indignation.

"Mr. Herriot," he said. "I have come to make a complaint. I strongly object to your allowing students to practise on my cat."

"Students? What students?" I was mystified.

"I think you know, Mr. Herriot. I brought my cat in a few days ago for a hysterectomy and I am referring to this operation."

I nodded. "Yes, I remember it very well . . . but where do the students come in?"

"Well the operation wound was rather large and I have it on good authority that it was made by somebody who was just learning the job." The old gentleman stuck out his chin fiercely.

"Right," I said. "Let's take one thing at a time. I did that operation myself and I had to enlarge the wound because your cat was in an advanced state of pregnancy. I couldn't squeeze the foetuses through my original incision."

"Oh? I didn't know that."

"Secondly, we have no students with us. They only come at holiday times and when they are here they certainly are not allowed to carry out operations."

"Well this lady seemed to be absolutely sure of her facts. She was adamant about it. She took one look at the cat and pronounced that it was the work of a student."

"Lady?"

"Yes," said the old gentleman. "She is very clever with animals and she came round to see if she could help in my cat's convalescence. She brought some excellent condition powders with her."

"Ah!" A blinding shaft pierced the fog in my mind. All was suddenly clear. "It was Mrs. Donovan, wasn't it?"

"Well . . . er, yes. That was her name."

Old Mrs. Donovan was a woman who really got around. No matter what was going on in Darrowby —weddings, funerals, house-sales—you'd find the dumpy little figure and walnut face among the spectators, the darting, black-button eyes taking everything in. And always, on the end of its lead, her terrier dog.

When I say "old", I'm only guessing, because she appeared ageless; she seemed to have been around a long time but she could have been anything between fifty five and seventy five. She certainly had the vitality of a young woman because she must have walked vast distances in her dedicated quest to keep abreast of events. Many people took an uncharitable view of her acute curiosity but whatever the motivation, her activities took her into almost every channel of life in the town. One of these channels was our veterinary practice.

Because Mrs. Donovan, among her other widely ranging interests, was an animal doctor. In fact I think it would be safe to say that this facet of her life transcended all the others.

She could talk at length on the ailments of small animals and she had a whole armoury of medicines and remedies at her command, her two specialties being her miracle working condition powders and a dog shampoo of unprecedented value for improving the coat. She had an uncanny ability to sniff out a sick animal and it was not uncommon when I was on my rounds to find Mrs. Donovan's dark gipsy face poised intently over what I had thought was my patient while she administered calf's foot jelly or one of her own patent nostrums.

I suffered more than Siegfried because I took a more active part in the small animal side of our practice. I was anxious to develop this aspect and to improve my image in this field and Mrs. Donovan didn't help at all. "Young Mr. Herriot," she would confide to my clients, "is all right with cattle and such like, but he don't know nothing about dogs and cats."

And of course they believed her and had implicit faith in her. She had the irresistible mystic appeal of the amateur and on top of that there was her habit, particularly endearing in Darrowby, of never charging for her advice, her medicines, her long periods of diligent nursing.

Older folk in the town told how her husband, an Irish farm worker, had died many years ago and how he must have had a "bit put away" because Mrs. Donovan had apparently been able to indulge all her interests over the years without financial strain. Since she inhabited the streets of Darrowby all day and every day I often encountered her and she always smiled up at me sweetly and told me how she had been sitting up all night with Mrs. So-and-so's dog that I'd been treating. She felt sure she'd be able to pull it through.

There was no smile on her face, however, on the day when she rushed into the surgery while Siegfried and I were having tea.

"Mr. Herriot!" she gasped. "Can you come? My little dog's been run over!"

I jumped up and ran out to the car with her. She sat in the passenger seat with her head bowed, her hands clasped tightly on her knees.

"He slipped his collar and ran in front of a car," she murmured. "He's lying in front of the school half way up Cliffend Road. Please hurry."

I was there within three minutes but as I bent over the dusty little body stretched on the pavement I knew there was nothing I could do. The fast-glazing eyes, the faint, gasping respirations, the ghastly pallor of the mucous membranes all told the same story.

"I'll take him back to the surgery and get some

saline into him, Mrs. Donovan," I said. "But I'm afraid he's had a massive internal haemorrhage. Did you see what happened exactly?"

She gulped. "Yes, the wheel went right over him."

Ruptured liver, for sure. I passed my hands under the little animal and began to lift him gently, but as I did so the breathing stopped and the eyes stared fixedly ahead.

Mrs. Donovan sank to her knees and for a few moments she gently stroked the rough hair of the head and chest. "He's dead, isn't he?" she whispered at last.

"I'm afraid he is," I said.

She got slowly to her feet and stood bewilderedly among the little group of bystanders on the pavement. Her lips moved but she seemed unable to say any more.

I took her arm, led her over to the car and opened the door. "Get in and sit down," I said. "I'll run you home. Leave everything to me."

I wrapped the dog in my calving overall and laid him in the boot before driving away. It wasn't until we drew up outside Mrs. Donovan's house that she began to weep silently. I sat there without speaking till she had finished. Then she wiped her eyes and turned to me.

"Do you think he suffered at all?"

"I'm certain he didn't. It was all so quick—he wouldn't know a thing about it."

She tried to smile. "Poor little Rex, I don't know what I'm going to do without him. We've travelled a few miles together, you know."

"Yes, you have. He had a wonderful life, Mrs. Donovan. And let me give you a bit of advice—you must get another dog. You'd be lost without one."

She shook her head. "No, I couldn't. That little dog meant too much to me. I couldn't let another take his place."

"Well I know that's how you feel just now but I wish you'd think about it. I don't want to seem callous—I tell everybody this when they lose an animal and I know it's good advice."

"Mr. Herriot, I'll never have another one." She shook her head again, very decisively. "Rex was my faithful friend for many years and I just want to remember him. He's the last dog I'll ever have."

I often saw Mrs. Donovan around the town after this and I was glad to see she was still as active as ever, though she looked strangely incomplete without the little dog on its lead. But it must have been over a month before I had the chance to speak to her.

It was on the afternoon that Inspector Halliday of the R.S.P.C.A. rang me.

"Mr. Herriot," he said, "I'd like you to come and see an animal with me. A cruelty case."

"Right, what is it?"

"A dog, and it's pretty grim. A dreadful case of neglect." He gave me the name of a row of old brick cottages down by the river and said he'd meet me there.

Halliday was waiting for me, smart and business-like in his dark uniform, as I pulled up in the back lane behind the houses. He was a big, blond man with cheerful blue eyes but he didn't smile as he came over to the car.

"He's in here," he said, and led the way towards one of the doors in the long, crumbling wall. A few curious people were hanging around and with a feeling of inevitability I recognised a gnome-like brown face. Trust Mrs. Donovan, I thought, to be among those present at a time like this.

We went through the door into the long garden. I had found that even the lowliest dwellings in Darrowby had long strips of land at the back as though the builders had taken it for granted that the country people who were going to live in them would want to occupy themselves with the pursuits of the soil; with vegetable and fruit growing, even stock keeping in a small way. You usually found a pig there, a few hens, often pretty beds of flowers.

But this garden was a wilderness. A chilling air of desolation hung over the few gnarled apple and plum trees standing among a tangle of rank grass as though the place had been forsaken by all living creatures.

Halliday went over to a ramshackle wooden shed with peeling paint and a rusted corrugated iron roof. He produced a key, unlocked the padlock and dragged the door partly open. There was no window and it wasn't easy to identify the jumble inside: broken gardening tools, an ancient mangle, rows of flower pots and partly used paint tins. And right at the back, a dog sitting quietly.

I didn't notice him immediately because of the gloom and because the smell in the shed started me coughing, but as I drew closer I saw that he was a big animal, sitting very upright, his collar secured by a chain to a ring in the wall. I had seen some thin dogs but this advanced emaciation reminded me of my text books on anatomy; nowhere else did the bones of pelvis, face and rib cage stand out with such horrifying clarity. A deep, smoothed out hollow in the earth floor showed where he had lain, moved about, in fact lived for a very long time.

The sight of the animal had a stupefying effect on me; I only half took in the rest of the scene—the filthy shreds of sacking scattered nearby, the bowl of scummy water.

"Look at his back end," Halliday muttered.

I carefully raised the dog from his sitting position and realised that the stench in the place was not entirely due to the piles of excrement. The hindquarters were a welter of pressure sores which had turned gangrenous and strips of sloughing tissue hung down from them. There were similar sores along the sternum and ribs. The coat, which seemed to be a dull yellow, was matted and caked with dirt.

The Inspector spoke again. "I don't think he's ever been out of here. He's only a young dog—about a year old—but I understand he's been in this shed since he was an eight week old pup. Somebody out in the lane heard a whimper or he'd never have been found."

I felt a tightening of the throat and a sudden nausea which wasn't due to the smell. It was the thought of this patient animal sitting starved and forgotten in the darkness and filth for a year. I looked again at the dog and saw in his eyes only a calm trust. Some dogs would have barked their heads off and soon been discovered, some would have become terrified and vicious, but this was one of the totally undemanding kind, the kind which had complete faith in people and accepted all their actions without complaint. Just an occasional whimper perhaps as he sat interminably in the empty blackness which had been his world and at times wondered what it was all about.

"Well, Inspector, I hope you're going to throw the book at whoever's responsible," I said.

Halliday grunted. "Oh, there won't be much done. It's a case of diminished responsibility. The owner's definitely simple. Lives with an aged mother who hardly knows what's going on either. I've seen the fellow and it seems he threw in a bit of food when he felt like it and that's about all he did. They'll fine him and stop him keeping an animal in the future but nothing more than that."

"I see." I reached out and stroked the dog's head and he immediately responded by resting a paw on my wrist. There was a pathetic dignity about the way he held himself erect, the calm eyes regarding me, friendly and unafraid. "Well, you'll let me know if you want me in court."

"Of course, and thank you for coming along." Halliday hesitated for a moment. "And now I expect you'll want to put this poor thing out of his misery right away."

I continued to run my hand over the head and ears while I thought for a moment. "Yes . . . yes, I suppose so. We'd never find a home for him in this state. It's the kindest thing to do. Anyway, push the door wide open will you so that I can get a proper look at him."

In the improved light I examined him more thoroughly. Perfect teeth, well-proportioned limbs with a fringe of yellow hair. I put my stethoscope on his chest and as I listened to the slow, strong thudding of the heart the dog again put his paw on my hand.

I turned to Halliday. "You know, Inspector, inside this bag of bones there's a lovely healthy Golden Retriever. I wish there was some way of letting him out."

As I spoke I noticed there was more than one figure in the door opening. A pair of black pebble eyes were peering intently at the dog from behind the Inspector's broad back. The other spectators had remained in the lane but Mrs. Donovan's curiosity had been too much for her. I continued conversationally as though I hadn't seen her.

"You know, what this dog needs first of all is a good shampoo to clean up his matted coat."

"Huh?" said Halliday.

"Yes. And then he wants a long course of some really strong condition powders."

"What's that?" The Inspector looked startled.

"There's no doubt about it," I said. "It's the only hope for him, but where are you going to find such things? Really powerful enough, I mean." I sighed and straightened up. "Ah well, I suppose there's nothing else for it. I'd better put him to sleep right away. I'll get the things from my car."

When I got back to the shed Mrs. Donovan was already inside examining the dog despite the feeble remonstrances of the big man.

"Look!" she said excitedly, pointing to a name roughly scratched on the collar. "His name's Roy." She smiled up at me. "It's a bit like Rex, isn't it, that name."

"You know, Mrs. Donovan, now you mention it, it is. It's very like Rex, the way it comes off your tongue." I nodded seriously.

She stood silent for a few moments, obviously in the grip of a deep emotion, then she burst out.

"Can I have 'im? I can make him better, I know I can. Please, please let me have 'im!"

"Well I don't know," I said. "It's really up to the Inspector. You'll have to get his permission."

Halliday looked at her in bewilderment, then he said: "Excuse me, Madam," and drew me to one side. We walked a few yards through the long grass and stopped under a tree.

"Mr. Herriot," he whispered, "I don't know what's going on here, but I can't just pass over an animal in this condition to anybody who has a casual whim. The poor beggar's had one bad break already—I think it's enough. This woman doesn't look a suitable person . . ."

I held up a hand. "Believe me, Inspector, you've nothing to worry about. She's a funny old stick but she's been sent from heaven today. If anybody in Darrowby can give this dog a new life it's her."

Halliday still looked very doubtful. "But I still don't get it. What was all that stuff about him needing shampoos and condition powders?"

"Oh never mind about that. I'll tell you some other time. What he needs is lots of good grub, care and affection and that's just what he'll get. You can take my word for it."

"All right, you seem very sure." Halliday looked at me for a second or two then turned and walked over to the eager little figure by the shed.

I had never before been deliberately on the look out for Mrs. Donovan: she had just cropped up wherever I happened to be, but now I scanned the streets of Darrowby anxiously day by day without sighting her. I didn't like it when Gobber Newhouse got drunk and drove his bicycle determinedly through a barrier into a ten foot hole where they were laying the new sewer and Mrs. Donovan was not in evidence among the happy crowd who watched the council workmen and two policemen trying to get him out; and when she was nowhere to be seen when they had to fetch the fire engine to the fish and chip shop the night the fat burst into flames, I became seriously worried.

Maybe I should have called round to see how she was getting on with that dog. Certainly I had trimmed off the necrotic tissue and dressed the sores before she took him away, but perhaps he needed something more than that. And yet at the time I had felt a strong conviction that the main thing was to get him out of there and clean him and feed him and nature would do the rest. And I had a lot of faith in Mrs. Donovan—far more than she had in me—when it came to animal doctoring; it was hard to believe I'd been completely wrong.

It must have been nearly three weeks and I was on the point of calling at her home when I noticed her stumping briskly along the far side of the market place, peering closely into every shop window exactly as before. The only difference was that she had a big yellow dog on the end of the lead.

I turned the wheel and sent my car bumping over the cobbles till I was abreast of her. When she saw me getting out she stopped and smiled impishly but she didn't speak as I bent over Roy and examined him. He was still a skinny dog but he looked bright and happy, his wounds were healthy and granulating and there was not a speck of dirt in his coat or on his skin. I knew then what Mrs. Donovan had been doing all this time; she had been washing and combing and teasing at that filthy tangle till she had finally conquered it.

As I straightened up she seized my wrist in a grip of surprising strength and looked up into my eyes.

"Now Mr. Herriot," she said. "Haven't I made a difference to this dog!"

"You've done wonders, Mrs. Donovan," I said. "And you've been at him with that marvellous shampoo of yours, haven't you?"

She giggled and walked away and from that day I saw the two of them frequently but at a distance

and something like two months went by before I
had a chance to talk to her again. She was passing
by the surgery as I was coming down the steps and
again she grabbed my wrist.

"Mr. Herriot," she said, just as she had done before.
"Haven't I made a difference to this dog!"

I looked down at Roy with something akin to awe.
He had grown and filled out and his coat, no longer
yellow but a rich gold, lay in luxuriant shining
swathes over the well-fleshed ribs and back. A new,
brightly studded collar glittered on his neck and his
tail, beautifully fringed, fanned the air gently. He
was now a Golden Retriever in full magnificence. As
I stared at him he reared up, plunked his fore paws
on my chest and looked into my face, and in his eyes
I read plainly the same calm affection and trust I
had seen back in that black, noisome shed.

"Mrs. Donovan," I said softly, "he's the most beautiful dog in Yorkshire." Then, because I knew she was
waiting for it. "It's those wonderful condition powders. Whatever do you put in them?"

"Ah, wouldn't you like to know!" She bridled and
smiled up at me coquettishly and indeed she was
nearer being kissed at that moment than for many
years.

I suppose you could say that that was the start of
Roy's second life. And as the years passed I often
pondered on the beneficent providence which had
decreed that an animal which had spent his first
twelve months abandoned and unwanted, staring uncomprehendingly into that unchanging, stinking darkness, should be whisked in a moment into an existence of light and movement and love. Because I
don't think any dog had it quite so good as Roy
from then on.

His diet changed dramatically from odd bread
crusts to best stewing steak and biscuit, meaty bones
and a bowl of warm milk every evening. And he never
missed a thing. Garden fetes, school sports, evictions,
gymkhanas—he'd be there. I was pleased to note
that as time went on Mrs. Donovan seemed to be

clocking up an even greater daily mileage. Her expenditure on shoe leather must have been phenomenal, but of course it was absolute pie for Roy—a busy round in the morning, home for a meal then straight out again; it was all go.

Mrs. Donovan didn't confine her activities to the town centre; there was a big stretch of common land down by the river where there were seats, and people used to take their dogs for a gallop and she liked to get down there fairly regularly to check on the latest developments on the domestic scene. I often saw Roy loping majestically over the grass among a pack of assorted canines, and when he wasn't doing that he was submitting to being stroked or patted or generally fussed over. He was handsome and he just liked people; it made him irresistible.

It was common knowledge that his mistress had bought a whole selection of brushes and combs of various sizes with which she laboured over his coat. Some people said she had a little brush for his teeth, too, and it might have been true, but he certainly wouldn't need his nails clipped—his life on the roads would keep them down.

Mrs. Donovan, too, had her reward; she had a faithful companion by her side every hour of the day and night. But there was more to it than that; she had always had the compulsion to help and heal animals and the salvation of Roy was the high point of her life—a blazing triumph which never dimmed.

I know the memory of it was always fresh because many years later I was sitting on the sidelines at a cricket match and I saw the two of them; the old lady glancing keenly around her, Roy gazing placidly out at the field of play, apparently enjoying every ball. At the end of the match I watched them move away with the dispersing crowd; Roy would be about twelve then and heaven only knows how old Mrs. Donovan must have been, but the big golden animal was trotting along effortlessly and his mistress, a little more bent, perhaps, and her head rather nearer the ground, was going very well.

When she saw me she came over and I felt the familiar tight grip on my wrist.

"Mr. Herriot," she said, and in the dark probing eyes the pride was still as warm, the triumph still as bursting new as if it had all happened yesterday.

"Mr. Herriot, haven't I made a difference to this dog!"

10

The thing that had changed everything was the tranquil basis of my home life. The vagaries of practice went on and would always go on but behind it all Helen's presence was a warm infinity, a measureless peace. When I looked back at the time before she was my wife it was an uncertain world and events like the Darrowby Show seemed an eternity ago.

I remembered when Siegfried first asked me about it.

"How would you like to officiate at Darrowby Show, James?" He threw the letter he had been reading on to the desk and turned to me.

"I don't mind, but I thought you always did it."

"I do, but it says in that letter that they've changed the date this year and it happens I'm going to be away that weekend."

"Oh well, fine. What do I have to do?"

Siegfried ran his eye down his list of calls. "It's a sinecure, really. More a pleasant day out than anything else. You have to measure the ponies and be on call in case any animals are injured. That's about all. Oh and they want you to judge the Family Pets."

"Family Pets?"

"Yes, they run a proper dog show but they have an expert judge for that. This is just a bit of fun—all kinds of pets. You've got to find a first, second and third."

"Right," I said. "I think I should just about be able to manage that."

"Splendid." Siegfried tipped up the envelope in

which the letter had come. "Here are your car park and luncheon tickets for self and friend if you want to take somebody with you. Also your vet's badge. O.K.?"

The Saturday of the show brought the kind of weather that must have had the organisers purring with pleasure; a sky of wide, unsullied blue, hardly a whiff of wind and the kind of torrid, brazen sunshine you don't often find in North Yorkshire

As I drove down towards the show ground I felt I was looking at a living breathing piece of old England; the group of tents and marquees vivid against the green of the riverside field, the women and children in their bright summer dresses, the cattle with their smocked attendants, a line of massive Shire horses parading in the ring.

I parked the car and made for the stewards' tent with its flag hanging limply from the mast. Tristan parted from me there. With the impecunious student's unerring eye for a little free food and entertainment he had taken up my spare tickets. He headed purposefully for the beer tent as I went in to report to the show secretary.

Leaving my measuring stick there I looked around for a while.

A country show is a lot of different things to a lot of different people. Riding horses of all kinds from small ponies to hunters were being galloped up and down and in one ring the judges hovered around a group of mares and their beautiful little foals.

In a corner four men armed with buckets and brushes were washing and grooming a row of young bulls with great concentration, twiddling and crimping the fuzz over the rumps like society hairdressers.

Wandering through the marquees I examined the bewildering variety of produce from stalks of rhubarb to bunches of onions, the flower displays, embroidery, jams, cakes, pies. And the children's section; a painting of "The Beach at Scarborough" by Annie Heseltine, aged nine; rows of wobbling copperplate handwriting—"A thing of beauty is a joy for ever" Bernard Peacock, aged twelve.

Drawn by the occasional gusts of melody I strolled across the grass to where the Darrowby and Houlton Silver Band was rendering Poet and Peasant. The bandsmen were of all ages from seventies down to one or two boys of about fourteen and most of them had doffed their uniform tunics as they sweated in the hot sun. Pint pots reposed under many of the chairs and the musicians refreshed themselves frequently with leisurely swigs.

I was particularly fascinated by the conductor, a tiny frail man who looked about eighty. He alone had retained his full uniform, cap and all, and he stood apparently motionless in front of the crescent of bandsmen, chin sunk on chest, arms hanging limply by his sides. It wasn't until I came right up to him that I realised his fingers were twitching in time with the music and that he was, in fact, conducting. And the more I watched him the more fitting it seemed that he should do it like that. The Yorkshireman's loathing of exhibitionism or indeed any outward show of emotion made it unthinkable that he should throw his arms about in the orthodox manner; no doubt he had spent weary hours rehearsing and coaching his players but here, when the results of his labours were displayed to the public, he wasn't going to swank about it. Even the almost imperceptible twitching of the finger-ends had something guilty about it as if the old man felt he was being caught out in something shameful.

But my attention was jerked away as a group of people walked across on the far side of the band. It was Helen with Richard Edmundson and behind them Mr. Alderson and Richard's father deep in conversation. The young man walked very close to Helen, his shining, plastered-down fair hair hovering possessively over her dark head, his face animated as he talked and laughed.

There were no clouds in the sky but it was as if a

dark hand had reached across and smudged away the brightness of the sunshine. I turned quickly and went in search of Tristan.

I soon picked out my colleague as I hurried into the marquee with "Refreshments" over the entrance. He was leaning with an elbow on the makeshift counter of boards and trestles chatting contentedly with a knot of cloth-capped locals, a Woodbine in one hand, a pint glass in the other. There was a general air of earthy bonhomie. Drinking of a more decorous kind would be taking place at the president's bar behind the stewards' headquarters with pink gins or sherry as the main tipple but here it was beer, bottled and draught, and the stout ladies behind the counter were working with the fierce concentration of people who knew they were in for a hard day.

"Yes, I saw her," Tristan said when I gave him my news. "In fact there she is now." He nodded in the direction of the family group as they strolled past the entrance. "I've had my eye on them for some time—I don't miss much from in here you know, Jim."

"Ah well." I accepted a half of bitter from him. "It all looks pretty cosy. The two dads like blood brothers and Helen hanging on to that bloke's arm."

Tristan squinted over the top of his pint at the scene outside and shook his head. "Not exactly. He's hanging on to HER arm." He looked at me judicially. "There's a difference, you know."

"I don't suppose it makes much difference to me either way," I grunted.

"Well don't look so bloody mournful." He took an effortless swallow which lowered the level in his glass by about six inches. "What do you expect an attractive girl to do? Sit at home waiting for you to call? If you've been pounding on her door every night you haven't told me about it."

"It's all right you talking. I think old man Alderson would set his dogs on me if I showed up there. I know he doesn't like me hanging around Helen and on top of that I've got the feeling he thinks I killed his cow on my last visit."

"And did you?"

"No, I didn't. But I walked up to a living animal, gave it an injection and it promptly died, so I can't blame him."

I took a sip at my beer and watched the Alderson party who had changed direction and were heading away from our retreat. Helen was wearing a pale blue dress and I was thinking how well the colour went with the deep brown of her hair and how I liked the way she walked with her legs swinging easily and her shoulders high and straight when the loudspeaker boomed across the show ground.

"Will Mr. Herriot, Veterinary Surgeon, please report to the stewards immediately."

It made me jump but at the same time I felt a quick stab of pride. It was the first time I had heard myself and my profession publicly proclaimed. I turned to Tristan. He was supposed to be seeing practice and this could be something interesting. But he was immersed in a story which he was trying to tell to a little stocky man with a fat, shiny face, and he was having difficulty because the little man, determined to get his full measure of enjoyment, kept throwing himself into helpless convulsions at the end of every sentence, and the finish was a long way away. Tristan took his stories very seriously; I decided not to interrupt him.

A glow of importance filled me as I hurried over the grass, my official badge with "Veterinary Surgeon" in gold letters dangling from my lapel. A steward met me on the way.

"It's one of the cattle. Had an accident, I think." He pointed to a row of pens along the edge of the field.

A curious crowd had collected around my patient which had been entered in the in-calf heifers class. The owner a stranger from outside the Darrowby practice came up to me, his face glum.

"She tripped coming off the cattle wagon and went 'ead first into the wall. Knocked one of 'er horns clean off."

The heifer, a bonny little light roan, was a pathetic sight. She had been washed, combed, powdered and primped for the big day and there she was with one horn dangling drunkenly down the side of her face and an ornamental fountain of bright arterial blood climbing gracefully in three jets from the broken surface high into the air.

I opened my bag. I had brought a selection of the things I might need and I fished out some artery forceps and suture material. The rational way to stop haemorrhage of this type is to grasp the bleeding vessel and ligate it, but it wasn't always as easy as that. Especially when the patient won't cooperate.

The broken horn was connected to the head only by a band of skin and I quickly snipped it away with scissors; then, with the farmer holding the heifer's nose I began to probe with my forceps for the severed vessels. In the bright sunshine it was surprisingly difficult to see the spurting blood and as the little animal threw her head about I repeatedly felt the warm spray across my face and heard it spatter on my collar.

It was when I was beginning to lose heart with my ineffectual groping that I looked up and saw Helen and her boy friend watching me from the crowd. Young Edmundson looked mildly amused as he watched my unavailing efforts but Helen smiled encouragingly as she caught my eye. I did my best to smile back at her through my bloody mask but I don't suppose it showed.

I gave it up when the heifer gave a particularly brisk toss which sent my forceps flying on to the grass. I did what I should probably have done at the beginning—clapped a pad of cotton wool and antiseptic powder on to the stump and secured it with a figure of eight bandage round the other horn.

"That's it, then," I said to the farmer as I tried to blink the blood out of my eyes. "The bleeding's stopped, anyway. I'd advise you to have her properly de-horned soon or she's going to look a bit odd."

Just then Tristan appeared from among the spectators.

"What's got you out of the beer tent?" I enquired with a touch of bitterness.

"It's lunch time, old lad," Tristan replied equably. "But we'll have to get you cleaned up a bit first. I can't be seen with you in that condition. Hang on, I'll get a bucket of water."

The show luncheon was so excellent that it greatly restored me. Although it was taken in a marquee the committee men's wives had somehow managed to conjure up a memorable cold spread. There was fresh salmon and home fed ham and slices of prime beef with mixed salads and apple pie and the big brimming jugs of cream you only see at farming functions. One of the ladies was a noted cheese maker and we finished with some delicious goat cheese and coffee. The liquid side was catered for too with a bottle of Magnet Pale Ale and a glass at every place.

I didn't have the pleasure of Tristan's company at lunch because he had strategically placed himself well down the table between two strict methodists so that his intake of Magnet was trebled.

I had hardly emerged into the sunshine when a man touched me on the shoulder.

"One of the dog show judges wants you to examine a dog. He doesn't like the look of it."

He led me to where a thin man of about forty with a small dark moustache was standing by his car. He held a wire-haired fox terrier on a leash and he met me with an ingratiating smile.

"There's nothing whatever the matter with my dog," he declared, "but the chap in there seems very fussy."

I looked down at the terrier. "I see he has some matter in the corner of his eyes."

The man shook his head vigorously. "Oh no, that's not matter. I've been using some white powder on him and a bit's got into his eyes, that's all."

"Hmm, well let's see what his temperature says, shall we?"

The little animal stood uncomplaining as I inserted the thermometer. When I took the reading my eyebrows went up.

"It's a hundred and four. I'm afraid he's not fit to go into the show."

"Wait a minute." The man thrust out his jaw. "You're talking like that chap in there. I've come a long way to show this dog and I'm going to show him."

"I'm sorry but you can't show him with a temperature of a hundred and four."

"But he's had a car journey. That could put up his temperature."

I shook my head. "Not as high as that it couldn't. Anyway he looks sick to me. Do you see how he's half closing his eyes as though he's frightened of the light? It's possible he could have distemper."

"What? That's rubbish and you know it. He's never been fitter!" The man's mouth trembled with anger.

I looked down at the little dog. He was crouching on the grass miserably. Occasionally he shivered, he had a definite photophobia and there was that creamy blob of pus in the corner of each eye. "Has he been inoculated against distemper?"

"Well no, he hasn't, but why do you keep on about it?"

"Because I think he's got it now and for his sake and for the sake of the other dogs here you ought to take him straight home and see your own vet."

He glared at me. "So you won't let me take him into the show tent?"

"That's right. I'm very sorry, but it's out of the question." I turned and walked away.

I had gone only a few yards when the loudspeaker boomed again. "Will Mr. Herriot please go to the measuring stand where the ponies are ready for him."

I collected my stick and trotted over to a corner of the field where a group of ponies had assembled; Welsh, Dales, Exmoor, Dartmoor—all kinds of breeds were represented.

For the uninitiated, horses are measured in hands

which consist of four inches and a graduated stick
is used with a cross piece and a spirit level which
rests on the withers, the highest point of the shoulders. I had done a fair bit of it in individual animals
but this was the first time I had done the job at a
show. With my stick at the ready I stood by the
two wide boards which had been placed on the turf
to give the animals a reasonably level standing surface.

A smiling young woman led the first pony, a smart
chestnut, on to the boards.

"Which class?" I asked.

"Thirteen hands."

I tried the stick on him. He was well under.

"Fine, next please."

A few more came through without incident then
there was a lull before the next group came up.
The ponies were arriving on the field all the time in
their boxes and being led over to me, some by their
young riders, others by the parents. It looked as
though I could be here quite a long time.

During one of the lulls a little man who had been
standing near me spoke up.

"No trouble yet?" he asked.

"No, everything's in order," I replied.

He nodded expressionlessly and as I took a closer
look at him his slight body, dark, leathery features
and high shoulders seemed to give him the appearance of a little brown gnome. At the same time there
was something undeniably horsy about him.

"You'll 'ave some awkward 'uns," he grunted.
"And they allus say the same thing. They allus tell
you the vet at some other show passed their pony."
His swarthy cheeks crinkled in a wry smile.

"Is that so?"

"Aye, you'll see."

Another candidate, led by a beautiful blonde, was
led on to the platform. She gave me the full blast
of two big greenish eyes and flashed a mouthful of
sparkling teeth at me.

"Twelve two," she murmured seductively.

I tried the stick on the pony and worked it around, but try as I might I couldn't get it down to that.

"I'm afraid he's a bit big," I said.

The blonde's smile vanished. "Have you allowed half an inch for his shoes?"

"I have indeed, but you can see for yourself, he's well over."

"But he passed the vet without any trouble at Hickley," she snapped and out of the corner of my eye I saw the gnome nodding sagely.

"I can't help that," I said. "I'm afraid you'll have to put him into the next class."

For a moment two green pebbles from the cold sea bed fixed me with a frigid glare then the blonde was gone taking her pony with her.

Next, a little bay animal was led on to the stand by a hard faced gentleman in a check suit and I must say I was baffled by its behaviour. Whenever the stick touched the withers it sank at the knees so that I couldn't be sure whether I was getting the right reading or not. Finally I gave up and passed him through.

The gnome coughed. "I know that feller."

"You do?"

"Aye, he's pricked that pony's withers with a pin so many times that it drops down whenever you try to measure 'im."

"Never!"

"Sure as I'm standing here."

I was staggered, but the arrival of another batch took up my attention for a few minutes. Some I passed, others I had to banish to another class and the owners took it in different ways—some philosophically, a few with obvious annoyance. One or two of the ponies just didn't like the look of the stick at all and I had to dance around them as they backed away and reared.

The last pony in this group was a nice grey led by a bouncy man wearing a great big matey smile.

"How are you, all right?" he inquired courteously. "This 'un's thirteen two."

The animal went under the stick without trouble but after he had trotted away the gnome spoke up again.

"I know that feller, too."

"Really?"

"Not 'alf. Weighs down 'is ponies before they're measured. That grey's been standing in 'is box for the last hour with a twelve stone sack of corn on 'is back. Knocks an inch off."

"Good God! Are you sure?"

"Don't worry, I've seen 'im at it."

My mind was beginning to reel just a little. Was the man making it all up or were there really those malign forces at work behind all this innocent fun?

"That same feller," continued the gnome. "I've seen 'im bring a pony to a show and get half an inch knocked off for shoes when it never 'ad no shoes on."

I wished he'd stop. And just then there was an interruption. It was the man with the moustache. He sidled up to me and whispered confidentially in my ear.

"Now I've just been thinking. My dog must have got over his journey by now and I expect his temperature will be normal. I wonder if you'd just try him again. I've still got time to show him."

I turned wearily. "Honestly, it'll be a waste of time. I've told you, he's ill."

"Please! Just as a favour." He had a desperate look and a fanatical light flickered in his eye.

"All right." I went over to the car with him and produced my thermometer. The temperature was still a hundred and four.

"Now I wish you'd take this poor little dog home," I said. "He shouldn't be here."

For a moment I thought the man was going to strike me. "There's nothing wrong with him!" he hissed, his whole face working with emotion.

"I'm sorry," I said, and went back to the measuring stand.

A boy of about fifteen was waiting for me with his

pony. It was supposed to be in the thirteen two class but was nearly one and a half inches over.

"Much too big, I'm afraid," I said. "He can't go in that class."

The boy didn't answer. He put his hand inside his jacket and produced a sheet of paper. "This is a veterinary certificate to say he's under thirteen two."

"No good, I'm sorry," I replied. "The stewards have told me not to accept any certificates. I've turned down two others today. Everything has to go under the stick. It's a pity, but there it is."

His manner changed abruptly. "But you've GOT to accept it!" he shouted in my face. "There doesn't have to be any measurements when you have a certificate."

"You'd better see the stewards. Those are my instructions."

"I'll see my father about this, that's what!" he shouted and led the animal away.

Father was quickly on the scene. Big, fat, prosperous-looking, confident. He obviously wasn't going to stand any nonsense from me.

"Now look here, I don't know what this is all about but you have no option in this matter. You have to accept the certificate."

"I don't, I assure you," I answered. "And anyway, it's not as though your pony was slightly over the mark. He's miles over—nowhere near the height."

Father flushed dark red. "Well let me tell you he was passed through by the vet at . . ."

"I know, I know," I said, and I heard the gnome give a short laugh. "But he's not going through here."

There was a brief silence then both father and son began to scream at me. And as they continued to hurl abuse I felt a hand on my arm. It was the man with the moustache again.

"I'm going to ask you just once more to take my dog's temperature," he whispered with a ghastly attempt at a smile. "I'm sure he'll be all right this time. Will you try him again?"

I'd had enough. "No, I bloody well won't!" I barked. "Will you kindly stop bothering me and take that poor animal home."

It's funny how the most unlikely things motivate certain people. It didn't seem a life and death matter whether a dog got into a show or not but it was to the man with the moustache. He started to rave at me.

"You don't know your job, that's the trouble with you! I've come all this way and you've played a dirty trick on me. I've got a friend who's a vet, a proper vet, and I'm going to tell him about you, yes I am. I'm going to tell him about you!"

At the same time the father and son were still in full cry, snarling and mouthing at me and I became suddenly aware that I was in the centre of a hostile circle. The blonde was there too, and some of the others whose ponies I had outed and they were all staring at me belligerently, making angry gestures.

I felt very much alone because the gnome, who had seemed an ally, was nowhere to be seen. I was disappointed in the gnome; he was a big talker but had vanished at the first whiff of danger. As I surveyed the threatening crowd I moved my measuring stick round in front of me; it wasn't much of a weapon but it might serve to fend them off if they rushed me.

And just at that moment, as the unkind words were thick upon the air, I saw Helen and Richard Edmundson on the fringe of the circle, taking it all in. I wasn't worried about him but again it struck me as strange that it should be my destiny always to be looking a bit of a clown when Helen was around.

Anyway, the measuring was over and I felt in need of sustenance. I retreated and went to find Tristan.

11

The atmosphere in the beer tent was just what I needed. The hot weather had made the place even more popular than usual and it was crowded; many of the inhabitants had been there since early morning and the air was thick with earthy witticisms, immoderate laughter, cries of joy; and the nice thing was that nobody in there cared a damn about the heights of ponies or the temperatures of dogs.

I had to fight my way through the crush to reach Tristan who was leaning across the counter in earnest conversation with a comely young barmaid. The other serving ladies were middle-aged but his practised eye had picked this one out; glossy red hair, a puckish face and an inviting smile. I had been hoping for a soothing chat with him but he was unable to give me his undivided attention, so after juggling with a glass among the throng for a few minutes I left.

Out on the field the sun still blazed, the scent of the trampled grass rose into the warm air, the band was playing a selection from Rose Marie and peace began to steal into my soul. Maybe I could begin to enjoy the show now the pinpricks were over; there was only the Family Pets to judge and I was looking forward to that.

For about an hour I wandered among the pens of mountainous pigs and haughty sheep; the rows of Shorthorn cows with their classical wedge-shaped grace, their level udders and dainty feet.

I watched in fascination a contest which was new to me; shirt-sleeved young men sticking a fork into a straw bale and hurling it high over a bar with a jerk of their thick brown arms.

Old Steve Bramley, a local farmer, was judging the heavy horses and I envied him his massive authority as he stumped, bowler-hatted and glowering around each animal, leaning occasionally on his stick as he took stock of the points. I couldn't imagine anyone daring to argue with him.

It was late in the afternoon when the loudspeaker called me to my final duty. The Family Pets contestants were arranged on wooden chairs drawn up in a wide circle on the turf. They were mainly children but behind them an interested ring of parents and friends watched me warily as I arrived.

The fashion of exotic pets was still in its infancy but I experienced a mild shock of surprise when I saw the variety of creatures on show. I suppose I must have had a vague mental picture of a few dogs and cats but I walked round the circle in growing bewilderment looking down at rabbits—innumerable rabbits of all sizes and colours—guinea pigs, white mice, several budgerigars, two tortoises, a canary, a kitten, a parrot, a Mynah bird, a box of puppies, a few dogs and cats and a goldfish in a bowl. The smaller pets rested on their owners' knees, the others squatted on the ground.

How, I asked myself, was I going to come to a decision here? How did you choose between a parrot and a puppy, a budgie and a bulldog, a mouse and a Mynah? Then as I circled it came to me; it couldn't be done. The only way was to question the children in charge and find which ones looked after their pets best, which of them knew most about their feeding and general husbandry. I rubbed my hands together and repressed a chuckle of satisfaction; I had something to work on now.

I don't like to boast but I think I can say in all honesty that I carried out an exhaustive scientific survey of that varied group. From the outset I adopted an attitude of cold detachment, mercilessly banishing any ideas of personal preference. If I had been pleasing only myself I would have given first prize to a gleaming black Labrador sitting by a chair with massive composure and offering me a gracious paw every time I came near. And my second would have been a benevolent tabby—I have always had a thing about tabby cats—which rubbed its cheek against my hand as I talked to its owner. The pups, crawling over each other and grunting obesely, would probably have come third. But I put away these unworthy thoughts and pursued my chosen course.

I was distracted to some extent by the parrot which kept saying "Hellow" in a voice of devastating refinement like a butler answering a telephone and the Mynah which repeatedly adjured me to "Shut door as you go out," in a booming Yorkshire baritone.

The only adult in the ring was a bosomy lady with glacial pop eyes and a white poodle on her knee. As I approached she gave me a challenging stare as though defying me to place her pet anywhere but first.

"Hello, little chap," I said, extending my hand. The poodle responded by drawing its lips soundlessly back from its teeth and giving me much the same kind of look as its owner. I withdrew my hand hastily.

"Oh you needn't be afraid of him," the lady said frigidly. "He won't hurt you."

I gave a light laugh. "I'm sure he won't." I held out my hand again. "You're a nice little dog, aren't you?" Once more the poodle bared his teeth and when I persevered by trying to stroke his ears he snapped noiselessly, his teeth clicking together an inch from my fingers.

"He doesn't like you, I can see that. Do you darling?" The lady put her cheek against the dog's head and stared at me distastefully as though she knew just how he felt.

"Shut door as you go out," commanded the Mynah gruffly from somewhere behind me.

I gave the lady my questionnaire and moved on.

And among the throng there was one who stood

out; the little boy with the goldfish. In reply to my promptings he discoursed knowledgeably about his fish, its feeding, life history and habits. He even had a fair idea of the common diseases. The bowl, too, was beautifully clean and the water fresh; I was impressed.

When I had completed the circuit I swept the ring for the last time with a probing eye. Yes, there was no doubt about it; I had the three prize winners fixed in my mind beyond any question and in an order based on strictly scientific selection. I stepped out into the middle.

"Ladies and gentlemen," I said, scanning the company with an affable smile.

"Hellow," responded the parrot fruitily.

I ignored him and continued. "These are the successful entrants. First, number six, the goldfish. Second, number fifteen, the guinea pig. And third, number ten, the white kitten."

I half expected a little ripple of applause but there was none. In fact my announcement was greeted by a tight-lipped silence. I had noticed an immediate change in the atmosphere when I mentioned the goldfish. It was striking—a sudden cold wave which swept away the expectant smiles and replaced them with discontented muttering.

I had done something wrong, but what? I looked around helplessly as the hum of voices increased. "What do you think of that then?" "Not fair, is it?" "Wouldn't have thought it of him?" "All them lovely rabbits and he hardly looked at them."

I couldn't make it out, but my job was done, anyway. I pushed between the chairs and escaped to the open field.

"Shut door as you go out," the Mynah requested in deepest bass as I departed.

I sought out Tristan again. The atmosphere in the beer tent had changed, too. The drinkers were long since past their peak and the hilarious babel which had met me on my last visit had died to an exhausted murmur. There was a general air of satiation.

Tristan, pint in hand, was being addressed with great solemnity by a man in a flat cap and braces. The man swayed slightly as he grasped Tristan's free hand and gazed into his eyes. Occasionally he patted him on the shoulder with the utmost affection. Obviously my colleague had been forging deep and lasting friendships in here while I was making enemies outside.

I sidled up to him and spoke into his ear. "Ready to go soon, Triss?"

He turned slowly and looked at me. "No, old lad," he said, articulating carefully. "I'm afraid I shan't be coming with you. They're having a dance here on the showfield later and Doreen has consented to accompany me." He cast a loving glance across the counter at the redhead who crinkled her nose at him.

I was about to leave when a snatch of conversation from behind made me pause.

"A bloody goldfish!" a voice was saying disgustedly.

"Aye, it's a rum 'un, George," a second voice replied.

There was a slurping sound of beer being downed.

"But tha knows, Fred," the first voice said. "That vet feller had to do it. Didn't 'ave no choice. He couldn't pass over t'squire's son."

"Reckon you're right, but it's a bugger when you get graft and corruption in t'Family Pets."

A heavy sigh, then "It's the way things are nowadays, Fred. Everything's hulterior."

"You're right there, George. It's hulterior, that's what it is."

I fought down a rising panic. The Pelhams had been Lords of the Manor of Darrowby for generations and the present squire was Major Pelham. I knew him as a friendly farmer client, but that was all. I'd never heard of his son.

I clutched at Tristan's arm. "Who is that little boy over there?"

Tristan peered out glassily across the sward. "The one with the goldfish bowl, you mean?"

"That's right."

"It's young Nigel Pelham, the squire's son."

"Oh Gawd," I moaned. "But I've never seen him before. Where's he been?"

"Boarding school down south, I believe. On holiday just now."

I stared at the boy again. Tousled fair hair, grey open-necked shirt, sunburned legs. Just like all the others.

George was at it again. "Lovely dogs and cats there was, but squire's lad won it with a bloody goldfish."

"Well let's be right," his companion put in. "If that lad 'ad brought along a bloody stuffed monkey he'd still 'ave got fust prize with it."

"No doubt about it, Fred. T'other kids might as well 'ave stopped at 'ome."

"Aye, it's not like it used to be, George. Nobody does owt for nowt these days."

"True, Fred, very true." There was a gloomy silence punctuated by noisy gulpings. Then, in weary tones: "Well you and me can't alter it. It's the kind of world we're living in today."

I reeled out into the fresh air and the sunshine. Looking round at the tranquil scene, the long stretch of grass, the loop of pebbly river with the green hills rising behind, I had a sense of unreality. Was there any part of this peaceful cameo of rural England without its sinister undertones? As if by instinct I made my way into the long marquee which housed the produce section. Surely among those quiet rows of vegetables I would find repose.

The place was almost empty but as I made my way down the long lines of tables I came upon the solitary figure of old John William Enderby who had a little grocer's shop in the town.

"Well how are things?" I enquired.

"Nobbut middlin' lad," the old man replied morosely.

"Why, what's wrong?"

"Well, ah got a second with me broad beans but only a highly commended for me shallots. Look at 'em."

I looked. "Yes, they're beautiful shallots, Mr. Enderby."

"Aye, they are, and nobbut a highly commended. It's a insult, that's what it is a insult."

"But Mr. Enderby . . . highly commended . . . I mean, that's pretty good isn't it?"

"No it isn't, it's a insult!"

"Oh bad luck."

John William stared at me wide-eyed for a moment. "It's not bad luck, lad, it's nowt but a twist."

"Oh surely not!"

"Ah'm tellin' you. Jim Houlston got first with 'is shallots and judge is his wife's cousin."

"Never!"

"It's true," grunted John William, nodding solemnly. "It's nowt but a twist."

"Well I've never heard such a thing!"

"You don't know what goes on, young man. Ah wasn't even placed with me taties. Frank Thompson got first wi' that lot." He pointed to a tray of noble tubers.

I studied them. "I must admit they look splendid potatoes."

"Aye, they are, but Frank pinched 'em."

"What?"

"Aye, they took first prize at Brisby show last Thursday and Frank pinched 'em off t'stand."

I clutched at the nearby table. The foundation of my world was crumbling. "That can't be true, Mr. Enderby."

"Ah'm not jokin' nor jestin'," declared John William. "Them's self and same taties, ah'd know them anywhere. It's nowt but a . . ."

I could take no more. I fled.

Outside the evening sunshine was still warm and the whole field was awash with the soft light which, in the Dales, seems to stream down in a golden flood from the high tops. But it was as if the forces of darkness were pressing on me; all I wanted was to get home.

I hurried to the stewards' tent and collected my

measuring stick, running a gauntlet of hostile stares from the pony people I had outed earlier in the day. They were still waving their certificates and arguing.

On the way to the car I had to pass several of the ladies who had watched me judge the pets and though they didn't exactly draw their skirts aside they managed to convey their message. Among the rows of vehicles I spotted the man with the moustache. He still hadn't taken his terrier away and his eyes, full of wounded resentment, followed my every step.

I was opening my door when Helen and her party, also apparently on the way home, passed about fifty yards away. Helen waved, I waved back, and Richard Edmundson gave me a nod before helping her into the front seat of a gleaming, silver Daimler. The two fathers got into the back.

As I settled into the seat of my little Austin, braced my feet against the broken floor boards and squinted through the cracked windscreen I prayed that just this once the thing would go on the starter. Holding my breath I pulled at the knob but the engine gave a couple of lazy turns then fell silent.

Fishing the starting handle from under the seat I crept out and inserted it in its hole under the radiator; and as I began the old familiar winding the silver monster purred contemptuously past me and away.

Dropping into the driver's seat again I caught sight of my face in the mirror and could see the streaks and flecks of blood still caked on my cheek and around the roots of my hair. Tristan hadn't done a very good job with his bucket of cold water.

I gazed back at the emptying field and at the Daimler disappearing round a distant bend. It seemed to me that in more ways than one the show was over.

12

As I looked at the group of sick young cattle on the hillside a mixture of apprehension and disbelief flooded through me. Surely not more trouble for the Dalbys.

The old saw "It never rains but it pours" seems to apply with particular force to farming. The husk outbreak last year and now this. It had all started with the death of Billy Dalby; big slow-smiling, slow-talking Billy. He was as strong and tough as any of the shaggy beasts which ranged his fields but he had just melted away in a few weeks. Cancer of the pancreas they said it was and Billy was gone before anybody could realise it and there was only his picture smiling down from the kitchen mantelpiece on his wife and three young children.

The general opinion was that Mrs. Dalby should sell up and get out. You needed a man to run this place and anyway Prospect House was a bad farm. Neighbouring farmers would stick out their lower lips and shake their heads when they looked at the boggy pastures on the low side of the house with the tufts of spiky grass sticking from the sour soil or at the rocky outcrops and scattered stones on the hillside fields. No, it was a poor place and a woman would never make a go of it.

Everybody thought the same thing except Mrs. Dalby herself. There wasn't much of her, in fact she must have been one of the smallest women I have ever seen—around five feet high—but there was a core of steel in her. She had her own mind and her own way of doing things.

I remember when Billy was still alive I had been injecting some sheep up there and Mrs. Dalby called me into the house.

"You'll have a cup of tea, Mr. Herriot?" She said it in a gracious way, not casually, her head slightly on one side and a dignified little smile on her face.

And when I went into the kitchen I knew what I would find; the inevitable tray. It was always a tray with Mrs. Dalby. The hospitable Dales people were continually asking me in for some kind of refreshment—a "bit o' dinner" perhaps, but if it wasn't midday there was usually a mug of tea and a scone or a hunk of thick-crusted apple pie—but Mrs. Dalby invariably set out a special tray. And there it was today with a clean cloth and the best china cup and saucer and side plates with sliced buttered scones and iced cakes and malt bread and biscuits. It was on its own table away from the big kitchen table.

"Do sit down, Mr. Herriot," she said in her precise manner. "I hope that tea isn't too strong for you."

Her speech was what the farmers would call "very proper" but it went with her personality which to me embodied a determination to do everything as correctly as possible.

"Looks perfect to me, Mrs. Dalby." I sat down feeling somewhat exposed in the middle of the kitchen with Billy smiling comfortably from an old armchair by the fire and his wife standing by my side.

She never sat down with us but stood there, very erect, hands clasped in front of her, head inclined, ceremoniously attending to my every wish. "Let me fill your cup, Mr. Herriot," or "Won't you try some of this custard tart?"

She wasn't what you would call pretty; it was a rough-skinned red little face with tiny, very dark eyes but there was a sweet expression and a quiet dignity. And as I say, there was strength.

Billy died in the spring and as everybody waited for Mrs. Dalby to make arrangement for the sale she went right on with the running of the farm. She did it with the help of a big farm worker called Charlie who had helped Billy occasionally but now came full time. During the summer I was called out a few times for trivial ailments among the cattle and I could see that Mrs. Dalby was managing to hang on; she looked a bit haggard because she was now helping in the fields and buildings as well as coping with her housework and young family, but she was still fighting.

It was half way through September when she asked me to call to see some young cattle—stirks of around nine months—which were coughing.

"They were really fit when they were turned out in May," she said as we walked across the grass to the gate in the corner. "But they've really gone down badly this last week or two."

I held the gate open, we walked through, and as I approached the group of animals I grew progressively uneasy. Even at this distance I could see that something was far wrong; they were not moving around or grazing as they should have been but were curiously immobile. There would be about thirty of them and many had their necks extended forward as if seeking air. And from the bunch a barking cough was carried to us on the soft breeze of late summer.

By the time we reached the cattle my uneasiness had been replaced by a dry-mouthed dread. They didn't seem to care as I moved in among them and I had to shout and wave my arms to get them moving; and they had barely begun to stir before the coughing broke out throughout the group; not just an occasional bark but a hacking chorus which seemed almost to be tearing the little animals apart. And they weren't just coughing; most of them were panting, standing straddle-legged, ribs heaving in a desperate fight for breath. A few showed bubbles of saliva at their lips and from here and there among the pack groans of agony sounded as the lungs laboured.

I turned as in a dream to Mrs. Dalby.

"They've got husk." Even as I said it it sounded a grimly inadequate description of the tragedy I was witnessing. Because this was neglected husk, a terrible doom-laden thing.

"Husk?" the little woman said brightly. "What causes it?"

I looked at her for a moment then tried to make my voice casual.

"Well it's a parasite. A tiny worm which infests the bronchial tubes and sets up bronchitis—in fact that's the proper name, parasitic bronchitis. The larvae climb up the blades of grass and the cattle eat them as they graze. Some pastures are badly affected with it." I broke off. A lecture was out of place at a time like this.

What I felt like saying was why in God's name hadn't I been called in weeks ago. Because this wasn't only bronchitis now; it was pneumonia, pleurisy, emphysema and any other lung condition you cared to name with not merely a few of the hair-like worms irritating the tubes, but great seething masses of them crawling everywhere, balling up and blocking the vital air passages. I had opened up a lot of calves like these and I knew how it looked.

I took a deep breath. "They're pretty bad, Mrs. Dalby. A mild attack isn't so bad if you can get them off the grass right away, but this has gone a long way beyond that. You can see for yourself, can't you —they're like a lot of little skeletons. I wish I'd seen them sooner."

She looked up at me apprehensively and I decided not to belabour the point. It would be like rubbing it in; saying what her neighbours had said all along, that her inexperience would land her in trouble sooner or later. If Billy had been here he probably would never have turned his young cattle on to this marshy field; or he would have spotted the trouble right at the start and brought them inside. Charlie would be no help in a situation like this; he was a good willing chap but lived up to the Yorkshire saying, "Strong in t'arm and thick in t'head." Farming is a skilful business and Billy, the planner, the stocksman, the experienced agriculturist who knew his own farm inside out, just wasn't there.

Mrs. Dalby drew herself up with that familiar gesture.

"Well what can we do about it, Mr. Herriot?"

An honest reply in those days would have been, "Medicinally nothing." But I didn't say that.

"We've got to get them all inside immediately. Every mouthful of this grass is adding to the worm burden. Is Charlie around to give us a hand?"

"Yes, he's in the next field, mending a wall." She trotted across the turf and in a minute or two returned with the big man ambling by her side.

"Aye, ah thought it were a touch of husk," he said amiably, then with a hint of eagerness. "Are ye goin' to give them the throat injection?"

"Yes . . . yes . . . but let's get them up to the buildings." As we drove the cattle slowly up the green slope I marvelled ruefully at this further example of faith in the intratracheal injection for husk. There was really no treatment for the condition and it would be another twenty years before one appeared in the shape of diethylcarbamazine, but the accepted procedure was to inject a mixture of chloroform, turpentine and creosote into the windpipe. Modern vets may raise their eyebrows at the idea of introducing this barbaric concoction directly into the delicate lung tissue and we old ones didn't think much of it either. But the farmers loved it.

When we had finally got the stirks into the fold yard I looked round them with something like despair. The short journey had exacerbated their symptoms tremendously and I stood in the middle of a symphony of coughs, grunts and groans while the cattle, tongues protruding, ribs pumping, gasped for breath.

I got a bottle of the wonderful injection from the car, and with Charlie holding the head and little Mrs. Dalby hanging on to the tail I began to go through the motions. Seizing the trachea in my left hand I inserted the needle between the cartilaginous rings and squirted a few c.c.'s into the lumen and, as always, the stirk gave a reflex cough, sending up the distinctive aroma of the medicaments into our faces.

"By gaw, you can smell it straight off, guvnor," Charlie said with deep satisfaction. "Ye can tell it's gettin' right to t'spot."

Most of the farmers said something like that. And they had faith. The books spoke comfortably about the chloroform stupefying the worms, the turpentine killing them and the creosote causing increased coughing which expelled them. But I didn't believe a word of it. The good results which followed were in my opinion due entirely to bringing the animals in from the infected pasture.

But I knew I had to do it and we injected every animal in the yard. There were thirty two of them and Mrs. Dalby's tiny figure was involved in the catching of all of them; clutching vainly at their necks, grabbing their tails, pushing them up against the wall. William, the eldest son, aged eight, came in from school and he plunged into the fray by his mother's side.

My repeated "Be careful, Mrs. Dalby!" or Charlie's gruff "Watch thissen, Missis, or you'll get lamed!" had no effect. During the melee both she and the little boy were kicked, trodden on and knocked down but they never showed the slightest sign of being discouraged.

At the end, the little woman turned to me, her face flushed to an even deeper hue. Panting, she looked up, "Is there anything else we can do, Mr. Herriot?"

"Yes there is." In fact the two things I was going to tell her were the only things which ever did any good. "First, I'm going to leave you some medicine for the worms which are in the stomach. We can get at them there, so Charlie must give every stirk a dose. Secondly, you'll have to start giving them the best possible food—good hay and high protein cake."

Her eyes widened. "Cake? That's expensive stuff. And hay ..."

I knew what she was thinking. The precious hay safely garnered for next winter's feed; to have to start using it now was a cruel blow, especially with all that beautiful grass out there; grass, the most natural, most perfect food for cattle but every blade carrying its own load of death.

"Can't they go out again ... ever?" she asked in a small voice.

"No, I'm sorry. If they had just had a mild attack you could have kept them in at nights and turned them out after the dew had left the grass in the mornings. The larvae climb up the grass mainly when it's wet. But your cattle have got too far. We daren't risk them picking up any more worms."

"Right ... thank you, Mr. Herriot. We know where we are, anyway." She paused. "Do you think we'll lose any of them?"

My stomach contracted into a tight ball. I had already told her to buy cake she couldn't afford and it was a certainty she would have to lay out more precious cash for hay in the winter. How was I going to tell her that nothing in the world was going to stop this batch of beasts dying like flies? When animals with husk started blowing bubbles it was nearly hopeless and the ones which were groaning with every breath were quite simply doomed. Nearly half of them were in these two categories and what about the rest? The pathetic barking other half? Well, they had a chance.

"Mrs. Dalby," I said. "It would be wrong of me to make light of this. Some of them are going to die, in fact unless there's a miracle you are going to lose quite a few of them." At the sight of her stricken face I made an attempt to be encouraging. "However, where there's life there's hope and sometimes you get pleasant surprises at this job." I held up a finger. "Worm them and get some good grub into them! That's your hope—to help them to fight it off themselves."

"I see." She lifted her chin in her characteristic way. "And now you must come in for a wash."

And of course there it was in its usual place in the kitchen; the tray with all the trimmings.

"Really, Mrs. Dalby. You shouldn't have bothered. You have enough to do without this."

"Nonsense," she said, the smile back on her face. "You take one spoonful of sugar don't you?"

As I sat there she stood in her habitual position, hands clasped in front of her, watching me while the middle boy, Dennis, who was five looked up at me solemnly and Michael, a mere toddler of two, fell over the coal scuttle and started to bawl lustily.

The usual procedure was to repeat the intratracheal injection in four days so I had to go through with it. Anyway, it gave me a chance to see how the cattle were faring.

When I drew up in the yard my first sight was of a long sack-covered mound on the cobbles. A row of hooves protruded from beneath the sacks. I had expected something of the sort but the reality was still like a blow in the face. It was still quite early in the morning and perhaps I wasn't feeling quite strong enough to have the evidence of my failure thrust before my eyes. Because failure it undoubtedly was; even though I had been in a hopeless position from the start there was something damning in those motionless hooves jutting from their rough blanket.

I made a quick count. There were four dead cattle under there. Wearily I made my way into the fold yard; I had no cheerful expectation of what I would find inside. Two of the stirks were down and unable to rise from the deep straw, the rest were still panting, but I noticed with a faint lifting of my gloom that several of them were doggedly munching at the cubes of cake in the troughs and others were pulling an occasional wisp of hay from the racks. It was incredible how animals with advanced respiratory symptoms would still eat; and it provided the only gleam of hope.

I walked over to the house. Mrs. Dalby greeted

me cheerfully as though those carcases outside didn't exist.

"It's time for the second injection," I said, and then after some hesitation, "I see you've lost four of them ... I'm sorry."

"Well you told me, Mr. Herriot." She smiled through the tired lines on her face. "You said I had to expect it so it wasn't as big a shock as it might have been." She finished washing the youngest child's face, seized a towel in her work-roughened hands and rubbed him briskly, then she straightened up. It was Saturday and William was at home and I noticed not for the first time that there was something about the little boy which suggested that even at his age he had decided he was going to be the man about the house. He pulled on his little wellingtons and marched resolutely with us across the yard to do his bit as he saw it. I rested my hand on his shoulder as he walked beside me; he would have to grow up a lot more rapidly than most youngsters but I had the feeling that the realities of life wouldn't bowl him over very easily.

We gave the animals their second injection with the two little Dalbys again throwing themselves fearlessly into the rough and tumble and that was about the last practical thing I did in the husk outbreak.

Looking back, there is a macabre fascination in recalling situations like this when we veterinary surgeons were utterly helpless in the face of inevitable disaster. Nowadays, thank heavens, the young members of the profession do not have to stand among a group of gasping, groaning creatures with the sick knowledge that they can't do a thing about it; they have an excellent oral vaccine to prevent husk and efficient therapeutic agents to treat it.

But with the Dalbys who needed my help so desperately I had nothing to offer; my memories are of repeated comfortless visits, of death, and of an all-pervading reek of chloroform, creosote and turpentine. When the business had finally come to an end a dozen of the stirks had died, about five were alive but blowing hard and would probably be stunted and unthrifty for the rest of their lives. The rest, thanks to the good feeding and not to my treatment, had recovered.

It was a crushing blow for any farmer to take but for a widow struggling to survive it could have been fatal. But on my last visit little Mrs. Dalby, hovering as usual, hands clasped above the tea tray, was undefeated.

"Only them as has them can lose them," she said firmly, her head tilted as always.

I had heard that said many times and they were brave Yorkshire words. But I wondered . . . did she have enough to be able to lose so many?

She went on. "I know you've told me not to turn the young beasts on to that field next year but isn't there anything we can give them to stop them getting husk?"

"No, Mrs. Dalby, I'm sorry." I put down my cup. "I don't think there's anything country vets need and want more than a husk vaccine. People keep asking us that question and we have to keep on saying no."

We had to keep on saying no for another twenty years as we watched disasters like I had just seen at the Dalbys', and the strange thing is that now we have a first rate vaccine it is taken completely for granted.

Driving away I stopped to open the gate at the end of the track and looked back at the old stone farmhouse crouching against the lower slopes. It was a perfect autumn day with mellow golden sunshine softening the harsh sweep of fell and moor with their striding walls and the air so still and windless that the whirring of a pigeon's wings overhead was loud in the silence. Across the valley on the hilltop a frieze of sparse trees stood as motionless as though they had been painted across the blue canvas of sky.

It seemed wrong that in the midst of this beauty was worry and anxiety, grinding struggle and the threat of ruin. I closed the gate and got back into the car. That little woman over there may have weathered this calamity but as I started the engine the thought was strong in my mind that another such thing would finish her.

13

I was vastly relieved when winter came and spring
followed and I saw virtually nothing of Mrs. Dalby.
It was one market day in midsummer that she came
to the surgery. I was just going to open the door
when Siegfried beat me to it. More than most people
he appreciated the hospitality we were shown on the
farms and he had sampled Mrs. Dalby's tray as often
as I had. On top of that he had the deepest admiration for her indomitable battle to keep the farm going
for her children, so that whenever she appeared at
Skeldale House he received her like royalty. His
manners, always impeccable, became those of a
Spanish grandee.

I watched him now as he threw the door wide and
hurried to the top step.

"Why, Mrs. Dalby! How very nice to see you! Do
come inside." He extended his hand towards the
house.

The little woman, dignified as ever, inclined her
head, smiled and walked past him while Siegfried
hastened to her side; and as they negotiated the passage he kept up a running fire of enquiries. "And
how is William . . . and Dennis . . . and little Michael?
Good, good, splendid."

At the sitting room door there was the same cere-
monious opening and courteous gestures and once inside a tremendous scraping of armchairs as he hauled
them around to make sure she was comfortable and
in the right position.

Next he galloped through to the kitchen to organise
some refreshment and when Mrs. Hall appeared with

the tray he raked it with an anxious glance as though he feared it may fall below the standard of Mrs. Dalby's. Apparently reassured, he poured the tea, hovered around solicitously for a moment or two then sat down opposite, the very picture of rapt attention.

The little woman thanked him and sipped at her cup.

"Mr. Farnon, I have called to see you about some young beasts. I turned a batch of thirty five out this spring and they looked in good condition but now they're losing ground fast—all of them."

My heart gave a great thump and something must have shown in my face because she smiled across at me.

"Oh don't worry, Mr. Herriot, it's not husk again. There's not a cough among the lot of them. But they are going thin and they're badly scoured."

"I think I know what that will be," Siegfried said, leaning across to push a plate of Mrs. Hall's flap-jack towards her. "They'll have picked up a few worms. Not lungworms but the stomach and intestinal kind. They probably just need a good dose of medicine to clear them out."

She nodded and took a piece of the flapjack. "Yes, that's what Charlie thought and we've dosed the lot of them. But it doesn't seem to have made any difference."

"That's funny." Siegfried rubbed his chin. "Mind you they sometimes need a repeat but you should have seen some improvement. Perhaps we'd better have a look at them."

"That's what I would like," she said. "It would set my mind at rest."

Siegfried opened the appointment book. "Right, and the sooner the better. Tomorrow morning all right? Splendid." He made a quick note then looked up at her. "By the way I'm going off for a week's holiday starting this evening, so Mr. Herriot will be coming."

"That will be fine," she replied, turning to me and smiling without a trace of doubt or misgiving. If she was thinking "This is the fellow who supervised the deaths of nearly half of my young stock last year" she certainly didn't show it. In fact when she finally finished her tea and left she waved and smiled again as though she could hardly wait to see me again.

And when I walked across the fields with Mrs. Dalby next day it was like turning the clock back to last year, except that we were going in the other direction; not down towards the marshy ground below the house but up to the stony pastures which climbed in an uneven checkerboard between their stone walls over the lower slopes of the hill.

The similarity persisted as we approached, too. These young beasts—roans, reds, red and whites— were an almost exact counterpart of last year's batch; shaggy little creatures, little more than calves, they stood spindly legged and knock-kneed regarding us apathetically as we came up the rise. And though their symptoms were entirely different from the previous lot there was one thing I could say for sure; they were very ill.

As I watched I could see the dark watery diarrhoea flowing from them without any lifting of the tails as though there was nothing they could do to control it. And every one of them was painfully thin, the skin stretched over the jutting pelvic bones and the protruding rows of ribs.

"I haven't neglected them this time," Mrs. Dalby said. "I know they look dreadful but this seems to have happened within a few days."

"Yes . . . yes . . . I see . . ." My eyes were hunting desperately among the little animals trying to find some sort of clue. I had seen unthriftiness from parasitism but nothing like this.

"Have you kept a lot of cattle in these fields over the last year or two?" I asked.

She paused in thought for a moment. "No . . . no . . . I don't think so. Billy used to let the milk cows graze up here now and then but that's all."

The grass wouldn't be likely to be "sick" with worms, then. In any case it didn't look like that. What it did look like was Johne's disease, but how in God's name could thirty five young things like this get Johne's at the same time? Salmonella . . . ? Coccidiosis . . . ? Some form of poisoning, perhaps . . . this was the time of year when cattle ate strange plants. I walked slowly round the field, but there was nothing unusual to be seen; it took even the grass all its time to grow on these wind-blown hillsides and there was no great range of other herbage. I could see bracken higher up the fell but none down here; Billy would have cleared it years ago.

"Mrs. Dalby," I said. "I think you'd better give these stirks another dose of the worm medicine just to be sure and in the meantime I'm going to take some samples of the manure for examination at the laboratory."

I brought up some sterile jars from the car and went painstakingly round the pasture scooping up as wide a range as possible from the pools of faeces.

I took them to the lab myself and asked them to phone the results through. The call came within twenty four hours; negative for everything. I resisted the impulse to dash out to the farm immediately; there was nothing I could think of doing and it wouldn't look so good for me to stand there gawping at the beasts and scratching my head. Better to wait till tomorrow to see if the second dose of worm medicine did any good. There was no reason why it should, because none of the samples showed a pathogenic worm burden.

In these cases I always hope that inspiration will come to me as I am driving around or even when I am examining other animals but this time as I climbed from the car outside Prospect House I was barren of ideas.

The young beasts were slightly worse. I had decided that if I still couldn't think of anything I would give the worst ones vitamin injections more or less for the sake of doing something; so with Charlie holding the heads I inserted the hypodermic under the taunt skins of ten of the little creatures, trying at the same time to put away the feeling of utter futility. We didn't have to drive them inside; they were easily caught in the open field and that was a bad sign in itself.

"Well you'll let me know, Mrs. Dalby," I said hoarsely as I got back into the car. "If that injection improves them I'll do the lot." I gave what I hoped was a confident wave and drove off.

I felt so bad that it had a numbing effect on me and over the next few days my mind seemed to shy away from the subject of the Dalby stirks as though by not thinking about them they would just go away. I was reminded that they were still very much there by a phone call from Mrs. Dalby.

"I'm afraid my cattle aren't doing any good, Mr. Herriot." Her voice was strained.

I grimaced into the reciever. "And the ones I injected . . . ?"

"Just the same as the others."

I had to face up to reality now and drove out to Prospect House immediately; but the feeling of cold emptiness, of having nothing to offer, made the journey a misery. I hadn't the courage to go to the farm house and face Mrs. Dalby but hurried straight up through the fields to where the young beasts were gathered.

And when I walked among them and studied them at close range the apprehension I had felt on the journey was nothing to the sick horror which rushed through me now. Another catastrophe was imminent here. The big follow-up blow which was all that was needed to knock the Dalby family out once and for all was on its way. These animals were going to die. Not just half of them like last year but all of them, because there was hardly any variation in their symptoms; there didn't seem to be a single one of them which was fighting off the disease.

But what disease? God almighty, I was a veterinary surgeon! Maybe not steeped in experience but I wasn't a new beginner any more. I should surely have some small inkling why a whole great batch of young beasts was sinking towards the knacker yard in front of my eyes.

I could see Mrs. Dalby coming up the field with little William striding in his tough, arm-swinging way by her side and Charlie following behind.

What the hell was I going to say to them? Shrug my shoulders with a light laugh and say I hadn't a single clue in my head and that it would probably be best to phone Mallock now and ask them to shoot the lot of them straight away for dog meat? They wouldn't have any cattle to bring on for next year but that wouldn't matter because they would no longer be farming.

Stumbling among the stricken creatures I gazed at them in turn, almost choking as I looked at the drooping, sunken-eyed heads, the gaunt little bodies, the eternal trickle of that deadly scour. There was a curious immobility about the group, probably because they were too weak to walk about; in fact as I watched, one of them took a few steps, swayed and almost fell.

Charlie was pushing open the gate into the field just a hundred yards away. I turned and stared at the nearest animal, almost beseeching it to tell me what was wrong with it, where it felt the pain, how this thing had all started. But I got no response. The stirk, one of the smallest, only calf-size, with a very dark roan-coloured head showed not the slightest interest but gazed back at me incuriously through its spectacles. What was that . . . what was I thinking about . . . spectacles? Was my reason toppling . . . ? But yes, by God, he did have spectacles . . . a ring of lighter hair surrounding each eye. And that other beast over there . . . he was the same. Oh glory be, now I knew! At last I knew!

Mrs. Dalby, panting slightly, had reached me.

"Good morning, Mr. Herriot," she said, trying to smile. "What do you think, then?" She looked around the cattle with anxious eyes.

"Ah, good morning to you, Mrs. Dalby," I replied expansively, fighting down the impulse to leap in the air and laugh and shout and perhaps do a few cartwheels. "Yes, I've had a look at them and it is pretty clear now what the trouble is."

"Really? Then what . . . ?"

"It's copper deficiency." I said it casually as though I had been turning such a thing over in my mind right from the beginning. "You can tell by the loss of the pigment in the coat, especially around the eyes. In fact when you look at them you can see that a lot of them are a bit paler than normal." I waved an airy hand in the general direction of the stirks.

Charlie nodded. "Aye, by gaw, you're right. Ah thowt they'd gone a funny colour."

"Can we cure it?" Mrs. Dalby asked the inevitable question.

"Oh yes, I'm going straight back to the surgery now to make up a copper mixture and we'll dose the lot. And you'll have to repeat that every fortnight while they are out at grass. It's a bit of a nuisance, I'm afraid, but there's no other way. Can you do it?"

"Oh aye, we'll do it," Charlie said.

And "Oh aye, we'll do it," little William echoed, sticking out his chest and strutting around aggressively as though he wanted to start catching the beasts right away.

The treatment had a spectacular effect. I didn't have the modern long-lasting copper injections at my disposal but the solution of copper sulphate which I concocted under the surgery tap at Skeldale House worked like magic. Within a few weeks that batch of stirks was capering, lively and fully fleshed, over those hillside fields. Not a single death, no lingering unthriftiness. It was as though the whole thing had never happened, as though the hand of doom had never hovered over, not only over the cattle, but the little family of humans.

It had been a close thing and, I realised, only a respite. That little woman had a long hard fight ahead of her still.

I have always abhorred change of any kind but it pleases me to come forward twenty years and spectate at another morning in the kitchen at Prospect House. I was seated at the same little table picking a buttered scone from the same tray and wondering whether I should follow it with a piece of malt bread or one of the jam tarts.

Billy still smiled down from the mantelpiece and Mrs. Dalby, hands clasped in front of her, was watching me, her head a little on one side, the same half smile curving her lips. The years had not altered her much; there was some grey in her hair but the little red, weathered face and the bright eyes were as I had always known them.

I sipped my tea and looked across at the vast bulk of William sprawled in his father's old chair, smiling his father's smile at me. There were about fifteen stones of William and I had just been watching him in action as he held a fully grown bullock's hind foot while I examined it. The animal had made a few attempts to kick but the discouragement on its face had been obvious as William's great hands effortlessly engulfed its fetlock and a corner of his wide shoulder span dug into its abdomen.

No, I couldn't expect William to be the same, nor Dennis and Michael clattering into the kitchen now in their heavy boots and moving over to the sink to wash their hands. They were six footers too with their father's high-shouldered easy slouching walk but without William's sheer bulk.

Their tiny mother glanced at them then up at the picture on the mantelpiece.

"It would have been our thirtieth anniversary today," she said conversationally.

I looked up at her, surprised. She never spoke of such things and I didn't know how to answer. I couldn't very well say "congratulations" when she had spent twenty of those years alone. She had never said a word about her long fight; and it had been a winning fight. She had bought the neighbouring farm lower down the Dale when old Mr. Mason retired; it was a good farm with better land and William had lived there after his marriage and they ran the two places as one. Things were pretty good now with her three expert stocksmen sons eliminating the need for outside labour except old Charlie who still pottered around doing odd jobs.

"Yes, thirty years," Mrs. Dalby said, looking slowly round the room as though she was seeing it for the first time. Then she turned back and bent over me, her face serious.

"Mr. Herriot," she said, and I was sure that at last, on this special day, she was going to say something about the years of struggle, the nights of worry and tears, the grinding toil.

For a moment she rested her hand lightly on my shoulder and her eyes looked into mine.

"Mr. Herriot, are you quite sure that tea is to your liking?"

14

One of the things Helen and I had to do was furnish our bed-sitter and kitchen. And when I say "furnish" I use the word in its most austere sense. We had no high-flown ideas about luxury; it was, after all, a temporary arrangement and anyway we had no money to throw around.

My present to Helen at the time of our marriage was a modest gold watch and this had depleted my capital to the extent that a bank statement at the commencement of our married life revealed the sum of twenty five shillings standing to my credit. Admittedly I was a partner now but when you start from scratch it takes a long time to get your head above water.

But we did need the essentials like a table, chairs, cutlery, crockery, the odd rug and carpet, and Helen and I decided that it would be most sensible to pick up these things at house sales. Since I was constantly going round the district I was able to drop in at these events and the duty of acquiring our necessities had been delegated to me. But after a few weeks it was clear that I was falling down on the job.

I had never realised it before but I had a blind spot in these matters. I would go to a sale and come away with a pair of brass candlesticks and a stuffed owl. On another occasion I acquired an ornate inkwell with a carved metal figure of a dog on it together with a polished wooden box with unnumerable fascinating little drawers and compartments for keeping homeopathic prescriptions. I could go on for a long time about the things I bought but they were nearly all useless.

Helen was very nice about it.

"Jim," she said one day when I was proudly showing her a model of a fully rigged sailing ship in a bottle which I had been lucky enough to pick up. "It's lovely, but I don't think we need it right now."

I must have been a big disappointment to the poor girl and also to the local auctioneers who ran the sales. These gentlemen, when they saw me hovering around the back of the crowd would cheer up visibly. They, in common with most country folk, thought all vets were rich and that I would be bidding for some of the more expensive items. When a nice baby grand piano came up they would look over the heads at me with an expectant smile and their disappointment was evident when I finally went away with a cracked-faced barometer or a glove stretcher.

A sense of my failure began to seep through to me and when I had to take a sample through to the Leeds Laboratory I saw a chance to atone.

"Helen," I said, "there's a huge sale room right in the city centre. I'll take an hour off and go in there. I'm bound to see something we need."

"Oh good!" my wife replied. "That's a great idea! There'll be lots to choose from there. You haven't had much chance to find anything at those little country sales." Helen was always kind.

After my visit to the Leeds lab I asked the way to the sale rooms.

"Leave your car here," one of the locals advised me. "You'll never park in the main street and you can get a tram right to the door."

I was glad I listened to him because when I arrived the traffic was surging both ways in a nonstop stream. The sale room was at the top of an extraordinarily long flight of smooth stone steps leading right to the top of the building. When I arrived, slightly out of breath, I thought immediately I had come to the right place, a vast enclosure strewn with furniture, cookers, gramophones, carpets—everything you could possibly want in a house.

I wandered around fascinated for quite a long time then my attention centred on two tall piles of books quite near to where the auctioneer was selling. I lifted one of them. It was The Geography of the World. I had never seen such beautiful books; as big as encyclopaedias and with thick embossed covers and gold lettering. The pages, too, were edged with gold and the paper was of a delightfully smooth texture. Quite enthralled I turned the pages, marvelling at the handsome illustrations, the coloured pictures each with its covering transparent sheet. They were a little old-fashioned, no doubt, and when I looked at the front I saw they were printed in 1858; but they were things of beauty.

Looking back, I feel that fate took a hand here because I had just reluctantly turned away when I heard the auctioneer's voice.

"Now then, here's a lovely set of books. The Geography of the World in Twenty Four Volumes. Just look at them. You don't find books like them today. Who'll give me a bid?"

I agreed with him. They were unique. But they must be worth pounds. I looked round the company but nobody said a word.

"Come on, ladies and gentlemen, surely somebody wants this wonderful addition to their library. Now what do I hear?"

Again the silence then a seedy looking man in a soiled mackintosh spoke up.

"Arf a crown," he said morosely.

I looked around expecting a burst of laughter at this sally, but nobody was amused. In fact the auctioneer didn't seem surprised.

"I have a half a crown bid." He glanced about him and raised his hammer. With a thudding of the heart I realised he was going to sell.

I heard my own voice, slightly breathless. "Three shillings."

"I have a bid of three shillings for The Geography

of the World in Twenty Four Volumes. Are you all done?" Bang went the hammer. "Sold to the gentleman over there."

They were mine! I couldn't believe my luck. This surely was the bargain to end all bargains. I paid my three shillings while one of the men tied a length of rough string round each pile. The first pause in my elation came when I tried to lift my purchases. Books are heavy things and these were massive specimens; and there were twenty four of them.

With a hand under each string I heaved like a weight-lifter and, pop-eyed, veins standing out on my forehead, I managed to get them off the ground and began to stagger shakily to the exit.

The first string broke on the top step and twelve of my volumes cascaded downwards over the smooth stone. After the first moment of panic I decided that the best way was to transport the intact set down to the bottom and come back for the others. I did this but it took me some time and I began to perspire before I was all tied up again and poised on the kerb ready to cross the road.

The second string broke right in the middle of the tram lines as I attempted a stiff-legged dash through a break in the traffic. For about a year I scrabbled there in the middle of the road while horns hooted, tram bells clanged and an interested crowd watched from the sidewalks. I had just got the escaped volumes balanced in a column and was reknotting the string when the other lot burst from their binding and slithered gently along the metal rails; and it was when I was retrieving them that I noticed a large policeman, attracted by the din and the long line of vehicles, walking with measured strides in my direction.

In my mental turmoil I saw myself for the first time in the hands of the law. I could be done on several charges—Breach of the Peace, Obstructing Traffic to name only two—but I perceived that the officer was approaching very slowly and rightly or wrongly I feel that when a policeman strolls towards you like that he is a decent chap and is giving you a chance to get away. I took my chance. He was still several yards off when I had my two piles reassembled and I thrust my hands under the strings, tottered to the far kerb and lost myself in the crowd.

When I finally decided there was no longer any fear of feeling the dread grip on my shoulder I stopped in my headlong flight and rested in a shop doorway. I was puffing like a broken-winded horse and my hands hurt abominably. The sale room string was coarse, hairy and abrasive and already it threatened to take the skin off my fingers.

Anyway, I thought, the worst was over. The tram stop was just at the end of the block there. I joined the queue and when the tram arrived, shuffled forward with the others. I had one foot on the step when a large hand was thrust before my eyes.

"Just a minute, brother, just a minute! Where d'you think you're goin'?" The face under the conductor's hat was the meaty, heavy jowled, pop-eyed kind which seems to take a mournful pleasure in imparting bad news.

"You're not bringin' that bloody lot on 'ere, brother, I'll tell tha now!"

I looked up at him in dismay. "But . . . it's just a few books . . ."

"Few books! You want a bloody delivery van for that lot. You're not usin' my tram—passengers couldn't stir inside!" His mouth turned down aggressively.

"Oh but really," I said with a ghastly attempt at an ingratiating smile, "I'm just going as far as . . ."

"You're not goin' anywhere in 'ere, brother! Ah've no time to argue—move your foot, ah'm off!"

The bell ding-dinged and the tram began to move. As I hopped off backwards one of the strings broke again.

After I had got myself sorted out I surveyed my situation and it appeared fairly desperate. My car must be over a mile away, mostly uphill, and I would defy the most stalwart Nepalese Sherpa to transport these books that far. I could of course just abandon the things; lean them against this wall and take to my heels . . . But no, that would be anti-social and anyway they were beautiful. If only I could get them home all would be well.

Another tram rumbled up to the stop and again I hefted my burden and joined the in-going passengers, hoping nobody would notice.

It was a female voice this time.

"Sorry, you can't come on, luv." She was middle-aged, motherly and her plump figure bulged her uniform tightly.

"We don't 'ave delivery men on our trams. It's against t'rules."

I repressed a scream. "But I'm not a . . . these are my own books. I've just bought them."

"Bought 'em?" Her eyebrows went up as she stared at the dusty columns.

"Yes . . . and I've got to get them home somehow."

"Well somebody'll tek 'em home for you luv. Hasta got far to go?"

"Darrowby."

"Eee, by gum, that's a long way. Right out in t'country." She peered into the tram's interior. "But there isn't no room in there, luv."

The passengers had all filed in and I was left alone standing between my twin edifices; and the conductress must have seen a desperate light in my eyes because she made a sudden gesture.

"Come on then, luv! You can stand out 'ere on the platform wi' me. I'm not supposed to, but ah can't see you stuck there."

I didn't know whether to kiss her or burst into tears. In the end I did neither but stacked the books in a corner of the platform and stood swaying over them till we arrived at the park where I had left my car.

The relief at my deliverance was such that I laughed off the few extra contretemps on my way to the car. There were in fact several more spills before I had the books tucked away on the back seat but when I finally drove away I felt like singing.

It was when I was threading my way through the traffic that I began to rejoice that I lived in the country, because the car was filled with an acrid reek which I thought could only come from the conglomeration of petrol fumes and industrial smoke. But even when the city had been left behind and I was climbing into the swelling green of the Pennines the aroma was still with me.

I wound down the window and gulped greedily as the sweet grassy air flowed in but when I closed it the strange pungency returned immediately. I stopped, leaned over and sniffed at the region of the back seat. And there was no doubt about it; it was the books.

Ah well, they must have been kept in a damp place or something like that. I was sure it would soon pass off. But in the meantime it certainly was powerful; it nearly made my eyes water.

I had never really noticed the long climb to our eyrie on top of Skeldale House but it was different today. I suppose my arms and shoulders were finally beginning to feel the strain and that string, bristly but fragile, was digging into my hands harder than ever, but it was true that every step was an effort and when I at last gained the top landing I almost collapsed against the door of our bed-sitter.

When, perspiring and dishevelled, I entered, Helen was on her knees, dusting the hearth. She looked up at me expectantly.

"Any luck, Jim?"

"Yes, I think so," I replied with a trace of smugness. "I think I got a bargain."

Helen rose and looked at me eagerly. "Really?"

"Yes," I decided to play my trump card. "I only had to spend three shillings!"

"Three shillings! What . . . where. . . ?"

"Wait there a minute." I went out to the landing and put my hand under those strings. This, thank heaven, would be the last time I would have to do this. A lunge and a heave and I had my prizes through the doorway and displayed for my wife's inspection.

She stared at the two piles. "What have you got there?"

"The Geography of the World in Twenty Four Volumes," I replied triumphantly.

"The Geography of the ... and is that all?"

"Yes, couldn't manage anything else, I'm afraid. But look—aren't they magnificent books!"

My wife's level gaze had something of disbelief, a little of wonder. For a moment one corner of her mouth turned up then she coughed and became suddenly brisk.

"Ah well, we'll have to see about getting some shelves for them. Anyway, leave them there for now." She went over and kneeled again by the hearth. But after a minute or two she paused in her dusting.

"Can you smell anything funny?"

"Well, er ... I think it's the books, Helen. They're just a bit musty ... I don't think it'll last long."

But the peculiar exhalation was very pervasive and it was redolent of extreme age. Very soon the atmosphere in our room was that of a freshly opened mausoleum.

I could see Helen didn't want to hurt my feelings but she kept darting looks of growing alarm at my purchases. I decided to say it for her.

"Maybe I'd better take them downstairs just for now."

She nodded gratefully.

The descent was torture, made worse by the fact that I had thought I was finished with such things. I finally staggered into the office and parked the books behind the desk. I was panting and rubbing my hands when Siegfried came in.

"Ah, James, had a nice run through to Leeds?"

"Yes, they said at the lab that they'd give us a ring about those sheep as soon as they've cultured the organisms."

"Splendid!" My colleague opened the door of the

cupboard and put some forms inside then he paused and began to sniff the air.

"James, there's a bloody awful stink in here."

I cleared my throat. "Well yes, Siegfried, I bought a few books while I was in Leeds. They seem a little damp." I pointed behind the desk.

Siegfried's eyes widened as he looked at the twin edifices. "What the devil are they?"

I hesitated. "The Geography of the World in Twenty Four Volumes."

He didn't say anything but looked from me to the books and back again. And he kept sniffing. There was no doubt that only his innate good manners were preventing him from telling me to get the damn things out of here.

"I'll find a place for them," I said, and with a great weariness pushed my hands yet again under the strings. My mind was in a ferment as I shuffled along the passage. What in heaven's name was I going to do with them? But as I passed the cellar door on my right it seemed to provide the answer.

There were great vaulted chambers beneath Skeldale House, a proper wine cellar in the grand days. The man who went down there to read the gas meter always described them as "The Cattycombs" and as I descended into the murky, dank-smelling depths I thought sadly that it was a fitting resting place for my books. We kept only coal and wood down here now and from the muffled thuds I judged that Tristan was chopping logs.

He was a great log chopper and when I rounded the corner he was whirling his axe expertly round his head. He stopped when he saw me with my burden and asked the inevitable question.

I answered for, I hoped, the last time, "The Geography of the World in Twenty Four Volumes." And I followed with a blow by blow account of my story.

As he listened he opened one tome after another, sniffed at it and replaced it hurriedly. And he didn't have to tell me, I knew already. My cherished books were down here to stay.

But the compassion which has always been and still is uppermost among the many facets of Tristan's character came to the fore now.

"Tell you what, Jim," he said. "We can put them in there." He pointed to a dusty wine bin just visible in the dim light which filtered through the iron grating at the top of the coal chute which led from the street.

"It's just like a proper book shelf."

He began to lift the volumes into the bin and when he had arranged them in a long row he ran his finger along the faded opulence of the bindings.

"There now, they look a treat in there, Jim." He paused and rubbed his chin. "Now all you want is somewhere to sit. Let's see now . . . ah, yes!" He retreated into the gloom and reappeared with an armful of the biggest logs. He made a few more journeys and in no time had rigged up a seat for me within arm's reach of the books.

"That'll do fine," he said with deep satisfaction.

"You can come down here and have a read whenever you feel like it."

And that is how it turned out. The books never came up those steps again but quite frequently when I had a few minutes to spare and wanted to improve my mind I went down and sat on Tristan's seat in the twilight under the grating and renewed my acquaintance with The Geography of the World in Twenty Four Volumes.

15

The flu epidemic sweeping through the Darrowby district hit the farming folk particularly hard. The townspeople could take a few days off till it passed but when there were cows to be milked twice a day it couldn't be done. On my rounds I saw stocksmen flushed with fever, staggering streaming-eyed from cow to cow when they should have been in bed.

Helen's father and Auntie Lucy were two of the victims and in need of help. I didn't wait for Helen to say anything about it but suggested right away that she should return to the farm for a few days to run the house. And it was so strange in the bed-sitter without her that I went back downstairs to my old room adjoining Tristan's to sleep and I ate with the brothers in the big dining room.

I was sitting at breakfast one morning with the feeling of having turned back the clock. My partner was refilling my coffee cup when his brother cleared his throat.

"You know, there's maybe something in this Raynes Ghost business after all." Tristan pushed his chair back from the breakfast table, stretched out his legs more comfortably and resumed his study of the *Darrowby and Houlton Times*. "It says here they've got a historian looking into it and this man has unearthed some interesting facts."

Siegfried didn't say anything, but his eyes narrowed as his brother took out a Woodbine and lit it. Siegfried had given up smoking a week ago and he didn't want to watch anybody lighting up; particularly somebody like Tristan who invested even the smallest action with quiet delight, rich fulfilment. My partner's mouth tightened to a grim line as the young man unhurriedly selected a cigarette, flicked his lighter and dragged the smoke deep with a kind of ecstatic gasp.

"Yes." Tristan continued, thin outgoing wisps mingling with his words. "This chap points out that several of the monks were murdered at Raynes Abbey in the fourteenth century."

"Well, so what?" snapped Siegfried.

Tristan raised his eyebrows. "This cowled figure that's been seen so often lately near the abbey—why shouldn't it be the spirit of one of those monks?"

"Whaat? What's that you say?"

"Well, after all it makes you think, doesn't it? Who knows what fell deeds might have been. . . ?"

"What the hell are you talking about?" Siegfried barked.

Tristan looked hurt. "That's all very well, and you may laugh, but remember what Shakespeare said." He raised a solemn finger. "There are more things in heaven and earth, Horatio, than are dreamt of in your . . ."

"Oh balls!" said Siegfried, bringing the discussion effectively to a close.

I took a last thankful swallow of coffee and put down my cup. I was pleased that the topic had petered out fairly peacefully because Siegfried was in an edgy condition. Up to last week he had been a dedicated puffer of pipe and cigarettes but he had also developed a classical smoker's cough and had suffered increasingly from violent stomach-ache. At times his long thin face had assumed the appearance of a skull, the cheeks deeply sunken, the eyes smouldering far down in their sockets. And the doctor had said he must give up smoking.

Siegfried had obeyed, felt immediately better and was instantly seized with the evangelical zeal of the convert. But he didn't just advise people to give up tobacco; I have seen him several times strike a cigarette from the trembling fingers of farm workers, push his face to within inches of theirs and grind out menacingly, "Now don't ever let me see you with one of those bloody things in your mouth again, do you hear?"

Even now there are grizzled men who tell me with a shudder, "Nay, ah've never had a fag sin' Mr. Farnon told me to stop, thirty years back. Nay, bugger it, the way 'e looked at me I dursn't do it!"

However the uncomfortable fact remained that his crusade hadn't the slightest effect on his brother. Tristan smoked almost continually but he never coughed and his digestion was excellent.

Siegfried looked at him now as he contentedly tapped off a little ash and took another blissful suck. "You smoke too many of those bloody cigarettes!"

"So do you."

"No I don't!" Siegfried retorted. "I'm a non-smoker and it's time you were, too! It's a filthy habit and you'll kill yourself the way you're going!"

Tristan gave him a benign look and again his words floated out on the fine Woodbine mist. "Oh I'm sure you're wrong. Do you know, I think it rather agrees with me."

Siegfried got up and left the room. I sympathised with him for he was in a difficult position. Being in loco parentis he was in a sense providing his brother with the noxious weeds and his innate sense of propriety prevented him from abusing his position by dashing the things from Tristan's hands as he did with others. He had to fall back on exhortation and it was getting him nowhere. And there was another thing—he probably wanted to avoid a row this morning as Tristan was leaving on one of his mysterious trips back to the Veterinary College; in fact my first job was to take him down to the Great North Road where he was going to hitch a lift.

After I had left him there I set off on my rounds and, as I drove, my thoughts kept going back to the conversation at breakfast. A fair number of people were prepared to swear that they had seen the Raynes ghost and though it was easy to dismiss some of them as sensation mongers or drunkards the fact remained that others were very solid citizens indeed.

The story was always the same. There was a hill beyond Raynes village and at the top a wood came right up to the roadside. Beyond lay the abbey. People driving up the hill late at night said they had seen the monk in their headlights—a monk in a brown habit just disappearing into the wood. They believed the figure had been walking across the road but they weren't sure because it was always a little too far away. But they were adamant about the other part; they had seen a cowled figure, head bowed, go into that wood. There must have been something uninviting about the apparition because nobody ever said they had gone into the wood after it.

It was strange that after my thoughts had been on Raynes during the day I should be called to the village at one o'clock the following morning. Crawling from bed and climbing wearily into my clothes I couldn't help thinking of Tristan curled up peacefully in his Edinburgh lodgings far away from the troubles of practice. But I didn't feel too bad about getting up; Raynes was only three miles away and the job held no prospect of hard labour—a colic in a little boy's Shetland pony. And it was a fine night—very cold with the first chill of autumn but with a glorious full moon to light my way along the road.

They were walking the pony round the yard when I got there. The owner was the accountant at my bank and he gave me a rueful smile.

"I'm very sorry to get you out of bed, Mr. Herriot, but I was hoping this bit of bellyache would go off. We've been parading round here for two hours. When we stop he tries to roll."

"You've done the right thing," I said. "Rolling can cause a twist in the bowel." I examined the little animal and was reassured. He had a normal temperature, a good strong pulse, and listening at his flank I could hear the typical abdominal sounds of spasmodic colic.

What he needed was a good evacuation of the

bowel, but I had to think carefully when computing the dose of arecoline for this minute member of the equine species. I finally settled on an eighth of a grain and injected it into the neck muscles. The pony stood for a few moments in the typical colic position, knuckling over and sinking down on one hind leg then the other and occasionally trying to lie down.

"Walk him on again slowly will you?" I was watching for the next stage and I didn't have long to wait; the pony's jaws began to champ and his lips to slobber and soon long dribbles of saliva hung down from his mouth. All right so far but I had to wait another fifteen minutes before he finally cocked his tail and deposited a heap of faeces on the concrete of the yard.

"I think he'll be O.K. now," I said. "So I'll leave you to it. Give me another ring if he's still in pain."

Beyond the village the road curved suddenly out of sight of the houses then began the long straight climb to the abbey. Just up there at the limits of my headlights would be where the ghost was always seen—walking across the road and into the black belt of trees. At the top of the hill, on an impulse, I drew in to the side of the road and got out of the car. This was the very place. At the edge of the wood, under the brilliant moon, the smooth boles of the beeches shone with an eerie radiance and, high above, the branches creaked as they swayed in the wind.

I walked into the wood, feeling my way carefully with an arm held before me till I came out on the other side. Raynes Abbey lay before me.

I had always associated the beautiful ruin with summer days with the sun warming the old stones of the graceful arches, the chatter of voices, children playing on the cropped turf; but this was 2.30 a.m. in an empty world and the cold breath of the coming winter on my face. I felt suddenly alone.

In the cold glare everything was uncannily distinct. But there was a look of unreality about the silent rows of columns reaching into the dark sky and throwing their long pale shadows over the grass.

Away at the far end I could see the monks' cells—gloomy black caverns deep in shadow—and as I looked an owl hooted, accentuating the heavy, blanketing silence.

A prickling apprehension began to creep over me, a feeling that my living person had no place here among these brooding relics of dead centuries. I turned quickly and began to hurry through the wood, bumping into the trees, tripping over roots and bushes, and when I reached my car I was trembling and more out of breath than I should have been. It was good to slam the door, turn the ignition and hear the familiar roar of the engine.

I was home within ten minutes and trotted up the stairs, looking forward to catching up on my lost sleep. Opening my bedroom door I flicked on the switch and felt a momentary surprise when the room remained in darkness. Then I stood frozen in the doorway.

By the window, where the moonlight flooded in, making a pool of silver in the gloom, a monk was standing. A monk in a brown habit, motionless, arms folded, head bowed. His face was turned from the light towards me but I could see nothing under the drooping cowl but a horrid abyss of darkness.

I thought I would choke. My mouth opened but no sound came. And in my racing mind one thought pounded above the others—there were such things as ghosts after all.

Again my mouth opened and a hoarse shriek emerged.

"Who in the name of God is that?"

The reply came back immediately in a sepulchral bass.

"Tristan."

I don't think I actually swooned, but I did collapse limply across my bed and lay there gasping, the blood thundering in my ears. I was dimly aware of the monk standing on a chair and screwing in the light bulb, giggling helplessly the while. Then he flicked on the switch and sat on my bed. With his cowl pushed back on his shoulders he lit a Woodbine and looked down at me, still shaking with laughter.

"Oh God, Jim, that was marvellous—even better than I expected."

I stared up at him and managed a whisper. "But you're in Edinburgh . . ."

"Not me, old lad. There wasn't much doing so I concluded my business and hitched straight back, I'd just got in when I saw you coming up the garden. Barely had time to get the bulb out and climb into my outfit—I couldn't miss the opportunity."

"Feel my heart," I murmured.

Tristan rested his hand on my ribs for a moment and as he felt the fierce hammering a fleeting concern crossed his face.

"Hell, I'm sorry, Jim." Then he patted my shoulder reassuringly. "But don't worry. If it was going to be fatal you'd have dropped down dead on the spot. And anyway, a good fright is very beneficial—acts like a tonic. You won't need a holiday this year."

"Thanks," I said. "Thanks very much."

"I wish you could have heard yourself." He began to laugh again. "That scream of terror . . . oh dear, oh dear!"

I hoisted myself slowly into a sitting position, pulled out the pillow, propped it against the bed head and leaned back against it. I still felt very weak.

I eyed him coldly. "So you're the Raynes ghost."

Tristan grinned in reply but didn't speak.

"You young devil! I should have known. But tell me, why do you do it? What do you get out of it?"

"Oh I don't know." The young man gazed dreamily at the ceiling through the cigarette smoke. "I suppose it's just getting the timing right so that the drivers aren't quite sure whether they've seen me or not. And then I get a hell of a kick out of hearing them revving up like mad and roaring off for home. None of them ever slows down."

"Well, somebody once told me your sense of humour was over-developed," I said. "And I'm telling you it'll land you in the cart one of these days."

"Not a chance. I keep my bike behind a hedge about a hundred yards down the road so that I can make a quick getaway if necessary. There's no problem."

"Well, please yourself." I got off the bed and made shakily for the door. "I'm going downstairs for a tot of whisky, and just remember this." I turned and glared at him. "If you try that trick on me again I'll strangle you."

A few days later at about eight o'clock in the evening I was sitting reading by the fireside in the big room at Skeldale House when the door burst open and Siegfried burst into the room.

"James," he rapped out. "Old Horace Dawson's cow has split its teat. Sounds like a stitching job. The old chap won't be able to hold the cow and he has no near neighbours to help him so I wonder if you'd come and give me a hand."

"Sure, glad to." I marked the place in my book, stretched and yawned then got up from the chair. I noticed Siegfried's foot tapping on the carpet and it occurred to me, not for the first time, that the only thing that would satisfy him would be some kind of ejector seat on my chair which would hurl me straight through the door and into action on the word of command. I was being as quick as I could but I had the feeling as always—when I was writing something for him or operating under his eyes—that I wasn't going nearly fast enough. There were elements of tension in the knowledge that the mere fact of watching me rise from the chair and replace my book in the fireside alcove was an almost unbearable strain for him.

By the time I was half way across the carpet he had disappeared into the passage. I followed at a trot and just made it into the street as he was starting the car. Grabbing the door I made a dive for the interior and felt the road whip away from under my foot as we took off into the darkness.

Fifteen minutes later we screeched to a halt in the yard behind a little smallholding standing on its own across a couple of fields. The engine had barely stopped before my colleague was out of the car and striding briskly towards the cow house. He called to me over his shoulder as he went.

"Bring the suture materials, James, will you . . . and the local and syringe . . . and that bottle of wound lotion . . ."

I heard the brief murmur of conversation from within then Siegfried's voice again, raised this time in an impatient shout.

"James! What are you doing out there? Can't you find those things?"

I had hardly got the boot open and I rummaged frantically among the rows of tins and bottles. I found what he required, galloped across the yard and almost collided with him as he came out of the building.

He was in mid shout. "James! What the hell's keeping you . . . oh, you're there. Right, let's have that stuff . . . what have you been doing all this time?"

He had been right about Horace Dawson, a tiny frail man of about eighty who couldn't be expected to do any strong-arm stuff. Despite his age he had stubbornly refused to give up milking the two fat shorthorn cows which stood in the little cobbled byre.

Our patient had badly damaged a teat; either she or her neighbour must have stood on it because there was a long tear running almost full length with the milk running from it.

"It's a bad one, Horace," Siegfried said. "You can see it goes right into the milk channel. But we'll do what we can for her—it'll need a good few stitches in there."

He bathed and disinfected the teat then filled a syringe with local anaesthetic.

"Grab her nose, James," he said, then spoke gently to the farmer. "Horace, will you please hold her tail

for me. Just catch it by the very end, that's the way
... lovely."

The little man squared his shoulders. "Aye, ah can
do that fine, Mr. Farnon."

"Good lad, Horace, that's splendid, thank you. Now
stand well clear." He bent over and as I gripped the
animal's nose he inserted the needle above the top
extremity of the wound.

There was an instant smacking sound as the cow
registered her disapproval by kicking Siegfried briskly half way up his wellington boot. He made no sound
but breathed deeply and flexed his knee a couple of
times before crouching down again.

"Cush pet," he murmured soothingly as he stuck
the needle in again.

This time the cloven foot landed on his forearm,
sending the syringe winging gracefully through the air
till it came to rest by a piece of good fortune in the
hay-rack. Siegfried straightened up, rubbed his arm
thoughtfully, retrieved his syringe and approached
the patient again.

For a few moments he scratched around the root of
her tail and addressed her in the friendliest manner.
"All right, old lady, it isn't very nice, is it?"

When he got down again he adopted a new stance,
burrowing with his head into the cow's flank and
stretching his long arms high he managed despite a
few more near misses to infiltrate the tissues round
the wound with local. Then he proceeded to thread a
needle unhurriedly, whistling tunelessly under his
breath.

Mr. Dawson watched him admiringly. "Ah know
why you're such a good feller wi' animals, Mr. Farnon. It's because you're so patient—I reckon you're
t'patientest man ah've ever seen."

Siegfried inclined his head modestly and recommenced work. And it was more peaceful now. The
cow couldn't feel a thing as my colleague put in a
long, even row of stitches, pulling the lips of the
wound firmly together.

When he had finished he put an arm round the old man's shoulders.

"Now, Horace, if that heals well the teat will be as good as new. But it won't heal if you pull at it, so I want you to use this tube to milk her." He held up a bottle of spirit in which a teat syphon gleamed.

"Very good," said Mr. Dawson firmly. "Ah'll use it."

Siegfried wagged a playful finger in his face. "But you've got to be careful, you know. You must boil the tube every time before use and keep it always in the bottle or you'll finish up with mastitis. Will you do that?"

"Mr. Farnon," the little man said, holding himself very erect. "Ah'll do exackly as you say."

"That's my boy, Horace." Siegfried gave him a final pat on the back before starting to pick up his instruments. "I'll pop back in about two weeks to take the stitches out."

As we were leaving, the vast form of Claude Blenkiron loomed suddenly in the byre door. He was the village policeman, though obviously off duty judging by the smart check jacket and slacks.

"I saw you had summat on, Horace, and I wondered if you wanted a hand."

"Nay, thank ye, Mr. Blenkiron. It's good of ye but you're ower late. We've done t'job," the old man replied.

Siegfried laughed. "Wish you'd arrived half an hour ago, Claude. You could have tucked this cow under your arm while I stitched her."

The big man nodded and a slow smile spread over his face. He looked the soul of geniality but I felt, as always, that there was a lot of iron behind that smile. Claude was a well-loved character in the district, a magnificent athlete who bestowed lavish help and friendship on all who needed it on his beat. But though he was a sturdy prop to the weak and the elderly he was also a merciless scourge of the ungodly.

I had no first hand knowledge but there were ru-

mours that Claude preferred not to trouble the magis-
trates with trivialities but dispensed his own form of
instant justice. It was said that he kept a stout stick
handy and acts of hooliganism and vandalism were
rapidly followed by a shrill yowling down some dark
alley. Second offenders were almost unknown and in
fact his whole district was remarkably law-abiding. I
looked again at the smiling face. He really was the
most pleasant looking man but as I say there was
something else there and nothing would ever have
induced me to pick a fight with him.

"Right, then," he said. "I was just on me way into
Darrowby so I'll say good night gentlemen."

Siegfried put a hand on his arm. "Just a moment,
Claude, I want to go on to see another of my cases. I
wonder if you'd give Mr. Herriot a lift into the town."

"I'll do that with pleasure, Mr. Farnon," the policeman replied and beckoned me to follow him.

In the darkness outside I got into the passenger
seat of a little Morris Eight and waited for a few
moments while Claude squeezed his bulk behind the
wheel. As we set off he began to talk about his recent
visit to Bradford where he had been taking part in a
wrestling match.

We had to go through Raynes village on the way
back and as we left the houses behind and began the
ascent to the abbey he suddenly stopped talking.
Then he startled me as he snapped upright in his
seat and pointed ahead.

"Look, look there, it's that bloody monk!"

"Where? Where?" I feigned ignorance but I had
seen it all right—the cowled, slow-pacing figure heading for the wood.

Claude's foot was on the boards and the car was
screaming up the hill. At the top he swung savagely
on to the roadside grass so that the headlights blazed
into the depth of the wood and as he lept from the
car there was a fleeting moment when his quarry was
in full view; a monk, skirts hitched high, legging it
with desperate speed among the trees.

The big man reached into the back of the car and

pulled out what looked like a heavy walking stick. "After the bugger!" he shouted, plunging eagerly forward.

I panted after him. "Wait a minute, what are you going to do if you catch him?"

"I'm goin' to come across his arse with me ash plant," Claude said with chilling conviction and galloped ahead of me till he disappeared from the circle of light. He was making a tremendous noise, beating against the tree trunks and emitting a series of intimidating shouts.

My heart bled for the hapless spectre blundering in the darkness with the policeman's cries dinning in his ears. I waited with tingling horror for the final confrontation and the tension increased as time passed and I could still hear Claude in full cry; "Come out of there, you can't get away! Come on, show yourself!" while his splintering blows echoed among the trees.

I did my own bit of searching but found nothing. The monk did indeed seem to have disappeared and when I finally returned to the car I found the big man already there.

"Well that's a rum 'un, Mr. Herriot," he said. "I can't find 'im and I can't think where he's got to. I was hard on his heels when I first spotted him and he didn't get out of the wood because I can see over the fields in the moonlight. I've 'ad a scout round the abbey too, but he isn't there. He's just bloody vanished."

I was going to say something like "Well, what else would you expect from a ghost?" but the huge hand was still swinging that stick and I decided against it.

"Well I reckon we'd better get on to Darrowby," the policeman grunted, stamping his feet on the frosty turf. I shivered. It was bitterly cold with an east wind getting up and I was glad to climb back into the car.

In Darrowby I had a few companionable beers with Claude at his favourite haunt, the Black Bull, and it was ten thirty when I got into Skeldale House.

There was no sign of Tristan and I felt a twinge of anxiety.

It must have been after midnight when I was awakened by a faint scuffling from the next room. Tristan occupied what had been the long, narrow "dressing room" in the grand days when the house was young. I jumped out of bed and opened the communicating door.

Tristan was in pyjamas and he cuddled two hot water bottles to his bosom. He turned his head and gave me a single haggard glance before pushing one of the bottles well down the bed. Then he crawled between the sheets and lay on his back with the second bottle clasped across his chest and his eyes fixed on the ceiling. I went over and looked down at him in some concern. He was shaking so much that the whole bed vibrated with him.

"How are you, Triss?" I whispered.

After a few moments a faint croak came up. "Frozen to the bloody marrow, Jim."

"But where the heck have you been?"

Again the croak. "In a drainpipe."

"A drainpipe!" I stared at him. "Where?"

The head rolled feebly from side to side on the pillow. "Up at the wood. Didn't you see those pipes by the roadside?"

A great light flashed. "Of course, yes! They're going to put a new sewer into the village, aren't they?"

"That's right," Tristan whispered. "When I saw that big bloke pounding into the wood I cut straight back and dived into one of the pipes. God only knows how long I was in there."

"But why didn't you come out after we left?"

A violent shudder shook the young man's frame and he closed his eyes briefly. "I couldn't hear a thing in there. I was jammed tight with my cowl over my ears and there was a ninety mile an hour wind screaming down the pipe. I didn't hear the car start and I daren't come out in case that chap was still standing there with his bloody great shillelagh." He took hold of the quilt with one hand and picked at it fiftully.

"Well never mind, Triss," I said. "You'll soon get warmed up and you'll be all right after a night's sleep."

Tristan didn't appear to have heard. "They're horrible things, drainpipes, Jim." He looked up at me with hunted eyes. "They're full of muck and they stink of cats' pee."

"I know, I know." I put his hand back inside the quilt and pulled the sheets up round his chin. "You'll be fine in the morning." I switched off the light and tiptoed from the room. As I closed the door I could still hear his teeth chattering.

Clearly it wasn't only the cold that was bothering him; he was still in a state of shock. And no wonder. The poor fellow had been enjoying a little session of peaceful haunting with never a care in the world when without warning there was a scream of brakes, a blaze of light and that giant bounding into the middle of it like the demon king. It had all been too much.

Next morning at the breakfast table Tristan was in poor shape. He looked very pale, he ate little and at intervals his body was racked by deep coughing spasms.

Siegfried looked at him quizzically. "I know what's done this to you. I know why you're sitting there like a zombie, coughing your lungs up."

His brother stiffened in his chair and a tremor crossed his face. "You do?"

"Yes, I hate to say I told you so, but I did warn you, didn't I? It's all those bloody cigarettes!"

Tristan never did give up smoking but the Raynes ghost was seen no more and remains an unsolved mystery to this day.

16

This was one for Granville Bennett. I liked a bit of small animal surgery and was gradually doing more as time went on but this one frightened me. A twelve year old spaniel bitch in the last stages of pyometritis, pus dripping from her vulva on to the surgery table, temperature a hundred and four, panting, trembling, and, as I held my stethoscope against her chest I could hear the classical signs of valvular insufficiency. A dicky heart was just what I needed on top of everything else.

"Drinking a lot of water, is she?" I asked.

Old Mrs. Barker twisted the strings of her shopping bag anxiously. "Aye, she never seems to be away from the water bowl. But she won't eat—hasn't had a bite for the last four days."

"Well I don't know," I took off my stethoscope and stuffed it in my pocket. "You should have brought her in long ago. She must have been ill for weeks."

"Not rightly ill, but a bit off it. I thought there was nothing to worry about as long as she was eating."

I didn't say anything for a few moments. I had no desire to upset the old girl but she had to be told.

"I'm afraid this is rather serious, Mrs. Barker. The condition has been building up for a long time. It's in her womb, you see, a bad infection, and the only cure is an operation."

"Well will you do it, please?" The old lady's lips quivered.

I came round the table and put my hand on her shoulder.

"I'd like to, but there are snags. She's in poor shape

and twelve years old. Really a poor operation risk. I'd like to take her through to the Veterinary Hospital at Hartington and let Mr. Bennett operate on her."

"All right," she said, nodding eagerly. "I don't care what it costs."

"Oh we'll keep it down as much as possible." I walked along the passage with her and showed her out of the door. "Leave her with me—I'll look after her, don't worry. What's her name, by the way?"

"Dinah," she replied huskily, still peering past me down the passage.

I went through and lifted the phone. Thirty years ago country practitioners had to turn to the small animal experts when anything unusual cropped in that line. It is different nowadays when our practices are more mixed. In Darrowby now we have the staff and equipment to tackle any type of small animal surgery but it was different then. I had heard it said that sooner or later every large animal man had to scream for help from Granville Bennett and now it was my turn.

"Hello, is that Mr. Bennett?"

"It is indeed." A big voice, friendly, full of give.

"Herriot here. I'm with Farnon in Darrowby."

"Of course! Heard of you, laddie, heard of you."

"Oh . . . er . . . thanks. Look, I've got a bit of a sticky job here. I wonder if you'd take it on for me."

"Delighted, laddie, what is it?"

"A real stinking pyo."

"Oh lovely!"

"The bitch is twelve years old."

"Splendid!"

"And toxic as hell."

"Excellent!"

"And one of the worst hearts I've heard for a long time."

"Fine, fine! When are you coming through?"

"This evening, if it's O.K. with you. About eight."

"Couldn't be better, laddie. See you."

Hartington was a fair sized town—about 200,000 inhabitants—but as I drove into the centre the traffic had thinned and only a few cars rolled past the rows of shop fronts. I hoped my twenty five mile journey had been worth it. Dinah, stretched out on a blanket in the back, looked as if she didn't care either way. I glanced behind me at the head drooping over the edge of the seat, at the white muzzle and the cataracts in her eyes gleaming palely in the light from the dash. She looked so old. Maybe I was wasting my time, placing too much faith in this man's reputation.

There was no doubt Granville Bennett had become something of a legend in northern England. In those days when specialisation was almost unknown he had gone all out for small animal work—never looked at farm stock—and had set a new standard by the modern procedures in his animal hospital which was run as nearly as possible on human lines. It was, in fact, fashionable for veterinary surgeons of that era to belittle dog and cat work; a lot of the older men who had spent their lives among the teeming thousands of draught horses in city and agriculture would sneer "Oh I've no time to bother with those damn things." Bennett had gone dead in the opposite direction.

I had never met him but I knew he was a young man in his early thirties. I had heard a lot about his skill, his business acumen, and about his reputation as a bon viveur. He was, they said, a dedicated devotee of the work-hard-play-hard school.

The Veterinary Hospital was a long low building near the top of a busy street. I drove into a yard and knocked at a door in the corner. I was looking with some awe at a gleaming Bentley dwarfing my own battered little Austin when the door was opened by a pretty receptionist.

"Good evening," she murmured with a dazzling smile which I thought must be worth another half crown on the bill for a start. "Do come in, Mr. Bennett is expecting you."

I was shown into a waiting room with magazines and flowers on a corner table and many impressive photographs of dogs and cats on the walls—taken, I learned later, by the principal himself. I was looking closely at a superb study of two white poodles when I heard a footstep behind me. I turned and had my first view of Granville Bennett.

He seemed to fill the room. Not over tall but of tremendous bulk. Fat, I thought at first, but as he came nearer it seemed to me that the tissue of which he was composed wasn't distributed like fat. He wasn't flabby, he didn't stick out in any particular place, he was just a big, wide, solid, hard-looking man. From the middle of a pleasant blunt-featured face the most magnificent pipe I had ever seen stuck forth shining and glorious, giving out delicious wisps of expensive smoke. It was an enormous pipe, in fact it would have looked downright silly with a smaller man but on him it was a thing of beauty. I had a final impression of a beautifully cut dark suit and sparkling shirt cuffs as he held out a hand.

"James Herriot!" He said it as somebody else might have said "Winston Churchill."

"That's right."

"Well, this is grand. Jim, is it?"

"Well yes, usually."

"Lovely. We've got everything laid on for you, Jim. The girls are waiting in the theatre."

"That's very kind of you, Mr. Bennett."

"Granville, Granville please!" He put his arm through mine and led me to the operating room.

Dinah was already there, looking very woebegone. She had had a sedative injection and her head nodded wearily. Bennett went over to her and gave her a swift examination.

"Mm, yes, let's get on, then."

The two girls went into action like cogs in a smooth machine. Bennett kept a large lay staff and these animal nurses, both attractive, clearly knew what they were about. While one of them pulled up the anaesthetic and instrument trolleys the other seized Dinah's foreleg expertly above the elbow, raised the radial vein by pressure and quickly clipped and disinfected the area.

The big man strolled up with a loaded needle and effortlessly slipped the needle into the vein.

"Pentothal," he said as Dinah slowly collapsed and lay unconscious on the table. It was one of the new short-acting anaesthetics which I had never seen used.

While Bennett scrubbed up and donned sterilised gown and cap the girls rolled Dinah on her back and secured her there with ties to loops on the operating table. They applied the ether and oxygen mask to her face then shaved and swabbed the operation site. The big man returned in time to have a scalpel placed in his hand.

With almost casual speed he incised skin and muscle layers and when he went through the peritoneum the horns of the uterus which in normal health would have been two slim pink ribbons now welled into the wound like twin balloons, swollen and turgid with pus. No wonder Dinah had felt ill, carrying that lot around with her.

The stubby fingers tenderly worked round the mass, ligated the ovarian vessels and uterine body then removed the whole thing and dropped it into an enamel bowl. It wasn't till he had begun to stitch that I realised that the operation was nearly over though he had been at the table for only a few minutes. It would all have looked childishly easy except that his total involvement showed in occasional explosive commands to the nurses.

And as I watched him working under the shadowless lamp with the white tiled walls around him and the rows of instruments gleaming by his side it came to me with a rush of mixed emotions that this was what I had always wanted to do myself. My dreams when I had first decided on veterinary work had been precisely of this. Yet here I was, a somewhat shaggy cow doctor; or perhaps more correctly a farm physician, but certainly something very different. The scene before me was a far cry from my routine of kicks and buffets, of muck and sweat. And yet I had no regrets; the life which had been forced on me by circumstances had turned out to be a thing of magical fulfilment. It came to me with a flooding certainty that I would rather spend my days driving over the unfenced roads of the high country than stooping over that operating table.

And anyway I couldn't have been a Bennett. I don't think I could have matched his technique and this whole set up was eloquent of a lot of things like business sense, foresight and driving ambition which I just didn't possess.

My colleague was finished now and was fitting up an intravenous saline drip. He taped the needle down in the vein then turned to me.

"That's it, then, Jim. It's up to the old girl now." He began to lead me from the room and it struck me how very pleasant it must be to finish your job and walk away from it like this. In Darrowby I'd have been starting now to wash the instruments, scrub the table, and the final scene would have been of Herriot the great surgeon swilling the floor with mop and bucket. This was a better way.

Back in the waiting room Bennett pulled on his jacket and extracted from a side pocket the immense pipe which he inspected with a touch of anxiety as if he feared mice had been nibbling at it in his absence. He wasn't satisfied with his examination because he brought forth a soft yellow cloth and began to polish the briar with intense absorption. Then he held the pipe high, moving it slightly from side to side, his eyes softening at the play of the light on the exquisite grain. Finally he produced a pouch of mammoth proportions, filled the bowl, applied a match with a touch of reverence and closed his eyes as a fragrant mist drifted from his lips.

"That baccy smells marvelous," I said. "What is it?"

"Navy Cut De Luxe." He closed his eyes again. "You know, I could eat the smoke."

I laughed. "I use the ordinary Navy Cut myself."

He gazed at me like a sorrowing Buddha. "Oh you

mustn't, laddie, you mustn't. This is the only stuff. Rich . . . fruity . . ." His hand made languid motions in the air. "Here, you can take some away with you."

He pulled open a drawer. I had a brief view of a stock which wouldn't have disgraced a fair sized tobacconist's shop; unnumerable tins, pipes, cleaners, reamers, cloths.

"Try this," he said. "And tell me if I'm not right."

I looked down at the first container in my hand. "Oh but I can't take all this. It's a four ounce tin!"

"Rubbish, my boy. Put it in your pocket." He became suddenly brisk. "Now I expect you'll want to hang around till old Dinah comes out of the anaesthetic so why don't we have a quick beer? I'm a member of a nice little club just across the road."

"Well fine, sounds great."

He moved lightly and swiftly for a big man and I had to hurry to keep up with him as he left the surgery and crossed to a building on the other side of the street.

17

Inside the club was masculine comfort, hails of welcome from some prosperous looking members and a friendly greeting from the man behind the bar.

"Two pints, Fred," murmured Bennett absently, and the drinks appeared with amazing speed. My colleague poured his down apparently without swallowing and turned to me.

"Another, Jim?"

I had just tried a sip at mine and began to gulp anxiously at the bitter ale. "Right, but let me get this one."

"No can do, laddie." He glanced at me with mild severity. "Only members can buy drinks. Same again, Fred."

I found I had two glasses at my elbow and with a tremendous effort I got the first one down. Gasping slightly I was surveying the second one timidly when I noticed that Bennett was three quarters down his. As I watched he drained it effortlessly.

"You're slow, Jim," he said, smiling indulgently. "Just set them up again will you, Fred."

In some alarm I watched the barman ply his handle and attacked my second pint resolutely. I surprised myself by forcing it over my tonsils then, breathing heavily, I got hold of the third one just as Bennett spoke again.

"We'll just have one for the road, Jim," he said pleasantly. "Would you be so kind, Fred?"

This was ridiculous but I didn't want to appear a piker at our first meeting. With something akin to desperation I raised the third drink and began to suck feebly at it. When my glass was empty I almost collapsed against the counter. My stomach was agonisingly distended and a light perspiration had broken out on my brow. As I almost lay there I saw my colleague moving across the carpet towards the door.

"Time we were off, Jim," he said. "Drink up."

It's wonderful what the human frame can tolerate when put to the test. I would have taken bets that it was impossible for me to drink that fourth pint without at least half an hour's rest, preferably in the prone position, but as Bennett's shoe tapped impatiently I tipped the beer a little at a time into my mouth, feeling it wash around my back teeth before incredibly disappearing down my gullet. I believe the water torture was a favourite with the Spanish Inquisition and as the pressure inside me increased I knew just how their victims felt.

When I at last blindly replaced my glass and splashed my way from the bar the big man was holding the door open. Outside in the street he placed an arm across my shoulder.

"The old Spaniel won't be out of it yet," he said. "We'll just slip to my house and have a bite—I'm a little peckish."

Sunk in the deep upholstery of the Bentley, cradling my swollen abdomen in my arms I watched the shop fronts flicker past the windows and give way to the darkness of the open countryside. We drew up outside a fine grey stone house in a typical Yorkshire village and Bennett ushered me inside.

He pushed me towards a leather armchair. "Make yourself at home, laddie. Zoe's out at the moment but I'll get some grub." He bustled through to the kitchen and reappeared in seconds with a deep bowl which he placed on a table by my side.

"You know, Jim," he said, rubbing his hands. "There's nothing better after beer than a few pickled onions."

I cast a timorous glance into the bowl. Everything in this man's life seemed to be larger than life, even the onions. They were bigger than golf balls, brownish-white, glistening.

"Well thanks Mr. Ben . . . Granville." I took one of them, held it between finger and thumb and stared at it helplessly. The beer hadn't even begun to sort itself out inside me; the idea of starting on this potent-looking vegetable was unthinkable.

Granville reached into the bowl, popped an onion into his mouth, crunched it quickly, swallowed and sank his teeth into a second. "By God, that's good. You know, my little wife's a marvellous cook. She even makes pickled onions better than anyone."

Munching happily he moved over to the sideboard and clinked around for a few moments before placing in my hand a heavy cut glass tumbler about two thirds full of neat whisky. I couldn't say anything because I had taken the plunge and put the onion in my mouth; and as I bit boldly into it the fumes rolled in a volatile wave into my nasal passages, making me splutter. I took a gulp at the whisky and looked up at Granville with watering eyes.

He was holding out the onion bowl again and when I declined he regarded it for a moment with hurt in his eyes. "It's funny you don't like them, I always thought Zoe did them marvellously."

"Oh you're wrong, Granville, they're delicious. I just haven't finished this one."

He didn't reply but continued to look at the bowl with gentle sorrow. I realised there was nothing else for it; I took another onion.

Immensely gratified, Granville hurried through to the kitchen again. This time when he came back he bore a tray with an enormous cold roast, a loaf of bread, butter and mustard.

"I think a beef sandwich would go down rather nicely, Jim," he murmured as he stropped his carving knife on a steel. Then he noticed my glass of whisky still half full.

"C'mon, c'mon, c'mon!" he said with some asperity, "You're not touching your drink." He watched me benevolently as I drained the glass then he refilled it to its old level. "That's better. And have another onion."

I stretched my legs out and rested my head on the back of the chair in an attempt to ease my internal turmoil. My stomach was a lake of volcanic lava bubbling and popping fiercely in its crater with each additional piece of onion, every sip of whisky setting up a fresh violent reaction. Watching Granville at work, a great wave of nausea swept over me. He was sawing busily at the roast, carving off slices which looked to be an inch thick, slapping mustard on them and enclosing them in the bread. He hummed with contentment as the pile grew. Every now and then he had another onion.

"Now then, laddie," he cried at length, putting a heaped plate at my elbow. "Get yourself round that lot." He took his own supply and collapsed with a sigh into another chair.

He took a gargantuan bite and spoke as he chewed. "You know, Jim, this is something I enjoy—a nice little snack. Zoe always leaves me plenty to go at when she pops out." He engulfed a further few inches of sandwich. "And I'll tell you something, though I say it myself, these are bloody good, don't you think so?"

"Yes indeed." Squaring my shoulders I bit, swallowed and held my breath as another unwanted foreign body slid down to the ferment below.

Just then I heard the front door open.

"Ah, that'll be Zoe," Granville said and was about to rise when a disgracefully fat Staffordshire Bull Terrier burst into the room, waddled across the carpet and leaped into his lap.

"Phoebles, my dear, come to daddykins!" he shouted. "Have you had nice walkies with mummy?"

The Staffordshire was closely followed by a Yorkshire Terrier which was also enthusiastically greeted by Granville.

"Yoo-hoo, Victoria, Yoo-hoo!"

The Yorkie, an obvious smiler, did not jump up but contented herself with sitting at her master's feet, baring her teeth ingratiatingly every few seconds.

I smiled through my pain. Another myth exploded; the one about these specialist small animal vets not being fond of dogs themselves. The big man crooned over the two little animals. The fact that he called Phoebe "Phoebles" was symptomatic.

I heard light footsteps in the hall and looked up expectantly. I had Granville's wife typed neatly in my mind; domesticated, devoted, homely; many of these dynamic types had wives like that, willing slaves content to lurk in the background. I waited confidently for the entrance of a plain little hausfrau.

When the door opened I almost let my vast sandwich fall. Zoe Bennett was a glowing warm beauty who would make any man alive stop for another look. A lot of soft brown hair, large grey-green friendly eyes, a tweed suit sitting sweetly on a slim but not too slim figure; and something else, a wholesomeness, an inner light which made me wish suddenly that I was a better man or at least that I looked better than I did.

In an instant I was acutely conscious of the fact that my shoes were dirty, that my old jacket and corduroy trousers were out of place here. I hadn't troubled to change but had rushed straight out in my working clothes, and they were different from Granville's because I couldn't go round the farms in a suit like his.

"My love, my love!" he carolled joyously as his wife bent over and kissed him fondly. "Let me introduce Jim Herriot from Darrowby."

The beautiful eyes turned on me.

"How d'you do, Mr. Herriot!" she looked as pleased to see me as her husband had done and again I had the desperate wish that I was more presentable; that my hair was combed, that I didn't have this mounting conviction that I was going to explode into a thousand pieces at any moment.

"I'm going to have a cup of tea, Mr. Herriot. Would you like one?"

"No-no, no, no, thank you very much but no, no, not at the moment." I backed away slightly.

"Ah well, I see you've got one of Granville's little sandwiches." She giggled and went to get her tea.

When she came back she handed a parcel to her husband. "I've been shopping today, darling. Picked up some of those shirts you like so much."

"My sweet! How kind of you!" He began to tear at the brown paper like a schoolboy and produced three elegant shirts in cellophane covers. "They're marvellous, my pet, you spoil me." He looked up at me. "Jim! These are the most wonderful shirts, you must have one." He flicked a shining package across the room on to my lap.

I looked down at it in amazement. "No, really, I can't . . ."

"Of course you can. You keep it."

"But Granville, not a shirt . . . it's too . . ."

"It's a very good shirt." He was beginning to look hurt again.

I subsided.

They were both so kind. Zoe sat right by me with her tea cup, chatting pleasantly while Granville beamed at me from his chair as he finished the last of the sandwiches and started again on the onions.

The proximity of the attractive woman was agreeable but embarrassing. My corduroys in the warmth of the room had begun to give off the unmistakable bouquet of the farmyard where they spent most of their time. And though it was one of my favourite scents there was no doubt it didn't go with these elegant surroundings.

And worse still, I had started a series of internal rumblings and musical tinklings which resounded only too audibly during every lull in the conversation. The only other time I have heard such sounds was in a cow with an advanced case of displacement of the abomasum. My companions delicately feigned deafness even when I produced a shameful, explosive belch which made the little fat dog start up in alarm, but when another of these mighty borborygmi escaped me and almost made the windows rattle I thought it time to go.

In any case I wasn't contributing much else. The alcohol had taken hold and I was increasingly conscious that I was just sitting there with a stupid leer on my face. In striking contrast to Granville who looked just the same as when I first met him back at the surgery. He was cool and possessed, his massive urbanity unimpaired. It was a little hard.

So, with the tin of tobacco bumping against my hip and the shirt tucked under my arm I took my leave.

Back at the hospital I looked down at Dinah. The old dog had come through wonderfully well and she lifted her head and gazed at me sleepily. Her colour was good and her pulse strong. The operative shock had been dramatically minimised by my colleague's skilful speedy technique and by the intravenous drip.

I knelt down and stroked her ears. "You know, I'm sure she's going to make it, Granville."

Above me the great pipe nodded with majestic confidence.

"Of course, laddie, of course."

And he was right. Dinah was rejuvenated by her hysterectomy and lived to delight her mistress for many more years.

On the way home that night she lay by my side on the passenger seat, her nose poking from a blanket. Now and then she rested her chin on my hand as it gripped the gear lever and occasionally she licked me lazily.

I could see she felt better than I did.

18

Ben Ashby the cattle dealer looked over the gate with his habitual deadpan expression. It always seemed to me that after a lifetime of buying cows from farmers he had developed a terror of showing any emotion which might be construed as enthusiasm. When he looked at a beast his face registered nothing beyond, occasionally, a gentle sorrow.

This was how it was this morning as he leaned on the top spar and directed a gloomy stare at Harry Sumner's heifer. After a few moments he turned to the farmer.

"I wish you'd had her in for me, Harry. She's too far away. I'm going to have to get over the top." He began to climb stiffly upwards and it was then that he spotted Monty. The bull hadn't been so easy to see before as he cropped the grass among the group of heifers but suddenly the great head rose high above the others, the nose ring gleamed, and an ominous, strangled bellow sounded across the grass. And as he gazed at us he pulled absently at the turf with a fore foot.

Ben Ashby stopped climbing, hesitated for a second then returned to ground level.

"Aye well," he muttered, still without changing expression. "It's not that far away. I reckon I can see all right from here."

Monty had changed a lot since the first day I saw him about two years ago. He had been a fortnight old then, a skinny, knock-kneed little creature, his head deep in a calf bucket.

"Well, what do you think of me new bull?" Harry

Sumner had asked, laughing. "Not much for a hundred quid is he?"

I whistled. "As much as that?"

"Aye, it's a lot for a new-dropped calf, isn't it? But I can't think of any other way of getting into the Newton strain. I haven't the brass to buy a big 'un."

Not all the farmers of those days were as far-seeing as Harry and some of them would use any type of male bovine to get their cows in calf.

One such man produced a gaunt animal for Siegfried's inspection and asked him what he thought of his bull. Siegfried's reply of "All horns and balls" didn't please the owner but I still treasure it as the most graphic description of the typical scrub bull of that period.

Harry was a bright boy. He had inherited a little place of about a hundred acres on his father's death and with his young wife had set about making it go. He was in his early twenties and when I first saw him I had been deceived by his almost delicate appearance into thinking that he wouldn't be up to the job; the pallid face, the large, sensitive eyes and slender frame didn't seem fitted for the seven days a week milking, feeding, mucking-out slog that was dairy farming. But I had been wrong.

The fearless way he plunged in and grabbed at the hind feet of kicking cows for me to examine and his clenched-teeth determination as he hung on to the noses of the big loose beasts at testing time made me change my mind in a hurry. He worked endlessly and tirelessly and it was natural that his drive should have taken him to the south of Scotland to find a bull.

Harry's was an Ayrshire herd—unusual among the almost universal shorthorns in the Dales—and there was no doubt an injection of the famous Newton blood would be a sure way of improving his stock.

"He's got prize winners on both his sire and dam's side," the young farmer said. "And a grand pedigree name, too. Newton Montmorency the Sixth—Monty for short."

As though recognising his name, the calf raised his head from the bucket and looked at us. It was a comic little face—wet-muzzled, milk slobbered half way up his cheeks and dribbling freely from his mouth. I bent over into the pen and scratched the top of the hard little head, feeling the tiny horn buds no bigger than peas under my fingers. Limpid-eyed and unafraid, Monty submitted calmly to the caress for a few moments then sank his head again in the bucket.

I saw quite a bit of Harry Sumner over the next few weeks and usually had a look at his expensive purchase. And as the calf grew you could see why he had cost £100. He was in a pen with three of Harry's own calves and his superiority was evident at a glance; the broad forehead and wide-set eyes; the deep chest and short straight legs; the beautifully even line of the back from shoulder to tail head. Monty had class; and small as he was he was all bull.

He was about three months old when Harry rang to say he thought the calf had pneumonia. I was surprised because the weather was fine and warm and I knew Monty was in a draught-free building. But when I saw him I thought immediately that his owner's diagnosis was right. The heaving of the rib cage, the temperature of 105 degrees—it looked fairly straightforward. But when I got my stethoscope on his chest and listened for the pneumonic sounds I heard nothing. His lungs were perfectly clear. I went over him several times but there was not a squeak, not a râle, not the slightest sign of consolidation.

This was a facer. I turned to the farmer. "It's a funny one, Harry. He's sick, all right, but his symptoms don't add up to anything recognisable."

I was going against my early training because the first vet I ever saw practice with in my student days told me once: "If you don't know what's wrong with an animal for God's sake don't admit it. Give it a name —call it McLuskie's Disease or Galloping Dandruff— anything you like, but give it a name." But no inspiration came to me. I looked at the panting, anxious-eyed little creature.

Treat the symptoms. That was the thing to do. He had a temperature so I'd try to get that down for a start. I brought out my pathetic armoury of febri-fuges; the injection of non-specific antiserum, the "fever drink" of sweet spirit of nitre; but over the next two days it was obvious that the time-honoured remedies were having no effect.

On the fourth morning, Harry Sumner met me as I got out of my car. "He's walking funny, this morning, Mr. Herriot—and he seems to be blind."

"Blind!" An unusual form of lead-poisoning—could that be it? I hurried into the calf pen and began to look round the walls, but there wasn't a scrap of paint anywhere and Monty had spent his entire life in there.

And anyway, as I looked at him I realised that he wasn't really blind; his eyes were staring and slightly upturned and he blundered unseeingly around the pen, but he blinked as I passed my hand in front of his face. To complete my bewilderment he walked with a wooden, stiff-legged gait almost like a mechan-ical toy and my mind began to snatch at diagnostic straws—tetanus, no—meningitis—no, no; I always tried to maintain the calm, professional exterior but I had to fight an impulse to scratch my head and stand gaping.

I got off the place as quickly as possible and set-tled down to serious thought as I drove away. My lack of experience didn't help, but I did have a knowledge of pathology and physiology and when stumped for a diagnosis I could usually work some-thing out on rational grounds. But this thing didn't make sense.

That night I got out my books, notes from college, back numbers of the Veterinary Record and anything else I could find on the subject of calf diseases. Somewhere here there would surely be a clue. But the volumes on medicine and surgery were barren of inspiration and I had about given up hope when I came upon the passage in a little pamphlet on calf diseases. "Peculiar, stilted gait, staring eyes with a tendency to gaze upwards, occasionally respiratory symptoms with high temperature." The words seemed to leap out at me from the printed page and it was as though the unknown author was patting me on the shoulder and murmuring reassuringly: "This is it, you see. It's all perfectly clear."

I grabbed the phone and rang Harry Sumner. "Harry, have you ever noticed Monty and those other calves in the pen licking each other?"

"Aye, they're allus at it, the little beggars. It's like a hobby with them. Why?"

"Well I know what's wrong with your bull. He's got a hair ball."

"A hair ball? Where?"

"In the abomasum—the fourth stomach. That's what's setting up all those strange symptoms."

"Well I'll go to hell. What do we do about it, then?"

"It'll probably mean an operation, but I'd like to try dosing him with liquid paraffin first. I'll put a pint bottle on the step for you if you'll come and collect it. Give him half a pint now and the same first thing in the morning. It might just grease the thing through. I'll see you tomorrow."

I hadn't a lot of faith in the liquid paraffin. I suppose I suggested it for the sake of doing something while I played nervously with the idea of operating. And next morning the picture was as I expected; Monty was still rigid-limbed, still staring sightlessly ahead of him, and an oiliness round his rectum and down his tail showed that the paraffin had by-passed the obstruction.

"He hasn't had a bite now for three days," Harry said. "I doubt he won't stick it much longer."

I looked from his worried face to the little animal trembling in the pen. "You're right. We'll have to open him up straight away to have any hope of saving him. Are you willing to let me have a go?"

"Oh aye, let's be at t'job—sooner the better." He

smiled at me. It was a confident smile and my stomach gave a lurch. His confidence could be badly misplaced because in those days abdominal surgery in the bovine was in a primitive state. There were a few jobs we had begun to tackle fairly regularly but removal of a hair ball wasn't one of them and my knowledge of the procedure was confined to some rather small-print reading in the text books.

But this young farmer had faith in me. He thought I could do the job so it was no good letting him see my doubts. It was at times like this that I envied our colleagues in human medicine. When a surgical case came up they packed their patient off to a hospital but the vet just had to get his jacket off on the spot and make an operating theatre out of the farm buildings.

Harry and I busied ourselves in boiling up the instruments, setting out buckets of hot water and laying a clean bed of straw in an empty pen. Despite his weakness the calf took nearly sixty c.c.'s of Nembutal into his vein before he was fully anaesthetised but finally he was asleep, propped on his back between two straw bales, his little hooves dangling above him. I was ready to start.

It's never the same as it is in the books. The pictures and diagrams look so simple and straightforward but it is a different thing when you are cutting into a living, breathing creature with the abdomen rising and falling gently and the blood oozing beneath your knife. The abomasum, I knew, was just down there, slightly to the right of the sternum but as I cut through the peritoneum there was this slippery mass of fat-streaked omentum obscuring everything; and as I pushed it aside one of the bales moved and Monty tilted to his left causing a sudden gush of intestines into the wound. I put the flat of my hand against the shining pink loops—it would be just great if my patient's insides started spilling out on to the straw before I had started.

"Pull him upright, Harry, and shove that bale back into place," I gasped. The farmer quickly com-

plied but the intestines weren't at all anxious to return to their place and kept intruding coyly as I
groped for the abomasum. Frankly I was beginning
to feel just a bit lost and my heart was thudding
when I came upon something hard. It was sliding
about beyond the wall of one of the stomachs—at
the moment I wasn't sure which. I gripped it and
lifted it into the wound. I had hold of the abomasum
and that hard thing inside must be the hair ball.

Repelling the intestines which had made another
determined attempt to push their way into the act,
I incised the stomach and had my first look at the
cause of the trouble. It wasn't a ball at all, rather a
flat plaque of densely matted hair mixed freely with
strands of hay, sour curd and a shining covering of
my liquid paraffin. The whole thing was jammed
against the pyloric opening.

Gingerly I drew it out through the incision and
dropped it in the straw. It wasn't till I had closed
the stomach wound with the gut, stitched up the
muscle layer and had started on the skin that I realised that the sweat was running down my face. As
I blew away a droplet from my nose end Harry
broke the silence.

"It's a hell of a tricky job, isn't it?" he said. Then
he laughed and thumped my shoulder. "I bet you
felt a bit queer the first time you did one of these!"

I pulled another strand of suture silk through and
knotted it. "You're right, Harry." I said. "How right
you are."

When I had finished we covered Monty with a
horse rug and piled straw on top of that, leaving
only his head sticking out. I bent over and touched
a corner of the eye. Not a vestige of a corneal reflex.
God, he was deep—had I given him too much
anaesthetic? And of course there'd be surgical shock,
too. As I left I glanced back at the motionless little
animal. He looked smaller than ever and very vulnerable under the bare walls of the pen.

I was busy for the rest of the day but that evening
my thoughts kept coming back to Monty. Had he

come out of it yet? Maybe he was dead. I hadn't the experience of previous cases to guide me and I simply had no idea of how a calf reacted to an operation like that. And I couldn't rid myself of the nagging consciousness of how much it all meant to Harry Sumner. The bull is half the herd, they say, and half of Harry's future herd was lying there under the straw—he wouldn't be able to find that much money again.

I jumped suddenly from my chair. It was no good, I had to find out what was happening. Part of me rebelled at the idea of looking amateurish and unsure of myself by going fussing back, but, I thought, I could always say I had returned to look for an instrument.

The farm was in darkness as I crept into the pen. I shone my torch on the mound of straw and saw with a quick bump of the heart that the calf had not moved. I dropped to my knees and pushed a hand under the rug; he was breathing anyway. But there was still no eye reflex—either he was dying or he was taking a hell of a time to come out.

In the shadows of the yard I looked across at the soft glow from the farmhouse kitchen. Nobody had heard me. I slunk over to the car and drove off with the sick knowledge that I was no further forward. I still didn't know how the job was going to turn out.

Next morning I had to go through the same thing again and as I walked stiffly across to the calf pen I knew for sure I'd see something this time. Either he'd be dead or better. I opened the outer door and almost ran down the passage. It was the third pen along and I stared hungrily into it.

Monty was sitting up on his chest. He was still under the rug and straw and he looked sorry for himself but when a bovine animal is on its chest I always feel hopeful. The tensions flowed from me in a great wave. He had survived the operation—the first stage was over; and as I knelt rubbing the top of his head I had the feeling that we were going to win.

And, in fact, he did get better, though I have always found it difficult to explain to myself scientifically why the removal of that pad of tangled fibres could cause such a dramatic improvement in so many directions. But there it was. His temperature did drop and his breathing returned to normal, his eyes did stop staring and the weird stiffness disappeared from his limbs.

But though I couldn't understand it, I was none the less delighted. Like a teacher with his favourite pupil I developed a warm proprietary affection for the calf and when I happened to be on the farm I found my feet straying unbidden to his pen. He always walked up to me and regarded me with friendly interest; it was as if he had a fellow feeling for me, too.

He was rather more than a year old when I noticed the change. The friendly interest gradually disappeared from his eyes and was replaced by a thoughtful, speculative look; and he developed a habit of shaking his head at me at the same time.

"I'd stop going in there, Mr. Herriot, if I were you," Harry said one day. "He's getting big and I reckon he's going to be a cheeky bugger before he's finished."

But cheeky was the wrong word. Harry had a long, trouble-free spell and Monty was nearly two years old when I saw him again. It wasn't a case of illness this time. One or two of Harry's cows had been calving before their time and it was typical of him that he should ask me to blood test his entire herd for Brucellosis.

We worked our way easily through the cows and I had a long row of glass tubes filled with blood in just over an hour.

"Well, that's the lot in here," the farmer said. "We only have bull to do and we're finished." He led the way across the yard through the door into the calf pens and along a passage to the bull box at the end. He opened the half door and as I looked inside I felt a sudden sense of shock.

Monty was enormous. The neck with its jutting humps of muscle supported a head so huge that the eyes looked tiny. And there was nothing friendly in those eyes now; no expression at all, in fact, only a cold black glitter. He was standing sideways to me, facing the wall, but I knew he was watching me as he pushed his head against the stones, his great horns scoring the whitewash with slow, menacing deliberation. Occasionally he snorted from deep in his chest but apart from that he remained ominously still. Monty wasn't just a bull—he was a vast, brooding presence.

Harry grinned as he saw me staring over the door. "Well, do you fancy popping inside to scratch his head? That's what you allus used to do."

"No thanks." I dragged my eyes away from the animal. "But I wonder what my expectation of life would be if I did go in."

"I reckon you'd last about a minute," Harry said thoughtfully. "He's a grand bull—all I ever expected —but by God he's a mean 'un. I never trust him an inch."

"And how," I asked without enthusiasm, "am I supposed to get a sample of blood from him?"

"Oh I'll trap his head in yon corner." Harry pointed to a metal yoke above a trough in an opening into the yard at the far side of the box. "I'll give him some meal to 'tice him in." He went back down the passage and soon I could see him out in the yard scooping meal into the trough.

The bull at first took no notice and continued to prod at the wall with his horns, then he turned with awesome slowness, took a few unhurried steps across the box and put his nose down to the trough. Harry, out of sight in the yard, pulled the lever and the yoke crashed shut on the great neck.

"All right," the farmer cried, hanging on to the lever, "I have 'im. You can go in now."

I opened the door and entered the box and though the bull was held fast by the head there was still the uneasy awareness that he and I were alone in

that small space together. And as I passed along the
massive body and put my hand on the neck I
sensed a quivering emanation of pent up power and
rage. Digging my fingers into the jugular furrow I
watched the vein rise up and poised my needle. It
would take a good hard thrust to pierce that leathery
skin.

The bull stiffened but did not move as I plunged
the needle in and with relief I saw the blood flowing
darkly into the syringe. Thank God I had hit the
vein the first time and didn't have to start poking
around. I was withdrawing the needle and thinking
that the job had been so simple after all when everything started to happen. The bull gave a tremendous
bellow and whipped round at me with no trace of
his former lethargy. I saw that he had got one horn
out of the yoke and though he couldn't reach me
with his head his shoulder knocked me on my back
with a terrifying revelation of unbelievable strength.
I heard Harry shouting from outside and as I scrambled up and headed for the box door I saw that the
madly plunging creature had almost got his second
horn clear and when I reached the passage I heard
the clang of the yoke as he finally freed himself.

Anybody who has travelled a narrow passage a
few feet ahead of about a ton of snorting, pounding
death will appreciate that I didn't dawdle. I was
spurred on by the certain knowledge that if Monty
caught me he would plaster me against the wall as
effortlessly as I would squash a ripe plum, and though
I was clad in a long oilskin coat and wellingtons
I doubt whether an olympic sprinter in full running
kit would have bettered my time.

I made the door at the end with a foot to spare,
dived through and crashed it shut. The first thing I
saw was Harry Sumner running round from the outside of the box. He was very pale. I couldn't see my
face but it felt pale; even my lips were cold and
numb.

"God, I'm sorry!" Harry said hoarsely. "The yoke
couldn't have closed properly—that bloody great neck

of his. The lever just jerked out of my hand. Damn, I'm glad to see you—I thought you were a goner!"

I looked down at my hand. The blood-filled syringe was still tightly clutched there. "Well I've got my sample anyway, Harry. And it's just as well, because it would take some fast talking to get me in there to try for another. I'm afraid you've just seen the end of a beautiful friendship."

"Aye, the big sod!" Harry listened for a few moments to the thudding of Monty's horns against the door. "And after all you did for him. That's gratitude for you."

19

Probably the most dramatic occurrence in the history of veterinary practice was the disappearance of the draught horse. It is an almost incredible fact that this glory and mainstay of the profession just melted quietly away within a few years. And I was one of those who were there to see it happen.

When I first came to Darrowby the tractor had already begun to take over, but tradition dies hard in the agricultural world and there were still a lot of horses around. Which was just as well because my veterinary education had been geared to things equine with everything else a poor second. It had been a good scientific education in many respects but at times I wondered if the people who designed it still had a mental picture of the horse doctor with his top hat and frock coat busying himself in a world of horse-drawn trams and brewers' drays.

We learned the anatomy of the horse in great detail, than that of the other animals much more superficially. It was the same with the other subjects; from animal husbandry with such insistence on a thorough knowledge of shoeing that we developed into amateur blacksmiths—right up to medicine and surgery where it was much more important to know about glanders and strangles than canine distemper. Even as we were learning, we youngsters knew it was ridiculous, with the draught horse already cast as a museum piece and the obvious potential of cattle and small animal work.

Still, as I say, after we had absorbed a vast store of equine lore it was a certain comfort that there were still a lot of patients on which we could try it out. I should think in my first two years I treated farm horses nearly every day and though I never was and never will be an equine expert there was a strange thrill in meeting with the age-old conditions whose names rang down almost from mediaeval times. Quittor, fistulous withers, poll evil, thrush, shoulder slip—vets had been wrestling with them for hundreds of years using very much the same drugs and procedures as myself. Armed with my firing iron and box of blister I plunged determinedly into what had always been the surging mainstream of veterinary life.

And now, in less than three years the stream had dwindled, not exactly to a trickle but certainly to the stage where the final dry-up was in sight. This meant, in a way, a lessening of the pressures on the veterinary surgeon because there is no doubt that horse work was the roughest and most arduous part of our life.

So that today, as I looked at the three year old gelding it occurred to me that this sort of thing wasn't happening as often as it did. He had a long tear in his flank where he had caught himself on barbed wire and it gaped open whenever he moved. There was no getting away from the fact that it had to be stitched.

The horse was tied by the head in his stall, his right side against the tall wooden partition. One of the farm men, a hefty six footer, took a tight hold of the head collar and leaned back against the manger as I puffed some iodoform into the wound. The horse didn't seem to mind, which was a comfort because he was a massive animal emanating an almost tangible vitality and power. I threaded my needle with a length of silk, lifted one of the lips of the wound and passed it through. This was going to be no trouble, I thought as I lifted the flap at the other side and pierced it, but as I was drawing the needle through, the gelding made a convulsive leap and I felt as though a great wind had whistled across the front of my body. Then, strangely, he was standing there against the wooden boards as if nothing had happened.

On the occasions when I have been kicked I have never seen it coming. It is surprising how quickly those great muscular legs can whip out. But there was no doubt he had had a good go at me because my needle and silk were nowhere to be seen, the big man at the head was staring at me with wide eyes in a chalk white face and the front of my clothing was in an extraordinary state. I was wearing a "gaberdine mac" and it looked as if somebody had taken a razor blade and painstakingly cut the material into narrow strips which hung down in ragged strips to ground level. The great iron-shod hoof had missed my legs by an inch or two but my mac was a write-off.

I was standing there looking around me in a kind of stupor when I heard a cheerful hail from the doorway.

"Now then, Mr. Herriot, what's he done at you?" Cliff Tyreman, the old horseman, looked me up and down with a mixture of amusement and asperity.

"He's nearly put me in hospital, Cliff," I replied shakily. "About the closest near miss I've ever had. I just felt the wind of it."

"What were you tryin' to do?"

"Stitch that wound, but I'm not going to try any more. I'm off to the surgery to get a chloroform muzzle."

The little man looked shocked. "You don't need no chloroform. I'll haul him and you'll have no trouble."

"I'm sorry, Cliff." I began to put away my suture materials, scissors and powder. "You're a good bloke, I know, but he's had one go at me and he's not getting another chance. I don't want to be lame for the rest of my life."

The horseman's small, wiry frame seemed to bunch into a ball of aggression. He thrust forward his head in a characteristic posture and glared at me. "I've never heard owt as daft in me life." Then he swung round on the big man who was still hanging on to the horse's head, the ghastly pallor of his face now tinged with a delicate green. "Come on out o' there, Bob! You're that bloody scared you're upsetting t'oss. Come on out of it and let me have 'im!"

Bob gratefully left the head and, grinning sheepishly moved with care along the side of the horse. He passed Cliff on the way and the little man's head didn't reach his shoulder.

Cliff seemed thoroughly insulted by the whole business. He took hold of the head collar and regarded the big animal with the disapproving stare of a schoolmaster at a naughty child. The horse, still in the mood for trouble, laid back his ears and began to plunge about the stall, his huge feet clattering ominously on the stone floor, but he came to rest quickly as the little man uppercutted him furiously in the ribs.

"Get stood up straight there, ye big bugger. What's the matter with ye?" Cliff barked and again he planted his tiny fist against the swelling barrel of the chest, a puny blow which the animal could scarcely have felt but which reduced him to quivering submission. "Try to kick, would you, eh? I'll bloody fettle you!" He shook the head collar and fixed the horse with a hypnotic stare as he spoke. Then he turned to me. "You can come and do your job, Mr. Herriot, he won't hurt tha."

I looked irresolutely at the huge, lethal animal. Stepping open-eyed into dangerous situations is something vets are called upon regularly to do and I suppose we all react differently. I know there were times when an over-vivid imagination made me acutely aware of the dire possibilities and now my mind seemed to be dwelling voluptuously on the frightful power in those enormous shining quarters, on the unyielding flintiness of the spatulate feet with their rim of metal. Cliff's voice cut into my musings.

"Come on, Mr. Herriot, I tell ye he won't hurt tha."

I reopened my box and tremblingly threaded another needle. I didn't seem to have much option; the little man wasn't asking me, he was telling me. I'd have to try again.

I couldn't have been a very impressive sight as I shuffled forwards, almost tripping over the tattered hula-hula skirt which dangled in front of me, my shaking hands reaching out once more for the wound, my heart thundering in my ears. But I needn't have worried. It was just as the little man had said; he didn't hurt me. In fact he never moved. He seemed to be listening attentively to the muttering which Cliff was directing into his face from a few inches' range. I powdered and stitched and clipped as though working on an anatomical specimen. Chloroform couldn't have done it any better.

As I retreated thankfully from the stall and began again to put away my instruments the monologue at the horse's head began to change its character. The menacing growl was replaced by a wheedling, teasing chuckle.

"Well, ye see, you're just a daft awd bugger, getting yourself all airigated over nowt. You're a good lad, really, aren't ye, a real good lad." Cliff's hand ran caressingly over the neck and the towering animal began to nuzzle his cheek, as completely in his sway as any Labrador puppy.

When he had finished he came slowly from the stall, stroking the back, ribs, belly and quarters, even giving a playful tweak at the tail on parting while what had been a few minutes ago an explosive mountain of bone and muscle submitted happily.

I pulled a packet of Gold Flake from my pocket. "Cliff, you're a marvel. Will you have a cigarette?"

"It 'ud be like givin' a pig a strawberry," the little man replied, then he thrust forth his tongue on which reposed a half-chewed gobbet of tobacco. "It's allus there. Ah push it in fust thing every mornin' soon as I get out of bed and there it stays. You'd never know, would you?"

I must have looked comically surprised because the

dark eyes gleamed and the rugged little face split
into a delighted grin. I looked at that grin—boyish,
invincible—and reflected on the phenomenon that
was Cliff Tyreman.

In a community in which toughness and durability
was the norm he stood out as something exceptional.
When I had first seen him nearly three years ago
barging among cattle, grabbing their noses and hanging on effortlessly, I had put him down as an
unusually fit middle-aged man; but he was in fact
nearly seventy. There wasn't much of him but he was
formidable; with his long arms swinging, his stumping, pigeon-toed gait and his lowered head he seemed
always to be butting his way through life.

"I didn't expect to see you today," I said. "I heard
you had pneumonia."

He shrugged. "Aye, summat of t'sort. First time I've
ever been off work since I was a lad."

"And you should be in your bed now, I should
say." I looked at the heaving chest and partly open
mouth. "I could hear you wheezing away when you
were at the horse's head."

"Nay, I can't stick that nohow. I'll be right in a
day or two." He seized a shovel and began busily
clearing away the heap of manure behind the horse,
his breathing loud and sterterous in the silence.

Harland Grange was a large, mainly arable farm
in the low country at the foot of the Dale, and there
had been a time when this stable had had a horse
standing in every one of the long row of stalls. There
had been over twenty with at least twelve regularly
at work, but now there were only two, the young
horse I had been treating and an ancient grey called
Badger.

Cliff had been head horseman and when the revolution came he turned to tractoring and other jobs
around the farm with no fuss at all. This was typical
of the reaction of thousands of other farm workers
throughout the country; they didn't set up a howl
at having to abandon the skills of a lifetime and

start anew—they just got on with it. In fact, the younger men seized avidly upon the new machines and proved themselves natural mechanics.

But to the old experts like Cliff, something had gone. He would say: "It's a bloody sight easier sitting on a tractor—it used to play 'ell with me feet walking up and down them fields all day." But he couldn't lose his love of horses; the fellow feeling between working man and working beast which had grown in him since childhood and was in his blood forever.

My next visit to the farm was to see a fat bullock with a piece of turnip stuck in his throat but while I was there, the farmer, Mr. Gilling, asked me to have a look at old Badger.

"He's had a bit of a cough lately. Maybe it's just his age, but see what you think."

The old horse was the sole occupant of the stable now. "I've sold the three year old," Mr. Gilling said. "But I'll still keep the old 'un—he'll be useful for a bit of light carting."

I glanced sideways at the farmer's granite features. He looked the least sentimental of men but I knew why he was keeping the old horse. It was for Cliff.

"Cliff will be pleased, anyway," I said.

Mr. Gilling nodded. "Aye, I never knew such a feller for 'osses. He was never happier than when he was with them." He gave a short laugh. "Do you know, I can remember years ago when he used to fall out with his missus he'd come down to this stable of a night and sit among his 'osses. Just sit here for hours on end looking at 'em and smoking. That was before he started chewing tobacco."

"And did you have Badger in those days?"

"Aye, we bred him. Cliff helped at his foaling—I remember the little beggar came arse first and we had a bit of a job pullin' him out." He smiled again. "Maybe that's why he was always Cliff's favourite. He always worked Badger himself—year in year out— and he was that proud of 'im that if he had to take him into the town for any reason he'd plait ribbons

into his mane and hang all his brasses on him first."
He shook his head reminiscently.

The old horse looked round with mild interest as I
went up to him. He was in his late twenties and
everything about him suggested serene old age; the
gaunt projection of the pelvic bones, the whiteness of
face and muzzle, the sunken eye with its benign expression. As I was about to take his temperature he
gave a sharp, barking cough and it gave me the first
clue to his ailment. I watched the rise and fall of his
breathing for a minute or two and the second clue
was there to be seen; further examination was unnecessary.

"He's broken winded, Mr. Gilling," I said. "Or he's
got pulmonary emphysema to give it its proper name.
Do you see that double lift of the abdomen as he
breathes out? That's because his lungs have lost their
elasticity and need an extra effort to force the air out."

"What's caused it, then?"

"Well it's to do with his age, but he's got a bit of
cold on him at the moment and that's brought it
out."

"Will he get rid of it in time?" the farmer asked.

"He'll be a bit better when he gets over his cold,
but I'm afraid he'll never be quite right. I'll give you
some medicine to put in his drinking water which
will alleviate his symptoms." I went out to the car for
a bottle of the arsenical expectorant mixture which
we used then.

It was about six weeks later that I heard from Mr.
Gilling again. He rang me about seven o'clock one
evening.

"I'd like you to come out and have a look at old
Badger," he said.

"What's wrong? Is it his broken wind again?"

"No, it's not that. He's still got the cough but it
doesn't seem to bother him much. No, I think he's got
a touch of colic. I've got to go out but Cliff will attend
to you."

The little man was waiting for me in the yard. He

was carrying an oil lamp. As I came up to him I exclaimed in horror.

"Good God, Cliff, what have you been doing to yourself?" His face was a patchwork of cuts and scratches and his nose, almost without skin, jutted from between two black eyes.

He grinned through the wounds, his eyes dancing with merriment. "Came off me bike t'other day. Hit a stone and went right over handlebars, arse over tip." He burst out laughing at the very thought.

"But damn it, man, haven't you been to a doctor? You're not fit to be out in that state."

"Doctor? Nay, there's no need to bother them fellers. It's nowt much." He fingered a gash on his jaw. "Ah lapped me chin up for a day in a bit o' bandage, but it's right enough now."

I shook my head as I followed him into the stable. He hung up the oil lamp then went over to the horse.

"Can't reckon t'awd feller up," he said. "You'd think there wasn't much ailing him but there's summat."

There were no signs of violent pain but the animal kept transferring his weight from one hind foot to the other as if he did have a little abdominal discomfort. His temperature was normal and he didn't show symptoms of anything else.

I looked at him doubtfully. "Maybe he has a bit of colic. There's nothing else to see, anyway. I'll give him an injection to settle him down."

"Right you are, maister, that's good." Cliff watched me get my syringe out then he looked around him into the shadows at the far end of the stable.

"Funny seeing only one 'oss standing here. I remember when there was a great long row of 'em and the barfins and bridles hangin' there on the stalls and the rest of the harness behind them all shinin' on t'wall." He transferred his plug of tobacco to the other side of his mouth and smiled. "By gaw, I were in here at six o'clock every morning feedin' them and gettin' them ready for work and ah'll tell you it was a sight to see us all goin' off ploughing at the start o' the day. Maybe six pairs of 'osses setting off with their harness jinglin' and the ploughmen sittin' sideways on their backs. Like a regular procession it was."

I smiled. "It was an early start, Cliff."

"Aye, by Gaw, and a late finish. We'd bring the 'osses home at night and give 'em a light feed and take their harness off, then we'd go and have our own teas and we'd be back 'ere again afterwards, curry-combing and dandy-brushin' all the sweat and dirt off 'em. Then we'd give them a right good stiff feed of chop and oats and hay to set 'em up for the next day."

"There wouldn't be much left of the evening then, was there?"

"Nay, there wasn't. It was about like work and bed, I reckon, but it never bothered us."

I stepped forward to give Badger the injection, then paused. The old horse had undergone a slight spasm, a barely perceptible stiffening of the muscles, and as I looked at him he cocked his tail for a second then lowered it.

"There's something else here," I said. "Will you bring him out of his stall, Cliff, and let me see him walk across the yard."

And watching him clop over the cobbles I saw it again; the stiffness, the raising of the tail. Something clicked in my mind. I walked over and rapped him under the chin and as the membrana nictitans flicked across his eye then slid slowly back I knew.

I paused for a moment. My casual little visit had suddenly become charged with doom.

"Cliff," I said. "I'm afraid he's got tetanus."

"Lockjaw, you mean?"

"That's right. I'm sorry, but there's no doubt about it. Has he had any wounds lately—especially in his feet?"

"Well he were dead lame about a fortnight ago and blacksmith let some matter out of his hoof. Made a right big 'ole."

There it was. "It's a pity he didn't get an anti-tetanus shot at the time," I said. I put my hand into the animal's mouth and tried to prise it open but the jaws were clamped tightly together. "I don't suppose he's been able to eat today."

"He had a bit this morning but nowt tonight. What's the lookout for him, Mr. Herriot?"

What indeed? If Cliff had asked me the same question today I would have been just as troubled to give him an answer. The facts are that seventy to eighty per cent of tetanus cases die and whatever you do to them in the way of treatment doesn't seem to make a whit of difference to those figures. But I didn't want to sound entirely defeatist.

"It's a very serious condition as you know, Cliff, but I'll do all I can. I've got some antitoxin in the car and I'll inject that into his vein and if the spasms get very bad I'll give him a sedative. As long as he can drink there's a chance for him because he'll have to live on fluids—gruel would be fine."

For a few days Badger didn't get any worse and I began to hope. I've seen tetanus horses recover and it is a wonderful experience to come in one day and find that the jaws have relaxed and the hungry animal can once more draw food into its mouth.

But it didn't happen with Badger. They had got the old horse into a big loose box where he could move around in comfort and each day as I looked over the half door I felt myself willing him to show some little sign of improvement; but instead, after that first few days he began to deteriorate. A sudden movement or the approach of any person would throw him into a violent spasm so that he would stagger stiff-legged round the box like a big wooden toy, his eyes terrified, saliva drooling from between his fiercely clenched teeth. One morning I was sure he would fall and I suggested putting him in slings. I had to go back to the surgery for the slings and it was just as I was entering Skeldale House that the phone rang.

It was Mr. Gilling. "He's beat us to it, I'm afraid. He's flat out on the floor and I doubt it's a bad job, Mr. Herriot. We'll have to put him down, won't we?"

"I'm afraid so."

"There's just one thing. Mallock will be taking him away but old Cliff says he doesn't want Mallock to shoot 'im. Wants you to do it. Will you come?"

I got out the humane killer and drove back to the farm, wondering at the fact that the old man should find the idea of my bullet less repugnant than the knacker man's. Mr. Gilling was waiting in the box and by his side Cliff, shoulders hunched, hands deep in his pockets. He turned to me with a strange smile.

"I was just saying to t'boss how grand t'awd lad used to look when I got 'im up for a show. By Gaw you should have seen him with 'is coat polished and the feathers on his legs scrubbed as white as snow and a big blue ribbon round his tail."

"I can imagine it, Cliff," I said. "Nobody could have looked after him better."

He took his hands from his pockets, crouched by the prostrate animal and for a few minutes stroked the white-flecked neck and pulled at the ears while the old sunken eye looked at him impassively.

He began to speak softly to the old horse but his voice was steady, almost conversational, as though he was chatting to a friend.

"Many's the thousand miles I've walked after you, awd lad, and many's the talk we've had together. But I didn't have to say much to tha, did I? I reckon you knew every move I made, everything I said. Just one little word and you always did what ah wanted you to do."

He rose to his feet. "I'll get on with me work now, boss," he said firmly, and strode out of the box.

I waited awhile so that he would not hear the bang which signaled the end of Badger, the end of the horses of Harland Grange and the end of the sweet core of Cliff Tyreman's life.

As I was leaving I saw the little man again. He was mounting the iron seat of a roaring tractor and I shouted to him above the noise.

"The boss says he's going to get some sheep in and you'll be doing a bit of shepherding. I think you'll enjoy that."

Cliff's undefeated grin flashed out as he called back to me.

"Aye, I don't mind learnin' summat new. I'm nobbut a lad yet!"

20

This was a different kind of ringing. I had gone to sleep as the great bells in the church tower down the street pealed for the Christmas midnight mass, but this was a sharper, shriller sound.

It was difficult at first to shake off the mantle of unreality in which I had wrapped myself last night. Last night—Christmas Eve. It had been like a culmination of all the ideas I had ever held about Christmas—a flowering of emotions I had never experienced before. It had been growing in me since the afternoon call to a tiny village where the snow lay deep on the single street and on the walls and on the ledges of the windows where the lights on the tinseled trees glowed red and blue and gold; and as I left it in the dusk I drove beneath the laden branches of a group of dark spruce as motionless as though they had been sketched against the white background of the fields. And when I reached Darrowby it was dark and around the market place the little shops were bright with decorations and the light from their windows fell in a soft yellow wash over the trodden snow of the cobbles. People, anonymously muffled, were hurrying about, doing their last minute shopping, their feet slithering over the rounded stones.

I had known many Christmases in Scotland but they had taken second place to the New Year celebrations; there had been none of this air of subdued excitement which started days before with folks shouting good wishes and coloured lights winking on the lonely fellsides and the farmers' wives plucking the fat geese, the feathers piled deep around their feet. And for fully two weeks you heard the children piping carols in the street then knocking on the door for sixpences. And best of all, last night the methodist choir had sung out there, filling the night air with rich, thrilling harmony.

Before going to bed and just as the church bells began I closed the door of Skeldale House behind me and walked again into the market place. Nothing stirred now in the white square stretching smooth and cold and empty under the moon, and there was a Dickens look about the ring of houses and shops put together long before anybody thought of town planning; tall and short, fat and thin, squashed in crazily around the cobbles, their snow-burdened roofs jagged and uneven against the frosty sky.

As I walked back, the snow crunching under my feet, the bells clanging, the sharp air tingling in my nostrils, the wonder and mystery of Christmas enveloped me in a great wave. Peace on earth, goodwill towards men; the words became meaningful as never before and I saw myself suddenly as a tiny particle in the scheme of things; Darrowby, the farmers, the animals and me seemed for the first time like a warm, comfortable entity. I hadn't been drinking but I almost floated up the stairs to our bed-sitter.

Helen was still asleep and as I crawled between the sheets beside her I was still wallowing in my Yuletide euphoria. There wouldn't be much work tomorrow; we'd have a long lie—maybe till nine—and then a lazy day, a glorious hiatus in our busy life. As I drifted into sleep it was as though I was surrounded by the smiling faces of my clients looking down at me with an all-embracing benevolence; and strangely I fancied I could hear singing, sweet and haunting, just like the methodist choir—God Rest Ye Merry Gentlemen . . .

But now there was this other bell which wouldn't stop. Must be the alarm. But as I pawed at the clock the noise continued and I saw that it was six o'clock. It was the phone of course. I lifted the receiver.

A metallic voice, crisp and very wide awake, jarred in my ear. "Is that the vet?"

"Yes, Herriot speaking," I mumbled.

"This is Brown, Willet Hill. I've got a cow down with milk fever. I want you here quick."

"Right, I'll see to it."

"Don't take ower long." Then a click at the far end.

I rolled on to my back and stared at the ceiling. So this was Christmas Day. The day when I was going to step out of the world for a spell and luxuriate in the seasonal spirit. I hadn't bargained for this fellow jerking me brutally back to reality. And not a word of regret or apology. No "sorry to get you out of bed" or anything else, never mind "Merry Christmas." It was just a bit hard.

Mr. Brown was waiting for me in the darkness of the farmyard. I had been to his place a few times before and as my headlights blazed on him I was struck, as always, by his appearance of perfect physical fitness. He was a gingery man of about forty with high cheekbones set in a sharp-featured clear-skinned face. Red hair peeped from under a check cap and a faint auburn down covered his cheeks, his neck, the backs of his hands. It made me feel a bit more sleepy just to look at him.

He didn't say good morning but nodded briefly then jerked his head in the direction of the byre. "She's in there" was all he said.

He watched in silence as I gave the injections and it wasn't until I was putting the empty bottles into my pocket that he spoke.

"Don't suppose I'll have to milk her today?"

"No," I replied. "Better leave the bag full."

"Anything special about feedin'?"

"No, she can have anything she likes when she wants it." Mr. Brown was very efficient. Always wanted to know every detail.

As we crossed the yard he halted suddenly and turned to face me. Could it be that he was going to ask me in for a nice hot cup of tea?

"You know," he said, as I stood ankle deep in the

snow, the frosty air nipping at my ears. "I've had a few of these cases lately. Maybe there's summat wrong with my routine. Do you think I'm steaming up my cows too much?"

"It's quite possible." I hurried towards the car. One thing I wasn't going to do was deliver a lecture on animal husbandry at this moment.

My hand was on the door handle when he said "I'll give you another ring if she's not up by dinner time. And there's one other thing—that was a hell of a bill I had from you fellers last month, so tell your boss not to be so savage with 'is pen." Then he turned and walked quickly towards the house.

Well that was nice, I thought as I drove away. Not even thanks or goodbye, just a complaint and a promise to haul me away from my roast goose if necessary. A sudden wave of anger surged in me. Bloody farmers! There were some miserable devils among them. Mr. Brown had doused my festive feeling as effectively as if he had thrown a bucket of water over me.

As I mounted the steps of Skeldale House the darkness had paled to a shivery grey. Helen met me in the passage. She was carrying a tray.

"I'm sorry, Jim," she said. "There's another urgent job. Siegfried's had to go out, too. But I've got a cup of coffee and some fried bread for you. Come in and sit down—you've got time to eat it before you go."

I sighed. It was going to be just another day after all. "What's this about, Helen?" I asked, sipping the coffee.

"It's old Mr. Kirby," she replied. "He's very worried about his nanny goat."

"Nanny goat!"

"Yes, he says she's choking."

"Choking! How the heck can she be choking?" I shouted.

"I really don't know. And I wish you wouldn't shout at me, Jim. It's not my fault."

In an instant I was engulfed by shame. Here I was, in a bad temper, taking it out on my wife. It is a common reaction for vets to blame the hapless person who passes on an unwanted message but I am not proud of it. I held out my hand and Helen took it.

"I'm sorry," I said and finished the coffee sheepishly. My feeling of goodwill was at a very low ebb.

Mr. Kirby was a retired farmer, but he had sensibly taken a cottage with a bit of land where he kept enough stock to occupy his time—a cow, a few pigs and his beloved goats. He had always had goats, even when he was running his dairy herd; he had a thing about them.

The cottage was in a village high up the Dale. Mr. Kirby met me at the gate.

"Ee, lad," he said. "I'm right sorry to be bothering you this early in the morning and Christmas an' all, but I didn't have no choice. Dorothy's real bad."

He led the way to a stone shed which had been converted into a row of pens. Behind the wire of one of them a large white Saanen goat peered out at us anxiously and as I watched her she gulped, gave a series of retching coughs, then stood trembling, saliva drooling from her mouth.

The farmer turned to me, wide-eyed. "You see, I had to get you out, didn't I? If I left her till tomorrow she'd be a goner."

"You're right, Mr. Kirby," I replied. "You couldn't leave her. There's something in her throat."

We went into the pen and as the old man held the goat against the wall I tried to open her mouth. She didn't like it very much and as I prised her jaws apart she startled me with a loud, long-drawn, human-sounding cry. It wasn't a big mouth but I have a small hand and, as the sharp back teeth tried to nibble me, I poked a finger deep into the pharynx.

There was something there all right. I could just touch it but I couldn't get hold of it. Then the animal began to throw her head about and I had to come out; I stood there, saliva dripping from my hand, looking thoughtfully at Dorothy.

After a few moments I turned to the farmer. "You know, this is a bit baffling. I can feel something in the back of her throat, but it's soft—like cloth. I'd been expecting to find a bit of twig, or something sharp sticking in there—it's funny what a goat will pick up when she's pottering around outside. But if it's cloth, what the heck is holding it there? Why hasn't she swallowed it down?"

"Aye, it's a rum 'un, isn't it?" The old man ran a gentle hand along the animal's back. "Do you think she'll get rid of it herself? Maybe it'll just slip down?"

"No, I don't. It's stuck fast, God knows how, but it is. And I've got to get it out soon because she's beginning to blow up. Look there." I pointed to the goat's left side, bulged by the tympanitic rumen, and as I did so, Dorothy began another paroxysm of coughs which seemed almost to tear her apart.

Mr. Kirby looked at me with a mute appeal, but just at that moment I didn't see what I could do. Then I opened the door of the pen. "I'm going to get my torch from the car. Maybe I can see something to explain this."

The old man held the torch as I once more pulled the goat's mouth open and again heard the curious child-like wailing. It was when the animal was in full cry that I noticed something under the tongue—a thin, dark band.

"I can see what's holding the thing now," I cried. "It's hooked round the tongue with string or something." Carefully I pushed my forefinger under the band and began to pull.

It wasn't string. It began to stretch as I pulled carefully at it . . . like elastic. Then it stopped stretching and I felt a real resistance . . . whatever was in the throat was beginning to move. I kept up a gentle traction and very slowly the mysterious obstruction came sliding up over the back of the tongue and into the mouth, and when it came within reach I let go the elastic, grabbed the sodden mass and hauled it forth. It seemed as if there was no end to it—a long snake of dripping material nearly two feet long—but at last I had it out on to the straw of the pen.

Mr. Kirby seized it and held it up and as he unravelled the mass wonderingly he gave a sudden cry.

"God 'elp us, it's me summer drawers!"

"Your what?"

"Me summer drawers. Ah don't like them long johns when weather gets warmer and I allus change into these little short 'uns. Missus was havin' a clear-out afore the end of t'year and she didn't know whether to wash 'em or mek them into dusters. She washed them at t'finish and Dorothy must have got 'em off the line." He held up the tattered shorts and regarded them ruefully. "By gaw, they've seen better days, but I reckon Dorothy's fettled them this time."

Then his body began to shake silently, a few low giggles escaped from him and finally he gave a great shout of laughter. It was an infectious laugh and I joined in as I watched him. He went on for quite a long time and when he had finished he was leaning weakly against the wire netting.

"Me poor awd drawers," he gasped, then leaned over and patted the goat's head. "But as long as you're all right, lass, I'm not worried."

"Oh, she'll be O.K." I pointed to her left flank. "You can see her stomach's going down already." As I spoke, Dorothy belched pleasurably and began to nose interestedly at her hay rack.

The farmer gazed at her fondly. "Isn't that grand to see! She's ready for her grub again. And if she hadn't got her tongue round the elastic that lot would have gone right down and killed her."

"I really don't think it would, you know," I said. "It's amazing what ruminants can carry around in their stomachs. I once found a bicycle tyre inside a cow when I was operating for something else. The tyre didn't seem to be bothering her in the least."

"I see." Mr. Kirby rubbed his chin. "So Dorothy might have wandered around with me drawers inside her for years."

"It's possible. You'd never have known what became of them."

"By gaw, that's right," Mr. Kirby said, and for a moment I thought he was going to start giggling again, but he mastered himself and seized my arm.

"But I don't know what I'm keeping you out here for, lad. You must come in and have a bit o' Christmas cake."

Inside the tiny living room of the cottage I was ushered to the best chair by the fireside where two rough logs blazed and crackled.

"Bring cake out for Mr. Herriot, mother," the farmer cried as he rummaged in the pantry. He reappeared with a bottle of whisky at the same time as his wife bustled in carrying a cake thickly laid with icing and ornamented with coloured spangles, toboggans, reindeers.

Mr. Kirby unscrewed the stopper. "You know, mother, we're lucky to have such men as this to come out on a Christmas mornin' to help us."

"Aye, we are that." The old lady cut a thick slice of the cake and placed it on a plate by the side of an enormous wedge of Wensleydale cheese.

Her husband meanwhile was pouring my drink. Yorkshiremen are amateurs with whisky and there was something delightfully untutored in the way he was sloshing it into the glass as if it was lemonade; he would have filled it to the brim if I hadn't stopped him.

Drink in hand, cake on knee, I looked across at the farmer and his wife who were sitting in upright kitchen chairs watching me with quiet benevolence. The two faces had something in common—a kind of beauty. You would find faces like that only in the country; deeply wrinkled and weathered, clear-eyed, alight with a cheerful serenity.

I raised my glass. "A happy Christmas to you both."

The old couple nodded and replied smilingly. "And the same to you, Mr. Herriot."

"Aye, and thanks again, lad," said Mr. Kirby. "We're right grateful to you for runnin' out here to save awd Dorothy. We've maybe mucked up your day for you but it would've mucked up ours if we'd lost the old lass, wouldn't it, mother?"

"Don't worry, you haven't spoiled anything for me," I said. "In fact you've made me realise again that it really is Christmas." And as I looked around the little room with the decorations hanging from the low-beamed ceiling I could feel the emotions of last night surging slowly back, a warmth creeping through me that had nothing to do with the whisky.

I took a bite of the cake and followed it with a moist slice of cheese. When I had first come to Yorkshire I had been aghast when offered this unheard-of combination, but time had brought wisdom and I had discovered that the mixture when chewed boldly together was exquisite; and, strangely, I had also found that there was nothing more suitable for washing it finally over the tonsils than a draught of raw whisky.

"You don't mind t'wireless, Mr. Herriot?" Mrs. Kirby asked. "We always like to have it on Christmas morning to hear t'old hymns but I'll turn it off if you like."

"No, please leave it, it sounds grand." I turned to look at the old radio with its chipped wooden veneer, the ornate scroll-work over the worn fabric; it must have been one of the earliest models and it gave off a tinny sound, but the singing of the church choir was none the less sweet . . . Hark the Herald Angels Sing—flooding the little room, mingling with the splutter of the logs and the soft voices of the old people.

They showed me a picture of their son, who was a policeman over in Houlton and their daughter who was married to a neighbouring farmer. They were bringing their grand-children up for Christmas dinner as they always did and Mrs. Kirby opened a box and ran a hand over the long row of crackers. The choir started on Once in Royal David's City, I finished my whisky and put up only feeble resistance as the farmer plied the bottle again. Through the small window I could see the bright berries of a holly tree pushing through their covering of snow.

It was really a shame to have to leave here and it

was sadly that I drained my glass for the second time and scooped up the last crumbs of cake and icing from my plate.

Mr. Kirby came out with me and at the gate of the cottage he stopped and held out his hand.

"Thank ye lad, I'm right grateful," he said. "And all the very best to you."

For a moment the rough dry palm rasped against mine, then I was in the car, starting the engine. I looked at my watch; it was still only half past nine but the first early sunshine was sparkling from a sky of palest blue.

Beyond the village the road climbed steeply then curved around the rim of the valley in a wide arc, and it was here that you came suddenly upon the whole great expanse of the Plain of York spread out almost at your feet. I always slowed down here and there was always something different to see, but today the vast chequerboard of fields and farms and woods stood out with a clarity I had never seen before. Maybe it was because this was a holiday and down there no factory chimney smoked, no lorries belched fumes, but the distance was magically fore-shortened in the clear, frosty air and I felt I could reach out and touch the familiar landmarks far below.

I looked back at the enormous white billows and folds of the fells, crowding close, one upon another into the blue distance, every crevice uncannily defined, the highest summits glittering where the sun touched them. I could see the village with the Kirby's cottage at the end. I had found Christmas and peace and goodwill and everything back there.

Farmers? They were the salt of the earth.

21

Marmaduke Skelton was an object of interest to me long before our paths crossed. For one thing I hadn't thought people were ever called Marmaduke outside of books and for another he was a particularly well known member of the honourable profession of unqualified animal doctors.

Before the Veterinary Surgeons' Act of 1948 anybody who fancied his chance at it could dabble in the treatment of animal disease. Veterinary students could quite legally be sent out to cases while they were seeing practice, certain members of the lay public did a bit of veterinary work as a sideline while others did it as a full time job. These last were usually called "quacks."

The disparaging nature of the term was often unjust because, though some of them were a menace to the animal population, others were dedicated men who did their job with responsibility and humanity and after the Act were brought into the profession's fold as Veterinary Practitioners.

But long before all this there were all sorts and types among them. The one I knew best was Arthur Lumley, a charming little ex-plumber who ran a thriving small animal practice in Brawton, much to the chagrin of Mr. Angus Grier MRCVS. Arthur used to drive around in a small van. He always wore a white coat and looked very clinical and efficient, and on the side of the van in foot-high letters which would have got a qualified man a severe dressing down from the Royal College was the legend, "Arthur

Lumley M.K.C., Canine and Feline Specialist." The lack of "letters" after their name was the one thing which differentiated these men from qualified vets in the eyes of the general public and I was interested to see that Arthur did have an academic attainment. However the degree of M.K.C. was unfamiliar to me and he was somewhat cagey when I asked him about it; I did find out eventually what it stood for; Member of the Kennel Club.

Marmaduke Skelton was a vastly different breed. I had been working long enough round the Scarburn district to become familiar with some of the local history and it seemed that when Mr. and Mrs. Skelton were producing a family in the early 1900's they must have thought their offspring were destined for great things; they named their four sons Marmaduke, Sebastian, Cornelius and, incredibly, Alonzo. The two middle brothers drove lorries for the Express Dairy and Alonzo was a small farmer; one of my vivid memories is the shock of surprise when I was filling up the forms after his tuberculin test and asked him for his first name. The exotic appellation pronounced in gruff Yorkshire was so incongruous that I thought he was pulling my leg; in fact I was going to make a light comment but something in his eye prompted me to leave it alone.

Marmaduke, or Duke as he was invariably called, was the colourful member of the family. I had heard a lot about him on my visits to the Scarburn farms; he was a "right good hand" at calving, foaling and lambing, and "as good as any vitnery" in the diagnosis and treatment of animals' ailments. He was also an expert castrator, docker and pig-killer. He made a nice living at his trade and in Ewan Ross he had the ideal professional opposition; a veterinary surgeon who worked only when he felt like it and who didn't bother to go to a case unless he was in the mood. Much as the farmers liked and in many cases revered Ewan, they were often forced to fall back on Duke's services. Ewan was in his fifties and unable to cope with the growing volume of testing in his Scarburn practice. I used to help him out with it and in consequence saw a lot of Ewan and his wife, Ginny.

If Duke had confined his activities to treating his patients I don't think Ewan would ever have spared him a thought; but Skelton liked to enliven his farm visits with sneers about the old Scotch vet who had never been much good and was definitely getting past it now. Maybe even that didn't get very far under Ewan's skin but at the mention of his rival's name his mouth would harden a little and a ruminative expression creep into the blue eyes.

And it wasn't easy to like Duke. There were the tales you heard about his savage brawls and about how he knocked his wife and children around when the mood was on him. I didn't find his appearance engaging either when I first saw him swaggering across Scarburn market place; a black bull of a man, a shaggy Heathcliffe with fierce, darting eyes and a hint of braggadocio in the bright red handkerchief tied round his neck.

But on this particular afternoon I wasn't thinking about Duke Skelton, in fact I wasn't thinking about anything much as I sprawled in a chair by the Ross's fireside. I had just finished one of Ginny's lunches; something with the unassuming name of fish pie but in truth a magical concoction in which the humble haddock was elevated to unimagined heights by the admixture of potatoes, tomatoes, eggs, macaroni and things only Ginny knew. Then the apple crumble and the chair close to the fire with the heat from the flames beating on my face.

The thoughts I had were slumberous ones; that this house and the people in it had come to have a magnetic attraction for me; that if this had been a big successful practice the phone would have been dinging and Ewan would be struggling into his coat as he chewed his last bite. And an unworthy thought as I glanced through the window at the white garden and the snow-burdened trees; that if I didn't hurry back to Darrowby, Siegfried might do double the work and finish the lot before I got home.

Playing with the soothing picture of the muffled figure of my boss battling round the farms I watched Ginny placing a coffee cup by her husband's elbow. Ewan smiled up into her face and just then the phone rang.

Like most vets I am bell-happy and I jumped, but Ewan didn't. He began quietly to sip his coffee as Ginny picked up the receiver and he didn't change expression when his wife came over and said, "It's Tommy Thwaite. One of his cows has put its calf bed out."

These dread tidings would have sent me leaping round the room but Ewan took a long swallow at his coffee before replying.

"Thank you, dear. Will you tell him I'll have a look at her shortly."

He turned to me and began to tell me something funny which had happened to him that morning and when he had finished he went into his characteristic laugh—showing nothing apart from a vibration of the shoulders and a slight popping of the eyes. Then he relaxed in his chair and recommenced his leisurely sipping.

Though it wasn't my case my feet were itching. A bovine prolapsed uterus was not only an urgent condition but it held such grim promise of hard labour that I could never get it over quickly enough. Some were worse than others and I was always in a hurry to find out what was in store.

Ewan, however, appeared to be totally incurious. In fact he closed his eyes and I thought for a moment he was settling down for a post prandial nap. But it was only a gesture of resignation at the wrecking of his afternoon's repose and he gave a final stretch and got up.

"Want to come with me, Jim?" he asked in his soft voice.

I hesitated for a moment then, callously abandoning Siegfried to his fate, I nodded eagerly and followed Ewan into the kitchen.

He sat down and pulled on a pair of thick woolen

over-socks which Ginny had been warming by the stove, then he put on his wellingtons, a short over-coat, yellow gloves and a check cap. As he strolled along the narrow track which had been dug through the garden snow he looked extraordinarily youthful and debonair.

He didn't go into his dispensary this time and I wondered what equipment he would use, thinking at the same time of Siegfried's words: "Ewan has his own way of doing everything."

At the farm Mr. Thwaite trotted over to meet us. He was understandably agitated but there was something else; a nervous rubbing of the hands, an uneasy giggle as he watched my colleague opening the car boot.

"Mr. Ross," he blurted out at last, "I don't want you to be upset, but I've summat to tell you." He paused for a moment. "Duke Skelton's in there with my cow."

Ewan's expression did not flicker. "Oh, right. Then you won't need me." He closed the boot, opened the door and got back into the car.

"Hey, hey, I didn't mean you to go away!" Mr. Thwaite ran round and cried through the glass. "Duke just happened to be in t'village and he said he'd help me out."

"Fine," Ewan said, winding down the window, "I don't mind in the least. I'm sure he'll do a good job for you."

The farmer screwed up his face in misery. "But you don't understand. He's been in there for about an hour and a half and he's no further forward. He's not doin' a bit o' good and he's about buggered an' all. I want you to take over, Mr. Ross."

"No, I'm sorry." Ewan gave him a level stare. "I couldn't possibly interfere. You know how it is, Tom-my. He's begun the job—I've got to let him finish." He started the engine.

"No, no, don't go!" shouted Mr. Thwaite, beating the car roof with his hands. "Duke's whacked, I tell ye. If you drive away now ah'm going to lose one of ma best cows. You've got to help me, Mr. Ross!" He seemed on the verge of tears.

My colleague looked at him thoughtfully as the engine purred. Then he bent forward and turned off the ignition. "All right, I'll tell you what—I'll go in there and see what he says. If he wants me to help, then I will."

I followed him into the byre and as we paused just inside the door Duke Skelton looked up from his work. He had been standing head down, one hand resting on the rump of a massive cow, his mouth hanging open, his great barrel chest heaving. The thick hair over his shoulders and ribs was matted with blood from the huge everted uterus which dangled behind the animal. Blood and filth streaked his face and covered his arms and as he stared at us from under his shaggy brows he looked like something from the jungle.

"Well now, Mr. Skelton," Ewan murmured conversationally, "How are you getting on?"

Duke gave him a quick malevolent glance. "Ah'm doin' all right." The words rumbled from deep down through his gaping lips.

Mr. Thwaite stepped forward, smiling ingratiatingly. "Come on, Duke, you've done your best. I think you should let Mr. Ross give you a 'and now."

"Well ah don't." The big man's jaw jutted suddenly. "If I was lookin' for help I wouldn't want 'IM." He turned away and seized the uterus. Hoisting it in his arms he began to push at it with fierce concentration.

Mr. Thwaite turned to us with an expression of despair and opened his mouth to lament again, but Ewan silenced him with a raised hand, pulled a milking stool from a corner and squatted down comfortably against a wall. Unhurriedly he produced his little pouch and, one-handed, began to make a cigarette; as he licked the paper, screwed up the end and applied a match he gazed with blank eyes at the sweating, struggling figure a few feet from him.

Duke had got the uterus about half way back. Grunting and gasping, legs straddled, he had worked the engorged mass inch by inch inside the vulva till he had just about enough cradled in his arms for one last push; and as he stood there taking a breather with the great muscles of his shoulders and arms rigid his immense strength was formidably displayed. But he wasn't as strong as that cow. No man is as strong as a cow and this cow was one of the biggest I had ever seen with a back like a table top and rolls of fat round her tail-head.

I had been in this position myself and I knew what was coming next. I didn't have to wait long. Duke took a long wheezing breath and made his assault, heaving desperately, pushing with arms and chest, and for a second or two he seemed to be winning as the mass disappeared steadily inside. Then the cow gave an almost casual strain and the whole thing welled out again till it hung down bumping against the animal's hocks.

As Duke almost collapsed against her pelvis in the same attitude as when we first came in I felt pity for the man. I found him uncharming but I felt for him. That could easily be me standing there; my jacket and shirt hanging on that nail, my strength ebbing, my sweat mingling with the blood. No man could do what he was trying to do. You could push back a calf bed with the aid of an epidural anaesthetic to stop the straining or you could sling the animal up to a beam with a block and tackle; you couldn't just stand there and do it from scratch as this chap was trying to do.

I was surprised Duke hadn't learned that with all his experience; but apparently it still hadn't dawned on him even now because he was going through all the motions of having another go. This time he got even further—a few more inches inside before the cow popped it out again. The animal appeared to have a sporting streak because there was something premeditated about the way she played her victim along before timing her thrust at the very last moment. Apart from that she seemed somewhat bored by the whole business; in fact with the possible exception of Ewan she was the calmest among us.

Duke was trying again. As he bent over wearily and picked up the gory organ I wondered how often he had done this since he arrived nearly two hours ago. He had guts, there was no doubt. But the end was near. There was a frantic urgency about his movements as though he knew himself it was his last throw and as he yet again neared his goal his grunts changed to an agonised whimpering, an almost tearful sound as though he were appealing to the recalcitrant mass, beseeching it to go away inside and stay away, just this once.

And when the inevitable happened and the poor fellow, panting and shaking, surveyed once more the ruin of his hopes I had the feeling that somebody had to do something.

Mr. Thwaite did it. "You've had enough, Duke," he said. "For God's sake come in the house and get cleaned up. Missus'll give you a bit o' dinner and while you're having it Mr. Ross'll see what he can do."

The big man, arms hanging limp by his sides, chest heaving, stared at the farmer for a few seconds then he turned abruptly and snatched his clothes from the wall.

"Aw right," he said and began to walk slowly towards the door. He stopped opposite Ewan but didn't look at him. "But ah'll tell you summat, Maister Thwaite. If ah can't put that calf bed back this awd bugger never will."

Ewan drew on his cigarette and peered up at him impassively. He didn't follow him with his eyes as he left the byre but leaned back against the wall, puffed out a thin plume of smoke and watched it rise and disappear among the shadows in the roof.

Mr. Thwaite was soon back. "Now, Mr. Ross," he said a little breathlessly, "I'm sorry about you havin' to wait but we can get on now. I expect you'll be needin' some fresh hot water and is there anything else you want?"

Ewan dropped his cigarette on the cobbles and ground it with his foot. "Yes, you can bring me a pound of sugar."

"What's that?"

"A pound of sugar."

"A pound of . . . right, right . . . I'll get it."

In no time at all the farmer returned with an unopened paper bag. Ewan split the top with his finger, walked over to the cow and began to dust the sugar all over the uterus. Then he turned to Mr. Thwaite again.

"And I'll want a pig stool, too. I expect you have one."

"Oh aye, we have one, but what the hangment . . . ?

Ewan cocked a gentle eye at him. "Bring it in, then. It's time we got this job done."

As the farmer disappeared at a stiff gallop I went over to my colleague. "What's going on, Ewan? What the devil are you chucking that sugar about for?"

"Oh it draws the serum out of the uterus. You can't beat it when the thing's engorged like that."

"It does?" I glanced unbelievingly at the bloated organ. "And aren't you going to give her an epidural . . . and some pituitrin . . . and a calcium injection?"

"Och no," Ewan replied with his slow smile. "I never bother about those things."

I didn't get the chance to ask him what he wanted with the pig stool because just then Mr. Thwaite trotted in with one under his arm.

Most farms used to have them. They were often called "creels" and the sides of bacon were laid on them at pig-killing time. This was a typical specimen—like a long low table with four short legs and a slatted concave top. Ewan took hold of it and pushed it carefully under the cow just in front of the udder while I stared at it through narrowed eyes. I was getting out of my depth.

Ewan then walked unhurriedly out to his car and

returned with a length of rope and two objects wrapped in the inevitable brown paper. As he draped the rope over the partition, pulled on a rubber parturition gown and began to open the parcels I realised I was once again watching Ewan setting out his stall.

From the first parcel he produced what looked like a beer tray but which I decided couldn't possibly be; but when he said, "Here, hold this a minute, Jim," and I read the emblazoned gold scroll, "John Smith's Magnet Pale Ale" I had to change my mind. It was a beer tray.

He began to unfold the brown paper from the other object and my brain reeled a little as he fished out an empty whisky bottle and placed it on the tray. Standing there with my strange burden I felt like the stooge in a conjuring act and I wouldn't have been a bit surprised if my colleague had produced a live rabbit next.

But all he did was to fill the whisky bottle with some of the clean hot water from the bucket.

Next he looped the rope round the cow's horns, passed it round the body a couple of times then leaned back and pulled. Without protest the big animal collapsed gently on top of the milk stool and lay there with her rear end stuck high in the air.

"Right now, we can start," Ewan murmured, and as I threw down my jacket and began to tear off my tie he turned to me in surprise.

"Here, here, what do you think you're doing?"

"Well I'm going to give you a hand, of course."

One corner of his mouth twitched upwards. "It's kind of you, Jim, but there's no need to get stripped off. This will only take a minute. I just want you and Mr. Thwaite to keep the thing level for me."

He gently hoisted the organ, which to my fevered imagination had shrunk visibly since the sugar, on to the beer tray and gave the farmer and me an end each to hold.

Then he pushed the uterus back.

He did literally only take a minute or not much

more. Without effort, without breaking sweat or exerting visible pressure he returned that vast mass to where it belonged while the cow, unable to strain or do a thing about it, just lay there with an aggrieved expression on her face. Then he took his whisky bottle, passed it carefully into the vagina and disappeared up to arm's length where he began to move his shoulder vigorously.

"What the hell are you doing now?" I whispered agitatedly into his ear from my position at the end of the beer tray.

"I'm rotating each horn to get it back into place and pouring a little hot water from the bottle into the ends of the horns to make sure they're completely involuted."

"Oh, I see." I watched as he removed the bottle, soaped his arms in the bucket and began to take off his overall.

"But aren't you going to stitch it in?" I blurted out.

Ewan shook his head. "No, Jim. If you put it back properly it never comes out again."

He was drying his hands when the byre door opened and Duke Skelton slouched in. He was washed and dressed, with his red handkerchief knotted again round his neck and he glared fierce-eyed at the cow which, tidied up and unperturbed, looked now just like all the other cows in the row. His lips moved once or twice before he finally found his voice.

"Aye, it's all right for some people," he snarled. "Some people with their bloody fancy injections and instruments! It's bloody easy that way, isn't it!" Then he swung round and was gone.

As I heard his heavy boots clattering across the yard it struck me that his words were singularly inapt. What was there even remotely fancy about a pig stool, a pound of sugar, a whisky bottle and a beer tray?

22

"I work for cats."

That was how Mrs. Bond introduced herself on my first visit, gripping my hand firmly and thrusting out her jaw defiantly as though challenging me to make something of it. She was a big woman with a strong, high-cheekboned face and a commanding presence and I wouldn't have argued with her anyway, so I nodded gravely as though I fully understood and agreed, and allowed her to lead me into the house.

I saw at once what she meant. The big kitchen-living room had been completely given over to cats. There were cats on the sofas and chairs and spilling in cascades on to the floor, cats sitting in rows along the window sills and right in the middle of it all, little Mr. Bond, pallid, wispy-moustached, in his shirt sleeves reading a newspaper.

It was a scene which was going to become very familiar. A lot of the cats were obviously uncastrated Toms because the atmosphere was vibrant with their distinctive smell—a fierce pungency which over-whelmed even the sickly wisps from the big sauce-pans of nameless cat food bubbling on the stove. And Mr. Bond was always there, always in his shirt sleeves and reading his paper, a lonely little island in a sea of cats.

I had heard of the Bonds, of course. They were Londoners who for some obscure reason had picked on North Yorkshire for their retirement. People said they had a "bit o' brass" and they had bought an old house on the outskirts of Darrowby where they kept themselves to themselves—and the cats. I had heard that Mrs. Bond was in the habit of taking in strays and feeding them and giving them a home if they wanted it and this had predisposed me in her favour, because in my experience the unfortunate feline species seemed to be fair game for every kind of cruelty and neglect. They shot cats, threw things at them, starved them and set their dogs on them for fun. It was good to see somebody taking their side.

My patient on this first visit was no more than a big kitten, a terrified little blob of black and white crouching in a corner.

"He's one of the outside cats," Mrs. Bond boomed.

"Outside cats?"

"Yes. All these you see here are the inside cats. The others are the really wild ones who simply refuse to enter the house. I feed them of course but the only time they come indoors is when they are ill."

"I see."

"I've had frightful trouble catching this one. I'm worried about his eyes—there seemed to be a skin growing over them, and I do hope you can do something for him. His name, by the way, is Alfred."

"Alfred? Ah yes, quite." I advanced cautiously on the little half-grown animal and was greeted by a waving set of claws and a series of open-mouthed spittings. He was trapped in his corner or he would have been off with the speed of light.

Examining him was going to be a problem. I turned to Mrs. Bond. "Could you let me have a sheet of some kind? An old ironing sheet would do. I'm going to have to wrap him up."

"Wrap him up?" Mrs. Bond looked very doubtful but she disappeared into another room and returned with a tattered sheet of cotton which looked just right.

I cleared the table of an amazing variety of cat feeding dishes, cat books, cat medicines and spread out the sheet, then I approached my patient again. You can't be in a hurry in a situation like this and it took me perhaps five minutes of wheedling and "Puss-pussing" while I brought my hand nearer and nearer. When I got as far as being able to stroke his cheek I made a quick grab at the scruff of his neck and finally bore Alfred, protesting bitterly and lashing out in all directions, over to the table. There, still holding tightly to his scruff, I laid him on the sheet and started the wrapping operation.

This is something which has to be done quite often with obstreperous felines and, although I say it, I am rather good at it. The idea is to make a neat, tight roll, leaving the relevant piece of cat exposed; it may be an injured paw, perhaps the tail, and in this case of course the head. I think it was the beginning of Mrs. Bond's unquestioning faith in me when she saw me quickly enveloping that cat till all you could see of him was a small black and white head protruding from an immovable cocoon of cloth. He and I were now facing each other, more or less eyeball to eyeball, and Alfred couldn't do a thing about it.

As I say, I rather pride myself on this little expertise and even today my veterinary colleagues have been known to remark: "Old Herriot may be limited in many respects but by God he can wrap a cat."

As it turned out, there wasn't a skin growing over Alfred's eyes. There never is.

"He's got a paralysis of the third eyelid, Mrs. Bond. Animals have this membrane which flicks across the eye to protect it. In this case it hasn't gone back, probably because the cat is in low condition—maybe had a touch of cat flu or something else which has weakened him. I'll give him an injection of vitamins and leave you some powder to put in his food if you could keep him in for a few days. I think he'll be all right in a week or two."

The injection presented no problems with Alfred furious but helpless inside his sheet and I had come to the end of my first visit to Mrs. Bond's.

It was the first of many. The lady and I established an immediate rapport which was strengthened by the fact that I was always prepared to spend time over her assorted charges; crawling on my stomach under piles of logs in the outhouses to reach the outside cats, coaxing them down from trees, stalking them endlessly through the shrubbery. But from my point of view it was rewarding in many ways.

For instance there was the diversity of names she had for her cats. True to her London upbringing she had named many of the Toms after the great Arsenal team of those days. There was Eddie Hapgood, Cliff Bastin, Ted Drake, Wilf Copping, but she did slip up in one case because Alex James had kittens three times a year with unfailing regularity.

Then there was her way of calling them home. The first time I saw her at this was on a still summer evening. The two cats she wanted me to see were out in the garden somewhere and I walked with her to the back door where she halted, clasped her hands across her bosom, closed her eyes and gave tongue in a mellifluous contralto.

"Bates, Bates, Bates, Ba-hates." She actually sang out the words in a reverant monotone except for a delightful little lilt on the "Ba-hates." Then once more she inflated her ample rib cage like an operatic prima donna and out it came again, delivered with the utmost feeling.

"Bates, Bates, Bates, Ba-hates."

Anyway it worked, because Bates the cat came trotting from behind a clump of laurel. There remained the other patient and I watched Mrs. Bond with interest.

She took up the same stance, breathed in, closed her eyes, composed her features into a sweet half-smile and started again.

"Seven-times-three, Seven-times-three, Seven-times-three-hee." It was set to the same melody as Bates with the same dulcet rise and fall at the end. She didn't get the quick response this time, though, and had to go through the performance again and again, and as the notes lingered on the still evening air the effect was startlingly like a muezzin calling the faithful to prayer.

At length she was successful and a fat tortoise-shell slunk apologetically along the wall-side into the house.

"By the way, Mrs. Bond," I asked, making my voice casual. "I didn't quite catch the name of that last cat."

"Oh, Seven-times-three?" She smiled reminiscently. "Yes, she is a dear. She's had three kittens seven times running, you see, so I thought it rather a good name for her, don't you?"

"Yes, yes, I do indeed. Splendid name, splendid."

Another thing which warmed me towards Mrs. Bond was her concern for my safety. I appreciated this because it is a rare trait among animal owners. I can think of the trainer after one of his racehorses had kicked me clean out of a loose box examining the animal anxiously to see if it had damaged its foot; the little old lady dwarfed by the bristling, teeth-bared Alsatian saying: "You'll be gentle with him won't you and I hope you won't hurt him—he's very nervous"; the farmer, after an exhausting calving which I feel certain has knocked about two years off my life expectancy, grunting morosely: "I doubt you've tired that cow out, young man."

Mrs. Bond was different. She used to meet me at the door with an enormous pair of gauntlets to protect my hands against scratches and it was an inexpressible relief to find that somebody cared. It became part of the pattern of my life; walking up the garden path among the innumerable slinking, wild-eyed little creatures which were the outside cats, the ceremonial acceptance of the gloves at the door, then the entry into the charged atmosphere of the kitchen with little Mr. Bond and his newspaper just visible among the milling furry bodies of the inside cats. I was never able to ascertain Mr. Bond's attitude to cats—come to think of it he hardly ever said anything—but I had the impression he could take them or leave them.

The gauntlets were a big help and at times they were a veritable godsend. As in the case of Boris. Boris was an enormous blue-black member of the outside cats and my bête noire in more senses than one. I always cherished a private conviction that he had escaped from a zoo; I had never seen a domestic cat with such sleek, writhing muscles, such dedicated ferocity. I'm sure there was a bit of puma in Boris somewhere.

It had been a sad day for the cat colony when he turned up. I have always found it difficult to dislike any animal; most of the ones which try to do us a mischief are activated by fear, but Boris was different; he was a malevolent bully and after his arrival the frequency of my visits increased because of his habit of regularly beating up his colleagues. I was forever stitching up tattered ears, dressing gnawed limbs.

We had one trial of strength fairly early. Mrs. Bond wanted me to give him a worm dose and I had the little tablet all ready held in forceps. How I ever got hold of him I don't quite know, but I hustled him on to the table and did my wrapping act at lightning speed, swathing him in roll upon roll of stout material. Just for a few seconds I thought I had him as he stared up at me, his great brilliant eyes full of hate. But as I pushed my loaded forceps into his mouth he clamped his teeth viciously down on them and I could feel claws of amazing power tearing inside the sheet. It was all over in moments. A long leg shot out and ripped its way down my wrist, I let go my tight hold of the neck and in a flash Boris sank his teeth through the gauntlet into the ball of my thumb and was away. I was left standing there stupidly, holding the fragmented worm tablet in a bleeding hand and looking at the bunch of ribbons which had once been my wrapping sheet. From then on Boris loathed the very sight of me and the feeling was mutual.

But this was one of the few clouds in a serene sky.
I continued to enjoy my visits there and life proceeded on a tranquil course except, perhaps, for
some legpulling from my colleagues. They could never understand my willingness to spend so much time
over a lot of cats. And of course this fitted in with
the general attitude because Siegfried didn't believe
in people keeping pets of any kind. He just couldn't
understand their mentality and propounded his views
to anybody who cared to listen. He himself, of course,
kept five dogs and two cats. The dogs, all of them,
travelled everywhere with him in the car and he fed
dogs and cats every day with his own hands—
wouldn't allow anybody else to do the job. In the
evening all seven animals would pile themselves
round his feet as he sat in his chair by the fire. To
this day he is still as vehemently anti-pet as ever,
though another generation of waving dogs' tails almost obscures him as he drives around and he also
has several cats, a few tanks of tropical fish and a
couple of snakes.

Tristan saw me in action at Mrs. Bond's on only
one occasion. I was collecting some long forceps
from the instrument cupboard when he came into
the room.

"Anything interesting, Jim?" he asked.

"No, not really. I'm just off to see one of the Bond
cats. It's got a bone stuck between its teeth."

The young man eyed me ruminatively for a moment. "Think I'll come with you. I haven't seen much
small animal stuff lately."

As we went down the garden at the cat establishment I felt a twinge of embarrassment. One of the
things which had built up my happy relationship
with Mrs. Bond was my tender concern for her
charges. Even with the wildest and the fiercest I exhibited only gentleness, patience and solicitude; it
wasn't really an act, it came quite naturally to me.
However, I couldn't help wondering what Tristan
would think of my cat bedside manner.

Mrs. Bond in the doorway had summed up the

situation in a flash and had two pairs of gauntlets waiting. Tristan looked a little surprised as he received his pair but thanked the lady with typical charm. He looked still more surprised when he entered the kitchen, sniffed the rich atmosphere and surveyed the masses of furry creatures occupying almost every available inch of space.

"Mr. Herriot, I'm afraid it's Boris who has the bone in his teeth," Mrs. Bond said.

"Boris!" My stomach lurched. "How on earth are we going to catch him?"

"Oh I've been rather clever," she replied. "I've managed to entice him with some of his favourite food into a cat basket."

Tristan put his hand on a big wicker cage on the table. "In here, is he?" he asked casually. He slipped back the catch and opened the lid. For something like a third of a second the coiled creature within and Tristan regarded each other tensely, then a sleek black body exploded silently from the basket past the young man's left ear on to the top of a tall cupboard.

"Christ!" said Tristan. "What the hell was that?"

"That," I said, "was Boris, and now we've got to get hold of him again." I climbed on to a chair, reached slowly on to the cupboard top and started "Puss-puss-puss'ing in my most beguiling tone.

After about a minute Tristan appeared to think he had a better idea; he made a sudden leap and grabbed Boris's tail. But only briefly, because the big cat freed himself in an instant and set off on a whirlwind circuit of the room; along the tops of cupboards and dressers, across the curtains, careening round and round like a wall of death rider.

Tristan stationed himself at a strategic point and as Boris shot past he swiped at him with one of the gauntlets.

"Missed the bloody thing!" he shouted in chagrin. "But here he comes again . . . take that, you black sod! Damn it, I can't nail him!"

The docile little inside cats, startled by the scattering of plates and tins and pans and by Tristan's cries and arm wavings, began to run around in their turn, knocking over whatever Boris had missed. The noise and confusion even got through to Mr. Bond because just for a moment he raised his head and looked around him in mild surprise at the hurtling bodies before returning to his newspaper.

Tristan, flushed with the excitement of the chase had really begun to enjoy himself. I cringed inwardly as he shouted over to me happily.

"Send him on, Jim, I'll get the bugger next time round!"

We never did catch Boris. We just had to leave the piece of bone to work its own way out, so it wasn't a successful veterinary visit. But Tristan as we got back into the car smiled contentedly.

"That was great, Jim. I didn't realise you had such fun with your pussies."

Mrs. Bond on the other hand, when I next saw her, was rather tight-lipped over the whole thing.

"Mr. Herriot," she said, "I hope you aren't going to bring that young man with you again."

23

I was back at Granville Bennett's again. Back in the tiled operating theatre with the great lamp pouring its harsh light over my colleague's bowed head, over the animal nurses, the rows of instruments, the little animal stretched on the table.

Until late this afternoon I had no idea that another visit to Hartington was in store for me; not until the doorbell rang as I was finishing a cup of tea and I went along the passage and opened the door and saw Colonel Bosworth on the step. He was holding a wicker cat basket.

"Can I trouble you for a moment, Mr. Herriot?" he said.

His voice sounded different and I looked up at him questioningly. Most people had to look up at Colonel Bosworth with his lean six feet three inches and his tough soldier's face which matched the D.S.O. and M.C. which he had brought out of the war. I saw quite a lot of him, not only when he came to the surgery but out in the country where he spent most of his time hacking along the quiet roads around Darrowby on a big hunter with two Cairn terriers trotting behind. I liked him. He was a formidable man but he was unfailingly courteous and there was a gentleness in him which showed in his attitude to his animals.

"No trouble," I replied. "Please come inside."

In the waiting room he held out the basket. His eyes were strained and there was shock and hurt in his face.

"It's little Maudie," he said.

225

"Maudie . . . your black cat?" When I had been to his house the little creature had usually been in evidence, rubbing down the colonel's ankles, jumping on his knee, competing assiduously with the terriers for his attention.

"What's the matter, is she ill?"

"No . . . no . . ." He swallowed and spoke carefully. "She's had an accident, I'm afraid."

"What kind of accident?"

"A car struck her. She never goes out into the road in front of the house but for some reason she did this afternoon."

"I see." I took the basket from him. "Did the wheel go over her?"

"No, I don't think it can have done that because she ran back into the house afterwards."

"Oh well," I said. "That sounds hopeful. It probably isn't anything very much."

The colonel paused for a moment. "Mr. Herriot, I wish you were right but it's . . . rather frightful. It's her face you see. Must have been a glancing blow but I . . . really don't see how she can live."

"Oh . . . as bad as that . . . I'm sorry. Anyway come through with me and I'll have a look."

He shook his head. "No, I'll stay here if you don't mind. And there's just one thing." He laid his hand briefly on the basket. "If you think, as I do, that it's hopeless, please put her to sleep immediately. She must not suffer any more."

I stared at him uncomprehendingly for a moment then hurried along the passage to the operating room. I put the basket on the table, slid the wooden rod from its loops and opened the lid. I could see the sleek little black form crouched in the depths and as I stretched my hand out gingerly towards it the head rose slowly and turned towards me with a long, open-mouthed wail of agony.

And it wasn't just an open mouth. The whole lower jaw was dangling uselessly, the mandible shattered and splintered, and as another chilling cry issued from the basket I had a horrific glimpse of jagged ends of bone gleaming from the froth of blood and saliva.

I closed the basket quickly and leaned on the lid. "Christ!" I gasped. "Oh Christ!"

I closed my eyes but couldn't dispel the memory of the grotesque face, the terrible sound of pain and worst of all the eyes filled with the terrified bewilderment which makes animal suffering so unbearable.

With trembling haste I reached behind me to the trolley for the bottle of Nembutal. This was the one thing vets could do, at any rate; cut short this agony with merciful speed. I pulled 5 c.c.'s into the syringe; more than enough—she'd drift into sleep and never wake up again. Opening the basket I reached down and underneath the cat and slipped the needle through the abdominal skin; an intraperitoneal injection would have to do. But as I depressed the plunger it was as though a calmer and less involved person was tapping me on the shoulder and saying, "Just a minute, Herriot, take it easy. Why don't you think about this for a bit?"

I stopped after injecting 1 c.c. That would be enough to anaesthetise Maudie. In a few minutes she would feel nothing. Then I closed the lid and began to walk about the room. I had repaired a lot of cat's broken jaws in my time; they seemed to be prone to this trouble and I had gained much satisfaction from wiring up symphyseal fractures and watching their uneventful healing. But this was different.

After five minutes I opened the basket and lifted the little cat, sound asleep and as limp as a rag doll, on to the table.

I swabbed out the mouth and explored with careful fingers, trying to piece the grisly jigsaw together. The symphysis had separated right enough and that could be fastened together with wire, but how about those mandibular rami, smashed clean through on both sides—in fact there were two fractures on the left. And some of the teeth had been knocked out and others slackened; there was nothing to get hold of. Could they be held together by metal plates screwed into the bone? Maybe . . . and was there a man with the skill and equipment to do such a job . . . ? I thought I just might know one.

I went over the sleeping animal carefully; there wasn't a thing amiss except that pathetically drooping jaw. Meditatively I stroked the smooth, shining fur. She was only a young cat with years of life in front of her and as I stood there the decision came to me with a surge of relief and I trotted back along the passage to ask the colonel if I could take Maudie through to Granville Bennett.

It had started to snow heavily when I set out and I was glad it was downhill all the way to Hartington; many of the roads higher up the Dale would soon be impassable on a night like this.

In the Veterinary Hospital I watched the big man drilling, screwing, stitching. It wasn't the sort of job which could be hurried but it was remarkable how quickly those stubby fingers could work. Even so, we had been in the theatre for nearly an hour and Granville's complete absorption showed in the long silences broken only by the tinkling of instruments, occasional barking commands and now and then a sudden flare of exasperation. And it wasn't only the nurses who suffered; I had scrubbed up and had been pressed into service and when I failed to hold the jaw exactly as my colleague desired he exploded in my face.

"Not that bloody way, Jim! . . . What the hell are you playing at? . . . No, no, no, no, NO! . . . Oh God Almighty!"

But at last all was finished and Granville threw off his cap and turned away from the table with that air of finality which made me envy him the first time. He was sweating. In his office he washed his hands, towelled his brow and pulled on an elegant grey jacket from the pocket of which he produced a pipe. It was a different pipe from the last time; I learned in time that all Granville's pipes were not only beautiful but big and this one had a bowl like a fair sized coffee cup. He rubbed it gently along the side of his nose, gave it a polish with the yellow cloth he always seemed to carry and held it lovingly against the light.

"Straight grain, Jim. Superb, isn't it?"

He contentedly scooped tobacco from his vast pouch, ignited it and puffed a cloud of delectable smoke at me before taking me by the arm. "Come on, laddie. I'll show you round while they're clearing up in there."

We did a tour of the hospital, taking in the waiting and consulting rooms, X-ray room, dispensary and of course the office with its impressive card index system with case histories of all patients, but the bit I enjoyed most was walking along the row of heated cubicles where an assortment of animals were recovering from their operations.

Granville stabbed his pipe at them as we went along. "Spay, enterotomy, aural haematoma, entropion." Then he bent suddenly, put a finger through the wire front and adopted a wheedling tone. "Come now, George, come on little fellow, don't be frightened, it's only Uncle Granville."

A small West Highland with a leg in a cast hobbled to the front and my colleague tickled his nose through the wire.

"That's George Wills-Fentham," he said in explanation. "Old Lady Wills-Fentham's pride and joy. Nasty compound fracture but he's doing very nicely. He's a bit shy is George but a nice little chap when you get to know him, aren't you, old lad?" He continued his tickling and in the dim light I could see the short white tail wagging furiously.

Maudie was lying in the very last of the recovery pens, a tiny, trembling figure. That trembling meant she was coming out of the anaesthetic and I opened the door and stretched my hand out to her. She still couldn't raise her head but she was looking at me and as I gently stroked her side, her mouth opened in a faint rusty miauw. And with a thrill of deep pleasure I saw that her lower jaw belonged to her again; she could open and close it; that hideous dangling tatter of flesh and bone was only a bad memory.

"Marvellous, Granville," I murmured. "Absolutely bloody marvellous."

Smoke plumed in quiet triumph from the noble pipe. "Yes, it's not bad, is it laddie. A week or two on fluids and she'll be as good as new. No problems there."

I stood up. "Great! I can't wait to tell Colonel Bosworth. Can I take her home tonight?"

"No, Jim, no. Not this time. I just want to keep an eye on her for a couple of days then maybe the colonel can collect her himself." He led me back into the brightly lit office where he eyed me for a moment.

"You must come and have a word with Zoe while you're here," he said. "But first, just a suggestion. I wonder if you'd care to slip over with me to ..."

I took a rapid step backward. "Well . . . er . . . really. I don't think so." I gabbled. "I enjoyed my visit to the club that other night but . . . er . . . perhaps not this evening."

"Hold on, laddie, hold on," Granville said soothingly. "Who said anything about the club? No, I just wondered if you'd like to come to a meeting with me?"

"Meeting?"

"Yes, Professor Milligan's come through from Edinburgh to speak to the Northern Veterinary Society about metabolic diseases. I think you'd enjoy it."

"You mean milk fever, acetonaemia and all that?"

"Correct. Right up your street, old son."

"Well it is, isn't it? I wonder . . ." I stood for a few moments deep in thought, and one of the thoughts was why an exclusively small animal man like Granville wanted to hear about cow complaints. But I was maybe doing him an injustice; he probably wanted to maintain a broad, liberal view of veterinary knowledge.

It must have been obvious that I was dithering because he prodded me a little further.

"I'd like to have your company, Jim, and anyway I see you're all dressed and ready for anything. Matter of fact when you walked in tonight I couldn't help thinking what a smart lad you looked."

He was right there. I hadn't dashed through in my farm clothes this time. With the memory of my last visit still painfully fresh in my mind I was determined that if I was going to meet the charming Zoe again I was going to be: (a) Properly dressed, (b) Sober, (c) in a normal state of health and not bloated and belching like an impacted bullock. Helen, agreeing that my image needed refurbishing, had rigged me out in my best suit.

Granville ran his hand along my lapel. "Fine piece of serge if I may say so."

I made up my mind. "Right, I'd like to come with you. Just let me ring Helen to say I won't be straight back and then I'm your man."

24

Outside it was still snowing; city snow drifting down in a wet curtain which soon lost itself in the dirty churned-up slush in the streets. I pulled my coat higher round my neck and huddled deeper in the Bentley's leather luxury. As we swept past dark buildings and shops I kept expecting Granville to turn up some side street and stop, but within a few minutes we were speeding through the suburbs up towards the North Road. This meeting, I thought, must be out in one of the country institutes, and I didn't say anything until we had reached Scotch Corner and the big car had turned on to the old Roman Road to Bowes.

I stretched and yawned. "By the way, Granville, where are they holding this meeting?"

"Appleby," my colleague replied calmly.

I came bolt upright in my seat then I began to laugh.

"What's the joke, old son?" Granville enquired.

"Well . . . Appleby . . . ha-ha-ha! Come on, where are we really heading?"

"I've told you, laddie, the Pemberton Arms, Appleby, to be exact."

"Do you mean it?"

"Of course."

"But hell, Granville, that's on the other side of the Pennines."

"Quite right. Always has been, laddie."

I ran a hand through my hair. "Wait a minute. Surely it isn't worth going about forty miles in weather like this. We'll never get over Bowes Moor you know—in fact I heard yesterday it was blocked. Anyway, it's nearly eight o'clock—we'd be too late."

The big man reached across and patted my knee.

"Stop worrying, Jim. We'll get there and we'll be in plenty of time. You've got to remember you're sitting in a proper motor car now. A drop of snow is nothing."

As if determined to prove his words he put his foot down and the great car hurtled along the dead straight stretch of road. We skidded a bit on the corner at Greta Bridge then roared through Bowes and up to the highest country. I couldn't see much. In fact on the moor top I couldn't see anything, because up there it was the real country snow; big dry flakes driving straight into the headlights and settling comfortably with millions of their neighbours on the already deep white carpet on the road. I just didn't know how Granville was able to see, never mind drive fast; and I had no idea how we were going to get back over here in a few hours time when the wind had drifted the snow across the road. But I kept my mouth shut. It was becoming increasingly obvious that I emerged as a sort of maiden aunt in Granville's company, so I held my peace and prayed.

I followed this policy through Brough and along the lower road where the going was easier until I climbed out with a feeling of disbelief in the yard of the Pemberton Arms. It was nine o'clock.

We slipped into the back of the room and I settled into my chair, prepared to improve my mind a little. There was a man on the platform holding forth and at first I had difficulty in picking up the substance of his words; he wasn't mentioning anything about animal diseases but suddenly everything clicked into place.

"We are indeed grateful," the man was saying "to Professor Milligan for coming all this way and for giving us a most interesting and instructive talk. I know I speak for the entire audience when I say we have enjoyed it thoroughly, so may I ask you to show your appreciation in the usual manner." There was a long round of applause then an outburst of talk and a pushing back of chairs.

I turned to Granville in some dismay. "That was the vote of thanks. It's finished."

"So it is, laddie." My colleague didn't seem unduly disappointed or even surprised. "But come with me—there are compensations."

We joined the throng of vets and moved across the richly carpeted hall to another room where bright lights shone down on a row of tables laden with food. Then I recognised Bill Warrington and Burroughs Wellcome representative and all became clear.

This was a commercially sponsored evening and the real action, in Granville's estimation, began right here. I remembered then that Siegfried had once told me that Granville hated to miss any of these occasions. Though the most generous of men there was some piquancy in the gratis food and drink which attracted him irresistibly.

Even now he was guiding me purposefully towards the bar. But our progress was slow due to a phenomenon peculiar to Granville; everybody seemed to know him. Since those days I have been with him to restaurants, pubs, dances and it has been just the same. In fact I have often thought that if I took him to visit some lost tribe in the jungles of the Amazon one of them would jump and say "Well hello, Granville old boy!" and slap him on the back.

Finally however he fought his way through his fellow vets and we reached the bar where two dark little men in white coats were already under pressure; they were working with the impersonal concentration of people who knew that the whisky always took a hammering on veterinary evenings, but they paused and smiled as my colleague's massive presence hovered at the counter.

"Now then, Mr. Bennett. How are you, Mr. Bennett?"

"Good evening, Bob. Nice to see you, Reg." Granville responded majestically.

I noticed that Bob put down his bottle of ordinary whisky and reached down for a bottle of Glenlivet Malt to charge Granville's glass. The big man sniffed the fine spirit appreciatively.

"And one for my friend, Mr. Herriot," he said.

The barmen's respectful expressions made me feel suddenly important and I found myself in possession of my own vast measure of Glenlivet. I had to get it down quickly followed by a few speedy refills since the barmen took their cue from my companion's consumption.

Then I followed in Granville's regal wake as he made his way among the tables with the air of a man in his natural environment. Messrs. Burroughs Wellcome had done us proud and we worked our way through a variety of canapes, savouries and cold meats. Now and again we revisited the bar for more of the Glenlivet then back to the tables.

I knew I had drunk too much and now I was eating too much. But the difficulty with Granville was that if I ever declined anything he took it as a personal insult.

"Try one of those prawn things," he would say, sinking his teeth into a mushroom vol au vent and if I hesitated a wounded look would come into his eyes.

But I was enjoying myself. Veterinary surgeons are my favourite people and I revelled as I always did in their tales of successes and failures. Especially the failures; they were particularly soothing. Whenever the thought of how we were going to get home stole into my mind I banished it quickly.

Granville seemed to have no qualms because he showed no signs of moving when the company began to thin out; in fact we were the last to leave, our departure being accorded a touch of ceremony by a final substantial stirrup cup from Bob and Reg.

As we left the hotel I felt fine; a little light-headed perhaps and with the merest hint of regret at being pressed to a second helping of trifle and cream, but

otherwise in excellent shape. As we settled once more
into the Bentley Granville was at his most expansive.

"Excellent meeting that, Jim. I told you it would be
worth the journey."

We were the only members of the company who
were headed eastward and were alone on the road.
In fact it occurred to me that we hadn't seen a single
car on the road to Appleby and now there was something uncomfortable in our total isolation. The snow
had stopped and the brilliant moon flooded its cold
light over a white empty world. Empty, that is, except for us, and our solitary state was stressed by the
smooth, virgin state of the glistening carpet ahead.

I was conscious of an increasing disquiet as the
great gaunt spine of the Pennines bulked before us
and as we drew nearer it reared up like an angry
white monster.

Past the snow-burdened roofs of Brough then the
long climb with the big car slipping from side to side
as it fought its way up the bending, twisting hill,
engine bellowing. I thought I'd feel better when we
reached the top but the first glimpse of the Bowes
Moor road sent my stomach into a lurch of apprehension; miles and miles of it coiling its way across the
most desolate stretch of country in all England. And
even from this distance you could see the drifts, satin
smooth and beautiful, pushing their deadly way
across our path.

On either side of the road a vast white desert rolled
and dipped endlessly toward the black horizon; there
was not a light, not a movement, not a sign of life
anywhere.

The pipe jutted aggressively as Granville roared
forward to do battle. We hit the first drift, slewed
sideways for a tense few seconds then we were on the
other side, speeding into the unbroken surface. Then
the next drift and the next and the next. Often I
thought we were stuck but always, wheels churning,
engine screaming we emerged. I had had plenty of
experience of snow driving and I could appreciate

Granville's expertise as, without slackening speed he picked out the shallowest, narrowest part of each obstruction for his attack. He had this heavy powerful car to help him but he could drive all right.

However, my trepidation at being stranded in this waste land was gradually being overshadowed by another uneasiness. When I had left the hotel I was pretty well topped up with food and drink and if I had been handled gently for the next few hours I'd have been all right. But on the bumpy journey to Brough I had been increasingly aware of a rising queasiness; my mind kept flitting back unhappily to that exotic cocktail, Reg's speciality, which Granville had said I must try; he had prevailed on me, too, to wash down the whiskies with occasional beers which, he said, were essential to maintain a balanced intake of fluids and solids. And that final trifle—it had been a mistake.

And now I wasn't just being bumped, I was being thrown around like a pea in a drum as the Bentley lurched and skidded and occasionally took off altogether. Soon I began to feel very ill indeed. And like a seasick man who didn't care if the ship foundered I lost all interest in our progress; I closed my eyes, braced my feet on the floor and shrunk into an inner misery.

I hardly noticed as, after an age of violent motion, we finally began to go downhill and thundered through Bowes. After that there was little danger of having to spend the night in the car but Granville kept his foot down and we rocked over the frozen ground while I felt steadily worse.

I would dearly have loved to ask my colleague to stop and allow me to be quietly sick by the roadside but how do you say such a thing to a man who never seemed to be in the least affected by over indulgence and who, even at that moment was chatting gaily as he refilled his pipe with his free hand. The internal pounding seemed to have forced extra alcohol into my bloodstream because on top of my other discomforts my vision was blurred, I was dizzy and had the strong conviction that if I tried to stand up I would fall flat on my face.

I was busy with these preoccupations when the car stopped.

"We'll just pop in and say hello to Zoe," Granville said.

"Wha's that?" I slurred.

"We'll go inside for a few minutes."

I looked around. "Where are we?"

Granville laughed. "Home old son. I can see a light, so Zoe's still up. You must come and have a quick cup of coffee."

I crawled laboriously from the seat and stood leaning on the car. My colleague tripped lightly to the door and rang the bell. He was as fit as a fiddle I thought bitterly as I reeled after him. I was slumped against the porch breathing heavily when the door opened and there was Zoe Bennett, bright eyed, glowing, beautiful as ever.

"Why Mr. Herriot!" she cried. "How nice to see you again!"

Slack-jawed, green-faced, rumpled-suited, I stared into her eyes, gave a gentle hiccup and staggered past her into the house.

Next morning Granville rang to say all was going to be well because Maudie had been able to lap a little milk. It was kind of him to let me know and I didn't want to sound churlish by saying that was all I had managed to do, too.

It happened that morning by a coincidence that I had a far outlying visit and had to pass the Scotch Corner turning on the North Road. I stopped the car and sat gazing at the long snow-covered road stretching towards the Pennines. I was starting my engine when an A.A. man came over and spoke at my window.

"You're not thinking of trying the Bowes Moor road, are you?" he said.

"No, no." I was just looking.

He nodded in satisfaction.

"I'm glad to hear that. It's blocked you know. There hasn't been a car over there for two days."

25

You could hardly expect to find a more unlikely character in Darrowby than Roland Partridge. The thought came to me for the hundredth time as I saw him peering through the window which looked on to Trengate just a little way up the other side of the street from our surgery.

He was tapping the glass and beckoning to me and the eyes behind the thick spectacles were wide with concern. I waited and when he opened the door I stepped straight from the street into his living room because these were tiny dwellings with only a kitchen in the rear and a single small bedroom overlooking the street above. But when I went in I had the familiar feeling of surprise. Because most of the other occupants of the row were farm workers and their furnishings were orthodox; but this place was a studio.

An easel stood in the light from the window and the walls were covered from floor to ceiling with paintings. Unframed canvases were stacked everywhere and the few ornate chairs and the table with its load of painted china and other bric a brac added to the artistic atmosphere.

The simple explanation was, of course, that Mr. Partridge was in fact an artist. But the unlikely aspect came into it when you learned that this middle-aged velvet-jacketed aesthete was the son of a small farmer, a man whose forbears had been steeped in the soil for generations.

"I happened to see you passing there, Mr. Herriot," he said. "Are you terribly busy?"

"Not too busy, Mr. Partridge. Can I help you?"

He nodded gravely. "I wondered whether you could spare a moment to look at Percy. I'd be most grateful."

"Of course," I replied. "Where is he?"

He was ushering me towards the kitchen when there was a bang on the outer door and Bert Hardisty the postman burst in. Bert was a rough-hewn character and he dumped a parcel unceremoniously on the table.

"There y'are, Rolie!" he shouted and turned to go.

Mr. Partridge gazed with unruffled dignity at the retreating back. "Thank you very much indeed, Bertram, good day to you."

Here was another thing. The postman and the artist were both Darrowby born and bred, had the same social background, had gone to the same school, yet their voices were quite different. Roland Partridge, in fact, spoke with the precise, well-modulated syllables of a barrister at law.

We went into the kitchen. This was where he cooked for himself in his bachelor state. When his father died many years ago he had sold the farm immediately. Apparently his whole nature was appalled by the earthy farming scene and he could not get out quickly enough. At any rate he had got sufficient money from the sale to indulge his interests and he had taken up painting and lived ever since in this humble cottage, resolutely doing his own thing. This had all happened long before I came to Darrowby and the dangling lank hair was silver now. I always had the feeling that he was happy in his way because I couldn't imagine that small, rather exquisite figure plodding around a muddy farmyard.

It was probably in keeping with his nature that he had never married. There was a touch of asceticism in the thin cheeks and pale blue eyes and it was possible that his self-contained imperturbable personality might denote a lack of warmth. But that didn't hold good with regard to his dog, Percy.

He loved Percy with a fierce protective passion

and as the little animal trotted towards him he bent over him, his face alight with tenderness.

"He looks pretty bright to me," I said. "He's not sick, is he?"

"No . . . no . . ." Mr. Partridge seemed strangely ill at ease. "He's perfectly well in himself, but I want you to look at him and see if you notice anything."

I looked. And I saw only what I had always seen, the snow-white, shaggy haired little object regarded by local dog breeders and other cognoscenti as a negligible mongrel but nevertheless one of my favourite patients. Mr. Partridge, looking through the window of a pet shop in Brawton about five years ago, had succumbed immediately to the charms of two soulful eyes gazing up at him from a six week old tangle of white hair and had put down his five bob and rushed the little creature home. Percy had been described in the shop somewhat vaguely as a "terrier" and Mr. Partridge had flirted fearfully with the idea of having his tail docked; but such was his infatuation that he couldn't bring himself to cause such a mutilation and the tail had grown in a great fringed curve almost full circle over the back.

To me, the tail nicely balanced the head which was undoubtedly a little too big for the body but Mr. Partridge had been made to suffer for it. His old friends in Darrowby who, like all country folks, considered themselves experts with animals, were free with their comments. I had heard them at it. When Percy was young it was:

"Time ye had that tail off, Rolie. Ah'll bite it off for ye if ye like." And later, again and again. "Hey Rolie, you should've had that dog's tail off when he were a pup. He looks bloody daft like that."

When asked Percy's breed Mr. Partridge always replied haughtily, "Sealyham Cross," but it wasn't as simple as that; the tiny body with its luxuriant bristling coat, the large, rather noble head with high, pricked ears, the short, knock-kneed legs and that tail made him a baffling mixture.

Mr. Partridge's friends again were merciless, referring to Percy as a "tripe-'ound" or a "mouse-'ound" and though the little artist received these railleries with a thin smile I knew they bit deep. He had a high regard for me based simply on the fact that the first time I saw Percy I exclaimed quite spontaneously, "What a beautiful little dog!" And since I have never had much time for the points and fads of dog breeding I really meant it.

"Just what is wrong, Mr. Partridge?" I asked. "I can't see anything unusual."

Again the little man appeared to be uneasy. "Well now, watch as he walks across the floor. Come, Percy my dear." He moved away from me and the dog followed him.

"No . . . no . . . I don't quite understand what you mean."

"Watch again." He set off once more. "It's at his . . . his er . . . back end."

I crouched down. "An now, yes, wait a minute. Just hold him there, will you?"

I went over and had a close look. "I see it now. One of his testicles is slightly enlarged."

"Yes . . . yes . . . quite." Mr. Partridge's face turned a shade pinker. "That is . . . er . . . what I thought."

"Hang on to him a second while I examine it." I lifted the scrotum and palpated gently. "Yes, the left one is definitely bigger and it is harder too."

"Is it . . . anything serious?"

I paused. "No, I shouldn't think so. Tumours of the testicles are not uncommon in dogs and fortunately they aren't inclined to metastasise—spread through the body—very readily. So I shouldn't worry too much."

I added the last bit hastily because at the mention of the word "tumour" the colour had drained from his face alarmingly.

"That's a growth, isn't it?" he stammered.

"Yes, but there are all kinds and a lot of them are not malignant. So don't worry but please keep an eye on him. It may not grow much but if it does you must let me know immediately."

"I see . . . and if it does grow?"

"Well the only thing would be to remove the testicle."

"An operation?" The little man stared at me and for a moment I thought he would faint.

"Yes, but not a serious one. Quite straightforward, really." I bent down and felt the enlargement again. It was very slight. From the front end, Percy kept up a continuous musical growling. I grinned. He always did that—when I took his temperature, cut his nails, anything; a nonstop grumble and it didn't mean a thing. I knew him well enough to realise there was no viciousness in him; he was merely asserting his virility, reminding me what a tough fellow he was, and it was not idle boasting because for all his lack of size he was a proud, mettlesome little dog, absolutely crammed with character.

After I had left the house I looked back and saw Mr. Partridge standing there watching me. He was clasping and unclasping his hands.

And even when I was back in the surgery half of me was still in that odd little studio. I had to admire Mr. Partridge for doing exactly what he wanted to do because in Darrowby he would never get any credit for it. A good horseman or cricketer would be revered in the town but an artist . . . never. Not even if he became famous, and Mr. Partridge would never be famous. A few people bought his paintings but he could not have lived on the proceeds. I had one of them hanging in our bed-sitter and to my mind he had a definite gift. In fact I would have tried to afford more of them but for the fact that he obviously shrank from that aspect of the Yorkshire Dales which I loved most.

If I had been able to paint I would have wanted to show how the walls climbed everywhere over the stark fell-sides. I would have tried to capture the magic of the endless empty moors with the reeds trembling over the black bog pools. But Mr. Partridge went only for the cosy things; willows hanging by a rustic bridge, village churches, rose-covered cottages.

Since Percy was a near neighbour I saw him nearly every day, either from our bed-sitter at the top of the house or from the surgery below. His master exercised him with great zeal and regularity and it was a common sight to see the artist passing on the other side of the road with the little animal trotting proudly beside him. But from that distance it was impossible to see if the tumour was progressing, and since I heard nothing from Mr. Partridge I assumed that all was well. Maybe that thing had grown no more. Sometimes it happened that way.

Keeping a close watch on the little dog reminded me of other incidents connected with him, particularly the number of times he was involved in a fight. Not that Percy ever started a brawl—at ten inches high he wasn't stupid enough for that—but somehow big dogs when they saw that dainty white figure prancing along were inclined to go for him on sight. I witnessed some of these attacks from our windows and the same thing happened every time; a quick flurry of limbs, a snarling and yelping and then the big dog retreated bleeding.

Percy never had a mark on him—that tremendous thick coat gave him complete protection—but he always got a nip in from underneath. I had stitched up several of the local street fighters after Percy had finished with them.

It must have been about six weeks later when Mr. Partridge came in again. He looked tense.

"I'd like you to have a look at Percy again, Mr. Herriot."

I lifted the dog on to the surgery table and I didn't need to examine him very closely.

"It's quite a lot bigger, I'm afraid." I looked across the table at the little man.

"Yes, I know." He hesitated. "What do you suggest?"

"Oh there's no doubt at all he'll have to come in for an operation. That thing must come off."

Horror and despair flickered behind the thick spectacles.

"An operation!" He leaned on the table with both hands.

"I hate the idea, I just can't bear the thought of it!"

I smiled reassuringly. "I know how you feel, but honestly there's nothing to worry about. As I told you before, it's quite a simple procedure."

"Oh I know, I know," he moaned. "But I don't want him to be . . . cut about, you understand . . . it's just the idea of it."

And I couldn't persuade him. He remained adamant and marched resolutely from the surgery with his pet. I watched him crossing the road to his house and I knew he had let himself in for a load of worry, but I didn't realise just how bad it was going to be.

It was to be a kind of martyrdom.

26

I do not think martyrdom is too strong a word for what Mr. Partridge went through over the next few weeks, because with the passage of time that testicle became more and more massive and due to the way Percy carried his tail the thing was lamentably conspicuous.

People used to turn and stare as man and dog made their way down the street, Percy trotting bravely, his master, eyes rigidly to the front, putting up a magnificent pretence of being quite unaware of anything unusual. It really hurt me to see them and I found the sight of the smart little dog's disfigurement particularly hard to bear.

Mr. Partridge's superior facade had always made him a natural target for a certain amount of leg-pulling which he bore stoically; but the fact that it now involved his pet pierced him to the soul.

One afternoon he brought him over to the surgery and I could see that the little man was almost in tears. Gloomily I examined the offending organ which was now about six inches long; gross, pendulous, undeniably ludicrous.

"You know, Mr. Herriot," the artist gasped. "Some boys chalked on my window. Roll up and see the famous Chinese dog, Wun Hung Lo. I've just been wiping it off."

I rubbed my chin. "Well that's an ancient joke Mr. Partridge. I shouldn't worry about that."

"But I do worry! I can't sleep because of the thing!"

"For heaven's sake, then, why don't you let me

operate? I could put the whole business right for you."

"No! No! I can't do that!" His head rolled on his shoulders; he was the very picture of misery as he stared at me. "I'm frightened, that's what it is. I'm frightened he'll die under the anaesthetic."

"Oh come now! He's a strong little animal. There's no reason at all for such fears."

"But there is a risk isn't there?"

I looked at him helplessly. "Well there's a slight risk in all operations if you come right down to it, but honestly in this case . . ."

"No! That's enough. I won't hear of it," he burst out and seizing Percy's lead he strode away.

Things went from bad to worse after that. The tumour grew steadily, easily visible now from my vantage point in the surgery window as the dog went by on the other side of the street, and I could see too that the stares and occasional ridicule were beginning to tell on Mr. Partridge. His cheeks had hollowed and he had lost some of his high colour.

But I didn't have words with him till one market day several weeks later. It was early afternoon—the time the farmers often came in to pay their bills. I was showing one of them out when I saw Percy and his master coming out of the house. And I noticed immediately that the little animal now had to swing one hind leg slightly to clear the massive obstruction.

On an impulse I called out and beckoned to Mr. Partridge.

"Look," I said as he came across to me. "You've just got to let me take that thing off. It's interfering with his walking—making him lame. He can't go on like this."

The artist didn't say anything but stared back at me with hunted eyes. We were standing there in silence when Bill Dalton came round the corner and marched up to the surgery steps, cheque book in hand. Bill was a large beefy farmer who spent most of market day in the bar of the Black Swan and he was preceded by an almost palpable wave of beer fumes.

"Nah then, Rolie lad, how ista?" he roared, slapping the little man violently on the back.

"I am quite well, William, thank you, and how are you?"

But Bill didn't answer. His attention was all on Percy who had strolled a few paces along the pavement. He watched him intently for a few moments then, repressing a giggle, he turned back to Mr. Partridge with a mock-serious expression.

"Tha knows, Rolie," he said, "That blood 'ound of yours reminds me of the young man of Devizes, whose balls were of different sizes. The one was so small it was no ball at all, but the other one won several prizes." He finished with a shout of laughter which went on and on till he collapsed weakly against the iron railings.

For a moment I thought Mr. Partridge was going to strike him. He glared up at the big man and his chin and mouth trembled with rage, then he seemed to gain control of himself and turned to me.

"Can I have a word with you, Mr. Herriot?"

"Certainly." I walked a few yards with him down the street.

"You're right," he said. "Percy will have to have that operation. When can you do him?"

"Tomorrow," I replied. "Don't give him any more food and bring him in at two in the afternoon."

It was with a feeling of intense relief that I saw the little dog stretched on the table the next day. With Tristan as anaesthetist I quickly removed the huge testicle, going well up the spermatic cord to ensure the complete excision of all tumour tissue. The only thing which troubled me was that the scrotum itself had become involved due to the long delay in operating. This is the sort of thing that can lead to a recurrence and as I carefully cut away the affected parts of the scrotal wall I cursed Mr. Partridge's procrastination. I put in the last stitch with my fingers crossed.

The little man was in such transports of joy at seeing his pet alive after my efforts and rid of that horrid excrescence that I didn't want to spoil everything by voicing my doubts; but I wasn't entirely happy. If the tumour did recur I wasn't sure just what I could do about it.

But in the meantime I enjoyed my own share of pleasure at my patient's return to normality. I felt a warm rush of satisfaction whenever I saw him tripping along, perky as ever and free from the disfigurement which had bulked so large in his master's life. Occasionally I used to stroll casually behind him on the way down Trengate into the market place, saying nothing to Mr. Partridge but shooting some sharp glances at the region beneath Percy's tail.

In the meantime I had sent the removed organ off to the pathology department at Glasgow Veterinary College and their report told me that it was a Sertoli Cell Tumour. They also added the comforting information that this type was usually benign and that metastasis into the internal organs occurred in only a very small proportion of cases. Maybe this lulled me into a deeper security than was warranted because I stopped following Percy around and in fact, in the nonstop rush of new cases, forgot all about his spell of trouble.

So that when Mr. Partridge brought him round to the surgery I thought it was for something else and when his master lifted him on to the table and turned him round to show his rear end I stared uncomprehendingly for a moment. But I leaned forward anxiously when I spotted the ugly swelling on the left side of the scrotum. I palpated quickly, with Percy's growls and grousings providing an irritable obligato, and there was no doubt about it, the tumour was growing again. It meant business, too, because it was red, angry-looking, painful; a dangerously active growth if ever I had seen one.

"It's come up quite quickly, has it?" I asked.

Mr. Partridge nodded. "Yes, indeed. I can almost see it getting bigger every day."

We were in trouble. There was no hope of trying to cut this lot away; it was a great diffuse mass without clear boundaries and I wouldn't have known where to start. Anyway, if I began any more poking about it would be just what was needed to start a spread into the internal organs, and that would be the end of Percy.

"It's worse this time, isn't it?" The little man looked at me and gulped.

"Yes . . . yes . . . I'm afraid so."

"Is there anything at all you can do about it?" he asked.

I was trying to think of a painless way of telling him that there wasn't when I remembered something I had read in the Veterinary Record a week ago. It was about a new drug, Stilboestrol, which had just come out and was supposed to be useful for hormonal therapy in animals; but the bit I was thinking about was a small print extract which said it had been useful in cancer of the prostate in men. I wondered . . .

"There's one thing I'd like to try," I said, suddenly brisk. "I can't guarantee anything, of course, because it's something new. But we'll see what a week or two's course does."

"Oh good, good," Mr. Partridge breathed, snatching gratefully at the straw.

I rang May and Baker's and they sent the Stilboestrol to me immediately.

I injected Percy with 10 mg of the oily suspension and put him on to 10 mg tablets daily. They were big doses for a little dog but in a desperate situation I felt they were justified. Then I sat back and waited.

For about a week the tumour continued to grow and I nearly stopped the treatment, then there was a spell lasting several days during which I couldn't be sure; but then with a surge of relief I realised there could be no further doubt—the thing wasn't getting any bigger. I wasn't going to throw my hat in the air and I knew anything could still happen but I had done something with my treatment; I had halted that fateful progress.

The artist's step acquired a fresh spring as he passed on his daily walk and then as the ugly mass actually began to diminish he would wave towards the surgery window and point happily at the little white animal trotting by his side.

Poor Mr. Partridge. He was on the crest of the wave but just ahead of him was the second and more bizarre phase of his martyrdom.

At first neither I nor anybody else realised what was going on. All we knew was there suddenly seemed to be a lot of dogs in Trengate—dogs we didn't usually see, from other parts of the town; big ones, small ones, shaggy mongrels and sleek aristocrats all hanging around apparently aimlessly, but then it was noticed that there was a focal point of attraction. It was Mr. Partridge's house.

And it hit me blindingly one morning as I looked out of our bedroom window. They were after Percy. For some reason he had taken on the attributes of a bitch in heat. I hurried downstairs and got out my pathology book. Yes, there it was. The Sertoli Cell tumour occasionally made dogs attractive to other male dogs. But why should it be happening now when the thing was reducing and not when it was at its height? Or could it be the Stilboestrol? The new drug was said to have a feminising effect, but surely not to that extent.

Anyway, whatever the cause, the undeniable fact remained that Percy was under siege, and as the word got around the pack increased, being augmented by several of the nearby farm dogs, a Great Dane who had made the journey from Houlton, and Magnus, the little dachschund from the Drovers' Arms. The queue started forming almost at first light and by ten o'clock there would be a milling throng almost blocking the street. Apart from the regulars the odd canine visitor passing through would join the company, and no matter what his breed or size he was readily accepted into the club, adding one more to the assortment of stupid expressions, lolling tongues and waving tails; because, motley crew though they were, they were all happily united in the roisterous, bawdy camaraderie of lust.

The strain on Mr. Partridge must have been almost intolerable. At times I noticed the thick spectacles glinting balefully at the mob through his window but most of the time he kept himself in hand, working calmly at his easel as though he were oblivious that every one of the creatures outside had evil designs on his treasure.

Only rarely did his control snap. I witnessed one of these occasions when he rushed screaming from his doorway, laying about him with a walking stick; and I noticed that the polished veneer slipped from him and his cries rang out in broadest Yorkshire.

"Gerrout, ye bloody rotten buggers! Gerrout of it!"

He might as well have saved his energy because the pack scattered only for a few seconds before taking up their stations again.

I felt for the little man but there was nothing I could do about it. My main feeling was of relief that the tumour was going down but I had to admit to a certain morbid fascination at the train of events across the street.

Percy's walks were fraught with peril. Mr. Partridge always armed himself with his stick before venturing from the house and kept Percy on a short lead, but his precautions were unavailing as the wave of dogs swept down on him. The besotted creatures, mad with passion, leaped on top of the little animal as the artist beat vainly on the shaggy backs and yelled at them; and the humiliating procession usually continued right across the market place to the great amusement of the inhabitants.

At lunch time most of the dogs took a break and at nightfall they all went home to bed, but there was one little brown spaniel type who, with the greatest dedication, never left his post. I think he must have gone almost without food for about two weeks because he dwindled practically to a skeleton and I think he might have died if Helen hadn't taken pieces of meat over to him when she saw him huddled trembling in the doorway in the cold darkness of the evening. I know he stayed there all night because every now and then a shrill yelping wakened me in the small hours and I deduced that Mr. Partridge had got home on him with some missile from his bedroom window. But it made no difference; he continued his vigil undaunted.

I don't quite know how Mr. Partridge would have survived if this state of affairs had continued indefinitely; I think his reason might have given way. But mercifully signs began to appear that the nightmare was on the wane. The mob began to thin as Percy's condition improved and one day even the little brown dog reluctantly left his beat and slunk away to his unknown home.

That was the very day I had Percy on the table for the last time. I felt a thrill of satisfaction as I ran a fold of the scrotal skin between my fingers.

"There's nothing there now, Mr. Partridge. No thickening, even. Not a thing."

The little man nodded. "Yes, it's a miracle, isn't it! I'm very grateful to you for all you've done. I've been so terribly worried."

"Oh, I can imagine. You've been through a bad time. But I'm really as pleased as you are yourself— it's one of the most satisfying things in practice when an experiment like this comes off."

But often over the subsequent years, as I watched dog and master pass our window, Mr. Partridge with all his dignity restored, Percy as trim and proud as ever, I wondered about that strange interlude.

Did the Stilboestrol really reduce that tumour or did it regress naturally? And were the extraordinary events caused by the treatment or the condition or both?

I could never be quite sure of the answer, but of the outcome I could be happily certain. That unpleasant growth never came back . . . and neither did all those dogs.

27

Every professional visit has its beginning in a call, a summons from the client which can take varying forms. . . .

"This is Joe Bentley speaking," said the figure on the surgery doorstep. It was an odd manner of address, made stranger by the fact that Joe was holding his clenched fist up by his jaw and staring vacantly past me.

"'ello, 'ello," Joe continued as though into space, and suddenly everything became clear. That was an imaginary telephone he was holding and he was doing his best to communicate with the vet; and not doing so badly considering the innumerable pints of beer that were washing around inside him.

On market days the pubs stayed open from ten o'clock till five and Joe was one of the now extinct breed who took their chance to drink themselves almost insensible. The modern farmer may have a few drinks on market day but the old reckless intake is rare now.

In Darrowby it was confined to a group of hard-bitten characters, all of them elderly, so even then the custom was on the wane. But it wasn't uncommon to see them when they came to pay their bills, leaning helplessly against the surgery wall and pushing their cheque books wordlessly at us. Some of them still used a pony and trap and the old joke about the horse taking them home was illustrated regularly. One old chap kept an enormously powerful ancient car simply for the purpose of getting him home; even if he engaged top gear by mistake when he collapsed into the driver's seat the vehicle would still take off. Some didn't go home at all on market day but spent the night carousing and playing cards till dawn.

As I looked at Joe Bentley swaying on the step I wondered what his programme might be for the rest of the evening. He closed his eyes, held his fist close to his face and spoke again.

"Hellow, who's there?" he asked in an affected telephone voice.

"Herriot speaking," I replied. Clearly Joe wasn't trying to be funny. He was just a little confused. It was only right to cooperate with him. "How are you, Mr. Bentley?"

"Nicely, thank ye," Joe answered solemnly, eyes still tightly closed. "Are you very well?"

"I'm fine, thanks. Now what can I do for you?"

This seemed to floor him temporarily because he remained silent for several seconds, opening his eyes occasionally and squinting somewhere over my left shoulder with intense concentration. Then something seemed to click; he closed his eyes again, cleared his throat and recommenced.

"Will you come up to ma place? I've a cow wants cleansin'."

"Do you want me to come tonight?"

Joe gave this serious thought, pursing his lips and scratching his ear with his free hand before answering.

"Nay, morning'll do. Goodbye and thank ye." He placed the phantom telephone carefully in its rest, swung round and made his way down the street with great dignity. He hardly staggered at all and there was something purposeful in his bearing which convinced me that he was heading back to the Red Bear. For a moment I thought he would fall outside Johnson's the ironmongers but by the time he rounded the corner into the market place he was going so well that I felt sure he'd make it.

And I can remember Mr. Biggins standing by the desk in our office, hands deep in his pockets, chin thrust forward stubbornly.

"I 'ave a cow gruntin' a bit."

"Oh, right, we'll have a look at her." I reached for a pen to write the visit in the book.

He shuffled his feet. "Well ah don't know. She's maybe not as bad as all that."

"Well, whatever you say . . ."

"No," he said. "It's what you say—you're t'vet."

"It's a bit difficult," I replied. "After all, I haven't seen her. Maybe I'd better pay you a visit."

"Aye, that's all very fine, but it's a big expense. It's ten bob every time you fellers walk on to ma place and that's before you start. There's all t'medicines and everything on top."

"Yes, I understand, Mr. Biggins. Well, would you like to take something away with you? A tin of stomach powder, perhaps?"

"How do you know it's t'stomach?"

"Well I don't actually . . ."

"It might be summat else."

"That's very true, but . . ."

"She's a right good cow, this," he said with a touch of aggression. "Paid fifty pun for her at Scarburn Market."

"Yes, I'm sure she is. And consequently I really think she'd be worth a visit. I could come out this afternoon."

There was a long silence. "Aye, but it wouldn't be just one visit, would it? You'd be comin' again next day and maybe the one after that and before we knew we'd 'ave a clonkin' great bill."

"Yes, I'm sorry, Mr. Biggins, everything is so expensive these days."

"Yes, by gawl" He nodded, vigorously. "Sometimes it ud be cheaper to give you t'cow at t'end of it."

"Well now, hardly that . . . but I do see your point."

I spent a few moments in thought. "How about

taking a fever drink as well as the stomach powder?
That would be safer."

He gave me a long blank stare. "But you still
wouldn't be sure, would you?"

"No, not quite sure, not absolutely . . ."

"She could even 'ave a wire in 'er."

"True, very true."

"Well then, shoving medicines down her neck isn't
goin' to do no good is it?"

"It isn't, you're right."

"Ah don't want to lose this cow, tha knows!" he
burst out truculently. "Ah can't afford to lose 'er!"

"I realise that, Mr. Biggins. That's why I feel I
should see her—I did suggest that if you remember."

He did not reply immediately and only the strain
in his eyes and a faint twitching of a cheek muscle
betrayed the inner struggle which was raging. When
he finally spoke it was in a hoarse croak.

"Aye, well, it might be best . . . but . . . er . . . we
could mebbes leave 'er till mornin' and see how she
is then."

"That's a good idea." I smiled in relief. "You have a
look at her first thing in the morning and give me a
ring before nine if she's no better."

My words seemed to deepen his gloom. "But what
if she doesn't last till mornin'?"

"Well of course there is that risk."

"Not much good ringin' you if she's dead, is it?"

"That's true, of course."

"Ah'd be ringin' Mallock the knacker man, wouldn't
I?"

"Afraid so, yes . . ."

"Well that's no bloody use to me, gettin' five quid
from Mallock for a good cow!"

"Mm, no . . . I can see how you feel."

"Ah think a lot about this cow!"

"I'm sure you do."

"It ud be a big loss for me."

"Quite."

Mr. Biggins hunched his shoulders and glared at

me belligerently. "Well then what are you goin' to do about 'er?"

"Let's see," I ran my fingers through my hair. "Perhaps you could wait till tonight and see if she recovers and if she isn't right by say, eight o'clock you could let me know and I'd come out."

"You'd come out then, would you?" he said slowly, narrowing his eyes.

I gave him a bright smile. "That's right."

"Aye, but last time you came out at night you charged extra, ah'm sure you did."

"Well, probably," I said, spreading my hands. "That's usual in veterinary practices."

"So we're worse off than afore, aren't we?"

"When you look at it like that . . . I suppose so . . ."

"Ah'm not a rich man, tha knows."

"I realise that."

"Takes me all ma time to pay t'ordinary bill without extras."

"Oh I'm sure . . ."

"So that idea's a bad egg, ain't it?"

"Seems like it . . . yes . . ." I lay back in my chair, feeling suddenly tired.

Mr. Biggins glowered at me morosely but I wasn't going to be tempted into any further gambits. I gave him what I fancied was a neutral stare and I hoped it conveyed the message that I was open to suggestions but wasn't going to make any myself.

The silence which now blanketed the room seemed to be of a durable nature. Down at the end of the street the church clock tolled the quarter hour, far off in the market place a dog barked, Miss Dobson the grocer's daughter glided past the window on her bicycle but no word was uttered.

Mr. Biggins, biting his lower lip, darting his eyes desperately from his feet to me and back again, was clearly at the end of his resources, and it came to me at last that I had to take a firm initiative.

"Mr. Biggins," I said. "I've got to be on my way. I have a lot of calls and one of them is within a mile of your farm, so I shall see your cow around three o'clock." I stood up to indicate that the interview was over.

The farmer gave me a hunted look. I had the feeling that he had been resigned to a long period of stalemate and this sudden attack had taken him out of his stride. He opened his mouth as though to speak then appeared to change his mind and turned to go. At the door he paused, raised his hand and looked at me beseechingly for a moment, then he sank his chin on his chest and left the room.

I watched him through the window and as he crossed the road he stopped half way in the same indeterminate way, muttering to himself and glancing back at the surgery; and as he lingered there I grew anxious that he might be struck by a passing car, but at length he squared his shoulders and trailed slowly out of sight.

And sometimes it isn't easy to get a clear picture over the telephone . . .

"This is Bob Fryer."

"Good morning, Herriot here."

"Now then, one of me sows is bad."

"Oh right, what's the trouble?"

A throaty chuckle. "Ah, that's what ah want YOU to tell ME!"

"Oh, I see."

"Aye, ah wouldn't be ringin' you up if I knew what the trouble was, would I? Heh, heh, heh, heh!"

The fact that I had heard this joke about two thousand times interfered with my full participation in the merriment but I managed a cracked laugh in return.

"That's perfectly true, Mr. Fryer. Well, why have you rung me?"

"Damn, I've told ye—to find out what the trouble is."

"Yes, I understand that, but I'd like some details. What do you mean when you say she's bad?"

"Well, she's just a bit off it."

"Quite, but could you tell me a little more?"

A pause. "She's dowly, like."

"Anything else?"

"No . . . no . . . she's a right poorly pig, though."

I spent a few moments in thought. "Is she doing anything funny?"

"Funny? Funny? Nay, there's nowt funny about t'job, I'll tell tha! It's no laughin' matter."

"Well . . . er . . . let me put it this way. Why are you calling me out?"

"I'm callin' ye out because you're a vet. That's your job, isn't it?"

I tried again. "It would help if I knew what to bring with me. What are her symptoms?"

"Symptoms? Well, she's just off colour, like."

"Yes, but what is she doing?"

"She's doin' nowt. That's what bothers me."

"Let's see." I scratched my head. "Is she very ill?"

"I reckon she's in bad fettle."

"But would you say it was an urgent matter?"

Another long pause. "Well, she's nobbut middlin'. She's not framin' at all."

"Yes . . . yes . . . and how long has she been like this?"

"Oh, for a bit."

"But how long exactly?"

"For a good bit."

"But Mr. Fryer, I want to know when she started these symptoms. How long has she been affected?"

"Oh . . . ever since we got 'er."

"Ah, and when was that?"

"Well, she came wi' the others. . . ."

28

I always liked having a student with us. These young men had to see at least six months' practice on their way through college and most of their vacations were spent going round with a vet.

We, of course, had our own resident student in Tristan but he was in a different category; he didn't have to be taught anything—he seemed to know things, to absorb knowledge without apparent effort or indeed without showing interest. If you took Tristan to a case he usually spent his time on the farm sitting in the car reading his Daily Mirror and smoking Woodbines.

There were all types among the others—some from the country, some from the towns, some dull-witted, some bright—but as I say, I liked having them.

For one thing, before I had Sam they were good company in the car. A big part of a country vet's life consists of solitary driving and it was a relief to be able to talk to somebody. It was wonderful, too, to have a gate-opener. Some of the outlying farms were approached through long, gated roads—one which always struck terror into me had eight gates—and it is hard to convey the feeling of sheer luxury when somebody else leaped out and opened them.

And there was another little pleasure; asking the students questions. My own days of studying and examinations were still fresh in my memory and on top of that I had all the vast experience of nearly three years of practice. It gave me a feeling of power to drop casual little queries about the cases we saw and watch the lads squirm as I had so recently squirmed myself. I suppose that even in those early days I was forming a pattern for later life; unknown to myself I was falling into the way of asking a series of my own pet questions as all examiners are liable to do and many years later I overheard one youngster asking another: "Has he grilled you on the causes of fits in calves yet? Don't worry, he will." That made me feel suddenly old but there was compensation on another occasion when a newly qualified ex-student rushed up to me and offered to buy me all the beer I could drink. "You know what the examiner asked me in the final oral? The causes of fits in calves! By God I paralysed him—he had to beg me to stop talking."

And students were useful in other ways. They ran and got things out of the car boot, they pulled a rope at calvings, they were skilled assistants at operations, they were a repository for my worries and doubts; it isn't too much to say that during their brief visits they revolutionised my life.

So this Easter I waited on the platform of Darrowby station with pleasant anticipation. This lad had been recommended by one of the Ministry officials. "A really first class chap. Final year London—several times gold medallist. He's seen mixed and town practice and thought he ought to have a look at some of the real rural stuff. I said I'd give you a ring. His name is Richard Carmody."

Veterinary students came in a variety of shapes and sizes but there were a few features most of them had in common and I always had a mental picture of an eager-faced lad in tweed jacket and rumpled slacks carrying a rucksack. He would probably jump on to the platform as soon as the train drew up. But this time there was no immediate sign of life and a porter had begun to load a stack of egg boxes into the guard's van before one of the compartment doors opened and a tall figure descended leisurely.

I was doubtful about his identity but he seemed to place me on sight. He walked over, held out a hand and surveyed me with a level gaze.

"Mr. Herriot?"

"Yes ... er ... yes. That's right."

"My name is Carmody."

"Ah yes, good. How are you?" We shook hands and I took in the fine check suit and tweedy hat, the shining brogues and pigskin case. This was a very superior student, in fact a highly impressive young man. About a couple of years younger than myself but with a mature air in the set of his broad shoulders and the assurance on his strong, high-coloured face.

I led him across the bridge out onto the station yard. He didn't actually raise his eyebrows when he saw my car but he shot a cold glance at the mud-spattered vehicle, at the cracked windscreen and smooth tyres; and when I opened the door for him I thought for a moment he was going to wipe the seat before sitting down.

At the surgery I showed him round. I was only the assistant but I was proud of our modest set-up and most people were impressed by their first sight of it. But Carmody said "Hm," in the little operating room, "Yes, I see," in the dispensary, and "Quite" at the instrument cupboard. In the stockroom he was more forthcoming. He reached out and touched a packet of our beloved Adrevan worm medicine for horses.

"Still using this stuff, eh?" he said with a faint smile.

He didn't go into any ecstasies but he did show signs of approval when I took him out through the french windows into the long, high-walled garden where the daffodils glowed among the unkempt tangle and the wisteria climbed high over the old bricks of the tall Georgian house. In the cobbled yard at the foot of the garden he looked up at the rooks making their din high in the overhanging elms and he gazed for a few moments through the trees to where you could see the bare ribs of the fells still showing the last white runnels of winter.

"Charming," he murmured. "Charming."

I was glad enough to see him to his lodgings that evening. I felt I needed time to readjust my thinking.

When we started out next morning I saw he had discarded his check suit but was still very smart in a hacking jacket and flannels.

"Haven't you any protective clothing?" I asked.

"I've got these." He indicated a spotless pair of wellingtons in the back of the car.

"Yes, but I mean an oilskin or a coat of some kind. Some of our jobs are pretty dirty."

He smiled indulgently. "Oh, I'm sure I'll be all right. I've been round the farms before, you know."

I shrugged my shoulders and left it at that.

Our first visit was to a lame calf. The little animal was limping round its pen, holding up a fore leg and looking very woebegone. The knee was visibly swollen and as I palpated it there seemed to be a lumpiness in the fluid within as if there might be a floccules of pus among it. The temperature was a hundred and four.

I looked up at the farmer. "This is joint ill. He probably got an infection through his navel soon after birth and it's settled in his knee. We'll have to take care of him because his internal organs such as the liver and lungs can be affected. I'll give him an injection and leave you some tablets for him."

I went out to the car and when I came back Carmody was bending over the calf, feeling at the distended knee and inspecting the navel closely. I gave my injection and we left.

"You know," Carmody said as we drove out of the yard, "that wasn't joint ill."

"Really?" I was a bit taken aback. I didn't mind students discussing the pros and cons of my diagnosis as long as they didn't do it in front of the farmer, but I had never had one tell me bluntly that I was wrong. I made a mental note to try to keep this fellow away from Siegfried; one remark like that and Siegfried would hurl him unhesitatingly out of the car, big as he was.

"How do you make that out, then?" I asked him.

"Well there was only the one joint involved and

the navel was perfectly dry. No pain or swelling there. I should say he just sprained that knee."

"You may be right, but wouldn't you say the temperature was a bit high for a sprain?"

Carmody grunted and shook his head slightly. Apparently he had no doubts.

A few gates cropped up in the course of our next batch of calls and Carmody got out and opened them just like any ordinary being except that he did it with a certain leisurely elegance. Watching his tall figure as he paced across, his head held high, the smart hat set at just the right angle, I had to admit again that he had enormous presence. It was remarkable at his age.

Shortly before lunch I saw a cow that the farmer had said on the phone might have T.B. "She's gone down t'nick ever since she calved, guvnor. I doubt she's a screw, but you'd better have a look at her, anyroad."

As soon as I walked into the byre I knew what the trouble was. I have been blessed with an unusually sensitive nose and the sickly sweet smell of ketone hit me right away. It has always afforded me a childish pleasure to be able to say suddenly in the middle of a tuberculin test "There's a cow in here about three weeks calved that isn't doing very well," and watch the farmer scratch his head and ask me how I knew.

I had another little triumph today. "Started going off her cake first didn't she?" and the farmer nodded assent. "And the flesh has just melted off her since then?"

"That's right," the farmer said, "I've never seen a cow go down as quick."

"Well you can stop worrying, Mr. Smith. She hasn't got T.B., she's got slow fever and we'll be able to put her right for you."

Slow fever is the local term for acetonaemia and the farmer smiled in relief. "Damn. I'm glad! I thowt she was dog meat. I nearly rang Mallock this morning."

I couldn't reach for the steroids which we use to-day, but I injected six ounces of glucose and 100 units of insulin intravenously—it was one of my pet remedies and might make modern vets laugh. But it used to work. The cow, dead-eyed and gaunt, was too weak to struggle as the farmer held her nose.

When I had finished I ran my hand over the jutting bones, covered, it seemed, only by skin.

"She'll soon fatten up now," I said. "But cut her down to once a day milking—that's half the battle. And if that doesn't work, stop milking her entirely for two or three days."

"Yes, I reckon she's putting it in t'bucket instead of on her back."

"That's it exactly, Mr. Smith."

Carmody didn't seem to appreciate this interchange of home-spun wisdom and fidgetted impatiently. I took my cue and headed for the car.

"I'll see her in a couple of days," I cried as we drove away, and waved to Mrs. Smith who was look-ing out from the farmhouse doorway. Carmody how-ever raised his hat gravely and held it a few inches above his head till we had left the yard, which was definitely better. I had noticed him doing this at every place we had visited and it looked so good that I was playing with the idea of starting to wear a hat so that I could try it too.

I glanced sideways at my companion. Most of a morning's work done and I hadn't asked him any questions. I cleared my throat.

"By the way, talking about that cow we've just seen, can you tell me something about the causes of acetonaemia?"

Carmody regarded me impassively. "As a matter of fact I can't make up my mind which theory I en-dorse at the moment. Stevens maintains it is the in-complete oxidation of fatty acids, Sjollema leans to-wards liver intoxication and Janssen implicates one of the centres of the autonomic nervous system. My own view is that if we could only pin point the exact cause of the production of diacetic acid and betaoxybutyric acid in the metabolism we'd be well on the way to understanding the problem. Don't you agree?"

I closed my mouth which had begun to hang open.

"Oh yes, I do indeed . . . it's that oxy . . . that old beta-oxy . . . yes, that's what it is, without a doubt." I slumped lower in my seat and decided not to ask Carmody any more questions; and as the stone walls flipped past the windows I began to face up to the gradually filtering perception that this was a superior being next to me. It was depressing to ponder on the fact that not only was he big, good-looking, completely sure of himself but brilliant as well. Also, I thought bitterly, he had every appearance of being rich.

We rounded the corner of a lane and came up to a low huddle of stone buildings. It was the last call before lunch and the gate into the yard was closed.

"We might as well go through," I murmured. "Do you mind?"

The student heaved himself from the car, unlatched the gate and began to bring it round. And he did it as he seemed to do everything; coolly, unhurriedly, with natural grace. As he passed the front of the car I was studying him afresh, wondering again at his style, his massive composure, when, apparently from nowhere, an evil looking little black cur dog glided silently out, sank its teeth with dedicated venom into Carmody's left buttock and slunk away.

Not even the most monolithic dignity can survive being bitten deeply and without warning in the backside. Carmody screamed, leaped in the air clutching his rear, then swarmed to the top of the gate with the agility of a monkey. Squatting on the top spar, his natty hat tipped over one eye, he glared about him wildly.

"What the hell?" he yelled. "What the bloody hell?"

"It's all right," I said, hurrying towards him and resisting the impulse to throw myself on the ground and roll about. "It was just a dog."

"Dog? What dog? Where?" Carmody's cries took on a frantic note.

"It's gone—disappeared. I only saw it for a couple of seconds." And indeed, as I looked around it was difficult to believe that that flitting little black shadow had ever existed.

Carmody took a bit of coaxing down from the top of the gate and when he finally did reach ground level he limped over and sat down in the car instead of seeing the case. And when I saw the tattered cloth on his bottom I couldn't blame him for not risking a further attack. If it had been anybody else I'd have told him to drop his pants so that I could slap on some iodine but in this instance I somehow couldn't bring myself to do it. I left him sitting there.

29

When Carmody turned up for the afternoon round he had completely recovered his poise. He had changed his flannels and adopted a somewhat lopsided sitting position in the car but apart from that the dog episode might never have happened. In fact we had hardly got under way when he addressed me with a touch of arrogance.

"Look, I'm not going to learn much just watching you do things. Do you think I could carry out injections and the like? I want actual experience with the animals themselves."

I didn't answer for a moment but stared ahead through the maze of fine cracks on the windscreen. I couldn't very well tell him that I was still trying to establish myself with the farmers and that some of them had definite reservations about my capabilities. Then I turned to him.

"O.K. I'll have to do the diagnosing but whenever possible you can carry on from there."

He soon had his first taste of action. I decided that a litter of ten week old pigs might benefit from an injection of E coli antiserum and handed him the bottle and syringe. And as he moved purposefully among the little animals I thought with gloomy satisfaction that though I may not be au fait with all the small print in the text books I did know better than to chase pigs into the dirty end of the pen to catch them. Because with Carmody in close pursuit the squealing creatures leaped from their straw bed and charged in a body towards a stagnant lake of urine against the far wall. And as the student

grabbed at their hind legs the pigs scrabbled among
the filth, kicking it back over him in a steady shower.
He did finally get them all injected but at the end
his smart outfit was liberally spattered and I had to
open the windows wide to tolerate his presence in
the car.

The next visit was to a big arable farm in the low
country, and it was one of the few places where they
had hung on to their horses; the long stable had several stalls in use and the names of the horses on the
wall above; Boxer, Captain, Bobby, Tommy, and the
mares Bonny and Daisy. It was Tommy the old cart
horse we had to see and his trouble was a "stoppage."

Tommy was an old friend of mine; he kept having
mild bouts of colic with constipation and I often wondered if he had a faecolith lurking about in his bow-
els somewhere. Anyway, six drachms of Istin in a pint
of water invariably restored him to normal health
and I began automatically to shake up the yellow
powder in a drenching bottle. Meanwhile the farmer
and his man turned the horse round in his stall, ran
a rope under his nose band, threw it over a beam in
the stable roof and pulled the head upwards.

I handed the bottle to Carmody and stepped back.
The student looked up and hesitated. Tommy was a
big horse and the head, pulled high, was far beyond reach; but the farm man pushed a ramshackle kitchen chair wordlessly forward and Carmody
mounted it and stood swaying precariously.

I watched with interest. Horses are awkward
things to drench at any time and Tommy didn't like
Istin, even though it was good for him. On my last
visit I had noticed that he was becoming very clever
at holding the bitter mixture at the back of his throat
instead of swallowing it. I had managed to foil him
by tapping him under the chin just as he was toying
with the idea of coughing it out and he had gulped
it down with an offended look. But it was more and
more becoming a battle of wits.

Carmody never really had a chance. He started
off well enough by grasping the horse's tongue and

thrusting the bottle past the teeth, but Tommy out-witted him effortlessly by inclining his head and al-lowing the liquid to flow from the far side of his mouth.

"It's coming out t'other side, young man!" the farmer cried with some asperity.

The student gasped and tried to direct the flow down the throat but Tommy had summed him up immediately as an amateur and was now in complete command of the situation. By judicious rolling of the tongue and a series of little coughs and snorts he kept ridding himself of most of the medicine and I felt a pang of pity at the sight of Carmody weaving about on the creaking chair as the yellow fluid cas-caded over his clothes.

At the end, the farmer squinted into the empty bottle.

"Well I reckon t'oss got SOME of it," he muttered sourly.

Carmody eyed him impassively for a moment, shook a few ounces of Istin solution from somewhere up his sleeve and strode out of the stable.

At the next farm I was surprised to detect a vein of sadism in my makeup. The owner, a breeder of pedigree Large White pigs, was exporting a sow abroad and it had to be subjected to various tests including a blood sample for Brucellosis. Extracting a few c.c.'s of blood from the ear vein of a struggling pig is a job which makes most vets shudder and it was clearly a dirty trick to ask a student to do it, but the memory of his coldly confident request at the beginning of the afternoon seemed to have stilled my conscience. I handed him the syringe with scarcely a qualm.

The pigman slipped a noose into the sow's mouth and drew it tight over the snout and behind the canine teeth. This common method of restraint isn't at all painful but the sow was one of those who didn't like any form of mucking about. She was a huge animal and as soon as she felt the rope she opened her mouth wide in a long-drawn, resentful scream.

The volume of sound was incredible and she kept it up effortlessly without any apparent need to draw breath. Conversation from then on was out of the question and I watched in the appalling din as Carmody put an elastic tourniquet at the base of the sow's ear, swabbed the surface with spirit and then poked with his needle at the small blood vessel. Nothing happened. He tried again but the syringe remained obstinately empty. He had a few more attempts then, as I felt the top of my head was going to come loose, I wandered from the pen into the peace of the yard.

I took a leisurely stroll round the outside of the piggery, pausing for a minute or two to look at the view at the far end where the noise was comparatively faint. When I returned to the pen the screaming hit me again like a pneumatic drill and Carmody, sweating and slightly pop-eyed, looked up from the ear where he was still jabbing fruitlessly. It seemed to me that everybody had had enough. Using sign language I indicated to the student that I'd like to have a go and by a happy chance my first effort brought a dark welling of blood into the syringe. I waved to the pigman to remove the rope and the moment he did so the big sow switched off the noise magically and began to nose, quite unperturbed, among the straw.

"Nothing very exciting at the next place." I kept the triumph out of my voice as we drove away. "Just a bullock with a tumour on his jaw. But it's an interesting herd—all Galloways, and this group we're going to see have been wintered outside. They're the toughest animals in the district."

Carmody nodded. Nothing I said seemed to rouse much enthusiasm in him. For myself this herd of untamed black cattle always held a certain fascination; contacts with them were always coloured by a degree of uncertainty—sometimes you could catch them to examine them, sometimes you couldn't.

As we approached the farm I could see a bunch of about thirty bullocks streaming down the scrubby hillside on our right. The farm men were driving them down through the scattered gorse bushes and the sparse groups of trees to where the stone walls met in a rough V at the front.

One of them waved to me. "We're going to try to get a rope on 'im down in the corner while he's among his mates. He's a wick bugger—you'd never get near him in t'field."

After a lot of shouting and waving and running about the bullocks were finally cornered and they stood in a tight, uneasy pack, their shaggy black polls bobbing among the steam rising from their bodies.

"There he is! You can see the thing on his face." A man pointed to a big beast about the middle of the bunch and began to push his way towards him. My admiration for the Yorkshire farm worker rose another notch as I watched him squeezing between the plunging, kicking animals. "When I get the rope on his head you'll all have to get on t'other end—one man'll never hold 'im." He gasped as he fought his way forward.

He was obviously an expert because as soon as he got within reach he dropped the halter on to the bullock's head with practised skill. "Right!" he shouted. "Give me a hand with him. We have 'im now."

But as he spoke the beast gave a great bellow and began to charge from the pack. The man cried out despairingly and disappeared among the hairy bodies. The rope whipped free out of reach of everybody. Except Carmody. As the bullock shot past him he grabbed the trailing rope with a reflex action and hung on.

I watched, fascinated, as man and beast careered across the field. They were travelling away from me towards the far slope, the animal head down, legs pistoning, going like a racehorse, the student also at full speed but very upright, both hands on the rope in front of him, a picture of resolution.

The men and I were helpless spectators and we stood in a silent group as the beast turned left suddenly and disappeared behind a clump of low trees.

It was gone for only a few moments but it seemed a long time and when it reappeared it was going faster than ever, hurtling over the turf like a black thunderbolt. Carmody, incredibly, was still there on the end of the rope and still very upright but his strides had increased to an impossible length till he seemed to be touching the ground only every twenty feet or so.

I marvelled at his tenacity but obviously the end was near. He took a last few soaring, swooping steps then he was down on his face. But he didn't let go. The bullock, going better than ever, had turned towards us now, dragging the inert form apparently without effort, and I winced as I saw it was headed straight for a long row of cow pats.

It was when Carmody was skidding face down through the third heap of muck that I suddenly began to like him. And when he finally did have to release his hold and lay for a moment motionless on the grass I hurried over to help him up. He thanked me briefly then looked calmly across the field at a sight which is familiar to every veterinary surgeon—his patient thundering out of sight across the far horizon.

The student was almost unrecognisable. His clothes and face were plastered with filth except where the saffron streaks of the Istin showed up like war paint, he smelt abominably, he had been bitten in the backside, nothing had really gone right for him all day yet he was curiously undefeated. I smiled to myself. It was no good judging this bloke by ordinary standards; I could recognise the seeds of greatness when I saw them.

Carmody stayed with us for two weeks and after that first day I got on with him not so badly. Of course it wasn't the same relationship as with other students; there was always a barrier of reserve. He spent a lot of time squinting down the practice microscope at blood films, skin scrapings, milk smears, and by the end of each day he had collected a fresh supply of samples from the cases he had seen. He would come and drink a polite beer with me after an evening call but there was none of the giggling over the day's events as with the other young lads. I had the feeling always that he would rather have been writing up his case book and working out his findings.

But I didn't mind. I found an interest in being in contact with a truly scientific mind. He was as far removed as he could be from the traditional studious swot—his was a cold, superior intellect and there was something rewarding in watching him at work.

I didn't see Carmody again for over twenty years. I picked out his name in the Record when he qualified with top marks then he disappeared into the great world of research for a while to emerge with a Ph.D. and over the years he added a string of further degrees and qualifications. Every now and then an unintelligible article would appear in the professional journals under his name and it became commonplace when reading scientific papers to see references to what Dr. Carmody had said on the subject.

When I finally did see him he was the guest of honour at a professional banquet, an international celebrity heavy with honours. From where I was sitting at the far end of one of the side tables I listened to his masterly speech with a feeling of inevitability; the wide grasp of his subject, the brilliant exposition —I had seen it all coming those many years ago.

Afterwards when we had left the tables he moved among us and I gazed with something like awe at the majestic figure approaching. Carmody had always been big, but with the tail coat tight across the massive shoulders and the vast expanse of gleaming shirt front stretched over the curving abdomen he was almost overpowering. As he passed he stopped and looked at me.

"It's Herriot, isn't it?" the handsome, high-coloured face still had that look of calm power.

"Yes, it is. It's good to see you again."

We shook hands. "And how is the practice at Darrowby?"

"Oh, as usual," I replied. "Bit too busy at times. We could do with some help if ever you felt like it."

Carmody nodded gravely. "I'd like that very much. It would be good for me."

He was about to move on when he paused. "Perhaps you'd let me know any time you want a pig bled." For a moment we looked into each other's eyes and I saw a small flame flicker briefly in the frosty blue. Then he was gone.

As I looked at the retreating back a hand gripped my arm. It was Brian Miller, a happily obscure practitioner like myself.

"Come on, Jim, I'll buy you a drink," he said.

We went into the bar and ordered two beers.

"That Carmody!" Brian said. "The man's got a tremendous brain, but by God he's a cold fish."

I sipped at the beer and looked thoughtfully into my glass for a few seconds.

"Oh I don't know," I said. "He certainly gives that impression, but Carmody's all right."

30

No vet likes to have his job made more difficult and as I worked inside the ewe I fought a rising tide of irritation.

"You know, Mr. Kitson," I said testily, "you should have got me out sooner. How long have you been trying to lamb this ewe?"

The big man grunted and shrugged his shoulders. "Oh for a bit—not ower long."

"Half an hour—an hour?"

"Nay, nay, nobbut a few minutes." Mr. Kitson regarded me gloomily along his pointed nose. It was his habitual expression, in fact I had never seen him smile and the idea of a laugh ever disturbing those pendulous cheeks was unthinkable.

I gritted my teeth and decided to say no more about it, but I knew it had taken more than a few minutes to cause the swelling of the vaginal wall, this sandpaper dryness of the little creatures inside. And it was a simple enough presentation—biggish twins, one anterior the other posterior, but of course as often happens the hind legs of one were laid alongside the head of the other giving the illusion that they belonged to the same lamb. I'd like to bet that Mr. Kitson had been guddling for ages inside here with his big rough hands in a dogged attempt to bring that head and those legs out together.

If I had been there at the start it would have been the work of a few moments but instead here I was without an inch of space, trying to push things around with one finger instead of my full hand and getting nowhere.

Fortunately the present day farmer doesn't often play this trick on us. The usual thing I hear at a lambing is "Nay, I just had a quick feel and I knew it wasn't a job for me," or something I heard from a farmer the other day, "Two men at one ewe's no good," and I think that says it very well.

But Mr. Kitson was of the old school. He didn't believe in getting the vet out until every other avenue had been explored and when he did finally have to fall back on our services he was usually dissatisfied with the result.

"This is no good," I said, withdrawing my hand and swilling it quickly in the bucket. "I'll have to do something about this dryness."

I walked the length of the old stable which had been converted into temporary lambing pens and lifted a tube of lubricating cream from the car boot. Coming in again I heard a faint sound from my left. The stable was dimly lit and an ancient door had been placed across the darkest corner to make a small enclosure. I looked inside and in the gloom could just discern a ewe lying on her chest, head outstretched. Her ribs rose and fell with the typical quick distressed respirations of a sheep in pain. Occasionally she moaned softly.

"What's the trouble here?" I asked.

Mr. Kitson regarded me impassively from the other end of the building. "She 'ad a roughish time lambin' yesterday."

"How do you mean, roughish?"

"Well . . . a big single lamb wi' a leg back and I couldn't fetch it round."

"So you just pulled it out as it was . . . with the leg back?"

"Aye, nowt else ah could do."

I leaned over the door and lifted the ewe's tail, filthy with faeces and discharge. I winced as I saw the tumefied, discoloured vulva and perineum.

"She could do with a bit of attention, Mr. Kitson."

The farmer looked startled. "Nay, nay, I don't want

none o' that. It's ower with her—there's nowt you can do."

"You mean she's dying?"

"That's right."

I put my hand on the sheep's head, feeling the coldness of the ears and lips. He could be right.

"Well have you rung Mallock to come and pick her up? She really should be put out of her pain as soon as possible."

"Aye . . . ah'll do that." Mr. Kitson shuffled his feet and looked away.

I knew what the situation was. He was going to let the ewe "take her chance." The lambing season was always a rewarding and fulfilling time for me but this was the other side of the coin. It was a hectic time in the farming year, a sudden onslaught of extra work on top of the routine jobs and in some ways it overwhelmed the resources of farmers and vets alike. The flood of new life left a pathetic debris behind it; a flotsam and jetsam of broken creatures; ewes too old to stand a further pregnancy, some debilitated by diseases like liver fluke and toxaemia, others with infected arthritic joints and others who had just had a "roughish time." You were inclined to find them lying half forgotten in dark corners like the one in this stable. They had been left there to "take their chance."

I returned in silence to my original patient. My lubricating cream made a great difference and I was able to use more than one finger to explore. I had to make up my mind whether to repel the posterior or anterior presentation and since the head was well into the vagina I decided to bring out the anterior first.

With the farmer's help I raised the ewe's hindquarters till they were resting on a straw bale. I could work downhill now and gently pushed the two hind limbs away into the depths of the uterus. In the space which this left I was able to hook a finger round the fore limbs which were laid back along the ribs of the anterior lamb and bring them into the passage. I only needed another application of the cream and a few moments' careful traction and the lamb was delivered.

But it was all too late. The tiny creature was quite dead and the knell of disappointment sounded in me as it always did at the sight of the perfectly formed body which lacked only the spark of life.

Hurriedly I greased my arm again and felt inside for the repelled lamb. There was plenty of room now and I was able to loop my hand round the hocks and draw the lamb out without effort. This time I had little hope of life and my efforts were solely to relieve the ewe's discomfort but as the lamb came into the cold outside air I felt the convulsive jerk and wriggle of the woolly little form in my hands which told me all was well.

It was funny how often this happened; you got a dead lamb—sometimes even a decomposed one—with a live one lurking behind it. Anyway it was a bonus and with a surge of pleasure I wiped the mucus from its mouth and pushed it forward for its mother to lick. A further exploration of the uterus revealed nothing more and I got to my feet.

"Well she's come to no harm, and I think she'll be all right now," I said. "And could I have some fresh water, Mr. Kitson, please?"

The big man wordlessly emptied the bucket on to the stable floor and went off towards the house. In the silence I could faintly hear the panting of the ewe in the far corner. I tried not to think of what lay in front of her. Soon I would drive off and see other cases, then I would have lunch and start my afternoon round while hidden in this cheerful place a helpless animal was gasping her life away. How long would it take her to die? A day? Two days?

It was no good. I had to do something about it. I ran out to my car, grabbed the bottle of nembutal and my big fifty c.c. syringe and hurried back into the stable. I vaulted over the rotting timbers of the door, drew out forty c.c.'s from the bottle and plunged the whole dose into the sheep's peritoneal cavity. Then I leaped back, galloped the length of the stable and when Mr. Kitson returned I was standing innocently where he had left me.

I towelled myself, put on my jacket and gathered up my bottle of antiseptic and the tube of cream which had served me so well.

Mr. Kitson preceded me along the stable and on the way out he glanced over the door in the corner.

"By gaw, she's goin' fast," he grunted.

I looked over his shoulder into the gloom. The panting had stopped and was replaced by slow, even respirations. The eyes were closed. The sheep was anaesthetised. She would die in peace.

"Yes," I said. "She's definitely sinking. I don't think it will be very long now." I couldn't resist a parting shaft. "You've lost this ewe and that lamb back there. I think I could have saved both of them for you if you'd given me a chance."

Maybe my words got through to Mr. Kitson, because I was surprised to be called back to the farm a few days later to a ewe which had obviously suffered very little interference.

The animal was in a field close to the house and she was clearly bursting with lambs; so round and fat she could hardly waddle. But she looked bright and healthy.

"There's a bloody mix-up in there," Mr. Kitson said morosely. "Ah could feel two heads and God only knows how many feet. Didn't know where the 'ell I was."

"But you didn't try very hard?"

"Nay, never tried at all."

Well, we were making progress. As the farmer gripped the sheep round the neck I knelt behind her and dipped my hands in the bucket. For once it was a warm morning. Looking back, my memories of lambing times have been of bitter winds searing the grass of the hill pastures, of chapped hands, chafed arms, gloves, scarves and cold-nipped ears. For years after

I left Glasgow I kept waiting for the balmy early springs of western Scotland. After thirty years I am still waiting and it has begun to dawn on me that it doesn't happen that way in Yorkshire.

But this morning was one of the exceptions. The sun blazed from a sky of soft blue, there was no wind but a gentle movement of the air rolled the fragrance of the moorland flowers and warm grass over and around me as I knelt there.

And I had my favourite job in front of me. I almost chuckled as I fished around inside the ewe. There was all the room in the world, everything was moist and fresh and unspoiled, and it was child's play to fit the various jigsaws together. In about thirty seconds I had a lamb wriggling on the grass; in a few moments more a second, then a third and finally to my delight I reached away forward and found another little cloven foot and whisked it out into the world.

"Quadruplets!" I cried happily, but the farmer didn't share my enthusiasm.

"Nowt but a bloody nuisance," he muttered. "She'd be far better wi' just two." He paused and gave me a sour look. "Any road, ah reckon there wasn't no need to call ye. I could've done that job meself."

I looked at him sadly from my squatting position. Sometimes in our job you feel you just can't win. If you take too long you're no good, if you're too quick the visit wasn't necessary. I have never quite subscribed to the views of a cynical old colleague who once adjured me: "Never make a lambing look easy. Hold the buggers in for a few minutes if necessary," but at times I felt he had a point.

Anyway, I had my own satisfaction in watching the four lambs. So often I had pitied these tiny creatures in their entry into an uncharitable world, sometimes even of snow and ice, but today it was a joy to see them trying to struggle to their feet under the friendly sun, their woolly coats already drying rapidly. Their mother, magically deflated, was moving among them in a bemused manner as though she couldn't quite believe what she saw. As she nosed and licked

them her deep-throated chuckles were answered by
the first treble quaverings of her family. I was listening, enchanted, to this conversation when Mr. Kitson
spoke up.

"There's t'ewe you lambed t'other day."

I looked up and there indeed she was, trotting
proudly past, her lamb close at her flank.

"Ah yes, she looks fine," I said. That was good to see
but my attention was caught by something else. I
pointed across the grass.

"That ewe away over there . . ." As a rule all sheep
look alike to me but there was something about this
one I recognised . . . a loss of wool from her back, a
bare strip of skin stretched over the jutting ridge of
her spinal column . . . surely I couldn't be mistaken.

The farmer followed my pointing finger. "Aye,
that's t'awd lass that was laid in the stable last time
you were here." He turned an expressionless gaze on
me. "The one you told me to get Mallock to fetch."

"But . . . but . . . she was dying!" I blurted out.

The corner of Mr. Kitson's mouth twitched upwards in what must have been the nearest possible
approach to a smile. "Well that's what you tellt me,
young feller." He hunched his shoulders. "Said she
'adn't long to go, didn't you?"

I had no words to offer. I just gaped at him. I must
have been the picture of bewilderment and it
seemed the farmer was puzzled too because he went
on.

"But I'll tell tha summat. Ah've been among sheep
all me life but ah've never seen owt like it. That ewe
just went to sleep."

"Is that so?"

"Aye, went to sleep, ah tell you and she stayed
sleepin' for two days!"

"She slept for two days?"

"She did, ah'm not jokin', nor jestin'. Ah kept goin'
into t'stable but she never altered. Lay there peaceful as you like all t'first day, then all t'second, then
when I went in on t'third morning she was standin'
there lookin' at me and ready for some grub."

"Amazing!" I got to my feet. "I must have a look at her."

I really wanted to see what had become of that mass of inflammation and tumefaction under her tail and I approached her carefully, jockeying her bit by bit into the bottom corner of the field. There we faced each other for a few tense moments as I tried a few feints and she responded with nimble side-steps; then as I made my final swoop to catch her fleece she eluded me effortlessly and shot past me with a thundering of hooves. I gave chase for twenty yards but it was too hot and wellingtons aren't the ideal gear for running. In any case I have long held the notion that if a vet can't catch his patient there's nothing much to worry about.

And as I walked back up the field a message was tapping in my brain. I had discovered something, discovered something by accident. That ewe's life had been saved not by medicinal therapy but simply by stopping her pain and allowing nature to do its own job of healing. It was a lesson I have never forgotten; that animals confronted with severe continuous pain and the terror and shock that goes with it will often retreat even into death, and if you can remove that pain amazing things can happen. It is difficult to explain rationally but I know that it is so.

By the time I had got back to Mr. Kitson the sun was scorching the back of my neck and I could feel a trickle of sweat under my shirt. The big man was still watching the ewe which had finished its gallop and was cropping the grass contentedly.

"Ah can't get over it," he murmured, scratching the thin bristle on his jaw. "Two whole days and never a move." He turned to me and his eyes widened.

"Ah'll tell tha, young man, you'd just think she'd been drugged!"

31

I found it difficult to get Mr. Kitson's ewe out of my mind but I had to make the effort because while all the sheep work was going on the rest of the practice problems rolled along unabated. One of these concerned the Flaxtons' Poodle, Penny.

Penny's first visit to the surgery was made notable by the attractiveness of her mistress. When I stuck my head round the waiting room door and said "Next please," Mrs. Flaxton's little round face with its shining tight cap of blue-black hair seemed to illumine the place like a beacon. It is possible that the effect was heightened by the fact that she was sitting between fifteen stone Mrs. Barmby who had brought her canary to have its claws clipped and old Mr. Spence who was nearly ninety and had called round for some flea powder for his cat but there was no doubt she was good to look at.

And it wasn't just that she was pretty; there was a round-eyed, innocent appeal about her and she smiled all the time. Penny, sitting on her knee, seemed to be smiling from under the mound of brown curls on her forehead.

In the consulting room I lifted the little dog on to the table. "Well now, what's the trouble?"

"She has a touch of sickness and diarrhoea," Mrs. Flaxton replied. "It started yesterday."

"I see." I turned and lifted the thermometer from the trolley. "Has she had a change of food?"

"No, nothing like that."

"Is she inclined to eat rubbish when she's out?"

Mrs. Flaxton shook her head. "No, not as a rule.

But I suppose even the nicest dog will have a nibble at a dead bird or something horrid like that now and then." She laughed and Penny laughed back at her.

"Well she has a slightly raised temperature but she seems bright enough." I put my hand round the dog's middle. "Let's have a feel at your tummy, Penny."

The little animal winced as I gently palpated the abdomen, and there was a tenderness throughout the stomach and intestines.

"She has gastroenteritis," I said. "But it seems fairly mild and I think it should clear up quite soon. I'll give you some medicine for her and you'd better keep her on a light diet for a few days."

"Yes, I'll do that. Thank you very much." Mrs. Flaxton's smile deepened as she patted her dog's head. She was about twenty three and she and her young husband had only recently come to Darrowby. He was a representative of one of the big agricultural firms which supplied meal and cattle cake to the farms and I saw him occasionally on my rounds. Like his wife, and indeed his dog, he gave off an ambience of eager friendliness.

I sent Mrs. Flaxton off with a bottle of bismuth, kaolin and chlorodyne mixture which was one of our cherished treatments. The little dog trotted down the surgery steps, tail wagging, and I really didn't expect any more trouble.

Three days later, however, Penny was in the surgery again. She was still vomiting and the diarrhoea had not taken up in the least.

I got the dog on the table again and carried out a further examination but there was nothing significant to see. She had now had five days of this weakening condition but though she had lost a bit of her perkiness she still looked remarkably bright. The Toy Poodle is small but tough and very game and this one wasn't going to let anything get her down easily.

But I still didn't like it. She couldn't go on like this. I decided to alter the treatment to a mixture of carbon and astringents which had served me well in the past.

"This stuff looks a bit messy," I said as I gave Mrs. Flaxton a powder box full of the black granules. "But I have had good results with it. She's still eating, isn't she, so I should mix it in her food."

"Oh thank you." She gave me one of her marvellous smiles as she put the box in her bag and I walked along the passage with her to the door. She had left her pram at the foot of the steps and I knew before I looked under the hood what kind of baby I would find. Sure enough the chubby face on the pillow gazed at me with round friendly eyes and then split into a delighted grin.

They were the kind of people I liked to see but as they moved off down the street I hoped for Penny's sake that I wouldn't be seeing them for a long time. However, it was not to be. A couple of days later they were back and this time the Poodle was showing signs of strain. As I examined her she stood motionless and dead-eyed with only the occasional twitch of her tail as I stroked her head and spoke to her.

"I'm afraid she's just the same, Mr. Herriot," her mistress said. "She's not eating much now and whatever she does goes straight through her. And she has a terrific thirst—always at her water bowl and then she brings it back."

I nodded. "I know. This inflammation inside her gives her a raging desire for water and of course the more she drinks the more she vomits. And this is terribly weakening."

Again I changed the treatment. In fact over the next few days I ran through just about the entire range of available drugs. I look back with a wry smile at the things I gave that little dog; powdered epicacuanha and opium, sodium salicylate and tincture of camphor, even way-out exotics like decoction of haematoxylin and infusion of caryophyllum which thank heavens have been long forgotten. I might have done a bit of good if I had had access to a gut-active antibiotic like neomycin but as it was I got nowhere.

I was visiting Penny daily as she was unfit to bring

to the surgery. I had her on a diet of arrowroot and boiled milk but that, like my medicinal treatment, achieved nothing. And all the time the little dog was slipping away.

The climax came about three o'clock one morning. As I lifted the bedside phone Mr. Flaxton's voice, with a tremor in it, came over the line.

"I'm terribly sorry to get you out of your bed at this hour, Mr. Herriot, but I wish you'd come round to see Penny."

"Why, is she worse?"

"Yes, and she's . . . well . . . she's suffering now, I'm afraid. You saw her this afternoon didn't you? Well since then she's been drinking and vomiting and this diarrhoea running away from her all the time till she's about at the far end. She's just lying in her basket crying. I'm sure she's in great pain."

"Right, I'll be there in a few minutes."

"Oh thank you." He paused for a moment. "And Mr. Herriot . . . you'll come prepared to put her down won't you?"

My spirits, never very high at that time in the morning, plummeted to the depths. "As bad as that, is it?"

"Well honestly we can't bear to see her. My wife is so upset . . . I don't think she can stand any more."

"I see." I hung up the phone and threw the bed-clothes back with a violence which brought Helen wide awake. Being disturbed in the small hours was one of the crosses a vet's wife had to bear, but normally I crept out as quietly as I could. This time, however, I stamped about the bedroom, dragging on my clothes and muttering to myself; and though she must have wondered what this latest crisis meant she wisely watched me in silence until I turned out the light and left.

I had not far to go. The Flaxtons lived in one of the new bungalows on the Brawton Road less than a mile away. The young couple, in their dressing gowns, let me into the kitchen and before I reached the dog basket in the corner I could hear Penny's whimperings. She was not lying comfortably curled up, but on her chest, head forward obviously acutely distressed. I put my hands under her and lifted her and she was almost weightless. A Toy Poodle in its prime is fairly insubstantial but after her long illness Penny was like a bedraggled little piece of thistle-down, her curly brown coat wet and soiled by vomit and diarrhoea.

Mrs. Flaxton's smile for once was absent. I could see she was keeping back the tears as she spoke.

"It really would be the kindest thing . . ."

"Yes . . . yes . . ." I replaced the tiny animal in her basket and crouched over her, chin in hand. "Yes, I suppose you're right."

But still I didn't move but stayed, squatting there, staring down in disbelief at the evidence of my failure. This dog was only two years old—a lifetime of running and jumping and barking in front of her; all she was suffering from was gastroenteritis and now I was going to extinguish the final spark in her. It was a bitter thought that this would be just about the only positive thing I had done right from the start.

A weariness swept over me that was not just due to the fact that I had been snatched from sleep. I got to my feet with the slow stiff movements of an old man and was about to turn away when I noticed something about the little animal. She was on her chest again, head extended, mouth open, tongue lolling as she panted. There was something there I had seen before somewhere . . . that posture . . . and the exhaustion, pain and shock . . . it slid almost imperceptibly into my sleepy brain that she looked exactly like Mr. Kitson's ewe in its dark corner. A different species, yes, but all the other things were there.

"Mrs. Flaxton," I said, "I want to put Penny to sleep. Not the way you think, but to anaesthetise her. Maybe if she has a rest from this nonstop drinking and vomiting and straining it will give nature a chance."

The young couple looked at me doubtfully for a few moments then it was the husband who spoke.

"Don't you think she has been through enough, Mr. Herriot?"

"She has, yes she has." I ran a hand through my rumpled uncombed hair. "But this won't cause her any more distress. She won't know a thing about it."

When they still hesitated I went on. "I would very much like to try it—it's just an idea I've got."

They looked at each other, then Mrs. Flaxton nodded. "All right, go ahead, but this will be the last, won't it?"

Out into the night air to my car for the same bottle of nembutal and a very small dose for the little creature. I went back to my bed with the same feeling I had had about the ewe; come what may there would be no more suffering.

Next morning Penny was still stretched peacefully on her side and when, about four o'clock in the afternoon, she showed signs of awakening I repeated the injection.

Like the ewe she slept for forty eight hours and when she finally did stagger to her feet she did not head immediately for her water bowl as she had done for so many days. Instead she made her feeble way outside and had a walk round the garden.

From then on, recovery, as they say in the case histories, was uneventful. Or as I would rather write it, she wonderfully and miraculously just got better and never ailed another thing throughout her long life.

Helen and I used to play tennis on the grass courts near the Darrowby cricket ground. So did the Flaxtons and they always brought Penny along with them. I used to look through the wire at her romping with other dogs and later with the Flaxtons' fast growing young son and I marvelled.

I do not wish to give the impression that I advocate wholesale anaesthesia for all animal ailments but I do know that sedation has a definite place. Nowadays we have a sophisticated range of sedatives and

tranquillisers to choose from and when I come up
against an acute case of gastroenteritis in dogs I use
one of them as an adjunct to the normal treatment;
because it puts a brake on the deadly exhausting
cycle and blots out the pain and fear which go with
it.

And over the years, whenever I saw Penny running
around, barking, bright-eyed, full of the devil, I felt a
renewed welling of thankfulness for the cure which
I discovered in a dark corner of a stable by accident.

32

This was the real Yorkshire with the clean limestone wall riding the hill's edge and the path cutting brilliant green through the crowding heather. And, walking face on to the scented breeze I felt the old tingle of wonder at being alone on the wide moorland where nothing stirred and the spreading miles of purple blossom and green turf reached away till it met the hazy blue of the sky.

But I wasn't really alone. There was Sam, and he made all the difference. Helen had brought a lot of things into my life and Sam was one of the most precious; he was a Beagle and her own personal pet. He would be about two years old when I first saw him and I had no way of knowing that he was to be my faithful companion, my car dog, my friend who sat by my side through the lonely hours of driving till his life ended at the age of fourteen. He was the first of a series of cherished dogs whose comradeship have warmed and lightened my working life.

Sam adopted me on sight. It was as though he had read the Faithful Hound Manual because he was always near me; paws on the dash as he gazed eagerly through the windscreen on my rounds, head resting on my foot in our bed-sitting room, trotting just behind me wherever I moved. If I had a beer in a pub he would be under my chair and even when I was having a haircut you only had to lift the white sheet to see Sam crouching beneath my legs. The only place I didn't dare take him was the cinema and on these occasions he crawled under the bed and sulked.

Most dogs love car riding but to Sam it was a passion which never waned—even in the night hours; he would gladly leave his basket when the world was asleep, stretch a couple of times and follow me out into the cold. He would be on to the seat before I got the car door fully open and this action became so much a part of my life that for a long time after his death I still held the door open unthinkingly, waiting for him. And I still remember the pain I felt when he did not bound inside.

And having him with me added so much to the intermissions I granted myself on my daily rounds. Whereas in offices and factories they had tea breaks I just stopped the car and stepped out into the splendour which was always at hand and walked for a spell down hidden lanes, through woods, or as today, along one of the grassy tracks which ran over the high tops.

This thing which I had always done had a new meaning now. Anybody who has ever walked a dog knows the abiding satisfaction which comes from giving pleasure to a loved animal, and the sight of the little form trotting ahead of me lent a depth which had been missing before.

Round the curve of the path I came to where the tide of heather lapped thickly down the hillside on a little slope facing invitingly into the sun. It was a call I could never resist. I looked at my watch; oh I had a few minutes to spare and there was nothing urgent ahead, just Mr. Dacre's tuberculin test. In a moment I was stretched out on the springy stems, the most wonderful natural mattress in the world.

Lying there, eyes half closed against the sun's glare, the heavy heather fragrance around me, I could see the cloud shadows racing across the flanks of the fells, throwing the gulleys and crevices into momentary gloom but trailing a fresh flaring green in their wake.

Those were the days when I was most grateful I was in country practice; the shirt sleeve days when the bleak menace of the bald heights melted into friendliness, when I felt at one with all the airy life and growth about me and was glad that I had become what I never thought I would be, a doctor of farm animals.

My partner would be somewhere out there, thrashing round the practice and Tristan would probably be studying in Skeldale House. This latter was quite a thought because I had never seen Tristan open a text book until lately. He had been blessed with the kind of brain which made swotting irrelevant but he would take his finals this year and even he had to get down to it. I had little doubt he would soon be a qualified man and in a way it seemed a shame that his free spirit should be shackled by the realities of veterinary practice. It would be the end of a luminous chapter.

A long-eared head blotted out the sunshine as Sam came and sat on my chest. He looked at me questioningly. He didn't hold with this laziness but I knew if I didn't move after a few minutes he would curl up philosophically on my ribs and have a sleep until I was ready to go. But this time I answered the unspoken appeal by sitting up and he leaped around me in delight as I rose and began to make my way back to the car and Mr. Dacre's test.

"Move over, Bill!" Mr. Dacre cried some time later as he tweaked the big bull's tail.

Nearly every farmer kept a bull in those days and they were all called Billy or Bill. I suppose it was because this was a very mature animal that he received the adult version. Being a docile beast he responded to the touch on his tail by shuffling his great bulk to one side, leaving me enough space to push in between him and the wooden partition against which he was tied by a chain.

I was reading a tuberculin test and all I wanted to do was to measure the intradermal reaction. I had to open my calipers very wide to take in the thickness of the skin on the enormous neck.

"Thirty," I called out to the farmer.

He wrote the figure down on the testing book and laughed.

"By heck, he's got some pelt on 'im."

"Yes," I said, beginning to squeeze my way out. "But he's a big fellow, isn't he?"

Just how big he was was brought home to me immediately because the bull suddenly swung round, pinning me against the partition. Cows did this regularly and I moved them by bracing my back against whatever was behind me and pushing them away. But it was different with Bill.

Gasping, I pushed with all my strength against the rolls of fat which covered the vast roan-coloured flank, but I might as well have tried to shift a house.

The farmer dropped his book and seized the tail again but this time the bull showed no response. There was no malice in his behaviour—he was simply having a comfortable lean against the boards and I don't suppose he even noticed the morsel of puny humanity wriggling frantically against his rib-cage.

Still, whether he meant it or not, the end result was the same; I was having the life crushed out of me. Pop-eyed, groaning, scarcely able to breathe, I struggled with everything I had, but I couldn't move an inch. And just when I thought things couldn't get any worse, Bill started to rub himself up and down against the partition. So that was what he had come round for; he had an itch and he just wanted to scratch it.

The effect on me was catastrophic. I was certain my internal organs were being steadily ground to pulp and as I thrashed about in complete panic the huge animal leaned even more heavily.

I don't like to think what would have happened if the wood behind me had not been old and rotten, but just as I felt my senses leaving me there was a cracking and splintering and I fell through into the next stall. Lying there like a stranded fish on a bed of shattered timbers I looked up at Mr. Dacre, waiting till my lungs started to work again.

The farmer, having got over his first alarm, was

rubbing his upper lip vigorously in a polite attempt to stop himself laughing. His little girl who had watched the whole thing from her vantage point in one of the hay racks had no such inhibitions. Screaming with delight, she pointed at me.

"Ooo, Dad, Dad, look at that man! Did you see him, Dad, did you see him? Ooo what a funny man!" She went into helpless convulsions. She was only about five but I had a feeling she would remember my performance all her life.

At length I picked myself up and managed to brush the matter off lightly, but after I had driven a mile or so from the farm I stopped the car and looked myself over. My ribs ached pretty uniformly as though a light road roller had passed over them and there was a tender area on my left buttock where I had landed on my calipers but otherwise I seemed to have escaped damage. I removed a few spicules of wood from my trousers, got back into the car and consulted my list of visits.

And when I read my next call a gentle smile of relief spread over my face. "Mrs. Tompkin, 14, Jasmine Terrace. Clip budgie's beak."

Thank heaven for the infinite variety of veterinary practice. After that bull I needed something small and weak and harmless and really you can't ask for much better in that line than a budgie.

Number 14 was one of a row of small mean houses built of the cheap bricks so beloved of the jerry builders after the first world war. I armed myself with a pair of clippers and stepped on to the narrow strip of pavement which separated the door from the road. A pleasant looking red haired woman answered my knock.

"I'm Mrs. Dodds from next door," she said. "I keep an eye on t'old lady. She's over eighty and lives alone. I've just been out gettin' her pension for her."

She led me into the cramped little room. "Here y'are, love," she said to the old woman who sat in a corner. She put the pension book and money on the mantelpiece. "And here's Mr. Herriot come to see Peter for you."

Mrs. Tompkin nodded and smiled. "Oh that's good. Poor little feller can't hardly eat with 'is long beak and I'm worried about him. He's me only companion, you know."

"Yes, I understand, Mrs. Tompkin." I looked at the cage by the window with the green budgie perched inside. "These little birds can be wonderful company when they start chattering."

She laughed. "Aye, but it's a funny thing. Peter never has said owt much. I think he's lazy! But I just like havin' him with me."

"Of course you do," I said. "But he certainly needs attention now."

The beak was greatly overgrown, curving away down till it touched the feathers of the breast. I would be able to revolutionise his life with one quick snip from my clippers. The way I was feeling this job was right up my street.

I opened the cage door and slowly inserted my hand.

"Come on, Peter," I wheedled as the bird fluttered away from me. And I soon cornered him and enclosed him gently in my fingers. As I lifted him out I felt in my pocket with the other hand for the clippers, but as I poised them I stopped.

The tiny head was no longer poking cheekily from my fingers but had fallen loosely to one side. The eyes were closed. I stared at the bird uncomprehendingly for a moment then opened my hand. He lay quite motionless on my palm. He was dead.

Dry mouthed, I continued to stare; at the beautiful iridescence of the plumage, the long beak which I didn't have to cut now, but mostly at the head dropping down over my forefinger. I hadn't squeezed him or been rough with him in any way but he was dead. It must have been sheer fright.

Mrs. Dodds and I looked at each other in horror and I hardly dared turn my head towards Mrs.

Tompkin. When I did, I was surprised to see that she was still nodding and smiling.

I drew her neighbour to one side. "Mrs. Dodds, how much does she see?"

"Oh she's very short sighted but she's right vain despite her age. Never would wear glasses. She's hard of hearin', too."

"Well look," I said. My heart was still pounding. "I just don't know what to do. If I tell her about this the shock will be terrible. Anything could happen."

Mrs. Dodds nodded, stricken-faced. "Aye, you're right. She's that attached to the little thing."

"I can only think of one alternative," I whispered. "Do you know where I can get another budgie?"

Mrs. Dodds thought for a moment. "You could try Jack Almond at t'town end. I think he keeps birds."

I cleared my throat but even then my voice came out in a dry croak. "Mrs. Tompkin, I'm just going to take Peter along to the surgery to do this job. I won't be long."

I left her still nodding and smiling and, cage in hand, fled into the street. I was at the town end and knocking at Jack Almond's door within three minutes.

"Mr. Almond?" I asked of the stout, shirt-sleeved man who answered.

"That's right, young man." He gave me a slow, placid smile.

"Do you keep birds?"

He drew himself up with dignity. "I do, and I'm t'president of the Darrowby and Houlton Cage Bird Society."

"Fine," I said breathlessly. "Have you got a green budgie?"

"Ah've got Canaries, Budgies, Parrots, Parraqueets. Cockatoos . . ."

"I just want a budgie."

"Well ah've got Albinos, Blue-greens, Barreds, Lutinos . . ."

"I just want a green one."

A slightly pained expression flitted across the

man's face as though he found my attitude of haste somewhat unseemly.

"Aye . . . well, we'll go and have a look," he said.

I followed him as he paced unhurriedly through the house into the back yard which was largely given over to a long shed containing a bewildering variety of birds.

Mr. Almond gazed at them with gentle pride and his mouth opened as though he was about to launch into a dissertation then he seemed to remember that he had an impatient chap to deal with and dragged himself back to the job in hand.

"There's a nice little green 'un here. But he's a bit older than t'others. Matter of fact I've got 'im talkin.'"

"All the better, just the thing. How much do you want for him?"

"But . . . there's some nice 'uns along here. Just let me show you . . ."

I put a hand on his arm. "I want that one. How much?"

He pursed his lips in frustration then shrugged his shoulders.

"Ten bob."

"Right. Bung him in this cage."

As I sped back up the road I looked in the driving mirror and could see the poor man regarding me sadly from his doorway.

Mrs. Dodds was waiting for me back at Jasmine Terrace.

"Do you think I'm doing the right thing?" I asked her in a whisper.

"I'm sure you are," she replied. "Poor awd thing, she hasn't much to think about and I'm sure she'd fret over Peter."

"That's what I thought." I made my way into the living room.

Mrs. Tompkin smiled at me as I went in. "That wasn't a long job, Mr. Herriot."

"No," I said, hanging the cage with the new bird up in its place by the window. "I think you'll find all is well now."

It was months before I had the courage to put my hand into a budgie's cage again. In fact to this day I prefer it if the owners will lift the birds out for me. People look at me strangely when I ask them to do this; I believe they think I am scared the little things might bite me.

It was a long time, too, before I dared go back to Mrs. Tompkin's but I was driving down Jasmine Terrace one day and on an impulse I stopped outside Number 14.

The old lady herself came to the door.

"How . . ." I said, "How is . . . er . . . ?"

She peered at me closely for a moment then laughed. "Oh I see who it is now. You mean Peter, don't you, Mr. Herriot. Oh 'e's just grand. Come in and see 'im."

In the little room the cage still hung by the window and Peter the Second took a quick look at me then put on a little act for my benefit; he hopped around the bars of the cage, ran up and down his ladder and rang his little bell a couple of times before returning to his perch.

His mistress reached up, tapped the metal and looked lovingly at him.

"You know, you wouldn't believe it," she said. "He's like a different bird."

I swallowed. "Is that so? In what way?"

"Well he's so active now. Lively as can be. You know 'e chatters to me all day long. It's wonderful what cuttin' a beak can do."

33

The name was on the garden gate—Lilac Cottage. I pulled out my list of visits and checked the entry again. "Cook, Lilac Cottage, Marston Hall. Bitch overdue for whelping." This was the place all right, standing in the grounds of the Hall, a nineteenth century mansion house whose rounded turrets reared above the fringe of pine tree less than half a mile away.

The door was opened by a heavy featured dark woman of about sixty who regarded me unsmilingly.

"Good morning, Mrs. Cook," I said. "I've come to see your bitch."

She still didn't smile. "Oh, very well. You'd better come in."

She led me into the small living room and as a little Yorkshire Terrier jumped down from an armchair her manner changed.

"Come here, Cindy my darlin'," she cooed. "This gentleman's come to make you better." She bent down and stroked the little animal, her face radiant with affection.

I sat down in another armchair. "Well what's the trouble, Mrs. Cook?"

"Oh I'm worried to death." She clasped her hands anxiously. "She should have had her pups yesterday and there's nothing happenin'. Ah couldn't sleep all night—I'd die if anything happened to this dog."

I looked at the terrier, tail wagging, gazing up, bright-eyed under her mistress' caress. "She doesn't seem distressed at all. Has she shown any signs of labour?"

"What d'you mean?"

"Well, has she been panting or uneasy in any way? Is there any discharge?"

"No, nothing like that."

I beckoned to Cindy and spoke to her and she came timidly across the lino till I was able to lift her on to my lap. I palpated the distended abdomen; there were a lot of pups in there but everything appeared normal. I took her temperature—normal again.

"Bring me some warm water and soap, Mrs. Cook, will you please?" I said. The terrier was so small that I had to use my little finger, soaped and disinfected, to examine her, and as I felt carefully forward the walls of the vagina were dry and clinging and the cervix, when I reached it, tightly closed.

I washed and dried my hands. "This little bitch isn't anywhere near whelping, Mrs. Cook. Are you sure you haven't got your dates wrong?"

"No, I 'aven't, it was sixty three days yesterday." She paused in thought for a moment. "Now ah'd better tell you this, young man. Cindy's had pups before and she did self and same thing—wouldn't get on with t'job. That was two years ago when I was livin' over in Listondale. I got Mr. Broomfield the vet to her and he just gave her an injection. It was wonderful—she had the pups half an hour after it."

I smiled. "Yes, that would be pituitrin. She must have been actually whelping when Mr. Broomfield saw her."

"Well whatever it was, young man, I wish you'd give her some now. Ah can't stand all this suspense."

"I'm sorry." I lifted Cindy from my lap and stood up. "I can't do that. It would be very harmful at this stage."

She stared at me and it struck me that that dark face could look very forbidding. "So you're not goin' to do anything at all?"

"Well . . ." There are times when it is a soothing procedure to give a client something to do even if it is unnecessary. "Yes, I've got some tablets in the car.

They'll help to keep the little dog fit until she whelps."

"But I'd far rather have that injection. It was just a little prick. Didn't take Mr. Broomfield more than a second to do."

"I assure you, Mrs. Cook, it can't be done at the moment. I'll get the tablets from the car."

Her mouth tightened. I could see she was grievously disappointed in me. "Oh well if you won't you won't, so you'd better get them things." She paused. "And me name isn't Cook!"

"It isn't?"

"No it isn't, young man." She didn't seem disposed to offer further information so I left in some bewilderment.

Out in the road, a few yards from my car, a farm man was trying to start a tractor. I called over to him.

"Hey, the lady in there says her name isn't Cook."

"She's right an' all. She's the cook over at the Hall. You've gotten a bit mixed up." He laughed heartily.

It all became suddenly clear; the entry in the day book, everything. "What's her right name, then?"

"Booby," he shouted just as the tractor roared into life.

Funny name, I thought, as I produced my harmless vitamin tablets from the boot and returned to the cottage. Once inside I did my best to put things right with plenty of "Yes, Mrs. Booby" and "No, Mrs. Booby" but the lady didn't thaw. I told her not to worry and that I was sure nothing would happen for several days but I could tell I wasn't impressing her.

I waved cheerfully as I went down the path.

"Goodbye, Mrs. Booby," I cried. "Don't hesitate to ring me if you're in doubt about anything."

She didn't appear to have heard.

"Oh I wish you'd do as I say," she wailed. "It was just a little prick."

The good lady certainly didn't hesitate to ring. She was at me again the next day and I had to rush out to her cottage. Her message was the same as before; she wanted the wonderful injection which would make those pups pop out and she wanted it right away. Mr. Broomfield hadn't messed about and wasted time like I had. And on the third, fourth and fifth mornings she had me out at Marston examining the little bitch and reciting the same explanations. Things came to a head on the sixth day.

In the room at Lilac Cottage the dark eyes held a desperate light as they stared into mine. "I'm about at the end of my tether, young man. I tell you I'll die if anything happens to this dog, I'll die. Don't you understand?"

"Of course I know how you feel about her, Mrs. Booby. Believe me, I fully understand."

"Then why don't you do something?" she snapped.

I dug my nails into my palms. "Look, I've told you. A pituitrin injection works by contracting the muscular walls of the uterus so it can only be given when labour has started and the cervix is open. If I find it is indicated I will do it, but if I gave this injection now it could cause rupture of the uterus. It could cause death." I stopped because I fancied little bubbles were beginning to collect at the corners of my mouth.

But I don't think she had listened to a word. She sunk her head in her hands. "All this time, I can't stand it."

I was wondering if I could stand much more of it myself. Bulging Yorkshire Terriers had begun to prance through my dreams at night and I greeted each new day with a silent prayer that the pups had arrived. I held out my hand to Cindy and she crept reluctantly towards me. She was heartily sick of this strange man who came every day and squeezed her and stuck fingers into her and she submitted again with trembling limbs and frightened eyes to the indignity.

"Mrs. Booby," I said. "Are you absolutely sure that dog didn't have access to Cindy after the service date you gave me?"

She sniffed. "You keep askin' me that and ah've

been thinking about it. Maybe he did come a week after, now I think on."

"Well that's it, then!" I spread my hands. "She's held to the second mating, so she should be due to-morrow."

"Ah would still far rather you would get it over with today like Mr. Broomfield did . . . it was just a little prick."

"But Mrs. Booby. . . !"

"And let me tell you another thing, me name's not Booby!"

I clutched at the back of the chair. "It's not?"

"Naw!"

"Well . . . what is it, then?"

"It's Dooley . . . Dooley!" she looked very cross.

"Right . . . right . . ." I stumbled down the garden path and drove away. It was not a happy departure.

Next morning I could hardly believe it when there was no call from Marston. Maybe all was well at last. But I turned cold when an urgent call to go to Lilac Cottage was passed on to one of the farms on my round. I was right at the far end of the practice area and was in the middle of a tough calving and it was well over three hours before I got out at the now familiar garden gate. The cottage door was open and as I ventured up the path a little brown missile hurtled out at me. It was Cindy, but a transformed Cindy, a snarling, barking little bundle of ferocity; and though I recoiled she fastened her teeth in my trouser cuff and hung on grimly.

I was hopping around on one leg trying to shake off the growling little creature when a peal of almost girlish laughter made me look round.

Mrs. Dooley, vastly amused, was watching me from the doorway. "My word, she's different since she had them pups. Just shows what a good little mother she is, guarding them like that." She gazed fondly at the tiny animal dangling from my ankle.

"Had the pups. . . ?"

"Aye, when they said you'd be a long time I rang

Mr. Farnon. He came right away and d'you know he gave Cindy that injection I've wanted all along. And I tell you 'e wasn't right out of t'garden gate before the pups started. She's had seven—beauties they are."

"Ah well that's fine, Mrs. Dooley . . . splendid." Siegfried had obviously felt a pup in the passage. I finally managed to rid myself of Cindy and when her mistress lifted her up I went into the kitchen to inspect the family.

They certainly were grand pups and I lifted the squawking little morsels one by one from their basket while their mother snarled from Mrs. Dooley's arms like a starving wolfhound.

"They're lovely, Mrs. Dooley," I murmured.

She looked at me pityingly. "I told you what to do, didn't I, but you wouldn't 'ave it. It only needed a little prick. Ooo, that Mr. Farnon's a lovely man—just like Mr. Broomfield."

This was a bit much. "But you must realise, Mrs. Dooley, he just happened to arrive at the right time. If I had come . . ."

"Now, now, young man, be fair. Ah'm not blamin' you, but some people have had more experience. We all 'ave to learn." She sighed reminiscently. "It was just a little prick—Mr. Farnon'll have to show you how to do it. I tell you he wasn't right out of t'garden gate . . ."

Enough is enough. I drew myself up to my full height. "Mrs. Dooley, madam," I said frigidly, "let me repeat once and for all . . ."

"Oh, hoity, toity, hoity toity, don't get on your high horse wi' me!" she exclaimed. "We've managed very nicely without you so don't complain." Her expression became very severe. "And one more thing—me name's not Mrs. Dooley."

My brain reeled for a moment. The world seemed to be crumbling about me. "What did you say?"

"I said me name's not Mrs. Dooley."

"It isn't?"

"Naw!" She lifted her left hand and as I gazed at it

dully I realised it must have been all the mental stress which had prevented me from noticing the total absence of rings.

"Naw!" she said. "It's Miss!"

34

"Is this the thing you've been telling me about?" I asked.

Mr. Wilkin nodded. "Aye, that's it, it's always like that."

I looked down at the helpless convulsions of the big dog lying at my feet; at the staring eyes, the wildly pedalling limbs. The farmer had told me about the periodic attacks which had begun to affect his sheep dog, Gyp, but it was coincidence that one should occur when I was on the farm for another reason.

"And he's all right afterwards, you say?"

"Right as a bobbin. Seems a bit dazed, maybe, for about an hour then he's back to normal." The farmer shrugged. "I've had lots o' dogs through my hands as you know and I've seen plenty of dogs with fits. I thought I knew all the causes—worms, wrong feeding, distemper—but this has me beat. I've tried everything."

"Well you can stop trying, Mr. Wilkin," I said. "You won't be able to do much for Gyp. He's got epilepsy."

"Epilepsy? But he's a grand, normal dog most of t'time."

"Yes, I know. That's how it goes. There's nothing actually wrong with his brain—it's a mysterious condition. The cause is unknown but it's almost certainly hereditary."

Mr. Wilkin raised his eyebrows. "Well that's a rum 'un. If it's hereditary why hasn't it shown up before now? He's nearly two years old and he didn't start this till a few weeks ago."

"That's typical," I replied. "Eighteen months to two years is about the time it usually appears."

Gyp interrupted us by getting up and staggering towards his master, wagging his tail. He seemed untroubled by his experience. In fact the whole thing had lasted less than two minutes.

Mr. Wilkin bent and stroked the rough head briefly. His craggy features were set in a thoughtful cast. He was a big powerful man in his forties and now as the eyes narrowed in that face which rarely smiled he looked almost menacing. I had heard more than one man say he wouldn't like to get on the wrong side of Sep Wilkin and I could see what they meant. But he had always treated me right and since he farmed nearly a thousand acres I saw quite a lot of him.

His passion was sheep dogs. A lot of farmers liked to run dogs at the trials but Mr. Wilkin was one of the top men. He bred and trained dogs which regularly won at the local events and occasionally at the national trials. And what was troubling me was that Gyp was his main hope.

He had picked out the two best pups from a litter —Gyp and Sweep—and had trained them with the dedication that had made him a winner. I don't think I have ever seen two dogs enjoy each other quite as much; whenever I was on the farm I would see them together, sometimes peeping nose by nose over the half door of the loose box where they slept, occasionally slinking devotedly round the feet of their master but usually just playing together. They must have spent hours rolling about in ecstatic wrestling matches, growling and panting, gnawing gently at each other's limbs.

A few months ago George Crossley, one of Mr. Wilkin's oldest friends and a keen trial man, had lost his best dog with nephritis and Mr. Wilkin had let him have Sweep. I was surprised at the time because Sweep was shaping better than Gyp in his training and looked like turning out a real champion. But it was Gyp who remained. He must have missed his friend but there were other dogs on the farm and if they didn't quite make up for Sweep he was never really lonely.

As I watched, I could see the dog recovering rapidly. It was extraordinary how soon normality was restored after that frightening convulsion. And I waited with some apprehension to hear what his master would say.

The cold, logical decision for him to make would be to have Gyp put down. And, looking at the friendly, tail-wagging animal I didn't like the idea at all. There was something very attractive about him. The big-boned, well-marked body was handsome but his most distinctive feature was his head where one ear somehow contrived to stick up while the other lay flat, giving him a lop-sided, comic appeal. Gyp, in fact, looked a bit of a clown. But a clown who radiated goodwill and camaraderie.

Mr. Wilkin spoke at last. "Will he get any better as he grows older?"

"Almost certainly not," I replied.

"Then he'll always 'ave these fits?"

"I'm afraid so. You say he has them every two or three weeks—well it will probably carry on more or less like that with occasional variations."

"But he could have one any time?"

"Yes."

"In the middle of a trial, like." The farmer sunk his head on his chest and his voice rumbled deep. "That's it, then."

In the long silence which followed, the fateful words became more and more inevitable. Sep Wilkin wasn't the man to hesitate in a matter which concerned his ruling passion. Ruthless culling of any animal which didn't come up to standard would be his policy. When he finally cleared his throat I had a sinking premonition of what he was going to say.

But I was wrong.

"If I kept him, could you do anything for him?" he asked.

"Well I could give you some pills for him. They

might decrease the frequency of the fits." I tried to
keep the eagerness out of my voice.

"Right . . . right . . . I'll come into t'surgery and get
some," he muttered.

"Fine. But . . . er . . . you won't ever breed from
him, will you?" I said.

"Naw, naw, naw," the farmer grunted with a touch
of irritability as though he didn't want to pursue the
matter further.

And I held my peace because I felt intuitively that
he did not want to be detected in a weakness; that
he was prepared to keep the dog simply as a pet. It
was funny how events began to slot into place and
suddenly make sense. That was why he had let
Sweep, the superior trial dog, go. He just liked Gyp.
In fact Sep Wilkin, hard man though he may be, had
succumbed to that off-beat charm.

So I shifted to some light chatter about the weather
as I walked back to the car, but when I was about to
drive off the farmer returned to the main subject.

"There's one thing about Gyp I never mentioned,"
he said bending to the window. "I don't know
whether it has owt to do with the job or not. He has
never barked in his life."

I looked at him in surprise. "You mean never,
ever?"

"That's right. Not a single bark. T'other dogs made
a noise when strangers come on the farm but I've
never heard Gyp utter a sound since he was born."

"Well that's very strange," I said. "But I can't see
that it is connected with his condition in any way."

And as I switched on the engine I noticed for the
first time that while a bitch and two half grown pups
gave tongue to see me on my way Gyp merely regarded me in his comradely way, mouth open,
tongue lolling, but made no noise. A silent dog.

The thing intrigued me. So much so that whenever
I was on the farm over the next few months I made
a point of watching the big sheep dog at whatever
he was doing. But there was never any change. Between the convulsions which had settled down to

around three weeks intervals he was a normal active happy animal. But soundless.

I saw him, too, in Darrowby when his master came in to market. Gyp was often seated comfortably in the back of the car, but if I happened to speak to Mr. Wilkin on these occasions I kept off the subject because, as I said, I had the feeling that he more than most farmers would hate to be exposed in keeping a dog for other than working purposes.

And yet I have always entertained a suspicion that most farm dogs were more or less pets. The dogs on sheep farms were of course indispensable working animals and on other establishments they no doubt performed a function in helping to bring in the cows. But watching them on my daily rounds I often wondered. I saw them rocking along on carts at haytime, chasing rats among the stooks at harvest, pottering around the buildings or roaming the fields at the side of the farmer; and I wondered . . . what did they really do?

My suspicions were strengthened at other times—as when I was trying to round up some cattle into a corner and the dog tried to get into the act by nipping at a hop or tail. There was invariably a hoarse yell of "Siddown, dog!" or "Gerrout, dog!"

So right up to the present day I still stick to my theory; most farm dogs are pets and they are there mainly because the farmer just likes to have them around. You would have to put a farmer on the rack to get him to admit it but I think I am right. And in the process those dogs have a wonderful time. They don't have to beg for walks, they are out all day long, and in the company of their masters. If I want to find a man on a farm I look for his dog, knowing the man won't be far away. I try to give my own dogs a good life but it cannot compare with the life of the average farm dog.

There was a long spell when Sep Wilkin's stock stayed healthy and I didn't see either him or Gryp, then I came across them both by accident at a sheep dog trial. It was a local event run in conjunction with the Mellerton Agricultural Show and since I was in the district I decided to steal an hour off.

I took Helen with me, too, because these trials have always fascinated us. The wonderful control of the owners over their animals, the intense involvement of the dogs themselves, the sheer skill of the whole operation always held us spellbound.

She put her arm through mine as we went in at the entrance gate to where a crescent of cars was drawn up at one end of a long field. The field was on the river's edge and through a fringe of trees the afternoon sunshine glinted on the tumbling water of the shallows and turned the long beach of bleached stones to a dazzling white. Groups of men, mainly competitors, stood around chatting as they watched. They were quiet, easy, bronzed men and as they seemed to be drawn from all social strata from prosperous farmers to working men their garb was varied; cloth caps, trilbies, deerstalkers or no hat at all; tweed jackets, stiff best suits, open necked shirts, fancy ties, sometimes neither collar nor tie. Nearly all of them leaned on long crooks with the handles fashioned from ram's horns.

Snatches of talk reached us as we walked among them.

"You got 'ere, then, Fred." "That's a good gather." "Nay, 'e's missed one, 'e'll get nowt for that." "Them sheep's a bit flighty." "Aye, they're buggers." And above it all the whistles of the man running a dog; every conceivable level and pitch of whistle with now and then a shout. "Sit!" "Get by!" Every man had his own way with his dog.

The dogs waiting their turn were tied up to a fence with a hedge growing over it. There were about seventy of them and it was rather wonderful to see that long row of waving tails and friendly expressions. They were mostly strangers to each other but there wasn't even the semblance of disagreement, never mind a fight. It seemed that the natural obedience of these little creatures was linked to an amicable disposition.

This appeared to be common to their owners, too. There was no animosity, no resentment at defeat, no unseemly display of triumph in victory. If a man overran his time he ushered his group of sheep quietly into the corner and returned with a philosophical grin to his colleagues. There was a little quiet leg-pulling but that was all.

We came across Sep Wilkin leaning against his car at the best vantage point about thirty yards away from the final pen. Gyp, tied to the bumper, turned and gave me his crooked grin while Mrs. Wilkin on a camp stool by his side rested a hand on his shoulder. Gyp, it seemed, had got under her skin too.

Helen went over to speak to her and I turned to her husband. "Are you running a dog today, Mr. Wilkin?"

"No, not this time, just come to watch. I know a lot o' the dogs."

I stood near him for a while watching the competitors in action, breathing in the clean smell of trampled grass and plug tobacco. In front of us next to the pen the judge stood by his post.

I had been there for about ten minutes when Mr. Wilkin lifted a pointing finger. "Look who's there!"

George Crossly with Sweep trotting at his heels was making his way unhurriedly to the post. Gyp suddenly stiffened and sat up very straight, his cocked ears accentuating the lop-sided look. It was many months since he had seen his brother and companion; it seemed unlikely, I thought, that he would remember him. But his interest was clearly intense, and as the judge waved his white handkerchief and the three sheep were released from the far corner he rose slowly to his feet.

A gesture from Mr. Crossley sent Sweep winging round the perimeter of the field in a wide, joyous gallop and as he neared the sheep a whistle dropped him on his belly. From then on it was an object lesson in the cooperation of man and dog. Sep Wilkin had always said Sweep would be a champion and he looked the part, darting and falling at his master's commands. Short piercing whistles, shrill plaintive whistles; he was in tune with them all.

No dog all day had brought his sheep through the three lots of gates as effortlessly as Sweep did now and as he approached the pen near us it was obvious that he would win the cup unless some disaster struck. But this was the touchy bit; more than once with other dogs the sheep had broken free and gone bounding away within feet of the wooden rails.

George Crossley held the gate wide and extended his crook. You could see now why they all carried those long sticks. His commands to Sweep, huddled flat along the turf, were now almost inaudible but the quiet words brought the dog inching first one way then the other. The sheep were in the entrance to the pen now but they still looked around them irresolutely and the game was not over yet. But as Sweep wriggled towards them almost imperceptibly they turned and entered and Mr. Crossley crashed the gate behind them.

As he did so he turned to Sweep with a happy cry of "GOOD LAD!" and the dog responded with a quick jerking wag of his tail.

At that, Gyp, who had been standing very tall, watching every move with the most intense concentration raised his head and emitted a single resounding bark.

"WOOF!" went Gyp as we all stared at him in astonishment.

"Did you hear that?" gasped Mrs. Wilkin.

"Well, by gaw!" her husband burst out, looking open-mouthed at his dog.

Gyp didn't seem to be aware that he had done anything unusual. He was too preoccupied by the reunion with his brother and within seconds the two dogs were rolling around, chewing playfully at each other as of old.

I suppose the Wilkins as well as myself had the feeling that this event might start Gyp barking like any other dog, but it was not to be.

Six years later I was on the farm and went to the house to get some hot water. As Mrs. Wilkin handed me the bucket she looked down at Gyp who was basking in the sunshine outside the kitchen window.

"There you are, then, funny fellow," she said to the dog.

I laughed. "Has he ever barked since that day?"

Mrs. Wilkin shook her head. "No he hasn't, not a sound. I waited a long time but I know he's not going to do it now."

"Ah well, it's not important. But still, I'll never forget that afternoon at the trial," I said.

"Nor will I!" She looked at Gyp again and her eyes softened in reminiscence. "Poor old lad, eight years old and only one woof "

35

Clerical work has never been my strong point and after an evening of writing letters it was a relief to trot down the stairs from our bed-sitter and stroll across the market place to the post office. I had just dropped the letters in the box when a burst of jazz music came over the cobbles from an open doorway. And in an instant I was back in my bachelor days, back to the night of that dance when my courtship of Helen had been progressing badly. . . .

The big room at Skeldale House had been full that night. It seemed to me that this room with its graceful alcoves, high, carved ceiling and french windows lay at the centre of our life in Darrowby. It was where Siegfried, Tristan and I gathered when the day's work was done, toasting our feet by the white wood fireplace with the glass-fronted cupboard on top, talking over the day's events. It was the heart of our bachelor existence, sitting there in a happy stupor, reading, listening to the radio, Tristan usually flipping effortlessly through the Daily Telegraph crossword.

It was where Siegfried entertained his friends and there was a constant stream of them—old and young, male and female. But tonight it was Tristan's turn and the pack of young people with drinks in their hands were there at his invitation. And they wouldn't need much persuasion. Though just about the opposite of his brother in many ways he had the same attractiveness which brought the friends running at the crook of a finger.

The occasion was the Daffodil Ball at the Drovers'

Arms and we were dressed in our best. This was a different kind of function from the usual village institute hop with the farm lads in their big boots and music from a scraping fiddle and piano. It was a proper dance with a popular local band—Sadie Butterfield and her Hot Shots—and was an annual affair to herald the arrival of spring.

I watched Tristan dispensing the drinks. The bottles of whisky, gin and sherry which Siegfried kept in the fireplace cupboard had taken some severe punishment but Tristan himself had been abstemious. An occasional sip from a glass of light ale perhaps, but nothing more. Drinking, to him, meant the bulk intake of draught bitter; all else was mere vanity and folly. Dainty little glasses were anathema and even now when I see him at a party where everybody is holding small drinks Tristan somehow contrives to have a pint in his hand.

"Nice little gathering, Jim," he said, appearing at my elbow. "A few more blokes than girls but that won't matter much."

I eyed him coldly. I knew why there were extra men. It was so that Tristan wouldn't have to take the floor too often. It fitted in with his general dislike of squandering energy that he was an unenthusiastic dancer; he didn't mind walking a girl round the floor now and again during the evening but he preferred to spend most of the time in the bar.

So, in fact, did a lot of the Darrowby folk. When we arrived at the Drovers the bar was congested while only a dedicated few circled round the ballroom. But as time went on more and more couples ventured out and by ten o'clock the dance floor was truly packed.

And I soon found I was enjoying myself. Tristan's friends were an effervescent bunch; likeable young men and attractive girls; I just couldn't help having a good time.

Butterfield's famed band in their short red jackets added greatly to the general merriment. Sadie herself looked about fifty five and indeed all four of the Hot Shots ensemble were rather elderly, but they made up for their grey hairs by sheer vivacity. Not that Sadie's hair was grey; it was dyed a determined black and she thumped the piano with dynamic energy, beaming out at the company through her horn-rimmed glasses, occasionally bawling a chorus into the microphone by her side, announcing the dances, making throaty wisecracks. She gave value for money.

There was no pairing off in our party and I danced with all the girls in turn. At the peak of the evening I was jockeying my way around the floor with Daphne and the way she was constructed made it a rewarding experience. I never have been one for skinny women but I suppose you could say that Daphne's development had strayed a little too far in the other direction. She wasn't fat just lavishly endowed.

Battling through the crush, colliding with exuberant neighbours, bouncing deliciously off Daphne, with everybody singing as they danced and the Hot Shots pouring out an insistent boom-boom beat, I felt I hadn't a care in the world. And then I saw Helen.

She was dancing with the inevitable Richard Edmundson, his shining gold head floating above the company like an emblem of doom. And it was uncanny how in an instant my cosy little world disintegrated leaving a chill gnawing emptiness.

When the music stopped I returned Daphne to her friends and went to find Tristan. The comfortable little bar in the Drovers was overflowing and the temperature like an oven. Through an almost impenetrable fog of cigarette smoke I discerned my colleague on a high stool holding court with a group of perspiring revellers. Tristan himself looked cool and as always, profoundly content. He drained his glass, smacked his lips gently as though it had been the best pint of beer he'd ever tasted, then, as he reached across the counter and courteously requested a refill he spotted me struggling towards him.

When I reached his stool he laid an affable hand

on my shoulder. "Ah, Jim, nice to see you. Splendid dance, this, don't you think?"

I didn't bring up the fact that I hadn't seen him on the floor yet, but making my voice casual I mentioned that Helen was there.

Tristan nodded benignly. "Yes, saw her come in. Why don't you go and dance with her?"

"I can't do that. She's with a partner—young Edmundson."

"Not at all." Tristan surveyed his fresh pint with a critical eye and took an exploratory sip. "She's with a party, like us. No partner."

"How do you know that?"

"I watched all the fellows hang their coats out there while the girls went upstairs. No reason at all why you shouldn't have a dance with her."

"I see." I hesitated for a few moments then made my way back to the ballroom.

But it wasn't as easy as that. I had to keep doing my duty with the girls in our group and whenever I headed for Helen she was whisked away by one of her men friends before I got near her. At times I fancied she was looking over at me but I couldn't be sure; the only thing I knew for certain was that I wasn't enjoying myself any more; the magic and gaiety had gone and I felt a rising misery at the thought that this was going to be another of my frustrating contacts with Helen when all I could do was look at her hopelessly. Only this time was worse —I hadn't even spoken to her.

I was almost relieved when the manager came up and told me there was a call for me. I went to the phone and spoke to Mrs. Hall. There was a bitch in trouble whelping and I had to go. I looked at my watch—after midnight, so that was the end of the dance for me.

I stood for a moment listening to the muffled thudding from the dance floor then slowly pulled on my coat before going in to say goodbye to Tristan's friends. I exchanged a few words with them,

waved, then turned back and pushed the swing door
open.

Helen was standing there, about a foot away from
me. Her hand was on the door, too. I didn't wonder
whether she was going in or out but stared dumbly
into her smiling blue eyes.

"Leaving already, Jim?" she said.

"Yes, I've got a call, I'm afraid."

"Oh what a shame. I hope it's nothing very serious."

I opened my mouth to speak, but her dark beauty
and the very nearness of her suddenly filled my
world and a wave of hopeless longing swept over
and submerged me. I slid my hand a few inches
down the door and gripped hers as a drowning man
might, and wonderingly I felt her fingers come round
and entwine themselves tightly in mine.

And in an instant there was no band, no noise,
no people, just the two of us standing very close in
the doorway.

"Come with me," I said.

Helen's eyes were very large as she smiled that
smile I knew so well.

"I'll get my coat," she murmured.

This wasn't really me, I thought, standing on the
hall carpet watching Helen trotting quickly up the
stairs, but I had to believe it as she reappeared on
the landing pulling on her coat. Outside, on the cobbles of the market place my car, too, appeared to
be taken by surprise because it roared into life at
the first touch of the starter.

I had to go back to the surgery for my whelping
instruments and in the silent moonlit street we got
out and I opened the big white door to Skeldale
House.

And once in the passage it was the most natural
thing in the world to take her in my arms and kiss
her gratefully and unhurriedly. I had waited a long
time for this and the minutes flowed past unnoticed
as we stood there, our feet on the black and red

eighteenth century tiles, our heads almost touching the vast picture of the Death of Nelson which dominated the entrance.

We kissed again at the first bend of the passage under the companion picture of the Meeting of Wellington and Blucher at Waterloo. We kissed at the second bend by the tall cupboard where Siegfried kept his riding coats and boots. We kissed in the dispensary in between searching for my instruments. Then we tried it out in the garden and this was the best of all with the flowers still and expectant in the moonlight and the fragrance of the moist earth and grass rising about us.

I have never driven so slowly to a case. About ten miles an hour with Helen's head on my shoulder and all the scents of spring drifting in through the open window. And it was like sailing from stormy seas into a sweet, safe harbour, like coming home.

The light in the cottage window was the only one showing in the sleeping village, and when I knocked at the door Bert Chapman answered. Bert was a council roadman—one of the breed for whom I felt an abiding affinity.

The council men were my brethren of the roads. Like me they spent most of their lives on the lonely by-ways around Darrowby and I saw them most days of the week, repairing the tarmac, cutting back the grass verges in the summer, gritting and snow ploughing in the winter. And when they spotted me driving past they would grin cheerfully and wave as if the very sight of me had made their day. I don't know whether they were specially picked for good nature but I don't think I have ever met a more equable body of men.

One old farmer remarked sourly to me once, "There's no wonder the buggers are 'appy, they've got nowt to do." An exaggeration, of course, but I knew how he felt; compared to farming every other job was easy.

I had seen Bert Chapman just a day or two ago, sitting on a grassy bank, his shovel by his side, a vast

sandwich in his hand. He had raised a corded forearm in salute, a broad smile bisecting his round,
sun-reddened face. He had looked eternally carefree
but tonight his smile was strained.

"I'm sorry to bother you this late, Mr. Herriot,"
he said as he ushered us into the house, "but I'm
gettin' a bit worried about Susie. Her pups are due
and she's been making a bed for them and messing
about all day but nowt's happened. I was goin' to
leave her till morning but about midnight she started panting like 'ell—I don't like the look of her."

Susie was one of my regular patients. Her big, burly
master was always bringing her to the surgery, a
little shame-faced at his solicitude, and when I saw
him sitting in the waiting room looking strangely out
of place among the ladies with their pets, he usually
said "T'missus asked me to bring Susie." But it was
a transparent excuse.

"She's nobbut a little mongrel, but very faithful,"
Bert said, still apologetic, but I could understand how
he felt about Susie, a shaggy little ragamuffin whose
only wile was to put her paws on my knees and
laugh up into my face with her tail lashing. I found
her irresistible.

But she was a very different character tonight. As
we went into the living room of the cottage the
little animal crept from her basket, gave a single indeterminate wag of her tail, then stood miserably
in the middle of the floor, her ribs heaving. As I
bent to examine her she turned a wide panting
mouth and anxious eyes up to me.

I ran my hands over her abdomen. I don't think
I have ever felt a more bloated little dog; she was
as round as a football, absolutely bulging with pups,
ready to pop, but nothing was happening.

"What do you think?" Bert's face was haggard under his sunburn and he touched the dog's head
briefly with a big calloused hand.

"I don't know yet, Bert," I said. "I'll have to have
a feel inside. Bring me some hot water, will you?"

I added some antiseptic to the water, soaped my

hand and with one finger carefully explored the vagina. There was a pup there, all right; my finger tip brushed across the nostrils, the tiny mouth and tongue; but he was jammed in that narrow passage like a cork in a bottle.

Squatting back on my heels I turned to the Chapmans.

"I'm afraid there's a big pup stuck fast. I have a feeling that if she could get rid of this chap the others would come away. They'd probably be smaller."

"Is there any way of shiftin' him, Mr. Herriot?" Bert asked.

I paused for a moment. "I'm going to put forceps on his head and see if he'll move. I don't like using forceps but I'm going to have one careful try and if it doesn't work I'll have to take her back to the surgery for a caesarian."

"An operation?" Bert said hollowly. He gulped and glanced fearfully at his wife. Like many big men he had married a tiny woman and at this moment Mrs. Chapman looked even smaller than her four foot eleven inches as she huddled in her chair and stared at me with wide eyes.

"Oh I wish we'd never had her mated," she wailed, wringing her hands. "I told Bert five years old was too late for a first litter but he wouldn't listen. And now we're maybe going to lose 'er."

I hastened to reassure her, "No, she isn't too old, and everything may be all right. Let's just see how we get on."

I boiled the instrument for a few minutes on the stove then kneeled behind my patient again. I poised the forceps for a moment and at the flash of steel a grey tinge crept under Bert's sunburn and his wife coiled herself into a ball in her chair. Obviously they were non-starters as assistants so Helen held Susie's head while I once more reached in towards the pup. There was desperately little room but I managed to direct the forceps along my finger till they touched the nose. Then very gingerly I opened the jaws and pushed them forward with the very gentlest pressure until I was able to clamp them on either side of the head.

I'd soon know now. In a situation like this you can't do any pulling, you can only try to ease the thing along. This I did and I fancied I felt just a bit of movement; I tried again and there was no doubt about it, the pup was coming towards me. Susie, too, appeared to sense that things were taking a turn for the better. She cast off her apathy and began to strain lustily.

It was no trouble after that and I was able to draw the pup forth almost without resistance.

"I'm afraid this one'll be dead," I said, and as the tiny creature lay across my palm there was no sign of breathing. But, pinching the chest between thumb and forefinger I could feel the heart pulsing steadily and I quickly opened his mouth and blew softly down into his lungs.

I repeated this a few times then laid the pup on his side in the basket. I was just thinking it was going to be no good when the little rib cage gave a sudden lift, then another and another.

"He's off!" Bert exclaimed happily. "That's champion! We want these puppies alive tha knows. They're by Jack Dennison's terrier and he's a grand 'un."

"That's right," Mrs. Chapman put in. "No matter how many she has, they're all spoken for. Everybody wants a pup out of Susie."

"I can believe that," I said. But I smiled to myself. Jack Dennison's terrier was another hound of uncertain ancestry, so this lot would be a right mixture. But none the worse for that.

I gave Susie half a c.c. of pituitrin. "I think she needs it after pushing against that fellow for hours. We'll wait and see what happens now."

And it was nice waiting. Mrs. Chapman brewed a pot of tea and began to slap butter on to home-made scones. Susie, partly aided by my pituitrin, pushed out a pup in a self-satisfied manner about every fifteen minutes. The pups themselves soon set up a bawling of surprising volume for such minute creatures. Bert, relaxing visibly with every minute, filled his pipe and regarded the fast-growing family with a grin of increasing width.

"Ee, it is kind of you young folks to stay with us like this." Mrs. Chapman put her head on one side and looked at us worriedly. "I should think you've been dying to get back to your dance all this time."

I thought of the crush at the Drovers. The smoke, the heat, the nonstop boom-boom of the Hot Shots and I looked around the peaceful little room with the old-fashioned black grate, the low, varnished beams, Mrs. Chapman's sewing box, the row of Bert's pipes on the wall. I took a firmer grasp of Helen's hand which I had been holding under the table for the last hour.

"Not at all, Mrs. Chapman," I said. "We haven't missed it in the least." And I have never been more sincere.

It must have been about half past two when I finally decided that Susie had finished. She had six fine pups which was a good score for a little thing like her and the noise had abated as the family settled down to feast on her abundant udder.

I lifted the pups out one by one and examined them. Susie didn't mind in the least but appeared to be smiling with modest pride as I handled her brood. When I put them back with her she inspected them and sniffed them over busily before rolling on to her side again.

"Three dogs and three bitches," I said. "Nice even litter."

Before leaving I took Susie from her basket and palpated her abdomen. The degree of deflation was almost unbelievable; a pricked balloon could not have altered its shape more spectacularly and she had made a remarkable metamorphosis to the lean, scruffy little extrovert I knew so well.

When I released her she scurried back and curled herself round her new family who were soon sucking away with total absorption.

Bert laughed. "She's fair capped wi' them pups."

He bent over and prodded the first arrival with a horny forefinger. "I like the look o' this big dog pup. I reckon we'll keep this 'un for ourselves, mother. He'll be company for t'awd lass."

It was time to go. Helen and I moved over to the door and little Mrs. Chapman with her fingers on the handle looked up at me.

"Well, Mr. Herriot," she said, "I can't thank you enough for comin' out and putting our minds at rest. I don't know what I'd have done wi' this man of mine if anything had happened to his little dog."

Bert grinned sheepishly. "Nay," he muttered. "Ah was never really worried."

His wife laughed and opened the door and as we stepped out into the silent scented night she gripped my arm and looked up at me roguishly.

"I suppose this is your young lady," she said.

I put my arm around Helen's shoulders.

"Yes," I said firmly. "This is my young lady."

36

A full surgery! But the ripple of satisfaction as I surveyed the packed rows of heads waned quickly as realisation dawned. It was only the Dimmocks again.

I first encountered the Dimmocks one evening when I had a call to a dog which had been knocked down by a car. The address was down in the old part of the town and I was cruising slowly along the row of decaying cottages looking for the number when a door burst open and three shock-headed little children ran into the street and waved me down frantically.

"He's in 'ere, Mister!" they gasped in unison as I got out, and then began immediately to put me in the picture.

"It's Bonzo!" "Aye, a car 'it 'im!" "We 'ad to carry 'im in, Mister!" They all got their word in as I opened the garden gate and struggled up the path with the three of them hanging on to my arms and tugging at my coat; and en route I gazed in wonder at the window of the house where a mass of other young faces mouthed at me and a tangle of arms gesticulated.

Once through the door which opened directly into the living room I was swamped by a rush of bodies and borne over to the corner where I saw my patient.

Bonzo was sitting upright on a ragged blanket. He was a large shaggy animal of indeterminate breed and though at a glance there didn't seem to be much ailing him he wore a pathetic expression of self pity. Since everybody was talking at once I decided to ignore them and carry out my examination. I worked my way over legs, pelvis, ribs and spine; no fractures. His mucous membranes were a good colour, there was no evidence of internal injury. In fact the only thing I could find was slight bruising over the left shoulder. Bonzo had sat like a statue as I felt over him, but as I finished he toppled over on to his side and lay looking up at me apologetically, his tail thumping on the blanket.

"You're a big soft dog, that's what you are," I said and the tail thumped faster.

I turned and viewed the throng and after a moment or two managed to pick out the parents. Mum was fighting her way to the front while at the rear Dad, a diminutive figure, was beaming at me over the heads. I did a bit of shushing and when the babel died down I addressed myself to Mrs. Dimmock.

"I think he's been lucky," I said. "I can't find any serious injury. I think the car must have bowled him over and knocked the wind out of him for a minute, or he may have been suffering from shock."

The uproar broke out again. "Will 'e die, Mister?" "What's the matter with 'im?" "What are you going to do?"

I gave Bonzo an injection of a mild sedative while he lay rigid, a picture of canine suffering, with the towsled heads looking down at him with deep concern and innumerable little hands poking out and caressing him.

Mrs. Dimmock produced a basin of hot water and while I washed my hands I was able to make a rough assessment of the household. I counted eleven little Dimmocks from a boy in his early teens down to a grubby faced infant crawling around the floor; and judging by the significant bulge in Mum's midriff the number was soon to be augmented. They were clad in a motley selection of hand-me downs; darned pullovers, patched trousers, tattered dresses, yet the general atmosphere in the house was of unconfined joie di vivre.

Bonzo wasn't the only animal and I stared in disbelief as another biggish dog and a cat with two half grown kittens appeared from among the crowding legs and feet. I would have thought that the problem of filling the human mouths would have been difficult enough without importing several animals.

But the Dimmocks didn't worry about such things; they did what they wanted to do, and they got by. Dad, I learned later, had never done any work within living memory. He had a "bad back" and lived what seemed to me a reasonably gracious life, roaming interestedly around the town by day and enjoying a quiet beer and a game of dominoes in a corner of the Four Horse Shoes by night.

I saw him quite often; he was easy to pick out because he invariably carried a walking stick which gave him an air of dignity and he always walked briskly and purposefully as though he were going somewhere important.

I took a final look at Bonzo, still stretched on the blanket, looking up at me with soulful eyes then I struggled towards the door.

"I don't think there's anything to worry about," I shouted above the chattering which had speedily broken out again, "but I'll look in tomorrow and make sure."

When I drew up outside the house next morning I could see Bonzo galloping around the garden with several of the children. They were passing a ball from one to the other and he was leaping ecstatically high in the air to try to intercept it.

He was clearly none the worse for his accident but when he saw me opening the gate his tail went down and he dropped almost to his knees and slunk into the house. The children received me rapturously.

"You've made 'im better, Mister!" "He's all right now, isn't he?" "He's 'ad a right big breakfast this mornin', Mister!"

I went inside with little hands clutching at my coat, Bonzo was sitting bolt upright on his blanket in the same attitude as the previous evening, but as I approached he slowly collapsed on to his side and lay looking up at me with a martyred expression.

I laughed as I knelt by him. "You're the original old

soldier, Bonzo, but you can't fool me. I saw you out there."

I gently touched the bruised shoulder and the big dog tremblingly closed his eyes as he resigned himself to his fate. Then when I stood up and he realised he wasn't going to have another injection he leaped to his feet and bounded away into the garden.

There was a chorus of delighted cries from the Dimmocks and they turned and looked at me with undisguised admiration. Clearly they considered that I had plucked Bonzo from the jaws of death. Mr. Dimmock stepped forward from the mass.

"You'll send me a bill, won't you," he said with the dignity that was peculiar to him.

My first glance last night had decided me that this was a no-charging job and I hadn't even written it in the book, but I nodded solemnly.

"Very well, Mr. Dimmock, I'll do that."

And throughout our long association though no money ever changed hands he always said the same thing—"You'll send me a bill, won't you."

This was the beginning of my close relationship with the Dimmocks. Obviously they had taken a fancy to me and wanted to see as much as possible of me. Over the succeeding weeks and months they brought in a varied selection of dogs, cats, budgies, rabbits at frequent intervals, and when they found that my services were free they stepped up the number of visits; and when one came they all came. I was anxiously trying to expand the small animal side of the practice and increasingly my hopes were raised momentarily then dashed when I opened the door and saw a packed waiting room.

And it increased the congestion when they started bringing their auntie, Mrs. Pounder, from down the road with them to see what a nice chap I was. Mrs. Pounder, a fat lady who always wore a greasy velour hat perched on an untidy mound of hair, evidently shared the family tendency to fertility and usually brought a few of her own ample brood with her.

That is how it was this particular morning. I swept the assembled company with my eye but could discern only beaming Dimmocks and Pounders; and this time I couldn't even pick out my patient. Then the assembly parted and spread out as though by a prearranged signal and I saw little Nellie Dimmock with a tiny puppy on her knee.

Nellie was my favourite. Mind you, I liked all the family; in fact they were such nice people that I always enjoyed their visits after that first disappointment. Mum and Dad were always courteous and cheerful and the children, though boisterous, were never ill-mannered; they were happy and friendly and if they saw me in the street they would wave madly and go on waving till I was out of sight. And I saw them often because they were continually scurrying around the town doing odd jobs—delivering milk or papers. Best of all, they loved their animals and were kind to them.

But as I say, Nellie was my favourite. She was about nine and had suffered an attack of "infantile paralysis" as it used to be called when very young. It had left her with a pronounced limp and a frailty which set her apart from her robust brothers and sisters. Her painfully thin legs seemed almost too fragile to carry her around but above the pinched face her hair, the colour of ripe corn, flowed to her shoulders and her eyes, though slightly crossed, gazed out calm and limpid blue through steel-rimmed spectacles.

"What's that you've got, Nellie?" I asked.

"It's a little dog," she almost whispered. " 'e's mine."

"You mean he's your very own?"

She nodded proudly. "Aye, 'e's mine."

"He doesn't belong to your brothers and sisters, too?"

"Naw, 'e's mine."

Rows of Dimmock and Pounder heads nodded in eager acquiescence as Nellie lifted the puppy to her cheek and looked up at me with a smile of a strange sweetness. It was a smile that always tugged at my heart; full of a child's artless happiness and trust but with something else which was poignant and maybe had to do with the way Nellie was.

"Well, he looks a fine dog to me," I said. "He's a Spaniel, isn't he?"

She ran a hand over the little head. "Aye, a Cocker. Mr. Brown said 'e was a Cocker."

There was a slight disturbance at the back and Mr. Dimmock appeared from the crush. He gave a respectful cough.

"He's a proper pure bred, Mr. Herriot," he said. "Mr. Brown from the bank's bitch had a litter and 'e gave this 'un to Nellie." He tucked his stick under his arm and pulled a long envelope from an inside pocket. He handed it to me with a flourish. "That's 'is pedigree."

I read it through and whistled softly. "He's a real blue-blooded hound, all right, and I see he's got a big long name. Darrowby Tobias the third. My word, that sounds great."

I looked down at the little girl again. "And what do YOU call him, Nellie?"

"Toby," she said softly. "I calls 'im Toby."

I laughed. "All right, then. What's the matter with Toby anyway. Why have you brought him?"

"He's been sick, Mr. Herriot." Mrs. Dimmock spoke from somewhere among the heads. "He can't keep nothin' down."

"Well I know what that'll be. Has he been wormed?"

"No, don't think so."

"I should think he just needs a pill," I said. "But bring him through and I'll have a look at him."

Other clients were usually content to send one representative through with their animals but the Dimmocks all had to come. I marched along with the crowd behind me filling the passage from wall to wall. Our consulting cum operating room was quite small and I watched with some apprehension as the procession filed in after me. But they all got in, Mrs. Pounder, her velour hat slightly askew, squeezing herself in with some difficulty at the rear.

My examination of the puppy took longer than

usual as I had to fight my way to the thermometer on the trolley then struggle in the other direction to get the stethoscope from its hook on the wall. But I finished at last.

"Well I can't find anything wrong with him," I said. "So I'm pretty sure he just has a tummy full of worms. I'll give you a pill now and you must give it to him first thing tomorrow morning."

Like a football match turning out, the mass of people surged along the passage and into the street and another Dimmock visit had come to an end.

I forgot the incident immediately because there was nothing unusual about it. The pot-bellied appearance of the puppy made my diagnosis a formality; I didn't expect to see him again.

But I was wrong. A week later my surgery was once more overflowing and I had another squashed-in session with Toby in the little back room. My pill had evacuated a few worms but he was still vomiting, still distended.

"Are you giving him five very small meals a day as I told you?" I asked.

I received an emphatic affirmative and I believed them. The Dimmocks really took care of their animals. There was something else here, yet I couldn't find it. Temperature normal, lungs clear, abdomen negative on palpation; I couldn't make it out. I dispensed a bottle of our antacid mixture with a feeling of defeat. A young puppy like this shouldn't need such a thing.

This was the beginning of a frustrating period. There would be a span of two or three weeks when I would think the trouble had righted itself then without warning the place would be full of Dimmocks and Pounders and I'd be back where I started.

And all the time Toby was growing thinner.

I tried everything; gastric sedatives, variations of diet, quack remedies. I interrogated the Dimmocks repeatedly about the character of the vomiting—how long after eating, what were the intervals between, and I received varying replies. Sometimes he brought his food straight back, at others he retained it for several hours. I got nowhere.

It must have been over eight weeks later—Toby would be about four months old—when I again viewed the assembled Dimmocks with a sinking heart. Their visits had become depressing affairs and I could not foresee anything better today as I opened the waiting room door and allowed myself to be almost carried along the passage. This time it was Dad who was the last to wedge himself into the consulting room then Nellie placed the little dog on the table.

I felt an inward lurch of sheer misery. Toby had grown despite his disability and was now a grim caricature of a Cocker Spaniel, the long silky ears drooping from an almost fleshless skull, the spindly legs pathetically feathered. I had thought Nellie was thin but her pet had outdone her. And he wasn't just thin, he was trembling slightly as he stood arch-backed on the smooth surface, and his face had the dull inward look of an animal which has lost interest.

The little girl ran her hand along the jutting ribs and the pale, squinting eyes looked up at me through the steel spectacles with that smile which pulled at me more painfully than ever before. She didn't seem worried. Probably she had no idea how things were, but whether she had or not I knew I'd never be able to tell her that her dog was slowly dying.

I rubbed my eyes wearily. "What has he had to eat today?"

Nellie answered herself. "He's 'ad some bread and milk."

"How long ago was that?" I asked, but before anybody could reply the little dog vomited, sending the half digested stomach contents soaring in a graceful arc to land two feet away on the table.

I swung round on Mrs. Dimmock. "Does he always do it like that?"

"Aye he mostly does—sends it flying out, like."

"But why didn't you tell me?"

The poor lady looked flustered. "Well . . . I don't know . . . I . . ."

I held up a hand. "That's all right, Mrs. Dimmock, never mind." It occurred to me that all the way through my totally ineffectual treatment of this dog not a single Dimmock or Pounder had uttered a word of criticism so why should I start to complain now?

But I knew what Toby's trouble was now. At last, at long last I knew.

And in case my present day colleagues reading this may think I had been more than usually thick-headed in my handling of the case I would like to offer in my defence that such limited text books as there were in those days made only a cursory reference to pyloric stenosis (narrowing of the exit of the stomach where it joins the small intestine) and if they did they said nothing about treatment.

But surely, I thought, somebody in England was ahead of the books. There must be people who were actually doing this operation . . . and if there were I had a feeling one might not be too far away . . .

I worked my way through the crush and trotted along the passage to the phone.

"Is that you Granville?"

"JIM" A bellow of pure unalloyed joy. "How are you laddie?"

"Very well, how are you?"

"Ab-so-lutely tip top, old son! Never better!"

"Granville, I've got a four month old spaniel pup I'd like to bring through to you. It's got pyloric stenosis."

"Oh lovely!"

"I'm afraid the little thing's just about on its last legs—a bag of bones."

"Splendid, splendid!"

"This is because I've been mucking about for weeks in ignorance."

"Fine, just fine!"

"And the owners are a very poor family. They can't pay anything I'm afraid."

"Wonderful!"

I hesitated a moment. "Granville, you do . . . er . . . you have . . . operated on these cases before?"

"Did five yesterday."

"What!"

A deep rumble of laughter. "I do but jest, old son, but you needn't worry, I've done a few. And it isn't such a bad job."

"Well that's great." I looked at my watch. "It's half past nine now, I'll get Siegfried to take over my morning round and I'll see you before eleven."

37

Granville had been called out when I arrived and I hung around his surgery till I heard the expensive sound of the Bentley purring into the yard. Through the window I saw yet another magnificent pipe glinting behind the wheel then my colleague, in an impeccable pin-striped suit which made him look like the Director of the Bank of England, paced majestically towards the side door.

"Good to see you, Jim!" he exclaimed, wringing my hand warmly. Then before removing his jacket he took his pipe from his mouth and regarded it with a trace of anxiety for a second before giving it a polish with his yellow cloth and placing it tenderly in a drawer.

It wasn't long before I was under the lamp in the operating room bending over Toby's small outstretched form while Granville—the other Granville Bennett—worked with fierce concentration inside the abdomen of the little animal.

"You see the gross gastric dilatation," he murmured. "Classical lesion." He gripped the pylorus and poised his scalpel. "Now I'm going through the serous coat." A quick deft incision. "A bit of blunt dissection here for the muscle fibers . . . down . . . down . . . a little more . . . ah there it is, can you see it—the mucosa bulging into the cleft. Yes . . . yes . . . just right. That's what you've got to arrive at."

I peered down at the tiny tube which had been the site of all Toby's troubles. "Is that all, then?"

"That's all, laddie." He stepped back with a grin. "The obstruction is relieved now and you can take bets that this little chap will start to put weight on now."

"That's wonderful, Granville. I'm really grateful."

"Nonsense, Jim, it was a pleasure. You can do the next one yourself now, eh?" He laughed, seized needle and sutures and sewed up the abdominal muscles and skin at an impossible pace.

A few minutes later he was in his office pulling on his jacket, then as he filled his pipe he turned to me. "I've got a little plan for the rest of the morning, laddie."

I shrank away from him and threw up a protective hand. "Well now, er . . . it's kind of you, Granville, but I really . . . I honestly must get back . . . we're very busy, you know . . . can't leave Siegfried too long . . . work'll be piling up . . ." I stopped because I felt I was beginning to gibber.

My colleague looked wounded. "All I meant, old son, was that we want you to come to lunch. Zoe is expecting you."

"Oh . . . oh, I see. We'll that's very kind. We're not going . . . anywhere else, then?"

"Anywhere else?" He blew out his cheeks and spread his arms wide. "Of course not. I just have to call in at my branch surgery on the way."

"Branch surgery? I didn't know you had one."

"Oh yes, just a stone's throw from my house." He put an arm round my shoulders. "Well let's go, shall we?"

As I lay back, cradled in the Bentley's luxury, I dwelt happily on the thought that at last I was going to meet Zoe Bennett when I was my normal self. She would learn this time that I wasn't a perpetually drunken oaf. In fact the next hour or two seemed full of rosy promise; an excellent lunch illumined by my witty conversation and polished manners, then back with Toby, magically resuscitated, to Darrowby.

I smiled to myself when I thought of Nellie's face when I told her her pet was going to be able to eat and grow strong and playful like any other pup. I was still smiling when the car pulled up on the outskirts of Granville's home village. I glanced idly through the window at a low stone building with leaded panes and a wooden sign dangling over the entrance. It read "Old Oak Tree Inn." I turned quickly to my companion.

"I thought we were going to your branch surgery?"

Granville gave me a smile of childish innocence. "Oh that's what I call this place. It's so near home and I transact quite a lot of business here." He patted my knee. "We'll just pop in for an appetizer, eh?"

"Now wait a minute," I stammered gripping the sides of my seat tightly. "I just can't be late today. I'd much rather . . ."

Granville raised a hand. "Jim, laddie, we won't be in for long." He looked at his watch. "It's exactly twelve thirty and I promised Zoe we'd be home by one o'clock. She's cooking roast beef and Yorkshire pudding and it would take a braver man than me to let her pudding go flat. I guarantee we'll be in that house at one o'clock on the dot—O.K.?"

I hesitated. I couldn't come to much harm in half an hour. I climbed out of the car.

As we went into the pub, a large man who had been leaning on the counter turned and exchanged enthusiastic greetings with my colleague.

"Albert!" cried Granville. "Meet Jim Herriot from Darrowby. Jim, this is Albert Wainwright, the landlord of the Wagon and Horses over in Matherley. In fact he's the president of the Licensed Victuallers' Association this year, aren't you, Albert?"

The big man grinned and nodded and for a moment I felt overwhelmed by the two figures on either side of me. It was difficult to describe the hard, bulky tissue of Granville's construction but Mr. Wainwright was unequivocally fat. A checked jacket hung open to display an enormous expanse of striped shirted abdomen overflowing the waistband of his trousers. Above a gay bowtie cheerful eyes twinkled at me from a red face and when he spoke his tone was rich and fruity. He embodied the rich ambience of the term "Licensed Victualler."

I began to sip at the half pint of beer I had ordered but when another appeared in two minutes I saw I was going to fall hopelessly behind and switched to the whiskies and sodas which the others were drinking. And my undoing was that both my companions appeared to have a standing account here; they downed their drinks, tapped softly on the counter and said "Yes please, Jack," whereupon three more glasses appeared with magical speed. I never had a chance to buy a round. In fact no money ever changed hands.

It was a quiet, friendly little session with Albert and Granville carrying on a conversation of the utmost good humour punctuated by the almost soundless taps on the bar. And as I fought to keep up with the two virtuosos the taps came more and more frequently till I seemed to hear them every few seconds.

Granville was as good as his word. When it was nearly one o'clock he looked at his watch.

"Got to be off now, Albert. Zoe's expecting us right now."

And as the car rolled to a stop outside the house dead on time I realised with a dull despair that it had happened to me again. Within me a witch's brew was beginning to bubble, sending choking fumes into my brain. I felt terrible and I knew for sure I would get rapidly worse.

Granville, fresh and debonnair as ever, leaped out and led me into the house.

"Zoe, my love!" he warbled, embracing his wife as she came through from the kitchen.

When she disengaged herself she came over to me. She was wearing a flowered apron which made her look if possible even more attractive.

"HelLO!" she cried and gave me that look which she shared with her husband as though meeting James Herriot was an unbelievable boon. "Lovely to see you again. I'll get lunch now." I replied with a foolish grin and she skipped away.

Flopping into an armchair I listened to Granville pouring steadily over at the sideboard. He put a glass in my hand and sat in another chair. Immediately the obese Staffordshire Terrier bounded on to his lap.

"Phoebles, my little pet!" he sang joyfully. "Daddy-kins is home again." And he pointed playfully at the tiny Yorkie who was sitting at his feet, baring her teeth repeatedly in a series of ecstatic smiles. "And I see you, my little Victoria, I see you!"

By the time I was ushered to the table I was like a man in a dream, moving sluggishly, speaking with slurred deliberation. Granville poised himself over a vast sirloin, stropped his knife briskly then began to hack away ruthlessly. He was a prodigal server and piled about two pounds of meat on my plate then he started on the Yorkshire puddings. Instead of a single big one, Zoe had made a large number of little round ones as the farmers' wives often did; delicious golden cups, crisply brown round the sides. Gran-ville heaped about six of these by the side of the meat as I watched stupidly. Then Zoe passed me the gravy boat.

With an effort I took a careful grip on the handle, closed one eye and began to pour. For some reason I felt I had to fill up each of the little puddings with gravy and I owlishly directed the stream into one then another till they were all overflowing. Once I missed and spilled a few drops of the fragrant liquid on the table cloth. I looked up guiltily at Zoe and giggled.

Zoe giggled back, and I had the impression that she felt that though I was a peculiar individual there was no harm in me. I just had this terrible weakness that I was never sober day or night, but I wasn't such a bad fellow at heart.

It usually took me a few days to recover from a visit to Granville and by the following Saturday I was convalescing nicely. It happened that I was in the market place and saw a large concourse of people crossing the cobbles. At first I thought from the mix-ture of children and adults that it must be a school outing but on closer inspection I realised it was only the Dimmocks and Pounders going shopping.

When they saw me they diverted their course and I was engulfed by a human wave.

"Look at 'im now, Mister!" "He's eatin' like a 'oss now!" "He's goin' to get fat soon, Mister!" The delighted cries rang around me.

Nellie had Toby on a lead and as I bent over the little animal I could hardly believe how a few days had altered him. He was still skinny but the hopeless look had gone; he was perky, ready to play. It was just a matter of time now.

His little mistress ran her hand again and again over the smooth brown coat.

"You are proud of your little dog, aren't you Nellie," I said, and the gentle squinting eyes turned on me.

"Yes, I am." She smiled that smile again. "Because 'e's mine."

38

It was almost as though I were looking at my own cows because as I stood in the little new byre and looked along the row of red and roan backs I felt a kind of pride.

"Frank," I said, "they look marvellous. You wouldn't think they were the same animals"

Frank Metcalfe grinned. "Just what I was thinking meself. It's wonderful what a change of setting'll do for livestock."

It was the cows' first day in the new byre. Previously I had seen them only in the old place—a typical Dales cowhouse, centuries old with a broken cobbled floor and gaping holes where the muck and urine lay in pools, rotting wooden partitions between the stalls and slit windows as though the place had been built as a fortress. I could remember Frank sitting in it milking, almost invisible in the gloom, the cobwebs hanging in thick fronds from the low roof above him.

In there, the ten cows had looked what they were—a motley assortment of ordinary milkers—but today they had acquired a new dignity and style.

"You must feel it's been worth all your hard work," I said, and the young farmer nodded and smiled. There was a grim touch about the smile as though he was reliving for a moment the hours and weeks and months of back-breaking labour he had put in there. Because Frank Metcalfe had done it all himself. The rows of neat, concreted standings, the clean, level sweep of floor, the whitewashed, cement-rendered walls all bathed in light from the spacious windows had been put there by his own two hands.

"I'll show you the dairy," Frank said.

We went into a small room which he had built at one end and I looked admiringly at the gleaming milk cooler, the spotless sinks and buckets, the strainer with its neat pile of filter pads.

"You know," I said. "This is how milk should be produced. All those mucky old places I see every day on my rounds—they nearly make my hair stand on end."

Frank leaned over and drew a jet of water from one of the taps. "Aye, you're right. It'll all be like this and better one day and it'll pay the farmers better too. I've got me T.T. licence now and the extra fourpence a gallon will make a hell of a difference. I feel I'm ready to start."

And when he did start, I thought, he'd go places. He seemed to have all the things it took to succeed at the hard trade of farming—intelligence, physical toughness, a love of the land and animals and the ability to go slogging on endlessly when other people were enjoying their leisure. I felt these qualities would overcome his biggest handicap which was simply that he didn't have any money.

Frank wasn't a farmer at all to start with. He was a steel worker from Middlesbrough. When he had first arrived less than a year ago with his young wife to take over the isolated small holding at Bransett I had been surprised to learn that he hailed from the city because he had the dark, sinewy look of the typical Dalesman—and he was called Metcalfe.

He had laughed when I mentioned this. "Oh, my great grandfather came from these parts and I've always had a hankering to come back."

As I came to know him better I was able to fill in the gaps in that simple statement. He had spent all his holidays up here as a small boy and though his father was a foreman in the steelworks and he himself had served his time at the trade the pull of the Dales had been like a siren song welling stronger till he had been unable to resist it any longer. He had worked on farms in his spare time, read all he could about agriculture and finally had thrown up his old life and rented the little place high in the fells at the end of a long, stony track.

With its primitive house and tumbledown buildings it seemed an unpromising place to make a living and in any case I hadn't much faith in the ability of townspeople to suddenly turn to farming and make a go of it; in my short experience I had seen quite a few try and fail. But Frank Metcalfe had gone about the job as though he had been at it all his life, repairing the broken walls, improving the grassland, judiciously buying stock on his shoe-string budget; there was no sign of the bewilderment and despair I had seen in so many others.

I had mentioned this to a retired farmer in Darrowby and the old man chuckled. "Aye, you've got to have farmin' inside you. There's very few people as can succeed at it unless it's in their blood. It matters nowt that young Metcalfe's been brought up in a town, he's still got it in 'im—he's got it through the titty, don't you see, through the titty."

Maybe he was right, but whether Frank had it through the titty or through study and brains he had transformed the holding in a short time. When he wasn't milking, feeding, mucking out, he was slaving at that little byre, chipping stones, mixing cement, sand and dust clinging to the sweat on his face. And now, as he said, he was ready to start.

As we came out of the dairy he pointed to another old building across the yard. "When I'm straightened out I aim to convert that into another byre. I've had to borrow a good bit but now I'm T.T. I should be able to clear it off in a couple of years. Sometime in the future if all goes well I might be able to get a bigger place altogether."

He was about my own age and a natural friendship had sprung up between us. We used to sit under the low beams of his cramped living room with its single small window and sparse furniture and as his young wife poured cups of tea he liked to talk of his plans.

And, listening to him, I always felt that a man like him would do well not only for himself but for farming in general.

I looked at him now as he turned his head and gazed for a few moments round his domain. He didn't have to say: "I love this place, I feel I belong here." It was all there in his face, in the softening of his eyes as they moved over the huddle of grass fields cupped in a hollow of the fells. These fields, clawed by past generations from the rough hillside and fighting their age-old battle with heather and bracken, ran up to a ragged hem of cliff and scree and above you could just see the lip of the moor—a wild land of bog and peat hag. Below, the farm track disappeared round the bend of a wooded hill. The pastures were poor and knuckles of rock pushed out in places through the thin soil, but the clean, turf-scented air and the silence must have been like a deliverance after the roar and smoke of the steelworks.

"Well we'd better see that cow, Frank," I said. "The new byre nearly made me forget what I came for."

"Aye, it's this red and white 'un. My latest purchase and she's never been right since I got her. Hasn't come on to her milk properly and she seems dosy, somehow."

The temperature was a hundred and three and as I put the thermometer away I sniffed. "She smells a bit, doesn't she?"

"Aye," Frank said. "I've noticed that myself."

"Better bring me some hot water, then. I'll have a feel inside."

The uterus was filled with a stinking exudate and as I withdrew my arm there was a gush of yellowish, necrotic material. "Surely she must have had a bit of a discharge," I said.

Frank nodded. "Yes, she has had, but I didn't pay much attention—a lot of them do it when they're clearing up after calving."

I drained the uterus by means of a rubber tube and irrigated it with antiseptic, then I pushed in a few acriflavine pessaries. "That'll help to clean her up, and I think she'll soon be a lot better in herself, but I'm going to take a blood sample from her."

"Why's that?"

"Well it may be nothing, but I don't like the look of that yellow stuff. It consists of decayed cotyledone—you know, the berries on the calf bed—and when they're that colour it's a bit suspicious of Brucellosis."

"Abortion, you mean?"

"It's possible, Frank. She may have calved before her time or she may have calved normally but still been infected. Anyway the blood will tell us. Keep her isolated in the meantime."

A few days later at breakfast time in Skeldale House I felt a quick stab of anxiety as I opened the lab report and read that the agglutination test on the blood had given a positive result. I hurried out to the farm.

"How long have you had this cow?" I asked.

"Just over three weeks," the young farmer replied.

"And she's been running in the same field as your other cows and the in-calf heifers?"

"Yes, all the time."

I paused for a moment. "Frank, I'd better tell you the implications. I know you'll want to know what might happen. The source of infection in Brucellosis is the discharges of an infected cow and I'm afraid this animal of yours will have thoroughly contaminated that pasture. Any or all of your animals may have picked up the bug."

"Does that mean they'll abort?"

"Not necessarily. It varies tremendously. Many cows carry their calves through despite infection." I was doing my best to sound optimistic.

Frank dug his hands deep into his pockets. His thin, dark-complexioned face was serious. "Damn, I wish I'd never seen the thing. I bought her at Houlton market—God knows where she came from, but it's too late to talk like that now. What can we do about the job?"

"The main thing is to keep her isolated and away

from the other stock. I wish there was some way to protect the others but there isn't much we can do. There are only two types of vaccine—live ones which can only be given to empty cows and yours are all in-calf, and dead ones which aren't reckoned to be of much use."

"Well I'm the sort that doesn't like to just sit back and wait. The dead vaccine won't do any harm if it doesn't do any good, will it?"

"No."

"Right, let's do 'em all with it and we'll hope for the best."

Hoping for the best was something vets did a lot in the thirties. I vaccinated the entire herd and we waited.

Nothing happened for a full eight weeks. Summer lengthened into autumn and the cattle were brought inside. The infected cow improved, her discharge cleared up and she began to milk a bit better. Then Frank rang early one morning.

"I've found a dead calf laid in the channel when I went in to milk. Will you come?"

It was a thinly-haired seven months foetus that I found. The cow looked sick and behind her dangled the inevitable retained placenta. Her udder which, if she had calved normally, would have been distended with milk, the precious milk which Frank depended on for his livelihood, was almost empty.

Obsessed by a feeling of helplessness I could only offer the same old advice; isolate, disinfect—and hope.

A fortnight later one of the in-calf heifers did it— she was a pretty little Jersey cross which Frank had hoped would push up his butter fat percentage—and a week after that one of the cows slipped a calf in her sixth month of pregnancy.

It was when I was visiting this third case that I met Mr. Bagley. Frank introduced him somewhat apologetically. "He says he has a cure for this trouble, Jim. He wants to talk to you about it."

In every sticky situation there is always somebody who knows better than the vet. Subconsciously I suppose I had been waiting for a Mr. Bagley to turn up and I listened patiently.

He was very short with bandy legs in cloth leggings, and he looked up at me intently. "Young man, I've been through this on ma own farm and ah wouldn't be here today if I hadn't found the remedy."

"I see, and what was that, Mr. Bagley?"

"I have it 'ere." The little man pulled a bottle from his jacket pocket. "It's a bit mucky—it's been stood in t'cow house window for a year or two."

I read the label. "Professor Driscoll's Abortion Cure. Give two tablespoonsful to each cow in the herd in a pint of water and repeat on the following day." The professor's face took up most of the label. He was an aggressive-looking, profusely whiskered man in a high Victorian collar and he glared out at me belligerently through a thick layer of dust. He wasn't so daft, either, because lower down the bottle I read, "If an animal has aborted a dose of this mixture will prevent further trouble." He knew as well as I did that they didn't often do it more than once.

"Yes," Mr. Bagley said. "That's the stuff. Most of my cows did it on me but I kept goin' with the medicine and they were right as a bobbin next time round."

"But they would be in any case. They develop an immunity you see."

Mr. Bagley put his head on one side and gave a gentle unbelieving smile. And who was I to argue, anyway? I hadn't a thing to offer.

"O.K., Frank," I said wearily. "Go ahead—like my vaccine, I don't suppose it can do any harm."

A fresh bottle of Driscoll's cure was purchased and little Mr. Bagley supervised the dosing of the herd. He was cock-a-hoop when, three weeks later, one of the cows calved bang on time.

"Now then, what do you say, young man? Ma stuff's working already, isn't it?"

"Well I expected some of them to calve normally," I replied and the little man pursed his lips as though he considered me a bad loser.

But I wasn't really worried about what he thought;

all I felt was an unhappy resignation. Because this sort of thing was always happening in those days before the modern drugs appeared. Quack medicines abounded on the farms and the vets couldn't say a lot about them because their own range of pharmaceuticals was pitifully inadequate.

And in those diseases like abortion which had so far defeated all the efforts of the profession at control the harvest for the quack men was particularly rich. The farming press and country newspapers were filled with confident advertisements for red drenches, block draughts, pink powders which were positively guaranteed to produce results. Professor Driscoll had plenty of competition.

When shortly afterwards another cow calved to time Mr. Bagley was very nice about it. "We all 'ave to learn, young man, and you haven't had much practical experience. You just hadn't heard of my medicine and I'm not blaming you, but I think we're on top of t'job now."

I didn't say anything. Frank was beginning to look like a man who could see a gleam of hope and I wasn't going to extinguish it by voicing my doubts. Maybe the outbreak had run its course—these things were unpredictable.

But the next time I heard Frank on the phone all my gloomy forebodings were realised. "I want you to come out and cleanse three cows."

"Three!"

"Aye, they did it one after the other—bang, bang, bang. And all before time. It's an absolute bugger, Jim—I don't know what I'm going to do."

He met me as I got out of the car at the top of the track. He looked ten years older, his face pale and haggard as though he hadn't slept. Mr. Bagley was there, too, digging a hole in front of the byre door.

"What's he doing?" I asked.

Frank looked down at his boots expressionlessly. "He's burying one of the calves. He says it does a lot of good if you put it in front of the door." He looked at me with an attempt at a smile. "Science can do nowt for me so we might as well try a bit of black magic."

I felt a few years older myself as I picked my way round the deep grave Mr. Bagley was digging. The little man looked up at me as I passed. "This is a very old remedy," he explained. "Ma medicine seems to be losing its power so we'll have to try summat stronger. The trouble is," he added with some asperity, "I was called in on this case far too late."

I removed the putrefying afterbirths from the three cows and got off the place as soon as possible. I felt such a deep sense of shame that I could hardly meet Frank's eye. And it was even worse on my next visit a fortnight later because as I walked across the yard I was conscious of a strange smell polluting the sweet hill air. It was a penetrating, acrid stink and though it rang a bell somewhere I couldn't quite identify it. As Frank came out of the house he saw me sniffing and looking round.

"Not very nice is it?" he said with a tired smile. "I don't believe you've met our goat."

"You've got a goat?"

"Well, we've got the loan of one—an old Billy. I don't see him around right now but by God you can always smell him. Mr. Bagley dug 'im up somewhere —says he did one of his neighbours a world of good when he was having my trouble. Burying the calves wasn't doing any good so he thought he'd better bring on the goat. It's the smell that does the trick, he says."

"Frank, I'm sorry," I said. "It's still going on, then?"

He shrugged his shoulders. "Aye, two more since I saw you. But I'm past worrying now, Jim, and for God's sake stop looking so bloody miserable yourself. You can't do anything, I know that. Nobody can do anything."

Driving home, I brooded on his words. Contagious Bovine Abortion has been recognised for centuries and I had read in old books of the filthy scourge which ravaged and ruined the ancient farmers just as it was doing to Frank Metcalfe today. The experts of those days said it was due to impure water, improper feeding, lack of exercise, sudden frights. They did note, however, that other cows which were allowed to sniff at the foetuses and afterbirths were likely to suffer the same fate themselves. But beyond that it was a black tunnel of ignorance.

We modern vets, on the other hand, knew all about it. We knew it was caused by a gram negative bacillus called Brucella abortus whose habits and attributes we had studied till we knew its every secret; but when it came to helping a farmer in Frank's situation we were about as much use as our colleagues of old who wrote those quaint books. True, dedicated researchers were working to find a strain of the bacillus which would form a safe and efficient vaccine to immunise cattle in calfhood and as far back as 1930 a certain strain 19 had been developed from which much was hoped. But even now it was still in the experimental stage. If Frank had had the luck to be born twenty years later the chances are that those cows he bought would have all been vaccinated and protected by that same strain 19. Nowadays we even have an efficient dead vaccine for the pregnant cows.

Best of all there is now a scheme under way for the complete eradication of Brucellosis and this has brought the disease to the notice of the general public. People are naturally interested mainly in the public health aspect and they have learned about the vast spectrum of illnesses which the infected milk can cause in humans. But few townsmen know what Brucellosis can do to farmers.

The end of Frank's story was not far away. Autumn was reaching into winter and the frost was sparkling on the steps of Skeldale House when he called one night to see me. We went into the big room and I opened a couple bottles of beer.

"I thought I'd come and tell you, Jim," he said in a matter of fact tone. "I'm having to pack up."

"Pack up?" Something in me refused to accept what he was saying.

"Aye, I'm going back to me old job in Middlesbrough. There's nowt else to do."

I looked at him helplessly. "It's as bad as that, is it?"

"Well just think." He smiled grimly. "I have three cows which calved normally out of the whole herd. The rest are a mucky, discharging, sickly lot with no milk worth talking about. I've got no calves to sell or keep as replacements. I've got nowt."

I hesitated. "There's no hope of raising the wind to get you over this?"

"No, Jim. If I sell up now I'll just about be able to pay the bank what I owe them. The rest I borrowed from my old man and I'm not goin' back to him for more. I promised him I'd return to the steelworks if this didn't work out and that's what I'm goin' to do."

"Oh hell, Frank," I said. "I can't tell you how sorry I am. You haven't had a scrap of luck all the way through."

He looked at me and smiled with no trace of self pity. "Aye well," he said. "These things happen."

I almost jumped at the words. "These things happen!" That's what farmers always said after a disaster. That old man in Darrowby had been right. Frank really did have it through the titty.

And in truth he wasn't the only man to be bankrupted in this way. What had hit Frank was called an "abortion storm" and the same sort of thing had driven a legion of good men to the wall. Some of them hung on, tightened their belts, spent their life savings and half starved till the storm abated and they could start again. But Frank had no savings to see him through; his venture had been a gamble from the beginning and he had lost.

I never heard of him again. At first I thought he might write, but then I realised that once the agonising break had been made it had to be complete.

From some parts of the northern Pennines you can see away over the great sprawl of Teesside and when the fierce glow from the blast furnaces set the night sky alight I used to think of Frank down there and wonder how he was getting on. He'd make a go of it all right, but how often did his mind turn to the high-blown green hollow where he had hoped to build something worth while and to live and bring up his children?

Some people called Peters bought the little farm at Bransett after he left. Strangely enough they were from Teesside, too, but Mr. Peters was a wealthy director of the I.C.I. and used the place only as a weekend retreat. It was ideal for the purpose because he had a young family all keen on riding and the fields were soon being grazed by an assortment of horses and ponies. In the summer Mrs. Peters used to spend months on end up there with the children. They were nice people who cared for their animals and I was a frequent visitor.

The dwelling house was renovated almost out of recognition and I drank coffee instead of tea in the living room which had become a place of grace and charm with an antique table, chintzy furniture and pictures on the walls. The old outbuildings were converted into loose boxes with shining, freshly painted doors.

The only thing which got no attention was Frank's little new byre; it was used as a storage place for corn and bedding for the horses.

I always felt a tug at my heart when I looked in there at the thick dust on the floor, the windows almost opaque with dirt, the cobwebs everywhere, the rusting water bowls, the litter of straw bales, peat moss and sacks of oats where once Frank's cows had stood so proudly.

It was all that was left of a man's dream.

39

I had never been married before so there was nothing in my past experience to go by but it was beginning to dawn on me that I was very nicely fixed.

I am talking, of course, of material things. It would have been enough for me or anybody else to be paired with a beautiful girl whom I loved and who loved me. I hadn't reckoned on the other aspects.

This business of studying my comfort, for instance. I thought such things had gone out of fashion, but not so with Helen. It was brought home to me again as I walked in to breakfast this morning. We had at last acquired a table—I had bought it at a farm sale and brought it home in triumph tied to the roof of my car—and now Helen had vacated the chair on which she used to sit at the bench and had taken over the high stool. She was perched away up there now, transporting her food from far below, while I was expected to sit comfortably in the chair. I don't think I am a selfish swine by nature but there was nothing I could do about it.

And there were other little things. The neat pile of clothing laid out for me each morning; the clean, folded shirt and handkerchief and socks so different from the jumble of my bachelor days. And when I was late for meals, which was often, she served me with my food but instead of going off and doing something else she would down tools and sit watching me while I ate. It made me feel like a sultan.

It was this last trait which gave me a clue to her behaviour. I suddenly remembered that I had seen her sitting by Mr. Alderson while he had a late meal;

358

sitting in the same pose, one arm on the table, quietly watching him. And I realised I was reaping the benefit of her lifetime attitude to her father. Mild little man though he was she had catered gladly to his every wish in the happy acceptance that the man of the house was number one; and the whole pattern was rubbing off on me now.

In fact it set me thinking about the big question of how girls might be expected to behave after marriage. One old farmer giving me advice about choosing a wife once said: "Have a bloody good look at the mother first, lad," and I am sure he had a point. But if I may throw in my own little word of counsel it would be to have a passing glance at how she acts towards her father.

Watching her now as she got down and started to serve my breakfast the warm knowledge flowed through me as it did so often that my wife was the sort who just liked looking after a man and that I was so very lucky.

And I was certainly blooming under the treatment. A bit too much, in fact, and I was aware I shouldn't be attacking this plateful of porridge and cream; especially with all that material sizzling in the frying pan. Helen had brought with her to Skeldale House a delicious dowry in the shape of half a pig and there hung from the beams of the topmost attic a side of bacon and a majestic ham; a constant temptation. Some samples were in the pan now and though I had never been one for large breakfasts I did not demur when she threw in a couple of big brown eggs to keep them company. And I put up only feeble resistance when she added some particularly tasty smoked sausage which she used to buy in a shop in the market place.

When I had got through it all I rose rather deliberately from the table and as I put on my coat I noticed it wasn't so easy to button as it used to be.

"Here are your sandwiches, Jim," Helen said, putting a parcel in my hand. I was spending a day in the Scarburn district, tuberculin testing for Ewan Ross, and my wife was always concerned lest I grow faint from lack of nourishment on the long journey.

I kissed her, made a somewhat ponderous descent of the long flights of stairs and went out the side door. Half way up the garden I stopped as always and looked up at the window under the tiles. An arm appeared and brandished a dishcloth vigorously. I waved back and continued my walk to the yard. I found I was puffing a little as I got the car out and I laid my parcel almost guiltily on the back seat. I knew what it would contain; not just sandwiches but meat and onion pie, buttered scones, ginger cake to lead me into further indiscretions.

There is no doubt that in those early days I would have grown exceedingly gross under Helen's treatment. But my job saved me; the endless walking between the stone barns scattered along the hillsides, the climbing in and out of calf pens, pushing cows around, and regular outbursts of hard physical effort in calving and foaling. So I escaped with only a slight tightening of my collar and the occasional farmer's remark, "By gaw, you've been on a good pasture, young man!"

Driving away, I marvelled at the way she indulged my little whims, too. I have always had a pathological loathing of fat, so Helen carefully trimmed every morsel from my meat. This feeling about fat, which almost amounted to terror, had been intensified since coming to Yorkshire, because back in the thirties the farmers seemed to live on the stuff. One old man, noticing my pop-eyed expression as I viewed him relishing his lunch of roast fat bacon, told me he had never touched lean meat in his life.

"Ah like to feel t'grease runnin' down ma chin!" he chuckled. He pronounced it "grayus" which made it sound even worse. But he was a ruddy faced octogenarian, so it hadn't done him any harm; and this held good for hundreds of others just like him. I used to think that the day in day out and hard labour of farming burned it up in their systems but if I had to eat the stuff it would kill me very rapidly.

The latter was, of course, a fanciful notion as was proved to me one day.

It was when I was torn from my bed one morning at 6 a.m. to attend a calving heifer at old Mr. Horner's small farm and when I got there I found there was no malpresentation of the calf but that it was simply too big. I don't like a lot of pulling but the heifer, lying on her bed of straw, was obviously in need of assistance. Every few seconds she strained to the utmost and a pair of feet came into view momentarily then disappeared as she relaxed.

"Is she getting those feet out any further?" I asked.

"Nay, there's been no change for over an hour," the old man replied.

"And when did the water bag burst?"

"Two hours since."

There was no doubt the calf was well and truly stuck and getting drier all the time, and if the labouring mother had been able to speak I think she would have said: "For Pete's sake get this thing away from me!"

I could have done with a big strong man to help me but Mr. Horner, apart from his advanced age, was a rather shaky lightweight. And since the farm was perched on a lonely eminence miles from the nearest village there was no chance of calling in a neighbour. I would have to do the job myself.

It took me nearly an hour. With a thin rope behind the calf's ears and through his mouth to stop the neck from telescoping I eased the little creature inch by inch into the world. Not so much pulling but rather leaning back and helping the heifer as she strained. She was a rather undersized little animal and she lay patiently on her side, accepting the situation with the resignation of her kind. She could never have calved without help and all the time I had the warm conviction that I was doing what she wanted and needed. I felt I should be as patient as she was so I didn't hurry but let things come in their normal sequence; the little nose with the nostrils twitching reassuringly, then the eyes wearing a preoccupied light during the tight squeeze, then the ears and with a final rush the rest of the calf.

The young mother was obviously none the worse because she rolled on to her chest almost immediately and began to sniff with the utmost interest at the new arrival. She was in better shape than myself because I discovered with some surprise that I was sweating and breathless and my arms and shoulders were aching.

The farmer, highly pleased, rubbed my back briskly with the towel as I bent over the bucket, then he helped me on with my shirt.

"Well that's champion, lad. You'll come in and have a cup of tea now, won't you?"

In the kitchen Mrs. Horner placed a steaming mug on the table and smiled across at me.

"Will you sit down along o' my husband and have a bit o' breakfast?" she asked.

There is nothing like an early calving to whet the appetite and I nodded readily. "That's very kind of you, I'd love to."

It is always a good feeling after a successful delivery and I sighed contentedly as I sank into a chair and watched the old lady set out bread, butter and jam in front of me. I sipped my tea and as I exchanged a word with the farmer I didn't see what she was doing next. Then my toes curled into a tight ball as I found two huge slices of pure white fat lying on my plate.

Shrinking back in my seat I saw Mrs. Horner sawing at a great hunk of cold boiled bacon. But it wasn't ordinary bacon, it was one hundred per cent fat without a strip of lean anywhere. Even in my shocked state I could see it was a work of art; cooked to a turn, beautifully encrusted with golden crumbs and resting on a spotless serving dish . . . but fat.

She dropped two similar slices on her husband's plate and looked at me expectantly.

My position was desperate. I could not possibly offend this sweet old person but on the other hand

I knew beyond all doubt that there was no way I
could eat what lay in front of me. Maybe I could
have managed a tiny piece if it had been hot and
fried crisp, but cold, boiled and clammy . . . never.
And there was an enormous quantity; two slices about
six inches by four and at least half an inch thick
with the golden border of crumbs down one side.
The thing was impossible.

Mrs. Horner sat down opposite me. She was wearing a flowered mob cap over her white hair and
for a moment she reached out, bent her head to one
side and turned the dish with the slab of bacon a
little to the left to show it off better. Then she turned
to me and smiled. It was a kind, proud smile.

There have been times in my life when, confronted
by black and hopeless circumstances, I have discovered in myself undreamed-of resources of courage
and resolution. I took a deep breath, seized knife
and fork and made a bold incision in one of the
slices, but as I began to transport the greasy white
segment to my mouth I began to shudder and my
hand stayed frozen in space. It was at that moment
I spotted the jar of piccalilli.

Feverishly I scooped a mound of it on to my plate.
It seemed to contain just about everything; onions,
apples, cucumber and other assorted vegetables jos-
tling each other in a powerful mustard-vinegar sauce.
It was the work of a moment to smother my loaded
fork with the mass, then I popped it into my mouth,
gave a couple of quick chews and swallowed. It was
a start and I hadn't tasted a thing except the piccalilli.

"Nice bit of bacon," Mr. Horner murmured.

"Delicious!" I replied, munching desperately at the
second forkful. "Absolutely delicious!"

"And you like ma piccalilli too!" The old lady
beamed at me. "Ah can tell by the way you're slap-
pin' it on!" She gave a peal of delighted laughter.

"Yes indeed," I looked at her with streaming eyes.
"Some of the best I've ever tasted."

Looking back, I realise it was one of the bravest

things I have ever done. I stuck to my task unwaveringly, dipping again and again into the jar, keeping my mind a blank, refusing grimly to think of the horrible thing that was happening to me. There was only one bad moment, when the piccalilli, which packed a tremendous punch and was never meant to be consumed in large mouthfuls, completely took my breath away and I went into a long coughing spasm. But at last I came to the end. A final heroic crunch and swallow, a long gulp at my tea and the plate was empty. The thing was accomplished.

And there was no doubt it had been worth it. I had been a tremendous success with the old folks. Mr. Horner slapped my shoulder.

"By gaw, it's good to see a young feller enjoyin' his food! When I were a lad I used to put it away sharpish, like that, but ah can't do it now." Chuckling to himself, he continued with his breakfast.

His wife showed me the door. "Aye, it was a real compliment to me." She looked at the table and giggled. "You've nearly finished the jar!"

"Yes, I'm sorry, Mrs. Horner," I said, smiling through my tears and trying to ignore the churning in my stomach. "But I just couldn't resist it."

Contrary to my expectations I didn't drop down dead soon afterwards but for a week I was oppressed by a feeling of nausea which I am prepared to believe was purely psychosomatic.

At any rate, since that little episode I have never knowingly eaten fat again. My hatred was transformed into something like an obsession from then on.

And I haven't been all that crazy about piccalilli either.

40

"Well, do you want t'job or don't you?"

Walt Barnett towered over me in the surgery doorway and his eyes flickered from my head to my feet and up again without expression. The cigarette dangling from his lower lip seemed to be a part of him as did the brown trilby hat and the shining navy blue serge suit stretched tightly over his bulky form. He must have weighed nearly twenty stones and with his red beefy brutal mouth and overbearing manner he was undeniably formidable.

"Well, er . . . yes. Of course we want the job," I replied. "I was just wondering when we could fit it in." I went over to the desk and began to look through the appointment book. "We're pretty full this week and I don't know what Mr. Farnon has fixed for the week after. Maybe we'd better give you a ring."

The big man had burst in on me without warning or greeting and barked, "I 'ave a fine big blood 'oss to geld. When can you do 'im?"

I had looked at him hesitantly for a few moments, taken aback partly by the arrogance of his approach, partly by his request. This wasn't good news to me; I didn't like castrating fine big blood 'osses—I much preferred the ordinary cart colts and if you came right down to it I had a particular preference for Shetland ponies. But it was all part of living and if it had to be done it had to be done.

"You can give me a ring if you like, but don't be ower long about it." The hard unsmiling stare still held me. "And I want a good job doin', think on!"

"We always try to do a good job, Mr. Barnett," I said, fighting a rising prickle of resentment at his attitude.

"Aye well I've heard that afore and I've had some bloody balls-ups," he said. He gave me a final trucu- lent nod, turned and walked out, leaving the door open.

I was still standing in the middle of the room seething and muttering to myself when Siegfried walked in. I hardly saw him at first and when he finally came into focus I found I was glowering into his face.

"What's the trouble, James?" he asked. "A little touch of indigestion, perhaps?"

"Indigestion? No . . . no . . . Why do you say that?"

"Well you seemed to be in some sort of pain, standing there on one leg with your face screwed up."

"Did I look like that? Oh it was just our old friend Walt Barnett. He wants us to cut a horse for him and he made the request in his usual charming way —he really gets under my skin, that man."

Tristan came in from the passage. "Yes, I was out there and I heard him. He's a bloody big lout."

Siegfried rounded on him. "That's enough! I don't want to hear that kind of talk in here." Then he turned back to me. "And really, James, even if you were upset I don't think it's an excuse for profanity."

"What do you mean?"

"Well, some of the expletives I heard you mutter- ing there were unworthy of you." He spread his hands in a gesture of disarming frankness. "Heaven knows I'm no prude but I don't like to hear such language within these walls." He paused and his fea- tures assumed an expression of deep gravity. "After all, the people who come in here provide us with our bread and butter and they should be referred to with respect."

"Yes, but . . ."

"Oh I know some are not as nice as others but you must never let them irritate you. You've heard the

old saying, 'The customer is always right.' Well I
think it's a good working axiom and I always abide
by it myself." He gazed solemnly at Tristan and me
in turn. "So I hope I make myself clear. No swearing
in the surgery—particularly when it concerns the clients."

"It's all right for you!" I burst out heatedly. "But
you didn't hear Barnett. I'll stand so much, but . . ."

Siegfried put his head on one side and a smile of
ethereal beauty crept over his face. "My dear old
chap, there you go again, letting little things disturb
you. I've had to speak to you about this before,
haven't I? I wish I could help you, I wish I could
pass on my own gift of remaining calm at all times."

"What's that you said?"

"I said I wanted to help you, James, and I will."
He held up a forefinger. "You've probably often wondered why I never get angry or excited."

"Eh?"

"Oh I know you have—you must have. Well I'll
let you into a little secret." His smile took on a
roguish quality. "If a client is rude to me I simply
charge him a little more. Instead of getting all
steamed up like you do I tell myself that I'm putting
ten bob extra on the bill and it works like magic."

"Is that so?"

"Yes indeed, my boy." He thumped my shoulder
then became very serious. "Of course I realise that I
have an advantage right at the start—I have been
blessed with a naturally even temperament while you
are blown about in all directions by every little wind
of circumstance. But I do think that this is something you could cultivate, so work at it, James, work
at it. All this fretting and fuming is bad for you—
your whole life would change if you could just ac-
quire my own tranquil outlook."

I swallowed hard. "Well thank you, Siegfried," I
said. "I'll try."

Walt Barnett was a bit of a mystery man in Darrowby. He wasn't a farmer, he was a scrap merchant,

a haulier, a dealer in everything from linoleum to second hand cars, and there was only one thing the local people could say for certain about him—he had brass, lots of brass. They said everything he touched turned to money.

He had bought a decaying mansion a few miles outside the town where he lived with a downtrodden little wife and where he kept a floating population of livestock; a few bullocks, some pigs and always a horse or two. He employed all the vets in the district in turn, probably because he didn't think much of any of us; a feeling which, I may say, was mutual. He never seemed to do any physical work and could be seen most days of the week shambling around the streets of Darrowby, hands in pockets, cigarette dangling, his brown trilby on the back of his head, his huge body threatening to burst through that shiny navy suit.

After my meeting with him we had a busy few days and it was on the following Thursday that the phone rang in the surgery. Siegfried lifted it and immediately his expression changed. From across the floor I could clearly hear the loud hectoring tones coming through the receiver and as my colleague listened a slow flush spread over his cheeks and his mouth hardened. Several times he tried to put in a word but the torrent of sound from the far end was unceasing. Finally he raised his voice and broke in but instantly there was a click and he found himself speaking to a dead line.

Siegfried crashed the receiver into its rest and swung round. "That was Barnett—playing hell because we haven't rung him." He stood staring at me for a few moments, his face dark with anger.

"The bloody bastard!" he shouted. "Who the hell does he think he is? Abusing me like that, then hanging up on me when I try to speak!"

For a moment he was silent then he turned to me. "I'll tell you this, James, he wouldn't have spoken to me like that if he'd been in this room with me." He

came over to me and held out his hands, fingers
crooked menacingly. "I'd have wrung his bloody
neck, big as he is! I would have, I tell you, I'd
have strangled the bugger!"

"But Siegfried," I said. "What about your system?"

"System? What system?"

"Well, you know the trick you have when people
are unpleasant—you put something on the bill, don't
you?"

Siegfried let his hands fall to his sides and stared
at me for some time, his chest rising and falling with
his emotion. Then he patted me on the shoulder and
turned away towards the window where he stood
looking out at the quiet street.

When he turned back to me he looked grim but
calmer. "By God, James, you're right. That's the answer. I'll cut Barnett's horse for him but I'll charge
him a tenner."

I laughed heartily. In those days the average
charge for castrating a horse was a pound, or if you
wanted to be more professional, a guinea.

"What are you laughing at?" my colleague enquired sourly.

"Well . . . at your joke. I mean, ten pounds . . .
ha-ha-ha!"

"I'm not joking, I'm going to charge him a tenner."

"Oh come on, Siegfried, you can't do that."

"You just watch me," he said. "I'm going to sort
that bugger."

Two mornings later I was going through the familiar motions of preparing for a castration; boiling up
the emasculator and laying it on the enamel tray
along with the scalpel, the roll of cotton wool, the
artery forceps, the tincture of iodine, the suture materials, the tetanus antitoxin and syringes. For the
last five minutes Siegfried had been shouting at me
to hurry.

"What the hell are you doing through there,
James? Don't forget to put in an extra bottle of chlor-

oform. And bring the sidelines in case he doesn't go down. Where have you hidden those spare scalpel blades, James?"

The sunshine streamed across the laden tray, filtering through the green tangle of the wistaria which fell untidily across the surgery window. Reminding me that it was May and that there was nowhere a May morning came with such golden magic as to the long garden at Skeldale House; the high brick walls with their crumbling mortar and ancient stone copings enfolding the sunlight in a warm clasp and spilling it over the untrimmed lawns, the banks of lupins and bluebells, the masses of fruit blossom. And right at the top the rooks cawing in the highest branches of the elms.

Siegfried, chloroform muzzle looped over one shoulder, made a final check of the items on the tray then we set off. In less than half an hour we were driving through the lodge gates of the old mansion then along a mossy avenue which wandered among pine and birch trees up to the house which looked out from its wooded background over the rolling miles of fell and moor.

Nobody could have asked for a more perfect place for the operation; a high-walled paddock deep in lush grass. The two-year-old, a magnificent chestnut, was led in by two characters who struck me as typical henchmen for Mr. Barnett. I don't know where he had dug them up but you didn't see faces like that among the citizens of Darrowby. One was a brown goblin who, as he conversed with his companion, repeatedly jerked his head and winked one eye as though they were sharing some disreputable secret. The other had a head covered with ginger stubble surmounting a countenance of a bright scrofulous red which looked as though a piece would fall off if you touched it; and deep in the livid flesh two tiny eyes darted.

The two of them regarded us unsmilingly and the dark one spat luxuriously as we approached.

"It's a nice morning," I said.

Ginger just stared at me while Winker nodded knowingly and closed one eye as if I had uttered some craftiness which appealed to him.

The vast hunched figure of Mr. Barnett hovered in the background, cigarette drooping, the bright sunshine striking brilliant shafts of light from the tight sheen of the navy suit.

I couldn't help comparing the aspect of the trio of humans with the natural beauty and dignity of the horse. The big chestnut tossed his head then stood looking calmly across the paddock, the large fine eyes alight with intelligence, the noble lines of the face and neck blending gently into the grace and power of the body. Observations I had heard about the higher and lower animals floated about in my mind.

Siegfried walked around the horse, patting him and talking to him, his eyes shining with the delight of the fanatic.

"He's a grand sort, Mr. Barnett," he said.

The big man glowered at him. "Aye well, don't spoil 'im, that's all. I've paid a lot o' money for that 'oss."

Siegfried gave him a thoughtful look then turned to me.

"Well, let's get on. We'll drop him over there on that long grass. Are you ready, James?"

I was ready, but I'd be a lot more at ease if Siegfried would just leave me alone. In horse work I was the anaesthetist and my colleague was the surgeon. And he was good; quick, deft, successful. I had no quarrel with the arrangement; he could get on with his job and let me do mine. But there was the rub; he would keep butting into my territory and I found it wearing.

Anaesthesia in the large animals has a dual purpose; it abolishes pain and acts as a means of restraint. It is obvious that you can't do much with these potentially dangerous creatures unless they are controlled.

That was my job. I had to produce a sleeping patient ready for the knife and very often I thought it was the most difficult part. Until the animal was properly under I always felt a certain tension and Siegfried didn't help in this respect. He would hover at my elbow, offering advice as to the quantity of chloroform and he could never bear to wait until the anaesthetic had taken effect. He invariably said, "He isn't going to go down, James." Then, "Don't you think you should strap a fore leg up?"

Even now, thirty years later, when I am using such intravenous drugs as thiopentone he is still at it. Stamping around impatiently as I fill my syringe, poking over my shoulder with a long fore-finger into the jugular furrow. "I'd shove it in just there, James."

I stood there irresolute, my partner by my side, the chloroform bottle in my pocket, the muzzle dangling from my hand. It would be wonderful, I thought, if just once I could be on my own to get on with it. And, after all, I had worked for him for nearly three years—surely I knew him well enough to be able to put it to him.

I cleared my throat. "Siegfried, I was just wondering. Would you care to go and sit down over there for a few minutes till I get him down?"

"What's that?"

"Well I thought it would be a good idea if you left me to it. There's a bit of a crowd round the horse's head—I don't want him excited. So why don't you relax for a while. I'll give you a shout when he's down."

Siegfried raised a hand. "My dear chap, anything you say. I don't know what I'm hanging around here for anyway. I never interfere with your end as you well know." He turned about and, tray under arm, marched off to where he had parked his car on the grass about fifty yards away. He strode round behind the Rover and sat down on the turf, his back against the metal. He was out of sight.

Peace descended. I became suddenly aware of the soft warmth of the sun on my forehead, of the bird song echoing among the nearby trees. Unhurriedly I fastened on the muzzle under the head collar and produced my little glass measure.

This once I had plenty of time. I'd start him off with just a couple of drachms to get him used to the smell of it without frightening him. I poured the clear fluid on to the sponge.

"Walk him slowly round in a circle," I said to Ginger and Winker. "I'm going to give him a little bit at a time, there's no hurry. But keep a good hold of that halter shank in case he plays up."

There was no need for my warning. The two-year-old paced round calmly and fearlessly and every minute or so I trickled a little extra on to the sponge. After a while his steps became laboured and he began to sway drunkenly as he walked. I watched him happily; this was the way I liked to do it. Another little dollop would just about do the trick. I measured out another half ounce and walked over to the big animal.

His head nodded sleepily as I gave it to him. "You're just about ready aren't you, old lad," I was murmuring when the peace was suddenly shattered.

"He isn't going to go down, you know, James!" It was a booming roar from the direction of the car and as I whipped round in consternation I saw a head just showing over the bonnet. There was another cry.

"Why don't you strap up a . . . ?"

At that moment the horse lurched and collapsed quietly on the grass and Siegfried came bounding knife in hand from his hiding place like a greyhound.

"Sit on his head!" he yelled. "What are you waiting for, he'll be up in a minute! And get that rope round that hind leg! And bring my tray! And fetch the hot water!" He panted up to the horse then turned and bawled into Ginger's face, "Come on, I'm talking to you. MOVE!"

Ginger went off at a bow-legged gallop and cannoned into Winker who was rushing forward with the bucket. Then they had a brief but frenzied tug of war with the rope before they got it round the pastern.

"Pull the leg forward," cried my partner, bending over the operation site, then a full blooded bellow, "Get the bloody foot out of my eye, will you! What's the matter with you, you wouldn't pull a hen off its nest the way you're going."

I knelt quietly at the head, my knee on the neck. There was no need to hold him down; he was beautifully out, his eyes blissfully closed as Siegfried worked with his usual lightning expertise. There was a mere few seconds of silence broken only by the tinkling of instruments as they fell back on the tray, then my colleague glanced along the horse's back. "Open the muzzle, James."

The operation was over.

I don't think I've ever seen an easier job. By the time we had washed our instruments in the bucket the two-year-old was on his feet, cropping gently at the grass.

"Splendid anaesthetic, James," said Siegfried, drying off the emasculator. "Just right. And what a grand sort of horse."

We had put our gear back in the boot and were ready to leave when Walt Barnett heaved his massive bulk over towards us. He faced Siegfried across the bonnet of the car.

"Well that were nowt of a job," he grunted, slapping a cheque book down on the shining metal, "How much do you want?"

There was an arrogant challenge in the words and, faced with the dynamic force, the sheer brutal presence of the man, most people who were about to charge a guinea would have changed their minds and said a pound.

"Well, I'm askin' yer," he repeated. "How much do you want?"

"Ah yes," said Siegfried lightly. "That'll be a tenner."

The big man put a meaty hand on the cheque book and stared at my colleague. "What?"

"That'll be a tenner," Siegfried said again.

"Ten pounds?" Mr. Barnett's eyes opened wider.

"Yes," said Siegfried, smiling pleasantly. "That's right. Ten pounds."

There was a silence as the two men faced each other across the bonnet. The bird song and the noises from the wood seemed abnormally loud as the seconds ticked away and nobody moved. Mr. Barnett was glaring furiously and I looked from the huge fleshy face which seemed to have swollen even larger across to the lean, strong-jawed, high-cheek-boned profile of my partner. Siegfried still wore the remains of a lazy smile but down in the grey depths of his eye a dangerous light glinted.

Just when I was at screaming point the big man dropped his head suddenly and began to write. When he handed the cheque over he was shaking so much that the slip of paper fluttered as though in a high wind.

"Here y'are, then," he said hoarsely.

"Thank you so much." Siegfried read the cheque briefly then stuffed it carelessly into a side pocket. "Isn't it grand to have some real May weather, Mr. Barnett. Does us all good. I'm sure."

Walt Barnett mumbled something and turned away. As I got into the car I could see the great expanse of navy blue back moving ponderously towards the house.

"He won't have us back, anyway," I said.

Siegfried started the engine and we moved away. "No, James, I should think he'd get his twelve bore out if we ventured down this drive again. But that suits me—I think I can manage to get through the rest of my life without Mr. Barnett."

Our road took us through the little village of Baldon and Siegfried slowed down outside the pub, a yellow-washed building standing a few yards back from the road with a wooden sign reading The Cross Keys and a large black dog sleeping on the sunny front step.

My partner looked at his watch. "Twelve fifteen —they'll just have opened. A cool beer would be rather nice wouldn't it. I don't think I've been in this place before."

After the brightness outside, the shaded interior was restful, with only stray splinters of sunshine filtering through the curtains on to the flagged floor, the fissured oak tables, the big fireplace with its high settle.

"Good morning to you, landlord," boomed my partner, striding over to the bar. He was in his most ducal mood and I felt it was a pity he didn't have a silver-knobbed stick to rap on the counter.

The man behind the counter smiled and knuckled a forelock in the approved manner. "Good morning to you, sir, and what can I get for you gentlemen?"

I half expected Siegfried to say, "Two stoups of your choicest brew, honest fellow," but instead he just turned to me and murmured "I think two halves of bitter, eh James?"

The man began to draw the beer.

"Won't you join us?" Siegfried enquired.

"Thank ye sir, I'll 'ave a brown ale with you."

"And possibly your good lady, too?" Siegfried smiled over at the landlord's wife who was stacking glasses at the end of the counter.

"That's very kind of you, I will." She looked up, gulped, and an expression of wonder crept over her face. Siegfried hadn't stared at her—it had only been a five second burst from the grey eyes—but the bottle rattled against the glass as she poured her small port and she spent the rest of the time gazing at him dreamily.

"That'll be five and sixpence," the landlord said.

"Right." My partner plunged a hand into his bulging side pocket and crashed down on the counter an extraordinary mixture of crumpled bank notes, coins, veterinary instruments, thermometers, bits of string. He stirred the mass with a forefinger, flicking

out a half crown and two florins across the woodwork.

"Wait a minute!" I exclaimed. "Aren't those my
curved scissors? I lost them a few days . . ."

Siegfried swept the pile out of sight into his pocket.

"Nonsense! What makes you think that?"

"Well, they look exactly like mine. Unusual shape
—lovely long, flat blades. I've been looking everywhere . . ."

"James!" He drew himself up and faced me with
frozen hauteur. "I think you've said enough. I may
be capable of stooping to some pretty low actions
but I'd like to believe that certain things are beneath me. And stealing a colleague's curved scissors
is one of them."

I relapsed into silence. I'd have to bide my time
and take my chance later. I was fairly sure I'd recognised a pair of my dressing forceps in there too.

In any case, something else was occupying Siegfried's mind. He narrowed his eyes in intense thought
then delved into his other pocket and produced a
similar collection which he proceeded to push around
the counter anxiously.

"What's the matter?" I asked.

"That cheque I've just taken. Did I give it to
you?"

"No, you put it in that pocket. I saw you."

"That's what I thought. Well it's gone."

"Gone?"

"I've lost the bloody thing!"

I laughed. "Oh you can't have. Go through your
other pockets—it must be on you somewhere."

Siegfried made a systematic search but it was in
vain.

"Well James," he said at length. "I really have lost
it, but I've just thought of a simple solution. I will
stay here and have one more beer while you slip
back to Walt Barnett and ask him for another cheque."

41

There is plenty of time for thinking during the long hours of driving and now as I headed home from a late call my mind was idly assessing my abilities as a planner.

I had to admit that planning was not one of my strong points. Shortly after we were married I told Helen that I didn't think we should have children just at present. I pointed out that I would soon be going away, we did not have a proper home, our financial state was precarious and it would be far better to wait till after the war.

I had propounded my opinions weightily, sitting back in my chair and puffing my pipe like a sage, but I don't think I was really surprised when Helen's pregnancy was positively confirmed.

From the warm darkness the grass smell of the Dales stole through the open window and as I drove through a silent village it was mingled briefly with the mysterious sweetness of wood smoke. Beyond the houses the road curved smooth and empty between the black enclosing fells. No . . . I hadn't organised things very well. Leaving Darrowby and maybe England for an indefinite period, no home, no money and a pregnant wife. It was an untidy situation. But I was beginning to realise that life was not a tidy little parcel at any time.

The clock tower showed 11 p.m. as I rolled through the market place and, turning into Trengate, I saw that the light had been turned off in our room. Helen had gone to bed. I drove round to the yard at the back, put away the car and walked down the long garden. It was the end to every day, this walk; sometimes stumbling over frozen snow but to-night moving easily through the summer darkness under the branches of the apple trees to where the house stood tall and silent against the stars.

In the passage I almost bumped into Siegfried.

"Just getting back from Allenby's, James?" he asked. "I saw on the book that you had a colic."

I nodded. "Yes, but it wasn't a bad one. Just a bit of spasm. Their grey horse had been feasting on some of the hard pears lying around the orchard."

Siegfried laughed. "Well I've just beaten you in by a few minutes. I've been round at old Mrs. Dewar's for the last hour holding her cat's paw while it had kittens."

We reached the corner of the passage and he hesitated. "Care for a nightcap, James?"

"I would, thanks," I replied, and we went into the sitting room. But there was a constraint between us because Siegfried was off to London early next morning to enter the Air Force—he'd be gone before I got up—and we both knew that this was a farewell drink.

I dropped into my usual armchair while Siegfried reached into the glass-fronted cupboard above the mantelpiece and fished out the whisky bottle and glasses. He carelessly tipped out two prodigal measures and sat down opposite.

We had done a lot of this over the years, often yarning till dawn, but naturally enough it had faded since my marriage. It was like turning back the clock to sip the whisky and look at him on the other side of the fireplace and to feel, as though it were a living presence, the charm of the beautiful room with its high ceiling, graceful alcoves and french window.

We didn't talk about his departure but about the things we had always talked about and still do; the miraculous recovery of that cow, what old Mr. Jenks said yesterday, the patient that knocked us flat, leaped the fence and disappeared for good. Then Siegfried raised a finger.

"Oh, James, I nearly forgot. I was tidying up the books and I find I owe you some money."

"You do?"

"Yes, and I feel rather bad about it. It goes back to your pre-partnership days when you used to get a cut from Ewan Ross's testing. There was a slip-up somewhere and you were underpaid. Anyway, you've got fifty pounds to come."

"Fifty pounds! Are you sure?"

"Quite sure, James, and I do apologise."

"No need to apologise, Siegfried. It'll come in very handy right now."

"Good, good . . . anyway, the cheque's in the top drawer of the desk if you'll have a look tomorrow." He waved a languid hand and started to talk about some sheep he had seen that afternoon.

But for a few minutes I hardly heard him. Fifty pounds! It was a lot of money in those days, especially when I would soon be earning three shillings a day as an A.C. 2 during my initial training. It didn't solve my financial problem but it would be a nice little cushion to fall back on.

My nearest and dearest are pretty unanimous that I am a bit slow on the uptake and maybe they are right because it was many years later before it got through to me that there never was any fifty pounds owing. Siegfried knew I needed a bit of help at that time and when it all became clear long afterwards I realised that this was exactly how he would do it. No embarrassment to me. He hadn't even handed me the cheque. . . .

As the level in the bottle went down the conversation became more and more effortless. At one point some hours later my mind seemed to have taken on an uncanny clarity and it was as if I was disembodied and looking down at the pair of us. We had slid very low in our chairs, our heads well down the backs, legs extended far across the rug. My partner's face seemed to stand out in relief and it struck me that though he was only in his early thirties he looked a lot older. It was an attractive face, lean, strong-boned with steady humorous eyes, but not young. In fact Siegfried in the time I had known him had never looked young, but he has the last laugh now because he has hardly altered with the years and is one of those who will never look old.

At that moment of the night when everything was warm and easy and I felt omniscient it seemed a pity that Tristan wasn't there to make up the familiar threesome. As we talked, the memories marched through the room like a strip of bright pictures; of November days on the hillsides with the icy rain driving into our faces, of digging the cars out of snow drifts, of the spring sunshine warming the hard countryside. And the thought recurred that Tristan had been part of it all and that I was going to miss him as much as I would miss his brother.

I could hardly believe it when Siegfried rose, threw back the curtains and the grey light of morning streamed in. I got up and stood beside him as he looked at his watch.

"Five o'clock, James," he said, and smiled. "We've done it again."

He opened the french window and we stepped into the hushed stillness of the garden. I was taking grateful gulps of the sweet air when a single bird call broke the silence.

"Did you hear that blackbird?" I said.

He nodded and I wondered if he was thinking the same thing as myself; that it sounded just like the same blackbird which had greeted the early daylight when we talked over my first case those years ago.

We went up the stairs together in silence. Siegfried stopped at his door.

"Well, James . . ." he held out his hand and his mouth twitched up at one corner.

I gripped the hand for a moment then he turned and went into his room. And as I trailed dumbly up the next flight it seemed strange that we had never said goodbye. We didn't know when, if ever, we would see each other again yet neither of us had said a word. I don't know if Siegfried wanted to say anything but there was a lot trying to burst from me.

I wanted to thank him for being a friend as well as a boss, for teaching me so much, for never letting me down. There were other things, too, but I never said them.

Come to think of it, I've never even thanked him for that fifty pounds ... until now.

42

"Look, Jim," Helen said. "This is one engagement we can't be late for. Old Mrs. Hodgson is an absolute pet —she'd be terribly hurt if we let her supper spoil."

I nodded. "You're right, my girl, that mustn't happen. But I've got only three calls this afternoon and Tristan's doing the evening. I can't see anything going wrong."

This nervousness about a simple action like going out for a meal might be incomprehensible to the layman but to vets and their wives it was very real, particularly in those days of one or two man practices. The idea of somebody preparing a meal for me then waiting in vain for me to turn up was singularly horrifying but it happened to all of us occasionally.

It remained a gnawing worry whenever Helen and I were asked out; especially to somebody like the Hodgsons. Mr. Hodgson was a particularly likeable old farmer, short-sighted to the point of semiblindness, but the eyes which peered through the thick glasses were always friendly. His wife was just as kind and she had looked at me quizzically when I had visited the farm two days ago.

"Does it make you feel hungry, Mr. Herriot?"

"It does indeed, Mrs. Hodgson. It's a marvellous sight."

I was washing my hands in the farm kitchen and stealing a glance at a nearby table where all the paraphernalia of the family pig-killing lay in their full glory. Golden rows of pork pies, spare ribs, a mound of newly made sausages, jars of brawn. Great pots were being filled with lard, newly rendered in the fireside oven.

She looked at me thoughtfully. "Why don't you bring Mrs. Herriot round one night and help us eat it?"

"Well that's most kind of you and I'd love to, but . . ."

"Now then, no buts!" She laughed. "You know there's far too much stuff here—we have to give so much away."

This was quite true. In the days when every farmer and many of the townsfolk of Darrowby kept pigs for home consumption, killing time was an occasion for feasting. The hams and sides were cured and hung up but the masses of offal and miscellaneous pieces had to be eaten at the time; and though farmers with big families could tackle it, others usually passed delicious parcels round their friends in the happy knowledge that there would be a reciprocation in due course.

"Well, thanks, Mrs. Hodgson," I said. "Tuesday evening, then, seven o'clock."

And here I was on Tuesday afternoon heading confidently into the country with the image of Mrs. Hodgson's supper hanging before me like a vision of the promised land. I knew what it would be; a glorious mixed grill of spare ribs, onions, liver and pork fillet garlanded with those divine farm sausages which are seen no more. It was something to dream about.

In fact I was still thinking about it when I drew into Edward Wiggin's farm yard. I walked over to the covered barn and looked in at my patients—a dozen half grown bullocks resting on the deep straw. I had to inject these fellows with Blackleg vaccine. If I didn't it was a fair bet that one or more of them would be found dead due to infection with the deadly Clostridium which dwelt in the pastures of that particular farm.

It was a common enough disease and stockholders had recognised it for generations and had resorted to some strange practices to prevent it; such as running a seton—a piece of twine or bandage—through the dewlap of the animal. But now we had an efficient vaccine.

I was thinking I'd be here for only a few minutes because Mr. Wiggin's man, Wilf, was an expert beast catcher; then I saw the farmer coming across the yard and my spirits sank. He was carrying his lassoo. Wilf, by his side, rolled his eyes briefly heavenwards when he saw me. He too clearly feared the worst.

We went into the barn and Mr. Wiggin began the painstaking process of arranging his long, white rope, while we watched him gloomily. He was a frail little man in his sixties and had spent some years of his youth in America. He didn't talk a lot about it but everybody in time gained the impression that he had been a sort of cowboy over there and indeed he talked in a soft Texan drawl and seemed obsessed with the mystique of the ranch and the open range. Anything to do with the Wild West was near to his heart and nearest of all was his lassoo.

You could insult Mr. Wiggin with many things and he wouldn't turn a hair but question his ability to snare the wildest bovine with a single twirl of his rope and the mild little man could explode into anger. And the unfortunate thing was that he was no good at it.

Mr. Wiggin had now got a long loop dangling from his hand and he began to whirl it round his head as he crept towards the nearest bullock. When he finally made his cast the result was as expected; the rope fell limply half way along the animal's back and dropped on to the straw.

"Tarnation!" said Mr. Wiggin and started again. He was a man of deliberate movements and there was something maddening in the way he methodically assembled his rope again. It seemed an age before he once more advanced on a bullock with the rope whirring round his head.

"Bugger it!" Wilf grunted as the loop end lashed him across the face.

His boss turned on him. "Keep out of the dad-blasted road, Wilf," he said querulously. "I gotta start again now."

This time he didn't even make contact with the animal and as he retrieved his lassoo from the straw Wilf and I leaned wearily against the wall of the barn.

Yet again the whizz of the rope and a particularly ambitious throw which sent it high into the criss-cross of beams in the roof where it stuck. The farmer tugged at it several times in vain.

"Goldurn it, it's got round a nail up there. Slip across the yard and fetch a ladder, Wilf."

As I waited for the ladder then watched Wilf climbing into the shadowy heights of the barn I pondered on Mr. Wiggin. The way he spoke, the expressions he used were familiar to most Yorkshire folk since they filtered continually across the Atlantic in films and books. In fact there were dark mutterings that Mr. Wiggin had learned them that way and had never been near a ranch in his life. There was no way of knowing.

At last the rope was retrieved, the ladder put away and the little man went into action once more. He missed again but one of the bullocks got its foot in the loop and for a few moments the farmer hung on with fierce determination as the animal produced a series of piston-like kicks to rid itself of the distraction. And as I watched the man's lined face set grimly, the thin shoulders jerking, it came to me that Mr. Wiggin wasn't just catching a beast for injection; he was roping a steer, the smell of the prairie was in his nostrils, the cry of the coyote in his ears.

It didn't take long for the bullock to free itself and with a grunt of "Ornery crittur!" Mr. Wiggin started again. And as he kept on throwing his rope ineffectually I was uncomfortably aware that time was passing and that our chances of doing our job were rapidly diminishing. When you have to handle a bunch of young beasts the main thing is not to upset them. If Mr. Wiggin hadn't been there we would have penned them quietly in a corner and Wilf would have moved among them and caught their noses in his powerful fingers.

They were thoroughly upset. They had been peacefully chewing the cud or having a mouthful of hay from the rack but now, goaded by the teasing rope, were charging around like racehorses. Wilf and I watched in growing despair as Mr. Wiggin for once managed to get a loop round one of them, but it was too wide and slipped down and round the body. The bullock shook it off with an angry bellow then went off at full gallop, bucking and kicking. I looked at the throng of frenzied creatures milling past; it was getting more like a rodeo every minute.

And it was a disastrous start to the afternoon. I had seen a couple of dogs at the surgery after lunch and it had been nearly two thirty when I set out. It was now nearly four o'clock and I hadn't done a thing.

And I don't think I ever would have if fate hadn't stepped in. By an amazing fluke Mr. Wiggin cast his loop squarely over the horns of a shaggy projectile as it thundered past him, the rope tightened on the neck and Mr. Wiggin on the other end flew gracefully through the air for about twenty feet till he crashed into a wooden feeding trough.

We rushed to him and helped him to his feet. Badly shaken but uninjured he looked at us.

"Doggone, I jest couldn't hold the blame thing," he murmured. "Reckon I'd better sit down in the house for a while. You'll have to catch that pesky lot yourselves."

Back in the barn, Wilf whispered to me. "By gaw it's an ill wind, guvnor. We can get on now. And maybe it'll make 'im forget that bloody lassoo for a bit."

The bullocks were too excited to be caught by the nose but instead Wilf treated me to an exhibition of roping, Yorkshire style. Like many of the local stocksmen he was an expert with a halter and it fascinated me to see him dropping it on the head of a moving animal so that one loop fell behind the ears and the other snared the nose.

With a gush of relief I pulled the syringe and bottle of vaccine from my pocket and had the whole batch inoculated within twenty minutes.

Driving off I glanced at my watch and my pulse quickened as I saw it was a quarter to five. The afternoon had almost slipped away and there were still two more calls. But I had till seven o'clock and surely I wouldn't come across any more Mr. Wiggins. And as the stone walls flipped past I ruminated again on that mysterious little man. Had he once been a genuine cowboy or was the whole thing fantasy?

I recalled that one Thursday evening Helen and I were leaving the Brawton cinema where we usually finished our half day; the picture had been a Western and just before leaving the dark interior I glanced along the back row and right at the far end I saw Mr. Wiggin all on his own, huddled in the corner and looking strangely furtive.

Ever since then I have wondered....

Five o'clock saw me hurrying into the smallholding belonging to the Misses Dunn. Their pig had cut its neck on a nail and my previous experience of this establishment suggested that it wouldn't be anything very serious.

These two maiden ladies farmed a few acres just outside Dollingsford village. They were objects of interest because they did most of the work themselves and in the process they lavished such affection on their livestock that they had become like domestic pets. The little byre held four cows and whenever I had to examine one of them I could feel the rough tongue of her neighbour licking at my back; their few sheep ran up to people in the fields and sniffed round their legs like dogs; calves sucked at your fingers; an ancient pony wandered around wearing a benign expression and nuzzling anyone within reach. The only exception among the amiable colony was the pig, Prudence, who was thoroughly spoiled.

I looked at her now as she nosed around the straw in her pen. She was a vast sow and the four inch

laceration in her neck muscles was obviously posing no
threat to her life; but it was gaping and couldn't be
left like that.

"I'll have to put a few stitches in there," I said, and
the big Miss Dunn gasped and put a hand to her
mouth.

"Oh dear! Will it hurt her? I shan't be able to look,
I'm afraid."

She was a tall muscular lady in her fifties with a
bright red face and often as I looked at the wide
shoulders and the great arms with their bulging biceps
I had the feeling that she could flatten me effortlessly
with one blow if she so desired. But strangely she was
nervous and squeamish about the realities of animal
doctoring and it was always her little wisp of a sister
who helped at lambings, calvings and the rest.

"Oh you needn't worry, Miss Dunn," I replied. "It'll
be all over before she knows what's happening." I
climbed into the pen, went up to Prudence and
touched her gently on the neck.

Immediately the sow unleased a petulant scream
as though she had been stabbed with a hot iron and
when I tried to give her back a friendly scratch the
huge mouth opened again and the deafening sound
blasted out. And this time she advanced on me threat-
eningly. I stood my ground till the yawning cavern
with its yellowed teeth was almost touching my leg
then I put a hand on the rail and vaulted out of the
pen.

"We'll have to get her into a smaller space," I said.
"I'll never be able to stitch her in that big pen. She
has too much room to move around and she's too big
to hold."

Little Miss Dunn held up her hand. "We have the
very place. In the calf house across the yard. If we
got her into one of those narrow stalls she wouldn't
be able to turn round."

"Fine!" I rubbed my hands. "And I'll be able to do
the stitching over the top from the passage. Let's
get her over there."

I opened the door and after a bit of poking and

pushing Prudence ambled majestically out on to the cobbles of the yard. But there she stood, grunting sulkily, a stubborn glint in her little eyes, and when I leaned my weight against her back end it was like trying to move an elephant. She had no intention of moving any further; and that calf house was twenty yards away.

I stole a look at my watch. Five fifteen, and I didn't seem to be getting anywhere.

The little Miss Dunn broke into my thoughts. "Mr. Herriot, I know how we can get her across the yard."

"You do?"

"Oh yes, Prudence has been naughty before and we have found a way of persuading her to move."

I managed a smile. "Great! How do you do it?"

"Well now," and both sisters giggled. "She is very fond of digestive biscuits."

"What's that?"

"She simply loves digestive biscuits."

"She does?"

"Adores them!"

"Well, that's very nice," I said. "But I don't quite see . . ."

The big Miss Dunn laughed. "Just you wait and I'll show you."

She began to stroll towards the house and it seemed to me that though those ladies were by no means typical Dales farmers they did share the general attitude that time was of no consequence. The door closed behind her and I waited . . . and as the minutes ticked away I began to think she was brewing herself a cup of tea. In my mounting tension I turned away and gazed down over the hillside fields to where the grey roofs and old church tower of Dollingsford showed above the riverside trees. The quiet peace of the scene was in direct contrast to my mental state.

Just when I was giving up hope, big Miss Dunn reappeared carrying a long round paper container. She gave me a roguish smile as she held it up to me.

"These are what she likes. Now just watch."

She produced a biscuit and threw it down on the

cobbles a few feet in front of the sow. Prudence eyed it impassively for a few moments then without haste strolled forward, examined it carefully and began to eat it.

When she had finished, big Miss Dunn glanced at me conspiratorially and threw another biscuit in front of her. The pig again moved on unhurriedly and started on the second course. This was gradually leading her towards the buildings across the yard but it was going to take a long time. I reckoned that each biscuit was advancing her about ten feet and the calf house would be all of twenty yards away, so allowing three minutes a biscuit it was going to take nearly twenty minutes to get there.

I broke out in a sweat at the thought, and my fears were justified because nobody was in the slightest hurry. Especially Prudence who slowly munched each titbit then snuffled around picking up every crumb while the ladies smiled down at her fondly.

"Look," I stammered. "Do you think you could throw the biscuits a bit further ahead of her . . . just to save time, I mean?"

Little Miss Dunn laughed gaily. "Oh we've tried that, but she's such a clever old darling. She knows she'll get less that way."

To demonstrate she threw the next biscuit about fifteen feet away from the pig but the massive animal surveyed it with a cynical expression and didn't budge until it was kicked back to the required spot. Miss Dunn was right; Prudence wasn't so daft.

So I just had to wait, gritting my teeth as I watched the agonising progress. I was almost at screaming point at the end though the others were thoroughly enjoying themselves. But at last the final biscuit was cast into the calf pen, the pig made her leisurely way inside and the ladies, with triumphant giggles, closed the door behind her.

I leaped forward with my needle and suture silk and of course as soon as I laid a finger on her skin Prudence set up an almost unbearable nonstop squeal of rage. Big Miss Dunn put her hands over her ears and fled in terror but her little sister stayed with me bravely and passed me my scissors and dusting powder whenever I asked in sign language above the din.

My head was still ringing as I drove away, but that didn't worry me as much as the time. It was six o'clock.

43

Tensely I assessed my position. The next and final visit was only a couple of miles away—I could make it in ten minutes. Then say twenty minutes on the farm, fifteen minutes back to Darrowby, a lightning wash and change and I could still be pushing my knees under Mrs. Hodgson's table by seven o'clock.

And the next job wasn't a long one; just a bull to ring. Nowadays since the advent of Artificial Insemination there aren't many bulls about—only the big dairy men and pedigree breeders keep them—but in the thirties nearly every farmer had one, and inserting rings in their noses was a regular job. The rings were put in when they were about a year old and were necessary to restrain the big animals when they had to be led around.

I was immensely relieved when I arrived to find the gaunt figure of old Ted Buckle the farmer and his two men waiting for me in the yard. A classical way for a vet to waste time is to go hollering around the empty buildings then do more of the same out in the empty fields, waving madly, trying to catch the eye of a dot on the far horizon.

"Now then, young man," Ted said, and even that short phrase took a fair time to come out. To me, the old man was a constant delight; speaking the real old Yorkshire—which you seldom hear now and which I won't try to reproduce here—with slow deliberation as though he were savouring every syllable as much as I was enjoying listening to him. "You've come, then."

"Yes, Mr. Buckle, and I'm glad to see you're ready and waiting for me."

"Aye ah doan't like keepin' you fellers hangin' about." He turned to his men. "Now then, lads, go into that box and get haud'n that big lubber for Mr. Herriot."

The "lads," Ernest and Herbert, who were both in their sixties, shuffled into the bull's loose box and closed the door after them. There was a few seconds of muffled banging against the wood, a couple of bellows and the occasional anglo-saxon expression from the men, then silence.

"Ah think they have 'im now," Ted murmured and, not for the first time, I looked wonderingly at his wearing apparel. I had never seen him in anything else but that hat and coat in the time I had known him. With regard to the coat, which countless years ago must have been some kind of mackintosh, two things puzzled me; why he put it on and how he put it on. The long tatter of unrelated ribbons tied round the middle with binder twine could not possibly afford him any protection from the elements and how on earth did he know which were the sleeve holes among all the other apertures? And the hat, an almost crownless trilby from the early days of the century whose brim drooped vertically in sad folds over ears and eyebrows; it seemed incredible that he actually hung the thing up on a peg each night and donned it again in the morning.

Maybe the answer was to be found in the utterly serene humorous eyes which looked out from the skeleton-thin face. Nothing changed for Ted and the passage of a decade was a fleeting thing. I remember him showing me the old fashioned "reckon" which held the pans and kettles over the fire on his farm kitchen. He pointed out the row of holes where you could adjust it for large pans or small as though it were some modern invention.

"Aye, it's a wonderful thing, and t'lad that put it in for me made a grand job!"

"When was that, Mr. Buckle?"

"It were eighteen ninety seven. Ah remember it well. He was a right good workman was t'lad."

But the men had reappeared with the young bull on a halter and they soon had him held in the accepted position for ringing.

There was a ritual about this job, a set pattern as unvarying as a classical ballet. Ernest and Herbert pulled the bull's head over the half door and held it there by pulling on a shank on either side of the halter. The portable crush had not yet been invented and this arrangement with the bull inside the box and the men outside was adopted for safety's sake. The next step was to make a hole through the tough tissue at the extremity of the nasal septum with the special punch which I had ready in its box.

But first there was a little refinement which I had introduced myself. Though it was the general custom to punch the hole without any preliminaries I always had the feeling that the bull might not like it very much; so I used to inject a couple of c.c.'s of local anaesthetic into the nose before I started. I poised my syringe now and Ernest, holding the left shank, huddled back apprehensively against the door.

"Tha's standin' middlin' to t'side, Ernest," Ted drawled. "Doesta think he's goin' to jump on top o' tha?"

"Naw, naw." The man grinned sheepishly and took a shorter hold of the rope.

But he jumped back to his former position when I pushed the needle into the gristle just inside the nostril because the bull let loose a sudden deep-throated bellow of anger and reared up above the door. Ted had delayed ringing this animal; he was nearly eighteen months and very big.

"Haud 'im, lads," Ted murmured as the two men clung to the ropes. "That's right—he'll settle down shortly."

And he did. With his chin resting on the top of the door, held by the ropes on either side, he was ready for the next act. I pushed my punch into the nose, gripped the handles and squeezed. I never felt much like a professional gentleman when I did this, but at least my local had worked and the big animal didn't stir as the jaws of the instrument clicked together, puncturing a small round hold in the hard tissue.

The next stage in the solemn rite was unfolded as I unwrapped the bronze ring from its paper covering, took out the screw and opened the ring wide on its hinge. I waited for the inevitable words.

"Take tha' cap off, Herbert. Tha woan't catch caud just for a minute." Ted supplied them.

It was always a cap. A big bucket, a basin would have been more practical to hold that stupid, tiny screw and equally foolish little screwdriver, but it was always a cap. And a greasy old cap such as Herbert now removed from his polished pate.

My next step would be to slip the ring through the hole I had made, close it, insert the screw and tighten it up. That was where the cap came in; it was held under the ring to guard against sudden movements, because if the screw fell and was lost in the dirt and straw then all was lost. Then Ted would hand me the long rasp or file which every farmer had around somewhere and I would carefully smooth off the rim of the screw whether it needed it or not.

But this time there was to be a modification of the stereotyped little drama. As I stepped forward with my ring the young bull and I stood face to face and for a moment the wide set eyes under the stubby horns looked into mine. And as I reached out he must have moved slightly because the sharp end of the ring pricked him a little on the muzzle; the merest touch, but he seemed to take it as a personal insult because his mouth opened in an exasperated bawl and again he reared on his hind legs.

He was a well grown animal and in that position he looked very large indeed; and when his fore feet clumped down on the half door and the great rib cage loomed above us he was definitely formidable.

"The bugger's comin' over!" Ernest gasped and released his hold on the halter shank. He had never had much enthusiasm for the job and he abandoned it now without regret. Herbert was made of sterner stuff and he hung on grimly to his end as the bull thrashed above him, but after a cloven hoof had whizzed past his ear and another whistled just over his gleaming dome he too let go and fled.

Ted, untroubled as always, was well out of range and there remained only myself dancing in front of the door and gesticulating frantically at the bull in the vain hope that I might frighten him back whence he came; and the only thing that kept me there was the knowledge that every inch he scrambled out was taking me further from Mrs. Hodgson's glorious supper.

I stood my ground until the snorting, bellowing creature was two thirds over, hanging grotesquely with the top of the door digging deep into his abdomen, then with a final plunge he was into the yard and I ran for cover. But the bull was not bent on mischief; he took one look at the open gate into the field and thundered through it like an express train.

From behind a stack of milk churns I watched sadly as he curveted joyously over the grass, revelling in his new found freedom. Bucking and kicking, tail in the air he headed for the far horizon where the wide pasture dipped to a beck which wandered along the floor of a shallow depression. And as he disappeared over the brow of the hill the last hope of my spare ribs went with him.

"It'll tek us an hour to catch that bugger," grunted Ernest gloomily.

I looked at my watch. Half past six. The bitter injustice of the whole thing overwhelmed me and I set up a wail of lamentation.

"Yes, dammit, and I've got an appointment in Darrowby at seven o'clock!" I stamped over the cobbles for a moment or two then swung round on old Ted. "I'll never make it now . . . I'll have to ring my wife . . . have you got a phone?"

Ted's drawl was lazier than ever. "Nay, we 'aven't got no phone. Ah don't believe in them things." He fished out a tobacco tin from his pocket, unscrewed

the lid and produced a battered timepiece which he
scrutinised without haste. "Any road, there's nowt to
stop ye bein' back i' Darrowby by seven."

"But . . . but . . . that's impossible . . . and I can't
keep these people waiting . . . I must get to a phone."

"Doan't get s'flustered, young man." The old man's
long face creased into a soothing smile. "Ah tell ye
you won't be late."

I waved my arms around. "But he's just said it'll
take an hour to catch that bull!"

"Fiddlesticks! Ernest allus talks like that . . . 'e's
never 'appy unless 'e's miserable. Ah'll get bull in i'
five minutes."

"Five minutes! That's ridiculous! I'll . . . I'll drive
down the road to the nearest phone box while you're
catching him."

"You'll do nowt of t'sort, lad." Ted pointed to a
stone water trough against the wall. "Go and sit thissen down and think of summat else . . . ah'll only
be five minutes."

Wearily I sank on to the rough surface and buried
my face in my hands. When I looked up the old man was
coming out of the byre and in front of him ambled
a venerable cow. By the number of rings on the long
curving horns she must have been well into her teens;
the gaunt pelvic bones stood out like a hatstand and
underneath her a pendulous udder almost touched
the ground.

"Get out there awd lass," Ted said and the old cow
trotted into the field, her udder swinging gently at
each step. I watched her until she had disappeared
over the hill, then turned to see Ted throwing cattle
cake into a bucket.

He strolled through the gate and as I gazed uncomprehendingly he began to beat the bucket with a stick.
At the same time he raised his voice in a reedy tenor
and called out across the long stretch of green.

"Cush, cush!" he cried. "Cush, pet, cush!"

Almost immediately the cow reappeared over the
brow and just behind her the bull. I looked with wonder as Ted banged on his bucket and the cow broke

into a stiff gallop with my patient close by her side. When she reached the old man she plunged her head in among the cake while the bull, though he was as big as she, pushed his nose underneath her and seized one of her teats in his great mouth. It was an absurd sight but she didn't seem to mind as the big animal, almost on his knees, sucked away placidly.

In fact it was like a soothing potion because when the cow was led inside he followed; and he made no complaint as I slipped the ring in his nose and fastened it in with the screw which mercifully had survived inside Herbert's cap.

"Quarter to seven!" I panted happily as I jumped into the driving seat. "I'll get there in time now." I could see Helen and me standing on the Hodgson's step and the door opening and the heavenly scent of the spare ribs and onions drifting out from the kitchen.

I looked again at the scarecrow figure with the hat brim drooping over the calm eyes. "You did a wonderful job there, Mr. Buckle. I wouldn't have believed it if I hadn't seen it. It was amazing how that bull followed the cow in like that."

The old man smiled and I had a sudden surging impression of the wisdom in that quiet mind.

"There's nowt amazin' about it, lad, it's most nat'ral thing in t'world. That's 'is mother."

44

I slowed down and gazed along the farm lane. That was Tristan's car parked against the byre and inside, behind that green door, he was calving a cow. Because Tristan's student days were over. He was a fully fledged veterinary surgeon now and the great world of animal doctoring with all its realities stretched ahead.

Not for long, though, because like many others he was bound for the army and would leave soon after myself. But it wouldn't be so bad for Tristan because at least he would be doing his own job. When Siegfried and I had volunteered for service there had been no need for our profession in the army so we had gone into R.A.F. aircrew which was the only branch open to our "reserved occupation." But when it came to Tristan's turn the fighting had escalated in the far east and they were crying out for vets to doctor the horses, mules, cattle, camels.

The timing suggested that the Gods were looking after him as usual. In fact I think the Gods love people like Tristan who sway effortlessly before the winds of fate and spring back with a smile, looking on life always with blithe optimism. Siegfried and I as second class aircraftmen pounded the parade ground for weary hours, Captain Tristan Farnon sailed off to the war in style.

But in the meantime I was glad of his help. After my departure he would run things with the aid of an assistant then when he left the practice would be in the hands of two strangers till we returned. It seemed strange but everything was impermanent at that time.

I drew up and looked thoughtfully at the car. This was Mark Dowson's place and when I had rung the surgery from out in the country Helen told me about this calving. I didn't want to butt in and fuss but I couldn't help wondering how Tristan was getting on, because Mr. Dowson was a dour, taciturn character who wouldn't hesitate to come down on the young man if things went wrong.

Still, I hadn't anything to worry about because since he qualified Tristan was doing fine. The farmers had always liked him during his sporadic visits as a student but now that he was on the job regularly the good reports were coming in thick and fast.

"I'll tell tha, that young feller does work! Doesn't spare 'imself," or "Ah've never seen a lad put his 'eart and soul into his job like this 'un." And one man drew me to one side and muttered "He meks some queer noises but he does try. I think he'd kill 'isself afore he'd give up."

That last remark made me think. Tristan's forte was certainly not brute effort and I had been a bit bewildered at some of the comments till I began to remember some of my experiences with him in his student days. He had always applied his acute intelligence to any situation in his own particular way and the way he reacted to the little accidents of country practice led me to believe he was operating a system.

The first time I saw this in action was when he was standing by the side of a cow watching me pulling milk from a teat. Without warning the animal swung round and brought an unyielding cloven hoof down on his foot. This is a common and fairly agonising experience and before the days of steel-tipped wellingtons I have frequently had the skin removed from my toes in neat parchment-like rolls. When it happened to me I was inclined to hop around and swear a bit and my performance was usually greeted with appreciative laughter from the farmers. Tristan, however, handled it differently.

He gasped, leaned with bowed head against the

cow's pelvic bone for a moment then opened his mouth wide and emitted a long groan. Then, as the cowman and I stared at him he reeled over the cobbles dragging the damaged limb uselessly behind him. Arrived at the far wall he collapsed against it, face on the stone, still moaning pitifully.

Thoroughly alarmed, I rushed to his aid. This must be a fracture and already my mind was busy with plans to get him to hospital with all possible speed. But he revived rapidly and when we left the byre ten minutes later he was tripping along with no trace of a limp. And I did notice one thing; nobody had laughed at him, he had received only sympathy and commiseration.

This sort of thing happened on other places. He sustained a few mild kicks, he was crushed between cows, he met with many of the discomforts which are part of our life and he reacted in the same histrionic way. And how it paid off! To a man, the farmers exhibited the deepest concern when he went into his act and there was something more; it actually improved his image. I was pleased about that because impressing Yorkshire farmers isn't the easiest task and if Tristan's method worked it was all right with me.

But I smiled to myself as I sat outside the farm. I couldn't see Mr. Dowson being affected by any sign of suffering. I had had my knocks there in the past and he obviously hadn't cared a damn.

On an impulse I drove down the lane and walked into the byre. Tristan, stripped off and soaped, was just inserting an arm into a large red cow while the farmer, pipe in hand, was holding the tail. My colleague greeted me with a pleasant smile but Mr. Dowson just nodded curtly.

"What have you got, Triss?" I asked.

"Both legs back," he replied. "And they're a long way in. Look at the length of her pelvis."

I knew what he meant. It wasn't a difficult presentation but it could be uncomfortable in these long cows. I leaned back against the wall; I might as well see how he fared.

He braced himself and reached as far forward as he could, and just then the cow's flanks bulged as she strained hard against him. This is never very nice; the powerful contractions of the uterus squeeze the arm relentlessly between calf and pelvis and you have to grit your teeth till it passes off.

Tristan, however, went a little further.

"Ooh! Aah! Ouch!" he cried. Then as the animal still kept up the pressure he went into a gasping groan. When she finally relaxed he stood there quite motionless for a few seconds, his head hanging down as though the experience had drained him of all his strength.

The farmer drew on his pipe and regarded him impassively. Throughout the years I had known Mr. Dowson I had never seen any particular emotion portrayed in those hard eyes and craggy features. In fact it had always seemed to me that I could have dropped down dead in front of him and he wouldn't even blink.

My colleague continued his struggle and the cow, entering into the spirit of the game, fought back with a will. Some animals will stand quietly and submit to all kinds of internal interference but this was a strainer; every movement of the arm within her was answered by a violent expulsive effort. I had been through it a hundred times and I could almost feel the grinding pressure on the wrist, the helpless numbing of the fingers.

Tristan showed what he thought about it all by a series of heartrending sounds. His repertoire was truly astounding and he ranged from long harrowing moans through shrill squeals to an almost tearful whimpering.

At first Mr. Dowson appeared oblivious to the whole business, puffing smoke, glancing occasionally through the byre door, scratching at the bristle on his chin. But as the minutes passed his eyes were dragged more and more to the suffering creature before him until his whole attention was riveted on the young man.

And in truth he was worth watching because Tristan added to his vocal performance an extraordinary display of facial contortions. He sucked in his cheeks, rolled his eyes, twisted his lips, did everything in fact but wiggle his ears. And there was no doubt he was getting through to Mr. Dowson. As the noises and grimaces became more extravagant the farmer showed signs of growing uneasiness; he darted anxious glances at my colleague and occasionally his pipe trembled violently. Like me, he clearly thought some dreadful climax was at hand.

As if trying to bring matters to a head the cow started to build up to a supreme effort. She straddled her legs wide, grunted deeply and went into a prolonged heave. As her back arched Tristan opened his mouth wide in a soundless protest then little panting cries began to escape him. This, I thought, was his most effective ploy yet; a long drawn "Aah . . . aah . . . aah . . ." creeping gradually up the scale and building increasing tension in his audience. My toes were curling with apprehension when, with superb timing, he released a sudden piercing scream.

That was when Mr. Dowson cracked. His pipe had almost wobbled from his mouth but now he stuffed it into his pocket and rushed to Tristan's side.

"Ista all right, young man?" he enquired hoarsely.

My colleague, his face a mask of anguish, did not reply.

The farmer tried again. "Will ah get you a cup o' tea?"

For a moment Tristan made no response, then, eyes closed, he nodded dumbly.

Mr. Dowson scampered eagerly from the byre and within minutes returned with a steaming mug. After that I had to shake my head to dispel the feeling of unreality. It couldn't be true, this vision of the hard-bitten farmer feeding the tea to the young man in sips, cradling the lolling head in a horny hand. Tristan was still inside the cow, still apparently semi-conscious with pain but submitting helplessly to the farmer's ministrations.

With a sudden lunge he produced one of the calf's legs and as he flopped against the cow's rump he was rewarded with another long gulp of tea. After the first leg the rest wasn't so bad and the second leg and the calf itself soon followed.

As the little creature landed wriggling on the floor Tristan collapsed on his knees beside it and extended a trembling hand towards a pile of hay, prepared to give the new arrival a rub down.

Mr. Dowson would have none of it.

"George!" he bellowed to one of his men in the yard. "Get in 'ere and wisp this calf!" Then solicitously to Tristan, "You maun come into t'house, lad, and have a drop o' brandy. You're about all in."

The dream continued in the farm kitchen and I watched disbelievingly as my colleague fought his way back to health and strength with the aid of several stiff measures of Martell Three Star. I had never had treatment like this and a wave of envy swept over me as I wondered whether it was worth adopting Tristan's system.

But I still have never found the courage to try it.

45

It was strange, but somehow the labels on the calves'
backs made them look even more pathetic; the auc-
tion mart labels stuck roughly with paste on the
hairy rumps, stressing the little creatures' role as
helpless merchandise.

As I lifted one sodden tail and inserted the thermometer a thin whitish diarrhoea trickled from the
rectum and streamed down the thighs and hocks.

"It's the old story, I'm afraid, Mr. Clark," I said.

The farmer shrugged and dug his thumbs under
his braces. In the blue overalls and peaked porter's
cap he always wore he didn't look much like a
farmer and for that matter this place did not greatly
resemble a farm; the calves were in a converted railway wagon and all around lay a weird conglomeration of rusting agricultural implements, pieces of
derelict cars, broken chairs. "Aye, it's a beggar isn't
it? I wish I didn't have to buy calves in markets
but you can't always find 'em on t'farms when you
want them. This lot looked all right when I got them
two days since."

"I'm sure they did." I looked at the five calves,
arch-backed, trembling, miserable. "But they've had
a tough time and it's showing now. Taken from their
mothers at a week old, carted for miles in a draughty
wagon, standing for most of the day at the mart
then the final journey here on a cold afternoon. They
didn't have a chance."

"Well ah gave them a good bellyful of milk as
soon as they came. They looked a bit starved and ah
thought it would warm them up."

"Yes, you'd think it would, Mr. Clark, but really their stomachs weren't in a fit state to accept rich food like that when they were cold and tired. Next time if I were you I'd just give them a drink of warm water with maybe a little glucose and make them comfortable till next day.

"White scour" they called it. It killed countless thousands of calves every year and the name always sent a chill through me because the mortality rate was depressingly high.

I gave each of them a shot of E coli antiserum. Most authorities said it did no good and I was inclined to agree with them. Then I rummaged in my car boot and produced a packet of our astringent powders of chalk, opium and catechu.

"Here, give them one of these three times a day, Mr. Clark," I said. I tried to sound cheerful but I'm sure my tone lacked conviction. Whiskered veterinary surgeons in top hats and tail coats had been prescribing chalk opium and catechu a hundred years ago and though it might have been helpful in mild diarrhoea it was almost useless against the lethal bacterial enteritis of white scour. It was a waste of time just trying to dry up the diarrhoea; what was wanted was a drug which would knock out the vicious bugs which caused it, but there wasn't such a thing around.

However there was one thing which we vets of those days used to do which is sometimes neglected since the arrival of the modern drugs; we attended to the comfort and nursing of the animals. The farmer and I wrapped each calf in a big sack which went right round its body and was fastened with binder twine round the ribs, in front of the brisket and under the tail. Then I fussed round the shed, plugging up draught holes, putting up a screen of straw bales between the calves and the door.

Before I left I took a last look at them; there was no doubt they were warm and sheltered now. They would need every bit of help with only my astringent powders fighting for them.

I didn't see them again until the following afternoon. Mr. Clark was nowhere around so I went over to the railway wagon and opened the half door.

This, to me, is the thing that lies at the very heart of veterinary practice; the wondering and worrying about how your patient is progressing then the long moment when you open that door and find out. I rested my elbows on the timbers and looked inside. The calves were lying quite motionless on their sides, in fact I had to look closely to make sure they were not dead. I banged the door behind me with deliberate force but not a head was raised.

Walking through the deep straw and looking down at the outstretched little animals, each in his rough sacking jacket, I swore softly to myself. It looked as though the whole lot was going to perish. Great, great, I thought as I kicked among the straw—not just one or two but a hundred per cent death rate this time.

"Well you don't look very 'opeful, young man." Mr. Clark's head and shoulders loomed over the half door.

I dug my hands into my pockets. "No, damn it, I'm not. They've gone down really fast, haven't they?"

"Aye, it's ower wi' them all right. I've just been in t'house ringing Mallock."

The knacker man's name was like the pealing of a mournful bell. "But they're not dead yet," I said.

"No, but it won't be long. Mallock allus gives a bob or two more if he can get a beast alive. Makes fresher dog meat, he says."

I didn't say anything and I must have looked despondent because the farmer gave a wry smile and came over to me.

"It isn't your fault, lad. I know all about this dang white scour. If you get the right bad sort there's nothing anybody can do. And you can't blame me for tryin' to get a bit back—I've got to make the best of a bad job."

"Oh I know," I said. "I'm just disappointed I can't have a go at them with this new medicine."

"What's that, then?"

I took the tin from my pocket and read the label. "It's called M and B 693, or sulphapyridine, to give it its scientific name. Just came in the post this morning. It's one of a completely new range of drugs —they're called the sulphonamides and we've never had anything like them before. They're supposed to actually kill certain germs, such as the organisms which cause scour."

Mr. Clark took the tin from me and removed the lid. "A lot of little blue tablets, eh? Well ah've seen a few wonder cures for this ailment but none of 'em's much good—this'll be another, I'll bet."

"Could be," I said. "But there's been a lot of discussion about these sulphonamides in our veterinary journals. They're not quack remedies, they're a completely fresh field. I wish I could have tried them on your calves."

"Well look at them." The farmer gazed gloomily over the five still bodies. "Their eyes are goin' back in their heads. Have you ever seen calves like that get better?"

"No I haven't, but I'd still like to have a go."

As I spoke a tall-sided wagon rumbled into the yard. A sprightly, stocky man descended from the driver's seat and came over to us.

"By gaw, Jeff," said Mr. Clark. "You 'aven't been long."

"Nay, they got me on t'phone at Jenkinson's, just down t'road." He gave me a smile of peculiar sweetness.

I studied Jeff Mallock as I always did with a kind of wonder. He had spent the greater part of his forty odd years delving in decomposing carcases, slashing nonchalantly with his knife at tuberculous abscesses, wallowing in infected blood and filthy uterine exudates yet he remained a model of health and fitness. He had the clear eyes and the smooth pink skin of a twenty year old and the effect was heightened by the untroubled serenity of his expression. To the best of my knowledge Jeff never took any hygienic precautions such as washing his hands and I have seen him enjoying a snack on his premises, seated on a heap of bones and gripping a cheese and onion sandwich with greasy fingers.

He peered over the door at the calves. "Yes, yes, a clear case of stagnation of t'lungs. There's a lot of it about right now."

Mr. Clark looked at me narrowly. "Lungs? You never said owt about lungs, young man." Like all farmers he had complete faith in Jeff's instant diagnosis.

I mumbled something. I had found it useless to argue this point. The knacker man's amazing ability to tell at a glance the cause of an animal's illness or death was a frequent source of embarrassment to me. No examination was necessary—he just knew, and of all his weird catalogue of diseases stagnation of t'lungs was the favourite.

He turned to the farmer. "Well, ah'd better shift 'em now, Willie. Reckon they won't last much longer."

I bent down and lifted the head of the nearest calf. They were all shorthorns, three roans, a red and this one which was pure white. I passed my fingers over the hard little skull, feeling the tiny horn buds under the rough hair. When I withdrew my hand the head dropped limply on to the straw and it seemed to me that there was something of finality and resignation in the movement.

My thoughts were interrupted by the roar of Jeff's engine. He was backing his wagon round to the door of the calf house and as the high unpainted boards darkened the entrance the atmosphere of gloom deepened. These little animals had suffered two traumatic journeys in their short lives. This was to be the last, the most fateful and the most sordid.

When the knacker man came in he stood by the farmer, looking at me as I squatted in the straw among the prostrate creatures. They were both waiting for me to quit the place, leaving my failure behind me.

"You know, Mr. Clark," I said. "Even if we could save one of them it would help to reduce your loss."

The farmer regarded me expressionlessly. "But they're all dyin', lad. You said so yourself."

"Yes, I did, I know, but the circumstances could be a bit different today."

"Ah know what it is." He laughed suddenly. "You've got your heart set on havin' a go with them little tablets, haven't you?"

I didn't answer but looked up at him with a mute appeal.

He was silent for a few moments then he put a hand on Mallock's shoulder. "Jeff, if this young feller is that concerned about ma stock I'll 'ave to humour 'im. You're not bothered, are you?"

"Nay, Willie, nay," replied Jeff, completely unruffled. "I can pick 'em up tomorrow, just as easy."

"Right," I said. "Let's have a look at the instructions." I fished out the pamphlet from the tin and read rapidly, working out the dose for the weights of the calves. "We'll have to give them a loading dose first. I think twelve tablets per calf then six every eight hours after that."

"How do you get 'em down their necks?" the farmer asked.

"We'll have to crush them and shake them up in water. Can we go into the house to do that?"

In the farm kitchen we borrowed Mrs. Clark's potato masher and pounded the tablets until we had five initial doses measured out. Then we returned to the shed and began to administer them to the calves. We had to go carefully as the little creatures were so weak they had difficulty in swallowing, but the farmer held each head while I trickled the medicine into the side of the mouth.

Jeff enjoyed every minute of it. He showed no desire to leave but produced a pipe richly decorated with nameless tissues, leaned on the top of the half door and, puffing happily, watched us with tranquil eyes. He was quite unperturbed by his wasted journey and when we had finished he climbed into his wagon and waved to us cordially.

"I'll be back to pick 'em up in t'mornin, Willie," he cried, quite without malice I'm sure. "There's no cure for stagnation of t'lungs."

I thought of his words next day as I drove back to the farm. He was just stating the fact; his supply of dog meat was merely being postponed for another twenty four hours. But at least, I told myself, I had the satisfaction of having tried, and since I expected nothing I wasn't going to be disappointed.

As I pulled up in the yard Mr. Clark walked over and spoke through the window. "There's no need for you to get out of the car." His face was a grim mask.

"Oh," I said, the sudden lurch in my stomach belying my calm facade. "Like that, is it?"

"Aye, come and look 'ere." He turned and I followed him over to the shed. By the time the door creaked open a slow misery had begun to seep into me.

Unwillingly I gazed into the interior.

Four of the calves were standing in a row looking up at us with interest. Four shaggy, rough-jacketed figures, bright-eyed and alert. The fifth was resting on the straw, chewing absently at one of the strings which held his sack.

The farmer's weathered face split into a delighted grin, "Well ah told you there was no need to get out of your car, didn't I? They don't need no vitnery, they're back to normal."

I didn't say anything. This was something which my mind, as yet, could not comprehend. As I stared unbelievingly the fifth calf rose from the straw and stretched luxuriously.

"He's wraxin', d'you see?" cried Mr. Clark. "There's nowt much wrong wi' them when they do that."

We went inside and I began to examine the little animals. Temperatures were normal, the diarrhoea had dried up, it was uncanny. As if in celebration the white calf which had been all but dead yesterday began to caper about the shed, kicking up his legs like a mustang.

"Look at that little bugger!" burst out the farmer. "By gaw I wish I was as fit meself!"

I put the thermometer back in its tube and dropped it into my side pocket. "Well, Mr. Clark," I said slowly, "I've never seen anything like this. I still feel stunned."

"Beats hen-racin', doesn't it," the farmer said, wide-eyed, then he turned towards the gate as a wagon appeared from the lane. It was the familiar doom-burdened vehicle of Jeff Mallock.

The knacker man showed no emotion as he looked into the shed. In fact it was difficult to imagine anything disturbing those pink cheeks and placid eyes, but I fancied the puffs of blue smoke from his pipe came a little faster as he took in the scene. The pipe itself showed some fresh deposits on its bowl—some fragments of liver, I fancied, since yesterday.

When he had looked his fill he turned and strolled towards his wagon. On the way he gazed expansively around him and then at the dark clouds piling in the western sky.

"Ah think it'll turn to rain afore t'day's out, Willie," he murmured.

I didn't know it at the time but I had witnessed the beginning of the revolution. It was my first glimpse of the tremendous therapeutic breakthrough which was to sweep the old remedies into oblivion. The long rows of ornate glass bottles with their carved stoppers and Latin inscriptions would not stand on the dispensary shelves much longer and their names, dearly familiar for many generations —Sweet Spirits of Nitre, Sal ammoniac, Tincture of Camphor—would be lost and vanish for ever.

This was the beginning and just around the corner a new wonder was waiting—Penicillin and the other antibiotics. At last we had something to work with, at last we could use drugs which we knew were going to do something.

All over the country, probably all over the world at that time, vets were having these first spectacular results, going through the same experience as myself; some with cows, some with dogs and cats, others with valuable racehorses, sheep, pigs in all kinds of environments. But for me it happened in that old converted railway wagon among the jumble of rusting junk on Willie Clark's farm.

Of course it didn't last—not the miraculous part of it anyway. What I had seen at Willie Clark's was the impact of something new on an entirely unsophisticated bacterial population, but it didn't go on like that. In time the organisms developed a certain amount of resistance and new and stronger sulphonamides and antibiotics had to be produced. And so the battle has continued. We have good results now but no miracles, and I feel I was lucky to be one of the generation which was in at the beginning when the wonderful things did happen.

Those five calves never looked behind them and the memory of them gives me a warm glow even now. Willie of course was overjoyed and even Jeff Mallock gave the occasion his particular accolade. As he drove away he called back at us:

"Them little blue tablets must have good stuff in 'em. They're fust things I've ever seen could cure stagnation of t'lungs."

46

There was one marvellous thing about the set-up in Darrowby. I had the inestimable advantage of being a large animal practitioner with a passion for dogs and cats. So that although I spent most of my time in the wide outdoors of Yorkshire there was always the captivating background of the household pets to make a contrast.

I treated some of them every day and it made an extra interest in my life; interest of a different kind, based on sentiment instead of commerce and because of the way things were it was something I could linger over and enjoy. I suppose with a very intensive small animal practice it would be easy to regard the thing as a huge sausage machine, an endless procession of hairy forms to prod with hypodermic needles. But in Darrowby we got to know them all as individual entities.

Driving through the town I was able to identify my ex-patients without difficulty; Rover Johnson, recovered from his ear canker, coming out of the ironmongers with his mistress, Patch Walker whose broken leg had healed beautifully, balanced happily on the back of his owner's coal wagon, or Spot Briggs who was a bit of a rake anyway and would soon be tearing himself again on barbed wire, ambling all alone across the market place cobbles in search of adventure. I got quite a kick out of recalling their ailments and mulling over their characteristics. Because they all had their own personalities and they were manifested in different ways.

One of these was their personal reaction to me and

my treatment. Most dogs and cats appeared to bear me not the slightest ill will despite the fact that I usually had to do something disagreeable to them.

But there were exceptions and one of these was Magnus, the Miniature Dachshund from the Drovers' Arms.

He was in my mind now as I leaned across the bar counter.

"A pint of Smiths, please, Danny," I whispered.

The barman grinned. "Coming up, Mr. Herriot." He pulled at the lever and the beer hissed gently into the glass and as he passed it over the froth stood high and firm on the surface.

"That ale looks really fit tonight," I breathed almost inaudibly.

"Fit? It's beautiful!" Danny looked fondly at the brimming glass. "In fact it's a shame to sell it."

I laughed, but pianissimo. "Well it's nice of you to spare me a drop." I took a deep pull and turned to old Mr. Fairburn who was as always sitting at the far corner of the bar with his own fancy flower-painted glass in his hand.

"It's been a grand day, Mr. Fairburn," I murmured sotto voce.

The old man put his hand to his ear. "What's that you say?"

"Nice warm day it's been." My voice was like a soft breeze sighing over the marshes.

I felt a violent dig at my back. "What the heck's the matter with you, Jim? Have you got laryngitis?"

I turned and saw the tall bald-headed figure of Dr. Allinson, my medical adviser and friend. "Hello, Harry," I cried. "Nice to see you." Then I put my hand to my mouth.

But it was too late. A furious yapping issued from the manager's office. It was loud and penetrating and it went on and on.

"Damn, I forgot," I said wearily. "There goes Magnus again."

"Magnus? What are you talking about?"

"Well, it's a long story." I took another sip at my

beer as the din continued from the office. It really shattered the peace of the comfortable bar and I could see the regulars fidgeting and looking out into the hallway.

Would that little dog ever forget? It seemed a long time now since Mr. Beckwith, the new young manager at the Drovers, had brought Magnus in to the surgery. He had looked a little apprehensive.

"You'll have to watch him, Mr. Herriot."

"What do you mean?"

"Well, be careful. He's very vicious."

I looked at the sleek little form, a mere brown dot on the table. He would probably turn the scale at around six pounds. And I couldn't help laughing.

"Vicious? He's not big enough, surely."

"Don't you worry!" Mr. Beckwith raised a warning finger. "I took him to the vet in Bradford where I used to manage the White Swan and he sank his teeth into the poor chap's finger."

"He did?"

"He certainly did! Right down to the bone! By God I've never heard such language but I couldn't blame the man. There was blood all over the place. I had to help him to put a bandage on."

"Mm, I see." It was nice to be told before you had been bitten and not after. "And what was he trying to do to the dog? Must have been something pretty major."

"It wasn't you know. All I wanted was his nails clipped."

"Is that all? And why have you brought him today?"

"Same thing."

"Well honestly, Mr. Beckwith," I said. "I think we can manage to cut his nails without bloodshed. If he'd been a Bull Mastiff or an Alsatian we might have had a problem, but I think that you and I between us can control a Miniature Dachshund."

The manager shook his head. "Don't bring me into it. I'm sorry, but I'd rather not hold him, if you don't mind."

"Why not?"

"Well, he'd never forgive me. He's a funny little dog."

I rubbed my chin. "But if he's as difficult as you say and you can't hold him, what do you expect me to do?"

"I don't know, really . . . maybe you could sort of dope him . . . knock him out?"

"You mean a general anaesthetic? To cut his claws. . . ?"

"It'll be the only way, I'm afraid." Mr. Beckwith stared gloomily at the tiny animal. "You don't know him."

It was difficult to believe but it seemed pretty obvious that this canine morsel was the boss in the Beckwith home. In my experience many dogs had occupied this position but none as small as this one. Anyway, I had no more time to waste on this nonsense.

"Look," I said. "I'll put a tape muzzle on his nose and I'll have this job done in a couple of minutes." I reached behind me for the nail clippers and laid them on the table, then I unrolled a length of bandage and tied it in a loop.

"Good boy, Magnus," I said ingratiatingly as I advanced towards him.

The little dog eyed the bandage unwinkingly until it was almost touching his nose then, with a surprising outburst of ferocity, he made a snarling leap at my hand. I felt the draught on my fingers as a row of sparkling teeth snapped shut half an inch away, but as he turned to have another go my free hand clamped on the scruff of his neck.

"Right, Mr. Beckwith," I said calmly. "I have him now. Just pass me that bandage again and I won't be long."

But the young man had had enough. "Not me!" he gasped. "I'm off!" He turned the door handle and I heard his feet scurrying along the passage.

Ah well, I thought, it was probably best. With boss dogs my primary move was usually to get the owner out of the way. It was surprising how quickly these tough guys calmed down when they found them-

selves alone with a no-nonsense stranger who knew
how to handle them. I could recite a list who were
raving tearaways in their own homes but apologetic
tail-waggers once they crossed the surgery threshold.
And they were all bigger than Magnus.

Retaining my firm grip on his neck I unwound another foot of bandage and as he fought furiously,
mouth gaping, lips retracted like a scaled-down Siberian wolf, I slipped the loop over his nose, tightened it and tied the knot behind his ears. His mouth
was now clamped shut and just to make sure, I applied a second bandage so that he was well and truly
trussed.

This was when they usually packed in and I looked
confidently at the dog for signs of submission. But
above the encircling white coils the eyes glared furiously and from within the little frame an enraged growling issued, rising and falling like the distant droning
of a thousand bees.

Sometimes a stern word or two had the effect of
showing them who was boss.

"Magnus!" I barked at him. "That's enough! Behave
yourself!" I gave his neck a shake to make it clear
that I wasn't kidding but the only response was a side-
long squint of pure defiance from the slightly bulging
eyes.

I lifted the clippers. "All right," I said wearily. "If
you won't have it one way you'll have it the other."
And I tucked him under one arm, seized a paw and
began to clip.

He couldn't do a thing about it. He fought and wriggled but I had him as in a vice. And as I methodically
trimmed the overgrown nails, wrathful bubbles escaped on either side of the bandage along with his
splutterings. If dogs could swear I was getting the
biggest cursing in history.

I did my job with particular care, taking pains to
keep well away from the sensitive core of the claw
so that he felt nothing, but it made no difference. The
indignity of being mastered for once in his life was
insupportable.

Towards the conclusion of the operation I began to change my tone. I had found in the past that once dominance has been established it is quite easy to work up a friendly relationship, so I started to introduce a wheedling note.

"Good little chap," I cooed. "That wasn't so bad, was it?"

I laid down the clippers and stroked his head as a few more resentful bubbles forced their way round the bandage. "All right, Magnus, we'll take your muzzle off now." I began to loosen the knot. "You'll feel a lot better then, won't you?"

So often it happened that when I finally removed the restraint the dog would apparently decide to let bygones be bygones and in some cases would even lick my hand. But not so with Magnus. As the last turn of bandage fell from his nose he made another very creditable attempt to bite me.

"All right, Mr. Beckwith," I called along the passage. "You can come and get him now."

My final memory of the visit was of the little dog turning at the top of the surgery steps and giving me a last dirty look before his master led him down the street.

It said very clearly, "Right, mate, I won't forget you."

That had been weeks ago but ever since that day the very sound of my voice was enough to set Magnus yapping his disapproval. At first the regulars treated it as a big joke but now they had started to look at me strangely. Maybe they thought I had been cruel to the animal or something. It was all very embarrassing because I didn't want to abandon the Drovers; the bar was always cosy even on the coldest night and the beer very consistent.

Anyway if I had gone to another pub I would probably have started to do my talking in whispers and people would have looked at me even more strangely then.

How different it was with Mrs. Hammond's Irish Setter. This started with an urgent phone call one night when I was in the bath. Helen knocked on the bathroom door and I dried off quickly and threw on my dressing gown. I ran upstairs and as soon as I lifted the receiver an anxious voice burst in my ear.

"Mr. Herriot, it's Rock! He's been missing for two days and a man has just brought him back now. He found him in a wood with his foot in a gin trap. He must . . ." I heard a half sob at the end of the line. "He must have been caught there all this time."

"Oh, I'm sorry! Is it very bad?"

"Yes it is." Mrs. Hammond was the wife of one of the local bank managers and a capable, sensible woman. There was a pause and I imagined her determinedly gaining control of herself. When she spoke her voice was calm.

"Yes, I'm afraid it looks as though he'll have to have his foot amputated."

"Oh I'm terribly sorry to hear that." But I wasn't really surprised. A limb compressed in one of those barbarous instruments for 48 hours would be in a critical state. These traps are now mercifully illegal but in those days they often provided me with the kind of jobs I didn't want and the kind of decisions I hated to make. Did you take a limb from an uncomprehending animal to keep it alive or did you bring down the merciful but final curtain of euthanasia? I was responsible for the fact that there were several three-legged dogs and cats running around Darrowby and though they seemed happy enough and their owners still had the pleasure of their pets, the thing, for me, was clouded with sorrow.

Anyway, I would do what had to be done.

"Bring him straight round, Mrs. Hammond," I said.

Rock was a big dog but he was the lean type of Setter and seemed very light as I lifted him on to the surgery table. As my arms encircled the unresisting body I could feel the rib cage sharply ridged under the skin.

"He's lost a lot of weight," I said.

His mistress nodded. "It's a long time to go without food. He ate ravenously when he came in, despite his pain."

I put a hand beneath the dog's elbow and gently lifted the leg. The vicious teeth of the trap had been clamped on the radius and ulna but what worried me was the grossly swollen state of the foot. It was at least twice its normal size.

"What do you think, Mr. Herriot?" Mrs. Hammond's hands twisted anxiously at the handbag which every woman seemed to bring to the surgery irrespective of the circumstances.

I stroked the dog's head. Under the light, the rich sheen of the coat glowed red and gold. "This terrific swelling of the foot. It's partly due to inflammation but also to the fact that the circulation was pretty well cut off for the time he was in the trap. The danger is gangrene—that's when the tissue dies and decomposes."

"I know," she replied. "I did a bit of nursing before I married."

Carefully I lifted the enormous foot. Rock gazed calmly in front of him as I felt around the metacarpals and phalanges, working my way up to the dreadful wound.

"Well, it's a mess," I said. "But there are two good things. First, the leg isn't broken. The trap has gone right down to the bone but there is no fracture. And second and more important, the foot is still warm."

"That's a good sign?"

"Oh yes. It means there's still some circulation. If the foot had been cold and clammy the thing would have been hopeless. I would have had to amputate."

"You think you can save his foot, then?"

I held up my hand. "I don't know, Mrs. Hammond. As I say, he still has some circulation but the question is how much. Some of this tissue is bound to slough off and things could look very nasty in a few days. But I'd like to try."

I flushed out the wound with a mild antiseptic in warm water and gingerly explored the grisly depths. As I snipped away the pieces of damaged muscle and cut off the shreds and flaps of dead skin the thought was uppermost that it must be extremely unpleasant for the dog; but Rock held his head high and scarcely flinched. Once or twice he turned his head towards me inquiringly as I probed deeply and at times I felt his moist nose softly brushing my face as I bent over the foot, but that was all.

The injury seemed a desecration. There are few more beautiful dogs than an Irish Setter and Rock was a picture; sleek coated and graceful with silky feathers on legs and tail and a noble, gentle-eyed head. As the thought of how he would look without a foot drove into my mind I shook my head and turned quickly to lift the sulphanilamide powder from the trolley behind me. Thank heavens this was now available, one of the new revolutionary drugs, and I packed it deep into the wound with the confidence that it would really do something to keep down the infection. I applied a layer of gauze then a light bandage with a feeling of fatalism. There was nothing else I could do.

Rock was brought in to me every day. And every day he endured the same procedure; the removal of the dressing which was usually adhering to the wound to some degree, then the inevitable trimming of the dying tissues and the rebandaging. Yet, incredibly, he never showed any reluctance to come. Most of my patients came in very slowly and left at top speed, dragging their owners on the end of the leads; in fact some turned tail at the door, slipped their collar and sped down Trengate with their owners in hot pursuit. Dogs aren't so daft and there is doubtless a dentist's chair type of association about a vet's surgery.

Rock, however, always marched in happily with a gentle waving of his tail. In fact when I went into the waiting room and saw him sitting there he usually offered me his paw. This had always been a characteristic gesture of his but there seemed something uncanny about it when I bent over him and saw the white-swathed limb outstretched towards me.

After a week the outlook was grim. All the time the dead tissue had been sloughing and one night when I removed the dressing Mrs. Hammond gasped and turned away. With her nursing training she had been very helpful, holding the foot this way and that intuitively as I worked, but tonight she didn't want to look.

I couldn't blame her. In places the white bones of the metacarpals could be seen like the fingers of a human hand with only random strands of skin covering them.

"Is it hopeless, do you think?" she whispered, still looking away.

I didn't answer for a moment as I felt my way underneath the foot. "It does look awful, but do you know, I think we have reached the end of the road and are going to turn the corner soon."

"How do you mean?"

"Well, all the under surface is sound and warm. His pads are perfectly intact. And do you notice, there's no smell tonight? That's because there is no more dead stuff to cut away. I really think this foot is going to start granulating."

She stole a look. "And do you think those . . . bones . . . will be covered over?"

"Yes, I do." I dusted on the faithful sulphanilamide. "It won't be exactly the same foot as before but it will do."

And it turned out just that way. It took a long time but the new healthy tissue worked its way upwards as though determined to prove me right and when, many months later, Rock came into the surgery with a mild attack of conjunctivitis he proferred a courteous paw as was his wont. I accepted the civility and as we shook hands I looked at the upper surface of the foot. It was hairless, smooth and shining, but it was completely healed.

"You'd hardly notice it, would you?" Mrs. Hammond said.

"That's right, it's marvellous. Just this little bare patch. And he walked in without a limp."

Mrs. Hammond laughed. "Oh, he's quite sound on that leg now. And do you know, I really think he's grateful to you—look at him."

I suppose the animal psychologists would say it was ridiculous even to think that the big dog realised I had done him a bit of good; that lolling-tongued open mouth, warm eyes and outstretched paw didn't mean anything like that.

Maybe they are right, but what I do know and cherish is the certainty that after all the discomforts I had put him through Rock didn't hold a thing against me.

I have to turn back to the other side of the coin to discuss Timmy Butterworth. He was a wire-haired Fox Terrier who resided in Gimber's yard, one of the little cobbled alleys off Trengate, and the only time I had to treat him was one lunch time.

I had just got out of the car and was climbing the surgery steps when I saw a little girl running along the street, waving frantically as she approached. I waited for her and when she panted up to me her eyes were wide with fright.

"Ah'm Wendy Butterworth," she gasped. "Me mam sent me. Will you come to our dog?"

"What's wrong with him?"

"Me mam says he's et summat!"

"Poison?"

"Ah think so."

It was less than a hundred yards away, not worth taking the car. I broke into a trot with Wendy by my side and within seconds we were turning into the narrow archway of the "yard." Our feet clattered along the tunnel-like passage then we emerged into one of the unlikely scenes which had surprised me so much when I first came to Darrowby; the miniature street with its tiny crowding houses, strips of garden, bow windows looking into each other across a few feet of cobbles. But I had no time to gaze around me today because Mrs. Butterworth, stout, red-faced and very flustered, was waiting for me.

"He's in 'ere, Mr. Herriot!" she cried and threw wide the door of one of the cottages. It opened straight into the living room and I saw my patient sitting on the hearth rug looking somewhat thoughtful.

"What's happened, then?" I asked.

The lady clasped and unclasped her hands. "I saw a big rat run down across t'yard yesterday and I got some poison to put down for 'im." She gulped agitatedly. "I mixed it in a saucer full o' porridge then somebody came to t'door and when ah came back, Timmy was just finishin' it off!"

The terrier's thoughtful expression had deepened and he ran his tongue slowly round his lips with the obvious reflection that that was the strangest porridge he had ever tasted.

I turned to Mrs. Butterworth. "Have you got the poison tin there?"

"Yes, here it is." With a violently trembling hand she passed it to me.

I read the label. It was a well known name and the very look of it sounded a knell in my mind recalling the many dead and dying animals with which it was associated. Its active ingredient was zinc phosphide and even today with our modern drugs we are usually helpless once a dog has absorbed it.

I thumped the tin down on the table. "We've got to make him vomit immediately! I don't want to waste time going back to the surgery—have you got any washing soda? If I push a few crystals down it'll do the trick."

"Oh dear!" Mrs. Butterworth bit her lip. "We 'aven't such a thing in the house . . . is there anything else we could . . ."

"Wait a minute!" I looked across the table, past the piece of cold mutton, the tureen of potatoes and a jar of pickles. "Is there any mustard in that pot?"

"Aye, it's full."

Quickly I grabbed the pot, ran to the tap and diluted the mustard to the consistency of milk.

"Come on!" I shouted. "Let's have him outside."

I seized the astonished Timmy, whisked him from the rug, shot through the door and dumped him on the cobbles. Holding his body clamped tightly between my knees and his jaws close together with my left hand I poured the liquid mustard into the side of his mouth whence it trickled down to the back of his throat. There was nothing he could do about it, he had to swallow the disgusting stuff, and when about a tablespoon had gone down I released him.

After a single affronted glare at me the terrier began to retch then to lurch across the smooth stones. Within seconds he had deposited his stolen meal in a quiet corner.

"Do you think that's the lot?" I asked.

"That's it," Mrs. Butterworth replied firmly. "I'll fetch a brush and shovel."

Timmy, his short tail tucked down, slunk back into the house and I watched him as he took up his favourite position on the hearthrug. He coughed, snorted, pawed at his mouth, but he just couldn't rid himself of that dreadful taste; and increasingly it was obvious that he had me firmly tagged as the cause of all the trouble. As I left he flashed me a glance which said quite plainly, "You rotten swine!"

There was something in that look which reminded me of Magnus from the Drovers, but the first sign that Timmy, unlike Magnus, wasn't going to be satisfied with vocal disapproval came within a few days. I was strolling meditatively down Trengate when a white missile issued from Gimber's Yard nipped me on the ankle and disappeared as silently as he had come. I caught only a glimpse of the little form speeding on its short legs down the passage.

I laughed. Fancy him remembering! But it happened again and again and I realised that the little dog was indeed lying in wait for me. He never actually sank his teeth into me—it was a gesture more than anything—but it seemed to satisfy him to see me jump as he snatched briefly at my calf or trouser leg. I was a sitting bird because I was usually deep in thought as I walked down the street.

And when I thought about it, I couldn't blame Timmy. Looking at it from his point of view he had been sitting by his fireside digesting an unusual meal and minding his own business when a total stranger had pounced on him, hustled him from the comfort of his rug and poured mustard into him. It was outrageous and he just wasn't prepared to let the matter rest there.

For my part there was a certain satisfaction in being the object of a vendetta waged by an animal who would have been dead without my services. And unpleasantly dead because the victims of phosphorus poisoning had to endure long days and sometimes weeks of jaundice, misery and creeping debility before the inevitable end.

So I suffered the attacks with good grace. But when I remembered I crossed to the other side of the street to avoid the hazard of Gimber's Yard; and from there I could often see the little white dog peeping round the corner waiting for the moment when he would make me pay for that indignity.

Timmy, I knew, was one who would never forget.

47

I suppose there was a wry humour in the fact that my call-up papers arrived on my birthday, but I didn't see the joke at the time.

The event is preserved in my memory in a picture which is as clear to me today as when I walked into our "dining room" that morning. Helen perched away up on her high stool at the end of the table, very still, eyes downcast. By the side of my plate my birthday present, a tin of Dobie's Blue Square tobacco, and next to it a long envelope. I didn't have to ask what it contained.

I had been expecting it for some time but it still gave me a jolt to find I had only a week before presenting myself at Lord's Cricket Ground, St. John's Wood, London. And that week went by at frightening speed as I made my final plans, tidying up the loose ends in the practice, getting my Ministry of Agriculture forms sent off, arranging for our few possessions to be taken to Helen's old home where she would stay while I was away.

Having decided that I would finish work at teatime on Friday I had a call from old Arnold Summergill at about three o'clock that afternoon; and I knew that would be my very last job because it was always an expedition rather than a visit to his smallholding which clung to a bracken strewn slope in the depths of the hills. I didn't speak directly to Arnold but to Miss Thompson the postmistress in Hainby village.

"Mr. Summergill wants you to come and see his dog," she said over the phone.

"What's the trouble?" I asked.

I heard a muttered consultation at the far end.

"He says its leg's gone funny."

"Funny? What d'you mean, funny?"

Again the quick babble of voices. "He says it's kind of stickin' out."

"All right," I said. "I'll be along very soon."

It was no good asking for the dog to be brought in. Arnold had never owned a car. Nor had he ever spoken on a telephone—all our conversations had been carried on through the medium of Miss Thompson. Arnold would mount his rusty bicycle, pedal to Hainby and tell his troubles to the postmistress. And the symptoms; they were typically vague and I didn't suppose there would be anything either "funny" or "sticking out" about that leg when I saw it.

Anyway, I thought, as I drove out of Darrowby, I wouldn't mind having a last look at Benjamin. It was a fanciful name for a small farmer's dog and I never really found out how he had acquired it. But after all he was an unlikely breed for such a setting, a massive Old English Sheep Dog who would have looked more in place decorating the lawns of a stately home than following his master round Arnold's stony pastures. He was a classical example of the walking hearthrug and it took a second look to decide which end of him was which. But when you did manage to locate his head you found two of the most benevolent eyes imaginable glinting through the thick fringe of hair.

Benjamin was in fact too friendly at times, especially in winter when he had been strolling in the farmyard mud and showed his delight at my arrival by planting his huge feet on my chest. He did the same thing to my car, too, usually just after I had washed it, smearing clay lavishly over windows and bodywork while exchanging pleasantries with Sam inside. When Benjamin made a mess of anything he did it right.

But I had to interrupt my musings when I reached the last stage of my journey. And as I hung on to the kicking, jerking wheel and listened to the creaking and groaning of springs and shock absorbers, the thought forced its way into my mind as it always did around here that it cost us money to come to Mr. Summergill's farm. There could be no profit from the visit because this vicious track must knock at least five pounds off the value of the car on every trip. Since Arnold did not have a car himself he saw no reason why he should interfere with the primeval state of his road.

It was simply a six foot strip of earth and rock and it wound and twisted for an awful long way. The trouble was that to get to the farm you had to descend into a deep valley before climbing through a wood towards the house. I think going down was worse because the vehicle hovered agonisingly on the top of each ridge before plunging into the yawning ruts beyond; and each time, listening to the unyielding stone grating on sump and exhaust I tried to stop myself working out the damage in pounds, shillings and pence.

And when at last, mouth gaping, eyes popping, tyres sending the sharp pebbles flying, I ground my way upwards in bottom gear over the last few yards leading to the house I was surprised to see Arnold waiting for me there alone. It was unusual to see him without Benjamin.

He must have read my questioning look because he jerked his thumb over his shoulder.

"He's in t'house," he grunted, and his eyes were anxious.

I got out of the car and looked at him for a moment as he stood there in a typical attitude, wide shoulders back, head high. I have called him "old" and indeed he was over seventy, but the features beneath the woollen tammy which he always wore pulled down over his ears were clean and regular and the tall figure lean and straight. He was a fine looking man and must have been handsome in his youth, yet he had never married. I often felt there was a story there but he seemed content to live here alone, a "bit of a 'ermit" as they said in the village. Alone, that is, except for Benjamin.

As I followed him into the kitchen he casually shooed out a couple of hens who had been perching on a dusty dresser. Then I saw Benjamin and pulled up with a jerk.

The big dog was sitting quite motionless by the side of the table and this time the eyes behind the over-hanging hair were big and liquid with fright. He appeared to be too terrified to move and when I saw his left fore leg I couldn't blame him. Arnold had been right after all; it was indeed sticking out with a vengeance, at an angle which made my heart give a quick double thud; a complete lateral dislocation of the elbow, the radius projecting away out from the humerus at an almost impossible obliquity.

I swallowed carefully. "When did this happen, Mr. Summergill?"

"Just an hour since." He tugged worriedly at his strange headgear. "I was changing the cows into an-other field and awd Benjamin likes to have a nip at their heels when he's behind 'em. Well he did it once ower often and one of them lashed out and got 'im on the leg."

"I see." My mind was racing. This thing was gro-tesque. I had never seen anything like it, in fact thirty years later I still haven't seen anything like it. How on earth was I going to reduce the thing away up here in the hills? By the look of it I would need general anaesthesia and a skilled assistant.

"Poor old lad," I said, resting my hand on the shag-gy head as I tried to think. "What are we going to do with you?"

The tail whisked along the flags in reply and the mouth opened in a nervous panting, giving a glimpse of flawlessly white teeth.

Arnold cleared his throat. "Can you put 'im right?"

Well it was a good question. An airy answer might give the wrong impression yet I didn't want to worry him with my doubts. It would be a mammoth task to get the enormous dog down to Darrowby; he nearly filled the kitchen, never mind my little car. And with that leg sticking out and with Sam already in residence. And would I be able to get the joint back in place when I got him there? And even if I did manage it I would still have to bring him all the way back up here. It would just about take care of the rest of the day.

Gently I passed my fingers over the dislocated joint and searched my memory for details of the anatomy of the elbow. For the leg to be in this position the processus anconeus must have been completely disengaged from the supracondyloid fossa where it normally lay; and to get it back the joint would have to be flexed until the anconeus was clear of the epicondyles.

"Now let's see," I murmured to myself. "If I had this dog anaesthetised and on the table I would have to get hold of him like this." I grasped the leg just above the elbow and began to move the radius slowly upwards. Benjamin gave me a quick glance then turned his head away, a gesture typical of good-natured dogs, conveying the message that he was going to put up with whatever I thought it necessary to do.

I flexed the joint still further until I was sure the anconeus was clear, then carefully rotated the radius and ulna inwards.

"Yes . . . yes . . ." I muttered again. "This must be about the right position . . ." But my soliloquy was interrupted by a sudden movement of the bones under my hand; a springing, flicking sensation.

I looked incredulously at the leg. It was perfectly straight.

Benjamin, too, seemed unable to take it in right away, because he peered cautiously round through his shaggy curtain before lowering his nose and sniffing around the elbow. Then he seemed to realise all was well and ambled over to his master.

And he was perfectly sound. Not a trace of a limp.

A slow smile spread over Arnold's face. "You've mended him, then."

"Looks like it, Mr. Summergill." I tried to keep my voice casual, but I felt like cheering or bursting into hysterical laughter. I had only been making an examination, feeling things out a little, and the joint had popped back into place. A glorious accident.

"Aye well, that's grand," the farmer said. "Isn't it, awd lad?" He bent and tickled Benjamin's ear.

I could have been disappointed by this laconic reception of my performance, but I realised it was a compliment to me that he wasn't surprised that I, James Herriot, his vet, should effortlessly produce a miracle when it was required.

A theatre-full of cheering students would have rounded off the incident or it would be nice to do this kind of thing to some millionaire's animal in a crowded drawing room, but it never happened that way. I looked around the kitchen, at the cluttered table, the pile of unwashed crockery in the sink, a couple of Arnold's ragged shirts drying before the fire, and I smiled to myself. This was the sort of setting in which I usually pulled off my spectacular cures. The only spectators here, apart from Arnold, were the two hens who had made their way back on to the dresser and they didn't seem particularly impressed.

"Well, I'll be getting back down the hill," I said, and Arnold walked with me across the yard to the car.

"I hear you're off to join up," he said as I put my hand on the door.

"Yes, I'm away tomorrow, Mr. Summergill."

"Tomorrow, eh?" he raised his eyebrows.

"Yes, to London. Ever been there?"

"Nay, nay, be damned!" The woollen cap quivered as he shook his head. "That'd be no good to me."

I laughed. "Why do you say that?"

"Well now, I'll tell ye." He scratched his chin ruminatively. "Ah nobbut went once to Brawton and that was enough. Ah couldn't walk on t'streetl"

"Couldn't walk?"

"Nay. There were that many people about. I 'ad to take big steps and little 'uns, then big steps and little 'uns again. Couldn't get goin'."

I had often seen Arnold stalking over his fields with the long, even stride of the hillman with nothing in

his way and I knew exactly what he meant. "Big
steps and little 'uns." That put it perfectly.

I started the engine and waved and as I moved
away the old man raised a hand.

"Tek care, lad," he murmured.

I spotted Benjamin's nose just peeping round the
kitchen door. Any other time he would have been out
with his master to see me off the premises but it had
been a strange day for him culminating with my de-
scending on him and mauling his leg about. He
wasn't taking any more chances.

I drove gingerly down through the wood and before starting up the track on the other side I stopped
the car and got out with Sam leaping eagerly after
me.

This was a little lost valley in the hills, a green cleft
cut off from the wild country above. One of the
bonuses in a country vet's life is that he sees these
hidden places. Apart from old Arnold nobody ever
came down here, not even the postman who left the
infrequent mail in a box at the top of the track and
nobody saw the blazing scarlets and golds of the autumn trees nor heard the busy clucking and murmuring of the beck among its clean-washed stones.

I walked along the water's edge watching the little
fish darting and flitting in the cool depths. In the
spring these banks were bright with primroses and
in May a great sea of bluebells flowed among the
trees but today, though the sky was an untroubled
blue, the clean air was touched with the sweetness
of the dying year.

I climbed a little way up the hillside and sat down
among the bracken now fast turning to bronze. Sam,
as was his way, flopped by my side and I ran a hand
over the silky hair of his ears. The far side of the valley rose steeply to where, above the gleaming ridge
of limestone cliffs, I could just see the sunlit rim of
the moor.

I looked back to where the farm chimney sent a
thin tendril of smoke from behind the brow of the
hill, and it seemed that the eipisode with Benjamin,

my last job in veterinary practice before I left Darrowby, was a fitting epilogue. A little triumph, intensely satisfying but by no means world shaking; like all the other little triumphs and disasters which make up a veterinary surgeon's life but go unnoticed by the world.

Last night, after Helen had packed my bag I had pushed Black's Veterinary Dictionary in among the shirts and socks. It was a bulky volume but I had been gripped momentarily by a fear that I might forget the things I had learned, and conceived on an impulse the scheme of reading a page or two each day to keep my memory fresh. And here among the bracken the thought came back to me; that it was the greatest good fortune not only to be fascinated by animals but to know about them. Suddenly the knowing became a precious thing.

I went back and opened the car door. Sam jumped on to the seat and before I got in I looked away down in the other direction from the house to the valley's mouth where the hills parted to give a glimpse of the plain below. And the endless wash of pale tints, the gold of the stubble, the dark smudges of woods, the mottled greens of the pasture land were like a perfect water colour. I found myself staring greedily as if for the first time at the scene which had so often lifted my heart, the great wide clean-blown face of Yorkshire.

I would come back to it all, I thought as I drove away; back to my work . . . how was it that book had described it . . . my hard, honest and fine profession.

But tomorrow I would be far from here; in London pushing my way through the crowds. Taking big steps and little 'uns.

48

I had to catch the early train and Bob Cooper was at the door with his ancient taxi before eight o'clock next morning.

Sam followed me across the room expectantly as he always did but I closed the door gently against his puzzled face. Clattering down the long flights of stairs I caught a glimpse through the landing window of the garden with the sunshine beginning to pierce the autumn mist, turning the dewy grass into a glittering coverlet, glinting on the bright colours of the apples and the last roses.

In the passage I paused at the side door where I had started my day's work so many times since coming to Darrowby, but then I hurried passed. This was one time I went out the front.

Bob pushed open the taxi door and I threw my bag in before looking up over the ivy-covered brick of the old house to our little room under the tiles. Helen was in the window. She was crying. When she saw me she waved gaily and smiled, but it was a twisted smile as the tears flowed. And as we drove round the corner and I swallowed the biggest ever lump in my throat a fierce resolve welled in me; men all over the country were leaving their wives and I had to leave Helen now, but nothing, nothing, nothing would ever get me away from her again.

The shops were still closed and nothing stirred in the market place. As we left I turned and looked back at the cobbled square with the old clock tower and the row of irregular roofs with the green fells quiet and peaceful behind, and it seemed that I was losing something for ever.

I wish I had known then that it was not the end of everything. I wish I had known that it was only the beginning.

ABOUT THE AUTHOR

JAMES HERRIOT is still a practicing veterinary surgeon. He grew up in Scotland and went to Glasgow Veterinary College. After qualifying he went to work in the Yorkshire Dales of northern England. Except for wartime service in the R.A.F., he has never left Yorkshire, and he still works with Siegfried and Tristan Farnon, the colorful characters in *All Creatures Great and Small* and *ALL THINGS BRIGHT AND BEAUTIFUL*. Outside his work, his interests are music, football and dog-walking. James Herriot is married, with a son who is a veterinary surgeon and a daughter who is a doctor.